Who Was Who at Waterloo

Who Was Who at Waterloo

at Waterloo

A Biography of the Battle

Christopher Summerville

PEARSON
Longman

Harlow, England • London • New York • Boston • San Francisco • Toronto • Sydney • Singapore • Hong Kong
Tokyo • Seoul • Taipei • New Delhi • Cape Town • Madrid • Mexico City • Amsterdam • Munich • Paris • Milan

PEARSON EDUCATION LIMITED

Edinburgh Gate
Harlow CM20 2JE
United Kingdom
Tel: +44 (0)1279 623623
Fax: +44 (0)1279 431059
Website: www.pearsoned.co.uk

First edition published in Great Britain in 2007

The right of Christopher Summerville to be identified as author
of this work has been asserted by him in accordance
with the Copyright, Designs and Patents Act 1988.

ISBN: 978-0-582-78405-5

British Library Cataloguing in Publication Data
A CIP catalogue record for this book can be obtained from the British Library

10 9 8 7 6 5 4 3 2 1
11 10 09 08 07

Set by in 10/14pt Plantin
Printed in Great Britain by Ashford Colour Press Ltd, Gosport

The Publisher's policy is to use paper manufactured from sustainable forests.

Contents

Author's note

You speak of the difficulties you have in reconciling different accounts
of eyewitnesses. This is only what invariably occurs. There is scarcely an
instance, I think, of two persons, even though only fifty yards distant
from each other, who give of such events a concurring account.

Sir George De Lacy Evans, Waterloo veteran,
to the historian William Siborne (1848).

After Waterloo Wellington observed: 'If writers would adhere to the
golden rule for an historian, *viz*. To write nothing which they did not
know to be true, the Duke apprehends they would have nothing but
little to tell.' It's a fair point. I was born 145 years after the battle,
which first invaded my consciousness via Sergei Bondarchuk's 1970
movie, *Waterloo*: how could I possibly know what *really* happened?
Indeed, if I committed to paper what I 'knew to be true' about
Waterloo I wouldn't get much further than: 'it was fought on
Sunday, 18 June 1815' – thus proving the Duke's observation correct. And yet a mountain of Waterloo books has been thrown up over
the years as successive generations revisit the events of 15–18 June
1815. Scrambling up the slippery slopes of this stack is the only realistic option for modern explorers seeking a greater understanding of
the battle – but the ascent could take a lifetime. The present volume
will, I hope, provide a convenient base camp.

In preparing the book I wanted to remain true to the random,
fragmentary, subjective nature of human experience. In particular,
I wanted to produce a book without a beginning or end. And so
I have endeavoured to present a history of the Waterloo campaign via
the personalities involved. Arranged in alphabetical order, and with
entries **highlighted** throughout the text – like links in a website – the

book constitues a labyrinthine journey into the events of 15–18 June 1815. Abandoning the usual 'Greek tragedy in five acts' approach, I have tried to view Waterloo through a kaleidoscope rather than a microscope. And by focusing on the personal stories of participants and eyewitnesses I hope to pick up the gauntlet thrown down by the Duke. For what I 'know to be true' about Waterloo is this: there were as many facets to the battle as faces on the field.

One of those faces belonged to Jonathan Leach of the 95th (Rifle) Regiment, and in concluding this brief introduction I can do no better than quote his preface to *Rough Sketches of the Life of an Old Soldier* (1831):

> As it is the fashion now-a-days for everyone to become an author, I see no reason why I should not try my hand at it also, and let my book run the same risk of being criticised, lashed, and abused by the literati (if, indeed, they deign to peruse it), as is the every day case with some production or other, and to which everyone, who is bold enough to make similar experiments, must make up his mind. Such as mine is, forth it goes to the world; and it must be taken for better for worse.

Finally, thanks are due to Josephine Bryan, Mary-Clare Connellan, Linda Cuddy, Natasha Dupont, Ewa Haren, Casey Mein, Hetty Reid and Christina Wipf-Perry for help, patience, encouragement and support.

Christopher Summerville
York 2007

Maps

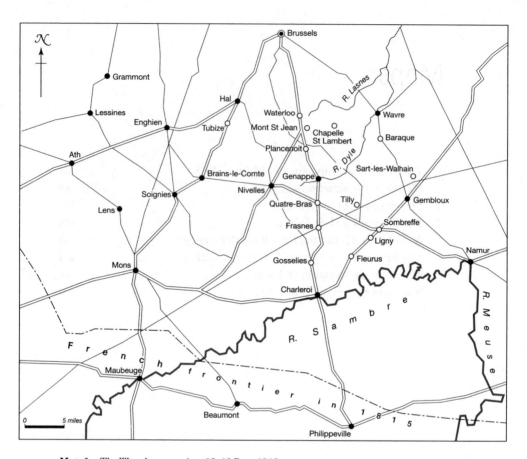

Map 1   *The Waterloo campaign, 15–18 June 1815*

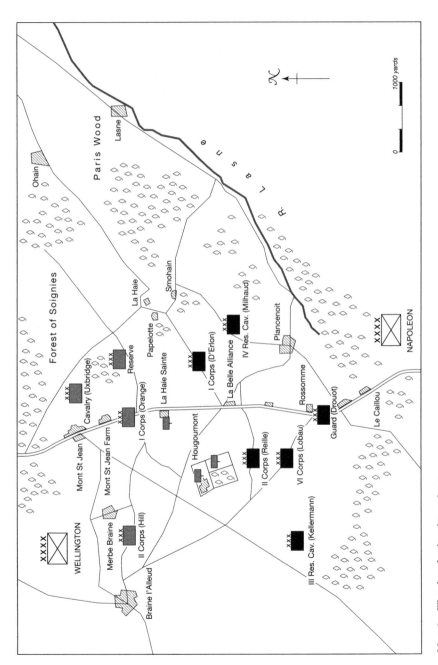

Map 2   *Waterloo: the situation at 1 p.m.*

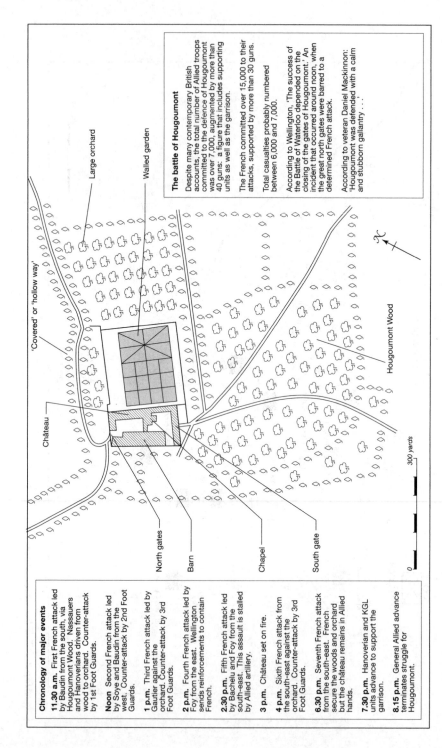

Map 3 · *The château of Hougoumont*

Chronology of major events

11.30 a.m. First French attack led by Baudin from the south, via Hougoumont Wood. Nassauers and Hanoverians driven from wood to orchard. Counter-attack by 1st Foot Guards.

Noon Second French attack led by Soye and Baudin from the west. Counter-attack by 2nd Foot Guards.

1 p.m. Third French attack led by Gautier against the orchard. Counter-attack by 3rd Foot Guards.

2 p.m. Fourth French attack led by Foy from the east. Wellington sends reinforcements to contain French.

2.30 p.m. Fifth French attack led by Bachelu and Foy from the south-east. This assault is stalled by Allied artillery.

3 p.m. Château set on fire.

4 p.m. Sixth French attack from the south-east against the orchard. Counter-attack by 3rd Foot Guards.

6.30 p.m. Seventh French attack from the south-east. French secure the woods and orchard but the château remains in Allied hands.

7.30 p.m. Hanoverian and KGL units advance to support the garrison.

8.15 p.m. General Allied advance terminates struggle for Hougoumont.

The battle of Hougoumont

Despite many contemporary British accounts, the total number of Allied troops committed to the defence of Hougoumont was over 7,000, augmented by more than 40 guns: a figure that includes supporting units as well as the garrison.

The French committed over 15,000 to their attacks, supported by more than 30 guns.

Total casualties probably numbered between 6,000 and 7,000.

According to Wellington, 'The success of the Battle of Waterloo depended on the closing of the gates of Hougoumont.' An incident that occurred around noon, when the great north gates were barred to a determined French attack.

According to veteran Daniel Mackinnon: 'Hougoumont was defended with a calm and stubborn gallantry . . .'

Large orchard

Walled garden

'Covered' or 'hollow way'

Château

North gates

Barn

Chapel

South gate

Hougoumont Wood

300 yards

0

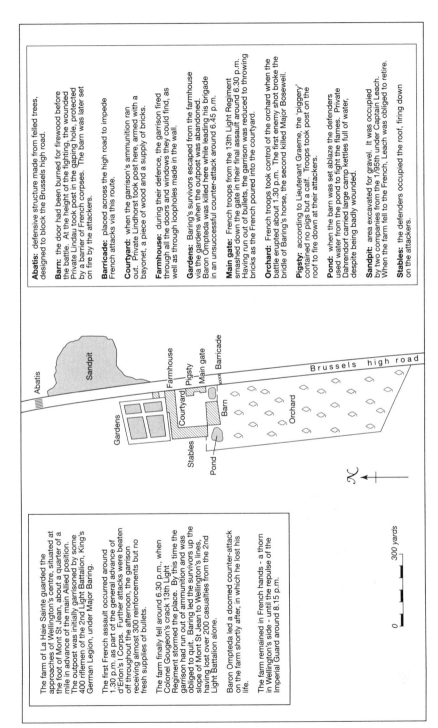

Map 4 *The farm of La Haie Sainte*

Abatis: defensive structure made from felled trees, designed to block the Brussels high road.

Barn: the door had been burned for firewood before the battle. At the height of the fighting, the wounded Private Lindau took post in the gaping hole, protected by a barrier of French corpses. The barn was later set on fire by the attackers.

Barricade: placed across the high road to impede French attacks via this route.

Courtyard: when the garrison's ammunition ran out. Private Lindhorst took post here, armed with a bayonet, a piece of wood and a supply of bricks.

Farmhouse: during their defence, the garrison fired through all the doors and windows they could find, as well as through loopholes made in the wall.

Gardens: Baring's survivors escaped from the farmhouse via the gardens when the outpost was abandoned. Baron Ompteda was killed here while leading his brigade in an unsuccessful counter-attack around 6.45 p.m.

Main gate: French troops from the 13th Light Regiment smashed down the gate in their final assault around 6.30 p.m. Having run out of bullets, the garrison was reduced to throwing bricks as the French poured into the courtyard.

Orchard: French troops took control of the orchard when the battle erupted about 1.30 p.m. The first enemy shot broke the bridle of Baring's horse, the second killed Major Bosewell.

Pigsty: according to Lieutenant Graeme, the 'piggery' contained no pigs but a calf. Troops took post on the roof to fire down at their attackers.

Pond: when the barn was set ablaze the defenders used water from the pond to fight the flames. Private Dahrendorf carried large camp kettles full of water, despite being badly wounded.

Sandpit: area excavated for gravel. It was occupied by two companies from the 1/95th under Captain Leach. When the farm fell to the French, Leach was obliged to retire.

Stables: the defenders occupied the roof, firing down on the attackers.

The farm of La Haie Sainte guarded the approaches of Wellington's centre, situated at the foot of Mont St Jean, about a quarter of a mile in advance of the main Allied position. The outpost was initially garrisoned by some 400 riflemen of the 2nd Light Battalion, King's German Legion, under Major Baring.

The first French assault occurred around 1.30 p.m. as part of the general advance of d'Erlon's I Corps. Further attacks were beaten off throughout the afternoon, the garrison receiving almost 300 reinforcements but no fresh supplies of bullets.

The farm finally fell around 6.30 p.m., when Colonel Gougeon's crack 13th Light Regiment stormed the place. By this time the garrison had run out of ammunition and was obliged to quit. Baring led the survivors up the slope of Mont St Jean to Wellington's lines, having lost over 200 casualties from the 2nd Light Battalion alone.

Baron Ompteda led a doomed counter-attack on the farm shortly after, in which he lost his life.

The farm remained in French hands - a thorn in Wellington's side - until the repulse of the Imperial Guard around 8.15 p.m.

0   300 yards

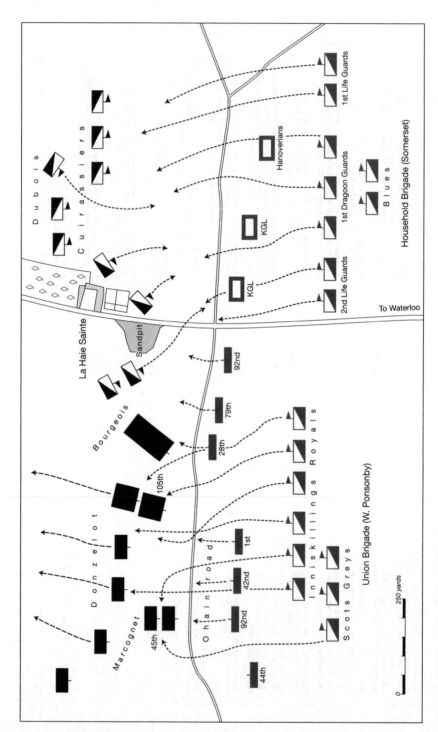

Map 5 *Waterloo at 2 p.m.: the British cavalry charges*

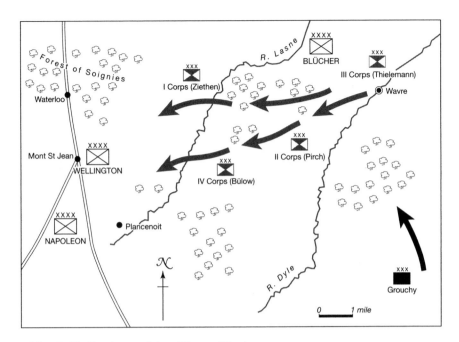

Map 6   *The Prussian march from Wavre to Waterloo*

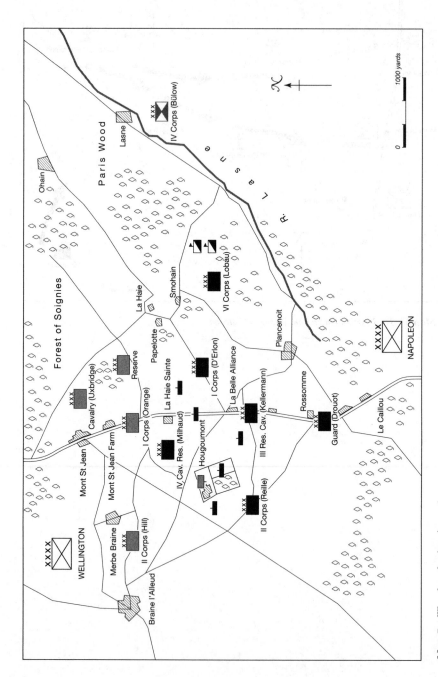

Map 7 *Waterloo: the situation at 4 p.m.*

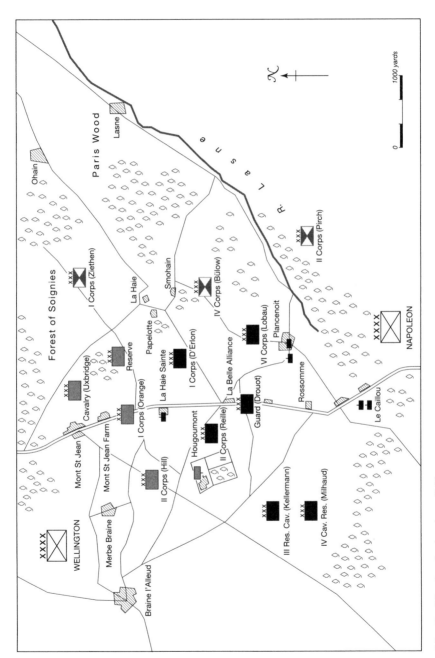

Map 8 *Waterloo: the situation at 7.30 p.m.*

Adam
Major General Sir Frederick William (1781–1853)

Commander of the 3rd British Brigade (part of Clinton's 2nd British Infantry Division), consisting of the 1/52nd, 71st and 2/95th Regiments: some 2,900 light infantrymen in total. A strict disciplinarian, Adam was a veteran of campaigns in Egypt, Sicily and Spain, having entered the army as an ensign in 1795.

On the morning of 18 June 1815, with 140,000 men squeezed on to a battlefront of just 3 miles, the 34-year-old Adam (younger than the four battalion commanders under him) dashed off a letter to his father, perceptively observing: 'It is believed we shall have a general action this afternoon.' Shortly afterwards the show began, with Adam's brigade held in reserve on **Wellington**'s right wing. But by late afternoon the Duke found it necessary to advance Adam's regiments to the heights north-east of Hougoumont, where, around 5.30 p.m., they drove off an infantry sortie by elements of **Reille**'s II Corps (though intense artillery fire obliged the brigade to seek shelter behind the ridge shortly thereafter).

About 7.30 p.m. came the decisive moment at Mont St Jean, when **Napoleon** threw forward 3,500 infantrymen of his Imperial

Guard, tasked with breaking Wellington's line. As the crisis loomed, one of Adam's regiments – the 52nd – swung forward from the firing line *en potence*, forming a right angle to take the approaching Frenchmen in the left flank. Attacked from front and flank, the Imperial Guard buckled then broke: bounced down the ridge at the point of the bayonet. Now, with the Imperial Guard beaten and the battle almost won, Wellington came across Adam, and indicating a battery of French guns defiantly slamming shot into the Allied lines (one of its final rounds shattering Lord **Uxbridge**'s right leg), declared: 'Adam, you must dislodge those fellows.' The General obliged, but in the battle's dying moments was badly wounded.

Adam was treated at Brussels, with some 20,000 other casualties from both sides. It was here, at noon on 19 June, Wellington finished his Waterloo Dispatch. Written with the Duke's customary self-restraint, it consisted of a brief summary of the four-day campaign, punctuated with encomia to the army's top brass. Included 'for His Royal Highness's approbation' was Adam, who was awarded the KCB (Knight Commander of the Most Honourable Order of the Bath). But having survived the battle in Belgium, Adam found himself at the centre of an unpleasant spat back in London. Since its foundation by George I in 1725, the Order of the Bath had been – with the exception of the Order of the Garter – the nation's most prestigious award for chivalry. The name derives from the medieval custom of bathing before the would-be knight's ceremonial 'dubbing' at the hands of the sovereign. The original regulations for the Order allowed for a maximum of 36 knights only, making it a very exlusive club. Its members were, in fact, the elite of the elite – and they wanted to keep it that way. But as a direct consequence of Waterloo, and the successful conclusion of the Napoleonic Wars, the Regent was swamped with requests for honours and rewards. The Prince solved the problem by enlarging the Order's membership to 2,258, subdividing it into three classes: Knights Grand Cross (GCB), Knights Commander (KCB) and Companions (CB). And while he was at it, 'Prinny' also abolished the archaic rituals of bathing, vigils and prayers for new initiates.

The result was a storm of controversy, as existing members bitterly complained their status had been eroded and the Order sullied. But if Adam was disturbed by the hullabaloo surrounding his knighthood, he may have taken comfort from yet more bounty bestowed by a grateful government on its Waterloo heroes. For, as a general officer, Adam received Waterloo prize money of £1,274, 10 shillings and 10¾ pennies, which converts to a modern equivalent of over £63,000. Indeed, all British soldiers present at the great battle were entitled to cash rewards. While generals received £1,274, 10 shillings and 10¾ pennies; field officers and colonels received £433, 2 shillings and 4¼ pennies; captains £90, 7 shillings and 3¾ pennies; subalterns £34, 14 shillings and 9½ pennies; sergeants £19, 4 shillings and 4 pennies; corporals, drummers, and privates £2, 11 shillings and 4 pennies. Wellington, as commander-in-chief, received £61,000 – over £3 million in modern reckoning. As for the widows and orphans of Britain's Waterloo dead, those of officers received one-off payments or annual allowances from a royal fund known as 'His Majesty's Royal Bounty'. Those of other ranks – most of whom subsisted on an income of less than 12 shillings a week – were obliged to rely on charity. This took the form of the Waterloo Subscription, a fund set up by the government, championed by celebrities – such as the poet and novelist Sir **Walter Scott** – but fuelled by public donations.

Adam, meanwhile, went on to reap more rewards: in 1817 he was given command of all British troops in the Mediterranean; in 1824 he was appointed Lord High Commissioner of the Ionian Islands; in 1832 he was made Governor of Madras; in 1846 he was promoted to full general; and he ended his career on the board of general officers responsible for the army's clothing. Adam also received more honours: becoming a Knight of the Austrian Order of Maria Theresa and the Russian Order of St Anne, as well as a Knight Grand Cross of the Order of St Michael and St George (GCMG). This serial chevalier died at the age of 72, having suffered an apoplectic fit on the platform of Greenwich railway station.

Alava
Miguel Ricardo de (1770–1843)

Spanish ambassador to the Nether-lands and friend of **Wellington**. Possessing probably the longest name of any Waterloo man, Miguel Ricardo Maria Juan de la Mata Domingo Vincente Ferrer Alava de Esquivel is simply referred to as 'Alava' in British accounts. An aristocrat, he entered the Spanish Navy as a youth, and holds the distinction (like **Drouot**, the French general) of having been present at

General Alava (1770–1843) by George Dawes

both Trafalgar and Waterloo: fighting against the British on the former occasion (aboard the *Principe de Asturias*), and with them on the latter. Alava served as a naval aide-de-camp during the time of Spain's disastrous alliance with France but switched sides following Napoleon's invasion of his homeland in 1808. Quitting the navy for the army, he joined the headquarters of Wellington's Peninsular Army as a military attaché, eventually becoming one of the Duke's closest companions. After **Napoleon**'s first abdication in 1814, Alava became Spain's convivial ambassador to the Netherlands.

On the morning of 18 June 1815, Mackinnon (1833) states that:

> General Alava went from Brussels to join his Grace, and found him in a tree observing the movements of the French Army. On the Duke turning round and seeing General Alava, he called out, 'How are you, Alava? Buonaparte shall see today how a General of Sepoys can defend a position!' – a remark which showed at once his contempt for an opinion given of him by Buonaparte, and a confidence in himself and in his troops, accompanied with a degree of cheerfulness almost amounting to an assurance of victory.

Having attached himself to Wellington's staff, Alava stuck close to the Duke during the Battle of Waterloo. Yet, despite being in the thick of the action, both Wellington and Alava survived the 10 hours' slaughter without so much as a scratch, the Duke declaring to his friend: 'The hand of Almighty God has been upon me this day.'

About 10 p.m., with the battle won and the Prussians pursuing Napoleon up the Charleroi Road, Wellington and Alava returned to their quarters, 5 miles away at Waterloo village. Wellington arrived at the inn of Jean de Nivelles (now the Wellington Museum) around 11 p.m. Was the Duke upbeat after victory? Alava describes a man overwrought with grief at lives lost, rather than overexcited at laurels gained. Indeed, according to Elizabeth Longford (1969), Wellington 'was in a state of emotional shock' at the slaughter. But how many men did the Duke lose? It is thought Wellington lost some 15,000 men killed and wounded on 18 June – about 21 per cent of his total Mont St Jean force of about 73,000. Losses among officers were high, the casualty rate for brass hats running at 30 per cent. In comparison, the Prussians lost about 7,000 men, or 14 per cent of forces engaged, while the French lost at least 31,000 or 40 per cent of forces engaged. Thus, out of a grand total of 199,700 men embattled at day's end, some 53,000 – over 25 per cent – became casualties. This was a butcher's bill of unprecedented proportions for Wellington, who, familiar with the comparatively small-scale operations of the Peninsular War, rarely sustained more than 5,000 casualties in battle. In percentage terms too, the Duke's Waterloo losses were

The village of Waterloo in 1815

high, though casualty rates of 25 per cent were not unknown to him, and had been sustained at Talavera (1809) and Badajoz (1812).

Contemporary British reports of the aftermath of battle often tell of appalling losses, with whole battalions wiped out, a few officers and men stoically preserving their regimental colours. Yet in the event, most units suffered casualty rates well below 50 per cent. But two factors rarely mentioned in primary sources added to the impression of total wastage: desertion and evacuation of the wounded. According to **Cotton** (1895) of the 7th Hussars: 'It is on record that upwards of 12,000 had sought refuge in the wood of Soigne, whose desertion caused great hardships on those who gallantly remained to achieve so glorious a victory.' Furthermore, the British practice of allotting four men for the removal of a single casualty must have thinned the ranks of those still standing at battle's end. Thus the spectacle of the battlefield in the late evening of 18 June – some 53,000 dead and wounded crammed into a space 3 miles square – made a sickening sight, and the absence of many thousands more Allied soldiers – either carrying wounded comrades to the surgeons' posts or sitting quietly in the Forest of Soignies – must have made the disaster look even worse.

No wonder Wellington and Alava, supping together at Waterloo, raised a glass 'To the memory of the Peninsular War'. After a meal

The Field of Waterloo – a contemporary print

prepared by his cook, **James Thornton,** Wellington is said to have
fallen asleep on a pallet on the floor, having given up his bed to
aide-de-camp Sir **Alexander Gordon,** whose leg had been
amputated. The story goes that Wellington was roused in the early
hours by Dr John Hume with news of Gordon's death and a list of
staff casualties, which caused the Duke to break down. Alava
confirms this reaction in a letter to the Spanish secretary of state,
dated 13 July 1815, and quoted by Christopher Kelly (1818):

> The Duke was unable to refrain from shedding tears on witnessing
> the death of so many brave and honourable men, and the loss of so
> many friends and faithful companions. Nothing but the importance
> of the triumph can compensate for a loss so dreadful.

Perhaps – but only just. For Wellington later admitted: 'I hope to
God that I have fought my last battle . . . I am wretched even at the
moment of victory, and I always say that next to a battle lost the
greatest misery is a battle gained.'

And what of Alava? Sadly for the Spaniard, Napoleon's downfall
did not bring peace to his troubled homeland. For though the flower
of France's army was crushed at Waterloo, the ideals of the French
Revolution continued to bloom. Consequently, Spain became an
ideological battleground between the reactionary forces of the
returning Bourbon monarchy (in the person of Ferdinand VII, the
ultra-conservative prince in whose name the Peninsular War had
been fought) and progressive elements seeking to pull the country
out of the Middle Ages. But Ferdinand was a force to be reckoned
with, and one of his first acts as king was to ditch the liberal constitution introduced by his 'intrusive' predecessor, Joseph Bonaparte. A
wholesale return to the powers and privileges of monarchy, church
and aristocracy followed, provoking a popular uprising in 1820. This
was repressed with French military aid – a bitter twist – and a
campaign of reprisals followed. Ferdinand continued to rule as a
tyrant until his death in 1833. His legacy was yet more bloodshed:
for, having failed to provide an heir, Ferdinand plunged Spain into
the first of the Carlist Wars from beyond the grave. Wisely, Alava
kept out of the way. Exploiting his friendship with Wellington, he
secured a series of diplomatic posts in London and Paris, eventually

settling in the latter place, and no doubt raising several more glasses 'To the memory of the Peninsular War'.

Allix de Vaux
General Jacques-Alexandre-François, Baron (1768–1836)

Original commander of **d'Erlon**'s 1st Infantry Division but not present at Waterloo. Mistakenly listed in many sources as attending the battle, his place was taken by General **Quiot du Passage**. Another officer sometimes listed as present at Waterloo – but who was actually on honeymoon – is General Sir **Galbraith Lowry Cole**. His place at the head of Wellington's 6th British Infantry Division was taken by Sir John Lambert.

Alten
Lieutenant General Sir Charles (1764–1840)

Commander of the 3rd British Infantry Division (part of the Prince of **Orange**'s I Corps), comprising the 5th British Brigade (Sir **Colin Halkett**), the 2nd King's German Legion Brigade (**Ompteda**) and the 1st Hanoverian Brigade (Kielmansegge): a force of over 8,000 men in all.

Alten was born at Burgwedel, Hanover, at this time a hereditary possession of the German-bred kings of Georgian Britain (the Elector of Hanover having acceded to the British throne in 1714 as George I). Thus, although separate political entities, the two states shared the same ruler, and when **Napoleon** seized Hanover in 1806 (annexing the northern half to France, while adding the remainder to his newly created puppet state of Westphalia), Hanoverians flocked to Britain to take up arms against the common foe. Alten was one of the first to leave, joining volunteers then assembling at Lymington, Hampshire. This unit became the King's

German Legion (KGL) and its numbers eventually swelled to some 18,000 recruits. The KGL was modelled on the British Army: its uniforms were of an almost identical pattern, weapons and equipment were standard British issue, and commands were given in English (except in the elite light companies, which retained their native German). There was even a fashion among Hanoverian officers for anglicising their Christian names: so Alten swapped 'Karl' for 'Charles'.

Alten was a keen soldier and gained a wealth of campaign experience: in Cathcart's expedition to Copenhagen (1807); Moore's expeditions to Sweden and Spain (1808); and Chatham's expedition to Walcheren (1809). Alten then transferred to **Wellington**'s Peninsular Army, fighting at Albuera before rising to command the Duke's Light Division. At Waterloo, this Hanoverian aristocrat was considered experienced enough to command Wellington's strongest infantry division, the 3rd British, which was in fact largely German in composition (around 38 per cent of the Duke's troops were ethnic Germans, mostly from Hanover).

Alten's division was situated at the centre of Wellington's position on the ridge of Mont St Jean, left of the paved Brussels–Charleroi high road (*chaussée*), and above the farm of La Haie Sainte, some 300 yards in advance. A detachment of 400 riflemen from Ompteda's brigade (2nd KGL Light Battalion under Major **Baring**) formed the garrison of this important bastion. Alten's division was destined to spend the entire day pummelled by artillery and mauled by cavalry. Meanwhile, the defenders of La Haie Sainte were obliged to endure a series of bloody assaults with little succour from their supports atop the ridge. Despite a stubborn and spirited resistance, Baring's garrison was overwhelmed around 6.30 p.m., their ammuntion having run out, despite a series of desperate pleas, which mysteriously went unanswered. Alten's failure to supply Baring with bullets was a blunder that led directly to the evacuation of La Haie Sainte: this in turn led to a another blunder, resulting in more wasted lives.

The loss of La Haie Sainte was a disaster for the Anglo-Allied army at Mont St Jean. As mentioned, the strong point lay within reach of Wellington's centre, making it the key to the Duke's position: if the enemy chose to use the farm as an advanced artillery emplacement – or the launch pad for an all-out attempt to break open the road to Brussels – there would be little anyone could do about it. As the divisional commander on the spot, Alten recognised the danger and knew he must do something. The French, meanwhile – superintended by the indefatigable Marshal **Ney** – lost no time in exploiting their new asset, and a multitude of men and guns began converging on the embattled farm. According to **Edward Cotton** (1895): 'Swarms of their skirmishers passed the buildings and established themselves immediately under the crest of our position.'

It was time for Alten to act. Turning to his countryman, Baron Christian von Ompteda, Alten commanded him to launch his 2nd KGL Brigade in a counter-attack to retake the farm. But Ompteda had spotted enemy cuirassiers nearby, waiting to ride down any Allied infantry foolish enough to break their defensive squares and form into line. He queried Alten's order. The command was repeated, and once again Ompteda objected. At this moment the Prince of Orange intervened. Prince William – an inexperienced youth of 23, whose appointment to the command of I Corps had been a political sop to his father, King William of the Netherlands – insisted Ompteda obey his superior officer. Ompteda, pointing at the enemy horsemen, suggested advancing in square rather than in line, but the Prince haughtily pronounced the hostile riders to be Dutch. When his error was pointed out, the Prince snapped: 'I will listen to no further arguments.' After a moment's silence, Ompteda mounted his horse and led forward his 5th and 8th Line Battalions. Cotton continues: 'the German Legion were led against the assailants; they pressed on at a good pace, the enemy giving ground'. But historian A.F. Becke (1914) provides the sequel: 'Immediately afterwards the French horsemen pounced on their defenceless foes. Taking them in front and flank they rode over them, inflicting tremendous slaughter. Colonel Ompteda was killed and less than twenty survived this fatal charge.'

The loss of Ompteda's brigade left a gaping hole in Wellington's centre, and Ney, convinced he was on the point of breaking through the Allied line, sent word to Napoleon for reinforcements. But the Emperor was already using his reserves against **Bülow**'s Prussians, pouring into the village of Plancenoit in the French rear. Meanwhile, Wellington plugged the gap in his centre with more Germans, in the form of the black-clad Brunswick Corps, and Ney's breakthrough never materialised. But the French still had La Haie Sainte, and more guns were wheeled up to rake the Allied line at close range, as Alten, quoted by Kelly (1818), descibes:

> The fire of artillery now became more tremendous, and was continued with a violence which the oldest soldiers never before witnessed. The attacks of the French infantry and cavalry were incessant, and directed on various points. Buonaparte was resolved to pierce the centre, and open for himself a way to Brussels. He every moment advanced nearer to us, and continually brought up fresh troops. His artillery played on our squares at the distance of one hundred and fifty paces; but not a single battalion yielded, the dead were thrust aside, and the ranks were immediately closed.

It was during this maelstrom that Alten was himself severely wounded and carried from the field: command of his division devolved upon Kielmansegge.

Some sources – notably William Siborne (1848) and more recently Jac Weller (1967) – omit Alten's name in connection with the Ompteda affair, attributing the fatal error to the Prince of Orange alone. But whether the Prince initiated the order or merely enforced it, there is no record of Alten intervening on Ompteda's behalf. Thus, Alten's sin – be it one of commission or omission – surely sealed Ompteda's fate. This being the case, he must, as Philip Haythornthwaite (1999) observes, 'bear some responsibility for the order which doomed Omteda'. And yet, praised by Wellington, ennobled by the Hanoverian court, honoured by Tsar Alexander, Alten escaped censure. Instead, history condemned the youthful Prince of Orange, highlighting his lack of military tact and experience.

Anton
Sergeant James (dates unknown)

Stalwart of the 1st Battalion 42nd (Royal Highland) Foot. For him, the highlight of the Battle of Waterloo – apart from surviving unscathed to record his reminiscences – was witnessing the spectacular opening phase of the celebrated charge of the Scots Greys, led by Lieutenant Colonel **Hamilton**, as it slammed into **d'Erlon**'s approaching infantry columns about 2.00 p.m. When d'Erlon launched his attack, Anton's battalion had been positioned on the reverse slope of the ridge of Mont St Jean, to the left of the crossroads above La Haie Sainte, with the rest of Pack's 1,500-strong 9th British Brigade (part of **Picton**'s 5th British Infantry Division). But as the Frenchmen toiled up the forward slope towards Picton's position, led by Marcognet's 4,000-strong division, the Highlanders were rushed forward to meet the foe. First, however, they had to negotiate the hedges that lined both sides of the Ohain road, running atop the ridge, and it was at this point that, according to Anton, 'Our general gave orders to open our ranks. In an instant our cavalry passed through, leaped both hedges, and plunged on the panic-stricken foe.' As is well known, the dragoons of the Scots Greys, having successfully stalled the French attack – with the rest of the 2nd British Cavalry Brigade to which they belonged – failed to heed the 'recall' and headed off across the valley on a wild and foolhardy rampage through the intervals between the French infantry divisions, until they eventually reached the muzzles of **Napoleon**'s grand battery.

Attacked in turn by French cuirassiers and lancers, only half the regiment managed to return unscathed: no longer an organised corps of cavalry but a collection of scattered detachments. Having done enough, in their own estimation, to satisfy honour, these survivors took little or no further part in the battle. But by the time Anton published his memoirs 25 years later (1841), the affair had passed into legend as a Homeric feat, glorious fuel for burning national pride. Indeed for Anton – whose regiment sustained around 45 casualties at Waterloo, including its commander, Lieutenant Colonel Sir Robert Macara, who was killed (the 42nd had already suffered some 300 casualties at Quatre-Bras, two days before) – the charge of the Scots Greys remained his most vivid recollection of the great battle, inspiring the following poetic vision:

'Scotland forever!' burst from the mouth of each Highlander, as the Scots Greys pass through our ranks. What pen can describe the scene? Horses' hoofs sinking in men's breasts, breaking bones and pressing out their bowels. Riders' swords streaming in blood, waving over heads and descending in deadly vengeance. Stroke follows stroke, like the turning of a flail in the hand of a dexterous thresher; the living stream gushes red from the ghastly wound, spouts in the victor's face, and stains him with brains and blood. There the piercing shrieks and dying groans; there the loud cheering of an exulting army, animating the slayers to deeds of signal vengeance upon a daring foe. Such is the music of the field . . . It was a scene of vehement destruction, yells and shrieks, wounds and death; and the bodies of the dead served as pillows for the dying.

Arentschildt
Lieutenant Colonel Sir Frederick, Baron von (dates unknown)

Hanoverian in command of the 7th Brigade of Lord **Uxbridge**'s Cavalry Corps. Arentschildt's command is sometimes described as consisting of the 3rd King's German Legion (KGL) Hussars and the 13th Light Dragoons: some 1,160 sabres in all. But, according to H.T. Siborne (1891), the latter regiment was transferred to Colquhoun Grant's 5th Cavalry Brigade as a replacement for the 2nd KGL Hussars, who were 'still on the frontier'. Thus Arentschildt was left with some 700 Hanoverians, initially posted in rear of **Wellington**'s centre, near the farm of Mont St Jean (with the Netherlands cavalry of **van Merlen** and Trip). But between 4 p.m. and 6 p.m. Arentschildt's hussars helped fend off successive sorties by massed French cavalry, as noted by Sir James Shaw Kennedy (1865):

> To understand these great cavalry attacks, it is necessary to bear in mind the extraordinary fact that the large bodies of Dutch–Belgian cavalry, and the regiment of Cumberland Hussars, that stood in reserve behind the 1st and 3rd divisions of infantry, took no part in the action; the only cavalry which did act being the small remains of Lord **Edward Somerset**'s brigade, the 3rd Hussars of the King's German Legion, and part of Grant's brigade.

Jac Weller (1967) underlines the contribution made by Arentschildt's Germans: 'The brigades of **Dörnberg**, Grant and Arentschildt never achieved so brilliant a success as **Ponsonby** and Somerset, but fought far longer at near full strength and were handled with more skill.'

In all, Arentschildt's hussars took some 130 casualties in their clashes with **Napoleon**'s steel-clad cuirassiers, including regimental CO, Lieutenant Colonel Frederick Meyer, who was killed. And yet Arentschildt's name is notable by its absence in Wellington's Waterloo Dispatch, which mentions – 'for His Royal Highness's approbation' – the remainder of Uxbridge's brigade commanders.

Arentschildt survived Waterloo to publish *Instructions For Officers and Non-Commissioned Officers of Cavalry On Outpost Duty* in 1854.

Bachelu
General Gilbert Désiré Joseph (1777–1849)

Commander of the 5th Infantry Division of **Reille**'s II Corps, numbering some 4,000 men in all. Coming from a middle-class background, Bachelu snubbed a cosy corner in his father's law practice to join the Revolutionary Army: first as an engineer and later as an infantryman. Consistently showing courage, initiative and ability, Bachelu was a general by the age of 33.

At Waterloo, Bachelu's command was initially placed in reserve, near the farm of La Belle Alliance, but by mid-afternoon his division was ordered to advance into the meat-grinding battle for Hougoumont. According to Victor Hugo, in *Les Misérables* (1862), Hougoumont was 'a fateful place, the beginning of the disaster, the first obstacle encountered at Waterloo by the great tree-feller of Europe whose name was **Napoleon**'. In fact, the Emperor had intended the assault to be a mere diversion, the idea being to tempt **Wellington** to weaken his line on Mont St Jean by sending troops to its defence. But the Duke did not significantly reinforce the château, relying instead on the fighting qualities of the elite troops stationed there. In the event, Wellington's men held out, weathering successive attacks, and the 'diversion' became a battle-within-a-battle, sucking in some 15,000 French troops.

It was around 2.30 p.m. when Bachelu entered the maelstrom, leading the fifth assault on Hougoumont in person, over a killing-ground raked by Allied cannon-fire. Marching in a north-westerly direction, in a diagonal from La Belle Alliance towards the château's orchard, Bachelu's division was obliged to cross Wellington's front: thus it was exposed to a storm of shot and shell. Unsurprisingly, the attack broke up before reaching its objective. Undeterred, Bachelu rallied his men and launched another sortie, but just as the orchard was reached, a barrage of Allied shells put paid to the heroics. Bachelu – whose horse was killed under him – was hit in the head by a shell splinter, courtesy of Captain Cleeves' battery of 9-pounders.

Bachelu was immediately evacuated to Paris – not the safest of places for Napoleonic officers in the wake of the Emperor's defeat. Napoleon abdicated for the second and final time on 22 June 1815 and was replaced by Louis XVIII. The new Bourbon monarch was the brother of Louis XVI, guillotined by Revolutionaries in 1793, and the uncle of Louis XVII, who died in prison two years after his father's execution, neglected and maltreated by his Republican captors. And so the incoming Royalists unleashed a savage backlash against their enemies. As Elaine Mokhtefi (2002) observes: 'the first year of Louis' reign was known as the White Terror, whose victims were Jacobins and Bonapartists'. In other words, it was open season on the survivors of Napoleon's Waterloo Army, and several generals were executed by the authorities or lynched by the mob. Many more were imprisoned or banished. Bachelu – recovering from his Waterloo wounds – fell into this latter category, being incarcerated on 15 October 1815 and then exiled.

Bachelu's fate, though not uncommon, was unfortunate, as he had never been a staunch Bonapartist. But he had been – indeed still was – a staunch Republican: it was for loyalty to the Revolution, rather than Napoleon, that Bachelu was persecuted by the Bourbons. Many of his fellow officers took a more pragmatic approach to principles, adapting political personas to the prevailing climate. But Bachelu stuck to his guns and remained an unrepentent Republican. Thus, his career – still full of potential – was effectively at an end.

Even when he returned to France, Bachelu continued to fall foul of the authorities for his politically incorrect stance, retiring from public life in 1848 – just days before Louis Blanc's socialist Revolution toppled the 'July Monarchy' of Louis Philippe. At last, Bachelu's beloved republic had been restored and Paris, in the words of Toqueville, 'was in the sole hands of those who owned nothing' (Mokhtefi 2002). But Bachelu did not enjoy this triumph for long. His health broken, the 72-year-old revolutionary died in Paris on 16 June 1849. The Second Republic died soon after: replaced in 1852 by Napoleon III's Second Empire.

Bailly de Monthion
General François Gédéon (1776–1850)

Deputy chief of staff to **Napoleon**'s Army of the North. According to Tony Linck (1993), Bailly de Monthion was 'possibly one of the most underestimated men to serve with the Army'. He had been appointed chief of staff to the Army of the North (*l'Armée du Nord*) on 8 April 1815, toiling ceaselessly to set up an efficient headquarters. Bailly was a good man for the job, having worked closely with Marshal Berthier, Napoleon's legendary chief of staff of the glory years. But Napoleon found Bailly too cool for his liking (and decidedly difficult to intimidate) so he declared protocol required a marshal for the post and Bailly, a mere general of division, was replaced by the inept but malleable Marshal **Soult** in May – the very eve of the Waterloo campaign. Bailly was retained as Soult's deputy. But the demotion came as a bitter blow and one with far-reaching consequences: for Bailly's seething resentment was unhappily wedded to Soult's sloppy inefficiency.

As mentioned above, Bailly had spent time as Berthier's understudy, and as far as staffwork was concerned, he could have had no better mentor. A gifted administrator, Berthier had the ability to translate Napoleon's broad-brush concepts and rapid changes of mind into crisp, concise, consistent orders. But by 1814 Berthier was sick of war, claiming, 'I'm being killed by work . . . An ordinary soldier is better off than I am.' Thus, when Napoleon returned from Elba, Berthier refused to answer his call. Within weeks, Berthier was dead: having mysteriously fallen to his death from a hotel balcony on 1 June 1815: some claim he was murdered by six masked men, but an accident seems more likely – or perhaps suicide, prompted by divided loyalties. At any rate, Berthier – the man who might have won the Waterloo campaign for Napoleon – had fought his last battle, and the fate of the army, having been initially placed in the hands of his talented protégé, was transferred to the weak grip of Marshal Soult.

It is generally put about that Soult, an able battlefield commander, was ill-suited to the post of chief of staff. According to historian Raymond Horricks (1995), 'He did not know how to intepret Napoleon's mind and his drafted orders were far from clear.' In theory, however, Soult was to be aided by Bailly, whose experience he could reasonably expect to draw on. But Bailly remained aloof, and instead of stepping in to help his new chief, stepped aside, allowing his illustrious master rope enough to hang himself. Unfortunately for Napoleon, the rope was long enough to hang the whole army: delays, muddled messages and a general operational carelessness marked the campaign, materially adding to its ultimate failure.

One of Soult's apparent oversights was his failure to dispatch orders in duplicate, or even triplicate, as Berthier had done. Consequently, orders went astray when single dispatch riders were delayed, causing mayhem. An example of this occurred on 15 June, when **Vandamme**'s corps failed to receive its marching orders, Soult's single dispatch rider having fallen from his horse and broken his leg. Naturally, Bailly was familiar with Berthier's system and could have advised Soult, but he elected to remain silent. But it was on the following day that a blizzard of botched orders and delayed dispatches ensured the collapse of Napoleon's carefully laid plans. Shortly after midday on 16 June, Napoleon, with some 60,000 troops, faced **Blücher**'s 84,000 Prussians at Ligny; while 10 miles to the north-east, at Quatre-Bras, Marshal **Ney**'s contingent of 25,000 faced the 8,000 Netherlanders of **Wellington**'s advanced guard. Having crossed the Sambre into Belgium and occupied the town of Charleroi, Napoleon's strategic aim was to drive a wedge between the two Allied armies, keep them apart, and defeat each one in turn. Ney had been detached from the main body to secure the vital crossroads at Quatre-Bras, before returning to help crush Blücher. But due to a misunderstanding, Ney was under the impression he was spearheading a major attack. Thus, while Napoleon was impatiently awaiting Ney's return before attacking at Ligny, Ney was impatiently waiting for Napoleon before attacking at Quatre-Bras. Having frittered away the entire morning, Ney finally launched a lukewarm assault on Wellington's rapidly concentrating army, as Napoleon – still confident of Ney's imminent arrival – eventually opened the Battle of Ligny. But the misunderstandings did not end there: **Lobau**'s VI Corps, languishing 20 miles to the rear at Charleroi, was still awaiting its marching orders; while **d'Erlon**'s I Corps spent the day marching between Quatre-Bras and Ligny, unsure which battle to fight, and in the event fighting neither.

The errors listed above highlight the shortcomings of French staffwork: orders failed to arrive, or were late, or were unclear. The upshot was an irretrievable loss of time. At Ligny, Napoleon's final attack was delayed by the non-appearance of Ney, the late arrival of Lobau, and the mistaking of d'Erlon's distant columns for enemy reinforcements. Consequently, Blücher's eventual defeat was cloaked by nightfall, allowing him to slip away unmolested to Wavre and remain in contact with Wellington. At Quatre-Bras, Ney also dallied, allowing Wellington time to concentrate, counter-attack, and shunt the French off the battlefield. Thus, French operations on 16 June – far from keeping the two Allied armies apart, as planned – helped facilitate their fateful junction two days later at Waterloo.

Bailly was among the wounded at Waterloo and, rightly anticipating Royalist reprisals, deserted a week after the battle. But in 1818 Bailly returned to France to pick up his career. After a series of promotions he rose to become a peer of France in 1837.

Baring

Major George (dates unknown)

Commander of the 2nd Light Battalion of the King's German Legion (KGL). An understrength unit, consisting of some 400 green-clad riflemen, the battalion formed part of **Ompteda**'s 2nd KGL Brigade, within Alten's 3rd British Infantry Division. It was posted in the centre of **Wellington**'s position, behind the sunken road atop the ridge of Mont St Jean.

Little is known of Baring's background, save that he joined the KGL as a captain, subsequently gaining campaign experience in the Baltic, Northern Europe and the Spanish Peninsula, where, at Albuera in 1811, he was wounded while serving as **Alten**'s aide-de-camp. This taste for soldiering did not, it seems, blunt the German's artistic sensibilities, for Baring apparently loved music and played the flute. The narrative of his Waterloo experiences, quoted by Beamish (1832–7), betrays a sensitive man with a flair for expressive prose.

On the morning of 18 June Baring found himself in charge at the farmhouse of La Haie Sainte, the battalion's commanding officer, Lieutenant Colonel David Martin, being absent. It was to be, perhaps, the most important post on the whole battlefield: for this bastion, lying a few hundred yards in advance of Wellington's centre, commanded its approaches and was crucial to its security. Described by **Edward Cotton** (1895) as 'a strong stone and brick building', La Haie Sainte was smaller than the château of Hougoumont, forming a picturesque farmstead lying at the foot of Wellington's ridge, abutting the Brussels high road. On the north side of the farmhouse – that facing Wellington's lines on Mont St Jean – was a small kitchen garden. On the south side was a farmyard, enclosed by various outbuildings, and terminating in a great barn. Beyond the barn was an orchard, and beyond the orchard, half a mile away, was **Napoleon**'s grand battery. Baring and his tiny garrison had spent the previous night at the farmstead, sheltering from the torrential rain. And although, by his own testimony, he fully expected to be attacked, Baring apparently allowed his men to chop up all available wood – including the huge barn door – to feed their fires. Perhaps even more surprising is the fact Baring neglected to stockpile ammunition. Thus, when the day of battle dawned, this vital outpost sported a large – and embarrassing – gap on the side facing the French (where the barn door had been), guarded by a mere 400 riflemen, each carrying only 60 rounds. As Baring himself admits: 'Important as the possession of this farm apparently was, the means of defending it were very insufficient.' (Beamish 1832–7).

The battle began in earnest around 1.30 p.m. with the attack of **d'Erlon**'s I Corps on Wellington's left-centre. As part of this grand operation, La Haie Sainte was assaulted by Colonel Charlet's infantry brigade, from **Quiot**'s 1st Infantry Division, which took possession of the orchard and the kitchen garden. But Baring's embattled garrison held firm: a defiant rock in a surging sea of soldiery. Baring recalled: 'The first shot broke the bridle of my horse close to my hand, and the second killed Major Böseweil, who was standing near me.' Alten, the divisional commander on Mont St Jean, decided to counter-attack Charlet's men, to relieve Baring, and sent the Lüneberg Light Battalion, under Colonel von Klencke, down to the farm. But they were caught in the open by cuirassiers, and those who were not cut to pieces fled back to the Allied lines.

Around 2 p.m., however, d'Erlon's mighty attack was stalled, and the deployment of British heavy cavalry helped clear La Haie Sainte of its invaders, giving the hard-pressed garrison a respite. Baring records: 'In this first attack I lost a considerable number of men, besides three officers killed, and six wounded.' Doubtless anticipating these casualties, Alten sent 170 men from the 1st KGL Light

La Haie Sainte – print by T. Sutherland, 1816

Battalion to bolster Baring's force. Meanwhile, two companies from the 1st Battalion 95th Rifles took up position at the sandpit in rear of the farm complex as supports. Perhaps an hour or so later, the French returned to the assault, two columns of infantry once more surrounding the stronghold. The German marksmen inside, armed with the deadly Baker rifle rather than standard-issue muskets, fired through loopholes in the farmhouse wall and all the doors and windows they could find. They even fired from the roof of the piggery (which according to Lieutenant George **Graeme**, a Scotsman serving with the garrison, contained no pigs but a calf) and as Baring states: 'every bullet of ours hurt'. But now more than ever, he regretted the burning of the barn door the previous night: 'many lives were sacrificed to the defence of the doors and gates; the most obstinate contest was carried on where the gate was wanting, and where the enemy seemed determined to enter'. And yet this attack also petered out, with the repulse of **Ney**'s cavalry assault on Wellington's line around 5.30 p.m., and once again Baring's garrison enjoyed a brief interlude.

It is at this juncture in Baring's narrative that he first admits to being alarmed by lack of ammunition, and notes that half the garrison's rounds had been used up. As mentioned above, Baring's men were armed with rifles, and though ten times more accurate than muskets, these weapons needed special cartridges. Baring was aware of this and took advantage of the lull to send an officer back up the hill with a request for bullets. The ammunition was promised, but never materialised. Soon after, Baring spotted fresh French battalions approaching and sent another officer to repeat the request. But instead of bullets, Baring was sent more troops: some 85 men from the Light Company of the 5th KGL Line Battalion under Captain Christian von Wurmb, who was killed by cannon-shot on the way. As Baring himself comments, these reinforcements 'could not compensate for want of ammuntion, which every moment increased'. When a third officer was dispatched to brigade headquarters, the result was 'as fruitless as the other two applications; however, 200 Nassau troops were sent me'.

Meanwhile, the farm was under attack again. The French, unable to force their way into the great barn, simply set the place alight (fortunately for Baring, the barn had already been emptied of its dry, inflammable straw by troops hunting for bedding or tinder). As it happened, the newly arrived Nassauers had brought their huge camp kettles with them, and these were used to carry water from the farmyard – Private Lewis Dahrendorf lending a hand, despite three bayonet wounds – and according to Graeme: 'Lieutenant Carey, in spite of the enemy's fire, went out, and with his men, poured water on the flames.' In his narrative, Baring praises the bravery and tenacity of his troops: 'Many of the men, although covered with wounds, could not be brought to retire. "So long as our officers fight, and we can stand", was their constant reply, "we will not stir from the spot." '

After an hour or so of frantic combat, interspersed with bouts of fire-fighting, came another interlude. Still uppermost in Baring's mind was the need for ammuntition. The men checked their pouches: on average, each soldier had four rounds left. The bodies of dead comrades were searched and a few more precious cartridges found. But soon the men were begging Baring for bullets: 'At this moment I would have blessed the ball that came to deprive me of my life.' All Baring could do was send a fourth man to ask for ammunition, and tell his men to husband their remaining rounds and make every shot count. 'I received one unanimous reply: "No man will desert you, we will fight and die with you!" ' And the soldiers were as good as their word: Private Frederick Lindau, wounded twice in the head and losing blood, refused to quit his post at the gaping entrance to the barn, partly blocked by French corpses; while Private Ernst Lindhorst guarded a breach in the courtyard wall armed with only a bayonet, a piece of wood and a supply of bricks.

The end came around 6.30 p.m., when, under Marshal Ney's personal direction, a hurricane hit La Haie Sainte, headed by the elite troops of the 13th Légère, under Colonel Gougeon. As the French swarmed up to the orchard, the defenders let fly a few final, scattered shots. But then silence betrayed their helplessness and Gougeon's men began smashing down the main gate. Meanwhile, French troops scaled the walls and after so many unsuccessful attempts, finally pushed their way into the great barn. According to A.F. Becke (1914): 'Even then the gallant defenders fought stubbornly, quarter being neither asked nor given'; while Baring states: 'Inexpressibly painful as the decision was of giving up the place, my feeling of duty as a man overcame that of honour, and I gave the order to retire through the house into the garden.' And so Baring and his band filed one at a time through the narrow passage of the farmhouse, making for the kitchen garden beyond, the French at their heels.

Outside, Baring sent his survivors back up the hill to the Allied position, before jumping on a riderless horse and making his own escape, bullets whistling about him. He gained the crest of the Allied ridge in time to witness French skirmishers pouring from the farmhouse below and advancing up the slope. His brigade commander, Baron von **Ompteda**, led the 5th and 8th KGL Line Battalions in a counter-attack: 'nothing seemed likely to terminate the slaughter but the entire destruction of one army or the other'. At that moment, Baring's horse was struck in the head by a bullet and the next instant Baring was trapped under its dead weight. Eventually dragged free and supplied with a fresh mount, Baring attached himself to the 1st KGL Hussars for the final advance against the French in the late evening, following the repulse of Napoleon's Imperial Guard.

After the battle, Baring went in search of his battalion:

> Out of nearly 400 men, with which I commenced the battle, only forty-two remained effective. Whoever I asked after, the answer was 'Killed' or 'Wounded'. I freely confess that tears came involuntarily into my eyes at this sad intelligence, and the many bitter feelings that seized upon me.

Many writers have misinterpreted Baring's words, declaring only 42 men escaped from La Haie Sainte alive, but this is incorrect. Baring is referring to those men from his own battalion still present and capable of bearing arms. Subsequent casualty returns, compiled after the battle, when scattered soldiers had regrouped, show that in reality the 2nd KGL Light Battalion lost some 202 men: almost 50 per cent of its initial strength.

Baring survived the Belgian campaign, later becoming a major general in the Hanoverian Army. Of his experiences at La Haie Sainte, he later wrote: 'Never had I felt myself so elevated; but never also placed in so painful a position, where honour contended with a feeling for the safety of the men who had given me such an unbounded proof of their confidence.'

As to the mystery surrounding the missing ammunition, it remains a controversy to this day. Most accounts of the battle pass over the matter or tread round it carefully. But who was to blame for the oversight? The staff at Ompteda's brigade headquarters must have known about Baring's shortage of ammunition, having, presumably, received four urgent requests from the embattled Major. Yet one of the first explanations to emerge from the British camp involved the claim that no door existed in the north wall of the farmhouse – the side facing the Allied lines – so supplies simply could not be delivered. This view was expressed by William Tomkinson of the 16th Light Dragoons, who recorded in his diary (Tomkinson 1894):

> It so happened that the communication with La Haie Sainte
> was on one side of the building, and not directly in its rear, so
> that the enemy, by occupying the ground on that side, rendered
> the approach impossible. There ought to have been a hole broken
> through the wall directly in the rear, which would have preserved
> the communication. The Duke said he ought to have ordered this,
> but, to use his own expression, 'it was impossible for me to think
> of everything'.

Yet Baring's defenders point out that a rear door did exist and, indeed, plans, drawings and early photographs of the complex clearly show a door and windows on the north side of the farmhouse, through which, presumably, ammunition could have been passed.

A second British explanation was that the communication between La Haie Sainte and Mont St Jean was intercepted by the French, prohibiting the delivery of supplies. This theory is disproved by the fact that numerous reinforcements – as well as Baring's various messengers – travelled to and fro between the farmhouse and the main position. Even when La Haie Sainte was overwhelmed by the final French attack, Baring and his survivors managed to escape from the farmhouse into the kitchen garden at its rear, and up the slopes of Mont St Jean beyond.

By 1848, however, William Siborne claimed to have solved the mystery:

It has been communicated to me from Hanover, upon excellent authority, that the cause of Major Baring's not having been supplied with ammunition arose from the circumstance, that there existed only one cart with rifle ammunition for the two light battalions of the King's German Legion, and that this cart was involved in the precipitate retreat of a great part of the baggage, etc., and thrown in a ditch.

At last, a plausible – if less than glorious – solution. But this still does not let Baring off the hook entirely, for some writers highlight his failure to call for extra ammuntion before the battle began. Baring himself remained tight-lipped over the issue, simply saying: 'I called for more, but none arrived.'

Barker
Henry Aston (1774–1856)

Artist and businessman who profited from the Battle of Waterloo. He was the younger son of Robert Barker, the Irish portrait artist and inventor of the 'panorama': a vehicle for presenting vast paintings designed to place viewers at the centre of spectacular scenes. Barker senior opened the world's first purpose-built panorama in 1793 at Leicester Square, London. His son Henry – who had studied at the Royal Academy with J.M.W. **Turner** – acted as chief assistant. Viewers were invited to step into a rotunda, there to sample the magical experience of witnessing exotic landscapes or famous battles unfold before their eyes. As Kristine Hughes (1998) describes, moving panoramas 'featured a long continuous picture measuring 30 feet high and 300 or 400 feet yards long, which slowly unrolled and passed before the seated spectators, who could then see "many miles of country and foreign scenes without trouble and at little cost"'. In the days before photography or cinema, the effect was astonishing: especially when heightened by atmospheric lighting, music and sound effects. It was an early – and successful – attempt at 'virtual reality'.

In 1806 Robert Barker died and Henry took over the business, promptly buying out his only rival: a panorama situated in the Strand, established by elder brother, Thomas, in 1802. Having married Maria Bligh – daughter of Captain William Bligh of HMS *Bounty* fame – Henry Barker toured Europe, in search of suitable subjects for panoramic paintings (these would include views of Constantinople and Paris, as well Nelson's victories at the Nile and Copenhagen). A stickler for detail, Barker personally made countless sketches on-site for his team of painters to copy back in London. Barker's work brought him into contact with many celebrities: he first met **Napoleon** in 1802, on a visit to Paris during the brief interval of tranquillity following the Peace of Amiens. Twelve years later, Barker journeyed to Elba to sketch the fallen Emperor in exile. Little did he realise the 'Corsican Adventurer' would shortly provide him with a fortune.

For in the aftermath of Waterloo, Barker visited the battlefield to make drawings and collect information. The plan was to produce a panoramic record of what was quickly becoming an event of sublime – almost spiritual – importance back in Britain. Exhibited at Leicester Square in 1815, Barker's depiction of the final stage of the battle – the rout of Napoleon's army – was an instant success. Barker charged 1 shilling admittance, yet within a few short months he grossed over £10,000 (some £500,000 in modern terms). His Waterloo panorama was the biggest box office hit of its day. Punters were not only treated to a view of the battle, they were invited to step into it; to see, perhaps, what **Wellington** himself had seen. An explanatory leaflet, a fold-out plan and a verbal commentary augmented the experience.

Acutely aware of Waterloo's growing commercial potential, Barker sent his panorama on a tour of England and Scotland. This was followed by a successful tour of the USA. On its return to Leicester Square, the Waterloo panorama was exhibited once again, remaining in place until it 'perished from damp and other causes'. Barker's formula was soon copied and rival panoramas were produced, including Marshall's 'Grand Historical Peristrephic Panorama of the Ever-Memorable Battles of Ligny, Les Quatre Bras, and Waterloo', which, accompanied by a military band, toured Britain and Ireland for 10 years before also making its way to the USA. And in 1912,

Barker's Waterloo panorama was surpassed – in scale at least – by Louis Dumoulin's depiction of **Ney**'s massed cavalry charge on Mont St Jean. Exhibited on the battlefield, Dumoulin's was the largest circular painting in the world. But none could compete with Barker's panorama for profit. In 1824 the 50-year-old Henry Aston Barker sold out and retired on its proceeds, having transformed a monstrous battle into a monster business opportunity.

Bell
Sir Charles (1774–1842)

Celebrated surgeon and anatomist, best known for his discovery of Bell's palsy: paralysis of the facial nerve leading to muscular atrophy in one side of the face. Born in Edinburgh, the fourth son of a local vicar, Bell followed his elder brother John into the medical profession. It was largely under his brother's tutelage that Bell learned his surgical and anatomical skills. Both brothers were skilled draughtsmen, making detailed anatomical sketches for use as reference material and teaching aids. As well as a practising surgeon, Bell was also a pioneer in the field of neurology, publishing several books on the topic, including the influential *Idea of a New Anatomy of the Brain* (1811). Keen to learn more about the treatment of extreme injuries, such as those sustained on the battlefield, Bell was among the civilian medicos who travelled to Portsmouth in 1809, to help treat Sir John Moore's Corunna survivors. The experience prompted Bell to publish *Dissertation on Gunshot Wounds* in 1814 – just in time for the surgeon's toughest challenge: the wounded of Waterloo.

The Battle of Waterloo was one of the bloodiest in modern history. Although estimates vary, it seems likely that, by battle's end, over 50,000 men had been killed or wounded. With **Napoleon**'s army in retreat and **Blücher**'s in pursuit, it largely fell to **Wellington**'s surgeons to treat the wounded of both sides. But the Duke's medical services were undermanned, underfunded and ill-prepared. Furthermore, medical knowledge was limited. Many medicos simply prescribed bleeding or an intake of alcohol or opium to patients, unaware that men suffering from severe blood loss need plenty of fresh water to stave off lethal levels of dehydration. And surgical techniques were basic: shattered bones were rounded off with a chisel; musket balls were extracted from limbs with skewers and forceps; amputations were performed with a knife or bone saw and live maggots sewn into wounds to consume the remaining dead tissue. Needles were unsterilised, drastically increasing the risk of infection, and there were no anaesthetics: casualties were expected to bear surgery patiently, without fuss. Little wonder, perhaps, that eyewitness accounts paint a picture of general neglect regarding wounded survivors in the immediate aftermath of the fighting.

But to be fair, military surgeons and local civilians felt themselves helpless in the face of an overwhelming and unprecedented human tragedy. And so Brussels became, in the words of its *Burgomaster*, Baron **d'Hoogvoorst**, the 'grand hospital of the Allied army'. The city fathers requisitioned carts and carriages for the evacuation of all the Waterloo wounded, beginning with Allied personnel (French casualties were still being ferried to Brussels a week after the battle). Soon the city was invested by an army of invalids some 20,000-strong, its six major hospitals swamped. A shortage of hospital beds led to further evacuations of casualties, mainly to Antwerp, almost 30 miles to the north. Some made the agonising journey in farm carts, others in canal boats. Meanwhile, Brussels became a charnel house, its citizens employed as nurses, porters, orderlies and gravediggers. With local resources exhausted, medical volunteers were drafted in from England.

Bell arrived in Brussels on 30 June, armed with his surgical instruments and his sketchbook. Accompanied by a small group of fellow civilians, Bell joined the military doctors – including the celebrated Baron **Larrey**, Napoleon's chief surgeon – in the humanitarian effort. Bell operated on soldiers of both sides, performing numerous amputations and working 12 hours a day, till, as he later recorded (1870), his clothes were 'stiff with blood and my arms powerless with the exertion of using the knife'. But as Philip Shaw (2002) points out:

Bell stood to gain a lot from his labours: in the aftermath of battle subjects were plentiful; the severity of the wounds meant that in many cases difficult or obscure areas of the body were already on display; on foreign soil the practice of dissection escaped legal censure. For Bell, therefore, Waterloo was also a locus of scientific curiosity: a zone of suffering, to be sure, but also a zone of knowledge and observation.

Nevertheless, Bell's primary concern was the care of the wounded, and in 1815 it was very much a 'hands on' affair. According to medical experts Crumplin and Starling (2005): 'Bell used his forefinger as his prime diagnostic aid. In the absence of X-rays or adequate operative exposure under anaesthesia, his forefinger gave him the information he required.' Bell also observed the military surgeons at work, recording case histories and jotting down copious notes. He also began sketching patients: the idea being to record the soldiers' injuries and the results of surgery, for future reference. Some two weeks after the battle, Bell used the sketches as the basis for a remarkable series of watercolours, depicting a wide range of wounds and surgical interventions. These studies (on display at the Royal College of Surgeons in Edinburgh) constitute an impressive visual record of contemporary battlefield injuries and treatments, and all are accompanied by Bell's own case notes. One of Bell's sitters (though not one of his own patients) was Sergeant Anthony Tuittmeyer of the 2nd Line Battalion King's German Legion. According to Bell:

> A round shot carried off his arm on the field of Waterloo. In this condition, unsubdued, he rode upright into Brussels, fifteen miles, and presented himself to Dr Bach at the hospital of St Elizabeth. When put into bed he fainted, and remained insensible for half an hour.

As Crumplin and Starling rightly observe: 'This is one of those almost incredible feats of stoicism by a wounded man.'

Bell quit Brussels on 7 July, returning to Britain with his Waterloo sketches and watercolours. He used the latter as teaching aids during lectures at University College London. From them, Bell later produced another set of paintings, this time in oils, which his widow presented to the Army Medical Department in 1866.

These are on permanent loan in the Wellcome Trust for the History of Medicine.

Bijlandt
Major General Willem Frederik van (dates unknown)

Often referred to as 'Bylandt' in British sources; commanded the 1st Brigade of **Perponcher**'s 2nd Netherlands Infantry Division. This brigade consisted of the 7th Regiment of the Line, the 27th Jägers, and the 5th, 7th, and 8th Militia Regiments: five battalions in all, numbering almost 3,000 men. The 7th Regiment of the Line was a Belgian outfit, the rest were Dutch. Although largely inexperienced, these soldiers of the newly created Kingdom of the United Netherlands (an uneasy marriage between Catholic Belgium and Protestant Holland, both former French satellites) had performed well at Quatre-Bras on 16 June. Yet at Waterloo, the conduct of van Bijlandt's troops would spark a controversy that rages to this day.

According to Ronald Pawly (2002): 'The British government still felt some distrust towards Dutch and Belgian veterans of **Napoleon**'s armies, who had been serving the Emperor until just a year before; there was always a nagging doubt that they might change sides.' It was for this reason **Wellington** mixed his Netherlands battalions with British: the idea being to thwart a last-minute mass desertion. Wellington was aware many Dutch officers had served in the armies of the old pro-French Batavian Republic and Louis Bonaparte's Kingdom of Holland. Belgium, meanwhile, had been annexed by France in 1795, Belgian sons having fought in Napoleon's Grand Army for almost 10 years. This fact was not lost on Napoleon, who penned a proclamation to the Belgian people on the eve

Dutch Jäger – print after W.B. van der Kooc

31

of battle: 'Napoleon is among you. You are worthy to be Frenchmen. Rise in mass, join my invincible phalanxes to exterminate the remainder of those barbarians who are your enemies and mine.' Yet both Dutch and Belgian troops fought hard during the Waterloo campaign, determined to prove their loyalty to the new Netherlands state: 'Napoleon thought that all the Belgians would range themselves on his side', wrote a veteran quoted by Demetrius C. Boulger (1901), 'but he very soon found that he was mistaken. We fought as if we were possessed.' This sentiment was echoed by the first battle reports of *The Times*, which declared: 'The Belgic and Dutch troops behaved admirably.'

But hardly had the gunsmoke cleared at Waterloo when the British turned on their Dutch–Belgian allies, charging them with cowardice. Singled out for particular attention was van Bijlandt's brigade, accused of ignominious flight at the start of the battle. Some say van Bijlandt's men fled before Napoleon unleashed his great barrage about 1 p.m.; some say they broke soon after; while others claim the Netherlanders ran before the advancing columns of **d'Erlon**'s I Corps about 2 p.m. That they did run – and in a base and unwarlike fashion – was taken as fact, quickly entering the British psyche. The following exchange, allegedly overheard by British cavalry officer William Tomkinson at the close of battle, and quoted in his diary (1894), neatly sums up the prevailing attitude:

> Prince of **Orange**: 'Well, **Alava**, what do you think your Spaniards would have done had they been present on this occasion?'
> Alava: 'Your Highness, I do not think they would have run away, as your Belgians did, before the first shot was fired.'

Sadly, the mud stuck – and stayed stuck. In 1848 William Siborne published his magisterial account of the campaign, *History of the War in France and Belgium*, in which he claimed: 'The Dutch–Belgians . . . commenced a hurried retreat, not partially and promiscuously, but collectively and simultaneously . . . As they rushed passed the British columns, hissings, hootings, and execrations were instantly heaped upon them.' While in *Vanity Fair*, published the same year, the novelist Thackeray bemoans Netherlandish squeamishness, lamenting that van Bijlandt's flight was 'only checked by the advance of the British in their rear'.

Successive Anglophile authors have more or less repeated the theme. But what really happened? According to Christopher Hibbert (1967), when Wellington assembled his army at Mont St Jean, he told his commanders to dispose their troops according to the 'usual' practice. Those familiar with the Duke's habits knew this meant deploying men on the reverse slope of the position. But van Bijlandt, for reasons that remain unclear, opted to deploy on the forward slope, in full view of the enemy. And there, it seems, he remained till midday 18 June. For according to a report written by a senior staff officer, it was at noon that van Bijlandt's exposed position was noticed by his countryman, General Perponcher, who, after consulting Wellington, ordered an immediate withdrawal. And so van Bijlandt's battalions were safe behind the crest of Wellington's ridge, flanked by the brigades of **Kempt** and Pack, before Napoleon's grand battery heralded d'Erlon's attack. As Boulger (1901) states: 'It is therefore clear from the evidence that the Bylandt brigade was withdrawn from the ground which under a mistaken view of the facts it was denounced for having abandoned.'

Boulger's comment seems reasonable: van Bijlandt's troops did not run before the first shot was fired, they withdrew out of the enemy's line of sight, in accordance with Perponcher's instructions and Wellington's wishes. But van Bijlandt must have left a small detachment of skirmishers on the forward slope of Mont St Jean. For when d'Erlon launched his columns against Wellington's left-centre about 1.30 p.m., these troops did indeed give way: hardly surprising, considering some 13,000 Frenchmen were advancing against them. **James Anton** of the 42nd Highlanders (part of Pack's brigade) recalled (Anton 1841) that: 'France now pushed forward on the line of our Belgic allies, drove them from their post, and rolled them into one promiscuous mass of con-fusion through the ranks of our brigade.' But presumably the bulk of van Bijlandt's troops were in line, Pack's men to their left, Kempt's to their right. Meanwhile, the French infantry reached the crest of the ridge, striking the Ohain road, lined on both sides with thick hedges. Ahead of them Allied troops were waiting. Including van Bijlandt's men. For according to an officer named Scheltens, adjutant of the Belgian 7th Regiment of the Line, quoted by Boulger (1901):

The battalion remained lying down behind the road until the head of the French column was at the distance of a pistol shot. The line then received the order to rise and commence firing. The French column, which was crossing the hollow road, committed the fault of halting in order to reply to our fire . . . The fire of the English very soon enveloped the column, which endeavoured to deploy instead of pushing on. The English cavalry arrived to take part in the fray. It passed like a whirlwind along the wings of our battalion, several of our men being knocked down by the horsemen. The battalion, which had to cease firing, for the cavalry were in front, immediately crossed the road and advanced. The enemy, taken in flank by **Picton**'s regiments, and in reverse by the cavalry, was compelled to retreat, leaving behind a great many prisoners. The battalion then took up again its first position, where it remained to the end of the battle.

But according to **Edward Cotton** (1895), British veteran and battlefield guide, 'Bylandt's brigade of the Netherlanders was overpowered and gave way . . . it was rallied again in rear of the ridge where it remained for the rest of the day.' The discrepancy is accounted for by historian Mark Adkin (2001), who explains that while the 7th Regiment held, the remainder of van Bijlandt's battalions melted. To substantiate this he quotes Major General **Constant de Rebecque**, chief of staff to the Prince of Orange, who noted that van Bijlandt's brigade: 'received the first shock and was cut up'.

Thus it would appear van Bijlandt's much-maligned Belgians stood firm, while his Dutchmen – inexperienced militia in the main – fled after a brief firefight, in the face of overwhelming numbers. Suffice it to say the British infantry were saved by the timely intervention of Sir **William Ponsonby**'s heavy cavalry. As for van Bijlandt, he was wounded in the melee, as was Colonel van Sanden of the 7th Line Regiment, and the colonels of all three Dutch militia regiments: surely a creditable performance by the Netherlands top brass? Meanwhile, having lost some 230 casualties at Waterloo, and a similar number at Quatre-Bras two days before, the Belgians of the 7th Regiment went on to become national heroes. Scheltens concludes:

In the evening we bivouacked on the very position we had held throughout the day. We were no more than 300 men all included; all the rest had been killed or wounded in this terrible affair – it was about half the effective. In a review held in the Bois de Boulogne by the Duke of Wellington, that general stopped before the battalion and complimented it on its fine conduct at Waterloo.

Blücher
Field Marshal Gebhard Leberecht von (1742–1819)

Commander of Prussian forces in the Netherlands, the so-called Army of the Lower Rhine. According to historian Jac Weller (1967), Blücher 'was not brainy. His greatest military virtues were steadfast courage, dash, fire and an intuitive grasp of how to handle an army in battle.' An assessment echoed by John R. Elting (1989), who adds: 'he loved to fight and he hated the French'. Lucky for the Allies he did: for without Blücher the Prussians would never have marched to Waterloo at all.

Field Marshal Blücher (1742–1819)

Born near Rostock, in what was then Mecklenberg, Blücher entered the Swedish Army aged 14, later transferring to a hussar regiment in the Prussian Army of Frederick the Great. By 1801 Blücher was a cavalry general and a bitter opponent of France. His loathing deepened after Prussia's humiliating defeat – and subsequent dismemberment – at **Napoleon**'s hands in 1806: Nostitz, Blücher's aide-de-camp observing, 'a thirst for bloody vengeance had taken possession of his will and of his intelligence' (Henderson 1911). Blücher's opportunity came in 1813, when, following Napoleon's catastrophic Russian campaign, Germany rose against French domination. It was during the German War of Liberation, as commander of the Army of Silesia, that Blücher took the talented General **Gneisenau** as his chief of staff. It proved a successful partnership, for as Philip Haythornthwaite (1998) states, 'They formed one of the greatest command partnerships in history, Gneisenau's calculating intelligence combining with Blücher's fire and determination.'

During the invasion of France the following year, Blücher proved himself a tireless fighter. Although defeated by Napoleon on four separate occasions, he beat the Emperor at Lâon, on 9–10 March 1814, following this up with a victory over Marshal Marmont at Fismes on 17 March. When Napoleon invaded Belgium on 16 June 1815, raising the curtain on the Waterloo campaign, he found Blücher occupying a series of low ridges north of Ligny. The Prussian Army numbered some 84,000, the French 80,000 (sources vary). But it was Blücher's force that gave way after a savage fight lasting over seven hours. **Jean-Roch Coignet**, a French guardsman, described Ligny in these terms: 'This was not a battle, it was a butchery' (Coignet 1928).

About 7.30 p.m., with his situation looking increasingly desperate, the septuagenarian Blücher led a cavalry charge. Gneisenau describes (1815) the sequel:

> A musket-shot struck the Field Marshal's horse; the animal, far from being stopped in his career by this wound, began to gallop more furiously, till it dropped down dead. The Field Marshal, stunned by the violent fall, lay entangled under the horse. The enemy's cuirassiers, following up their advantage, advanced; the last Prussian horseman had already passed by the Field Marshal, an adjutant

Blücher's Fall at Ligny
by George Jones

alone remained with him, and had just alighted to share his fate. The danger was great, but Heaven watched over him. The enemy, pursuing their charge, passed rapidly by the Field Marshal without seeing him; the next moment, a second charge of cavalry repelled them, they again passed by him, with the same precipitation, not perceiving him any more than they had done the first time. Then, but not without difficulty, the Field Marshal was disengaged from under the dead animal, and he immediately mounted a dragoon horse.

With Blücher apparently missing in action, Gneisenau took command and ordered a retreat. But instead of heading east to Germany, as Napoleon expected, the Prussians went north to Wavre because it was the only recognisable name on their maps. And so, as Geoffrey Wootten (1992) observes:

Wavre was chosen as a first stage before retiring eastward towards Liège. By almost pure accident, it was the one place Napoleon did not expect, and the one direction that would allow the Prussians the slightest option of joining up with **Wellington** before Brussels . . . Not that Gneisenau had any intention of moving to join Wellington; not only was he highly suspicious of his allies, almost to the point of Anglophobia in fact, but he was fully expecting the French pursuit to keep him fully occupied as he fell back.

It was at Wavre, about 12 miles north of Ligny, that the bruised Blücher rejoined his army later that night. According to biographer E.F. Henderson (1911):

While stretched on his couch at Wavre . . . [Blücher] wrote letters in the most courageous strain: 'If Napoleon fights a few more battles like this he and his army are done for!' And again: 'My troops fought like lions, but we were too weak; for two of my corps were not with me. Now I have drawn them all together.'

Having taken a day to recover from his ordeal, Blücher overruled Gneisenau and promised Wellington his aid. As Henderson states:

When he made this promise scarcely twelve hours had elapsed since his troops had suffered one of the great defeats in history, and the horrible harvest of dead and wounded had not yet been gathered in . . . When on the morning of the fateful 18th of June, Bietzke the physician proposed to rub ointment on the bruises he had incurred in his fall, he refused, saying that it was indifferent to him whether he went *balsamirt* or *nicht balsamirt*, anointed or unanointed, into eternity. 'But if things go well today,' he concluded, 'we shall soon all be washing and bathing in Paris!'

Thus, at 7 a.m. on 18 June, Blücher's order of the day concluded with these stirring words: 'I shall once more lead you against the enemy; we shall defeat him for we must!' As Nostitz remarked: 'no matter what his condition he would rather have himself tied on his horse than resign the command of the army' (Henderson 1911).

And so the 10-mile slog to Waterloo – or rather Plancenoit, the village situated on Napoleon's right flank – began. But it soon bogged down. Bülow's corps was chosen to lead the Prussian advance, but it was on the wrong side of town: the advance stalled while Bülow's troops pushed their way to the head of the queue. Then a fire broke out in one of Wavre's narrow streets, holding up the Prussian march for a further two hours. When clear of Wavre, the Prussians were obliged to wade through muddy lanes waterlogged from the recent downpours. According to Henderson:

> The march from Wavre to Waterloo would have been no remarkable achievement under ordinary circumstances; and Blücher, when he gave his promise to be present with his whole army, had not the slightest doubt of being able to be on hand at the beginning of the battle. But the circumstances were not ordinary, for everything conspired to make the march as toilsome as possible . . . The Prussian soldiers – wearied by the long fighting at Ligny and the subsequent night march – had lain down on the bare ground, seeking by preference the hollows and the furrows. They awoke in the morning wet to the skin and covered with a thick slime. They were hungry and could not be fed because, for the most part, the supplies had gone astry. The mud made it difficult to drag the cannon and ammunition, so that at every rising of the ground the infantry had to put their shoulders to the wheels . . . The men were spurred on to incredible efforts; 'Forward, boys!' he [Blücher] cried, 'some I hear say it cannot be done, but it must be done! I have promised my brother Wellington. You would not make me a perjurer?'

The Prussian troops did not let Blücher down. Marching to victory while recovering from defeat, they arrived on the eastern edge of the battlefield just after 4 p.m., smashing into Napoleon's right wing. Blücher allegedly met Wellington at the farm of La Belle Alliance, the mid-point between Plancenoit and Mont St Jean, about 10 p.m. According to Wellington, Blücher embraced and kissed him, exclaiming, 'Mein lieber Kamerad!' and then 'Quelle affaire!' Which, as the Duke observed, 'was pretty much all he knew of French'. Blücher's son wrote of this meeting: 'Father Blücher embraced Wellington in so hearty a manner, that every one present said it was the most touching scene that could be imagined.'

After the battle, Blücher found time to dash off a letter to his wife (quoted by Henderson):

You well remember what I promised you; and I have kept my word. The enemy's superiority of numbers [*sic*] obliged me to give way on the 17th; but on the 18th, in conjunction with my friend Wellington, I put an end to Napoleon's dancing. His army is completely routed, and the whole of his artillery, baggage, caissons, and equipages are in my hands. The insignia of all the different orders he had won have just been brought to me, having been found in his carriage in a casket. I had two horses killed under me yesterday [*sic*]. It will soon be all over with Bonaparte.

Blücher's report to General von Kalkreuth, the governor of Berlin, arrived at the Prussian capital on 24 June:

I inform your Excellency that in conjunction with the English Army under Field Marshal the Duke of Wellington, I yesterday gained the most complete victory over Napoleon Bonaparte that could possibly be won. The battle was fought in the neighbourhood of some isolated buildings on the road from here to Brussels, bearing the name 'La Belle Alliance' and a better name can hardly be given to this important day. The French Army is in complete dissolution, and an extraordinary number of guns have been captured. Time does not at this moment permit me to send further details to your Excellency. I reserve them for a future occasion, and beg you duly to communicate the joyful news to the good Berliners.

And so Blücher won the 'Battle of La Belle Alliance', while Wellington won the 'Battle of Waterloo'. The French, meanwhile – at least initially – claimed to have won the 'Battle of Mont St Jean'.

Bolton
Captain Samuel (?–1815)

Officer commanding a Royal Artillery Foot Battery attached to Clinton's 2nd British Infantry Division (part of **Hill**'s II Corps). Bolton's command consisted of five 9-pounder guns and one 5.5-inch howitzer, serviced by five officers, 17 NCOs, three drummers, and 116 gunners. The British Army had five Royal Artillery Foot Batteries at Waterloo and six Royal Horse Artillery Troops. Between them they fired almost 10,500 rounds. Besides his British artillery,

Driver of the British Royal Artillery, 1815

Wellington also had three King's German Legion batteries, four Hanoverian, four Netherlands, and two Brunswick: making 157 guns against **Napoleon**'s 250.

Bolton's battery began the battle 700 yards in rear of the château of Hougoumont. But some time after 3 p.m. it was moved to the centre of Wellington's line, the Brigade of Guards to its left. It was in this position, in the early evening, the battery aided in the repulse of Napoleon's Imperial Guard. According to eyewitnesses, Bolton's battery poured case-shot into the advancing foe at 50 yards. The French weathered the storm of shot and shell for at least 10 minutes before falling back, Wellington's infantry hard on their heels.

But Bolton did not live to see victory. According to author Charles Dalton (1904), Bolton 'was killed towards the close of the battle, when directing the fire of his battery against the Imperial Guards in their historical advance'. And yet Lieutenant William Sharpin, a member of Bolton's battery quoted by Siborne (1891), affirms the Captain died before the Imperial Guard assault (command passing to Captain Napier, who was subsequently wounded). Of the circumstances of Bolton's death, Sharpin writes:

> Captain Bolton at the time he was killed was on horseback. I was standing on his left with my hand on his stirrup talking with him. The shot from a French battery at that time flew very thick amongst us, and one passed between me and Bolton, upon which he coolly remarked that he thought we had passed the greatest danger for that day; but scarcely were the words uttered before another ball, which I saw strike the ground a little in front of us, hit him in his left breast. The shot having first severely wounded the horse in the left shoulder caused the animal to stagger backwards, thereby preventing my catching poor Bolton as he fell from his horse.

Bourmont
General Louis Auguste Victor de Ghaisnes, Count (1773–1846)

Commander of **Napoleon**'s 14th Infantry Division, who deserted to the Prussians. Desertion was a common practice in Napoleonic armies. According to Evelyn Wood (1895), some 180,000 soldiers had deserted the French colours during the campaign of 1814, and all armies would be prone to the evil during that of 1815. On the eve of the Belgian battles, **Thomas Creevey** asked **Wellington** if he could expect any desertions from Napoleon's ranks. The Duke shrewdly replied: 'Not a man from the colonel to the private in a regiment – both inclusive . . . we may pick up a marshal or two, perhaps; but not worth a damn!' In the event, the first known French deserter was General Bourmont.

Bourmont was an experienced soldier and a capable commander. But he was not a Bonapartist: instead his sympathies lay with the dethroned Bourbons. During the 1790s the aristocratic Bourmont had served both as an officer and an agent provocateur for émigré forces opposing Revolutionary France. In December 1800 he became embroiled in Cadoudal's plot to blow up Bonaparte with an 'infernal machine'. The failure of this enterprise led to Bourmont's imprisonment: though he made good his escape and fled to Spain. Thus, when French troops entered Madrid in 1807, igniting the Peninsular War (Napoleon's 'Spanish ulcer'), Bourmont moved to Portugal. So did the French. When General Junot's victorious army entered Lisbon in December the same year, Bourmont's only option was to throw himself on the conqueror's mercy. The move paid off. Junot patronised Bourmont, who 'volunteered' his services, and the former Bourbon terrorist became a veteran of several hard-fought Napoleonic campaigns.

Proximity to Junot ensured Bourmont's protection and eventual promotion to general. But Bourmont was distrusted by Napoleon's inner circle. Thus, when the Emperor returned to power in March 1815, Davout advised against his employment. But Napoleon – presumably more interested in recruiting experienced officers than in exacting revenge on a man who had once plotted his murder – ignored the warning, presenting Bourmont with command of the 14th Infantry Division, part of **Gérard**'s IV Corps.

Napoleon's thrust into Belgium aimed at driving a wedge between the armies of **Blücher** and Wellington. Preparations for the attack were made in total secrecy and by 14 June all was ready. Napoleon concentrated his Army of the North behind the River Sambre before launching the offensive. Bourmont's division was the first to arrive on the Belgian border. Next day, between 5 a.m. and 7 a.m. (sources vary) Bourmont crossed into Belgium and defected to the first Prussian picket he could find. According to John Naylor (1960):

> General Bourmont, commander of the 14th Infantry Division, accompanied by his staff, rode into **Ziethen**'s lines to surrender himself and reveal Napoleon's strength and his plan of campaign. The news was taken as quickly as possible to Blücher's headquarters at Namur. The Field Marshal made no alteration to his orders in the face of Napoleon's undoubted possession of the initiative.

In fact, Blücher was disgusted by Bourmont's action, refusing to profit by the vital information freely proffered. Historian Georges Blond (1979) states that:

> Bourmont declared to Colonel Schutter: 'The French will attack this afternoon.' Then he met Colonel de Reiche, who asked him what was the strength of the French Army and Bourmont told him: 120,000 men and he produced the order of march of his division for the day. At about 3 p.m. near Sombreffe, he was presented to Blücher, who only addressed a few words to him. A Prussian officer observed to the Field Marshal that Bourmont was wearing the white [i.e. Bourbon] cockade: 'What does it matter what he is wearing? A scoundrel is still a scoundrel!'

Henderson (1911) gives Blücher's retort as: 'Einerlei was das volk einen zettel ansteckt! Hundsfott bleibt hundsfott!' (It is all one what a man sticks in his hat for a mark, a scoundrel remains a scoundrel!)

Thus Bourmont's desertion did not impress the Allies, who altered their plans not a jot. But the desertion did impact on the French. For a start, Gérard's advance on Charleroi stalled with serious consequences. A.F. Becke (1914) describes the fallout:

> Bourmont's open desertion occasioned some consternation in Gérard's column. It necessitated further delay whilst a report was made to the Emperor; thus it was late when Gérard reached the river line . . . In consequence the corps was late in concentrating at Ligny on the 16th, and the opening of that battle was delayed. This delay contributed partly to the late hour at which the

Battle of Ligny ended, and to the consequent impossibility in the darkness of recognizing the true direction of the Prussian retreat. Gérard's late arrival on the Sambre had unfortunate and far-reaching results.

In other words, Bourmont's desertion caused a series of delays that possibly cost Napoleon the campaign. Meanwhile, morale was dented as soldiers began questioning their officers' loyalty: whispers that would reach a crescendo by sunset on 18 June. Bourmont's desertion helped create a climate of suspicion and distrust among the French, who would eventually buckle on the Waterloo battlefield amid cries of 'Trahison!' and 'Sauve qui peut!'

Bourmont, however, continued his charmed life, being handsomely rewarded by the incoming Bourbons. After Waterloo, while many Bonapartist officers faced exile, imprisonment or worse, Bourmont's career rocketed with a string of top appointments, including Minister of War in 1829. An ardent Royalist to the last, he died at his château in 1846.

Brack
Captain Prosper Fortuné, de (1789–c.1848)

Sometimes referred to as 'Antoine de Brack' in Waterloo literature; fought the battle as a captain in the famous Red Lancers of **Napoleon**'s Imperial Guard. Dubbed 'Mademoiselle' by comrades on account of his good looks, Parisian de Brack joined the elite unit in 1813, already a veteran of the Polish, Austrian and Russian campaigns. De Brack fought throughout 1813 and 1814, ending up at Waterloo, where his regiment joined the massed cavalry attacks on **Wellington**'s indomitable infantry squares.

The reason why the cavalry of the Imperial Guard was frittered away in this fashion has remained something of a mystery. **Ney** – mistakenly thinking Wellington's line on the point of cracking – only ever intended **Milhaud**'s *cuirassiers* to attack. Yet he ended up leading Napoleon's whole cavalry arm in a series of reckless assaults, including the Guard, which the Emperor had been holding in reserve. Historians have looked for a scapegoat ever since: Ney, Milhaud, **Lefebvre-Desnouëttes** and **Colbert** all being singled out for blame. And yet, in a letter written to General Pelet some 20 years after the event, de Brack appears to suggest (Brack 1876) that he was responsible – at least in part – for triggering the attack of the Guard cavalry:

> Flushed with our recent successes against **Ponsonby** and the advances of our cuirassiers on the right, I shouted, 'The English are lost! The position to which they have been thrown back shows it quite clearly. The only escape open to them is a narrow pathway between impassable woods. One false step and their army is ours!' . . . My words, spoken in a loud voice, could be easily heard by officers at the front of the regiment, who pushed forward to join our group. The detachments on the right closed up, followed in their turn by others, trying to keep in line. These were followed by the Chasseurs of the Guard. Although they all moved but a few paces to the right, it seemed more than that from the left-hand side, and suddenly, the brigade of Dragoons and Grenadiers assumed the order to charge had been given: it set off, and we followed! That is how the charge of the cavalry of the Imperial Guard really took place, and about which there has been so much discussion and deliberation.

After Waterloo the Red Lancers were disbanded, with the rest of the fallen Emperor's Guard. De Brack was dismissed from the army, but returned in 1830 as colonel of the 13th Chasseurs à Cheval. Further cavalry posts followed and in 1838 he was appointed commandant of the Military Cavalry School. Suffering a stroke in 1840, de Brack quit the cavalry to become commandant of the Department of Eure in Normandy. He held this post until 1848, when he retired. Several years earlier, de Brack published a book, *Avant Postes de Cavalerie Légère – Souvenirs*. It appeared in English in 1876 as *Light Cavalry Outposts – Recollections of General F. de Brack*.

Brewer
Joseph (dates unknown)

Private in the Royal Waggon Train, who heroically supplied the garrison of Hougoumont with ammunition. By early afternoon the foot guards defending this bastion on **Wellington**'s right flank were running low on ammuntion. Captain **Seymour**, Lord **Uxbridge**'s aide-de-camp, takes up the story, as quoted by Siborne (1891):

> Late in the day of the 18th I was called by some officers of the 3rd Guards defending Hougoumont, to use my best endeavours to send them musket ammunition. Soon afterwards I fell in with a private of the Waggon Train in charge of a tumbril on the crest of the position. I merely pointed out to him where he was wanted, when he gallantly started his horses, and drove straight down the hill to the farm, to the gate of which I saw him arrive. He must have lost his horses, as there was a severe fire kept on him. I feel convinced to that man's service the Guards owe their ammunition.

The man in question was Brewer, who was later accepted into the ranks of the 3rd Foot Guards, rising to the rank of corporal. His heroic deed was the inspiration behind Sir Arthur Conan Doyle's 1894 short story, *A Straggler of '15*, though the hero's name is changed to Brewster.

Brô
Colonel Louis (1781–1844)

Commander of **Napoleon**'s 4th Lancers at Waterloo. Brô joined the cavalry in 1801 as a hussar: 10 years later he was a major and an aide-de-camp to the cavalry's top brass. A veteran of campaigns in Prussia, Poland, Russia and Germany, Brô's career stalled in April 1814 with that of his imperial master. Napoleon's first abdication left the cavalryman kicking his heels, but on the Emperor's return in March 1815, Brô's loyalty was rewarded with the colonelcy of the 4th Lancers.

Although the lance was the traditional weapon of Poles, Tartars and Cossacks, most armies of the period included a few regiments of lancers: the British Army being an exception, not adopting the weapon till 1816, when hostilities were over. Impressed by the performance of Polish lancers – led by fanatical pro-French officers like **Jerzmanowski** – Napoleon began converting French and Dutch hussars and dragoons into Light Horse Lancers (Chevaux-Légers Lanciers) around 1811. Equipping these new regiments with 9-foot lances, Napoleon hoped to create a lethal cavalry force, capable of slaughtering broken or retreating enemy units with a weapon more accurate than a musket, and more deadly than a sabre. In other words, French lancers were to come into their own as counter-attackers and pursuers, spearing retreating enemy troops before they had a chance to defend themselves: a perfect example of this occurring at Waterloo.

On 18 June 1815, the 300 sabres of Brô's 4th Lancers (raised in 1811 from the 9th Regiment of Dragoons) formed part of **Jacquinot**'s 1st Cavalry Division, attached to **d'Erlon**'s I Corps. This force consisted of four regiments divided into two brigades: the 1st Brigade comprised the 7th Hussars and the 3rd Chasseurs à Cheval, perhaps 800 riders in all; the 2nd Brigade comprised the 3rd and 4th Lancers, some 700 riders in all.

Stationed on the extreme right of the French line, Jacquinot's troopers successfully counter-charged the British heavy cavalry brigades of **Somerset** and Sir **William Ponsonby**, which, having smashed d'Erlon's infantry, failed to rally. Brô recalled the action in his memoirs (Brô 1914):

Of the terrible Battle of Waterloo, this is what I have seen, and what I shall see until the time of my death: At 1 p.m. Donzelot's division, preceded by guns, marched . . . driving back a Belgian division and scattering them over hilly ground. The English corps of **Picton** attacked Donzelot's left flank. Macrognet's division speeded up but couldn't save a battery taken by Ponsonby, who charged at the head of the grey Scottish dragoons. Our infantry, split into sections, broke up. D'Erlon ordered the cavalry to charge. A waterlogged field prevented us manoeuvring with ease. I set my 4th Lancers in motion. On right-hand side of the little wood, we saw the English cavalry, which having promptly reformed, threatened to turn the 3rd

The Field of Waterloo – a contemporary visualisation

Chasseurs. At the head of the leading squadron I cried: 'Let us go, my children! We must knock over this rabble!' The soldiers replied: 'Forward! Vive l'Empereur!'

Two minutes later the shock took place. Three enemy ranks were overthrown. We struck the others hard! The clash was dreadful. Our horses trampled the corpses and the cries of the wounded drowned everything. For a moment I was lost in a fog of gunsmoke. When it cleared I saw some English officers surrounding Lieutenant Verrand, the Eagle-bearer. Gathering some riders I went to his aid. Sergeant Orban killed General Ponsonby with a blow of his lance. My sabre felled three of his captains. Two others fled. I turned around to save my adjutant-major. I had fired my second pistol when I suddenly felt paralysis in my right arm. With my left hand I blocked an attacker who faced me . . . A dizziness forced me to grab the mane of my horse. I had not the strength to say to Major Perrot: 'Take command of the regiment!'

General Jacquinot, arriving suddenly, saw the blood flowing down my uniform and supported me, saying: 'You must withdraw!' And he joined the charge. Major Motet cut open my tunic and applied a dressing, pronouncing: 'This is not a mortal wound, but you should not remain here.' The grief at having to leave my squadrons reduced me to tears.

A noteworthy fragment of Brô's account is his description of Ponsonby's death, seemingly at odds with the accepted British version repeated in countless books. According to most British historians – starting with Waterloo veteran **Edward Cotton** (1895) – Ponsonby, his blown horse bogged down in mud, was virtually alone when a posse of lancers arrived to put him to death. Brô, however, gives the impression that Ponsonby died in the thick of the mêlée, surrounded by officers, two of whom apparently bolted.

Whatever the truth of this incident, shortly afterwards Brô found himself among the wounded at an ambulance post at Montplaisir:

> M. Robert, the surgeon in charge, wanted to dress my wound personally. He observed that the flesh of my right arm, above the elbow, was cut to the bone. Blood had flowed in abundance, and weakened by this, I turned to my servant to support me.

Unfit for further service, Brô went to the rear. Hiring a barouche, he made for Genappe, where he heard news of the French defeat – and a rumour that Napoleon had been killed. Pressing on to Nivelles, he paid a Belgian farmer to convey him to Binch, where Belgian policemen apparently tried to arrest him: 'My servant, showing his pistols, made it clear that he meant to defend me to the last: so the gendarmes abandoned us, and on 19 June at 5 p.m. I returned to my old billet at Sobre-sur-Sambre. No one there knew of our disaster.' His wound worsening, Brô pressed on to Paris, entering the capital on 22 June, the day of Napoleon's second and final abdication.

A period in the wilderness followed for Brô, as the returning Bourbon authorities dismissed Napoleon's veterans on half-pay. But all this changed with the July Revolution of 1830, which toppled Charles X and his ultra-conservative faction. Suddenly, Bonapartists were back in fashion and Brô's career received a kick-start. A series of regimental commands followed, plus more campaigning: this time in Algeria with fellow veteran **Jean-Baptiste de Marbot** (France invaded in 1830, finally annexing the territory 40 years later). Returning home in 1838 as a Grand Officer of the Legion of Honour, Brô went on to become a departmental commandant, a lieutenant general and an inspector of cavalry. He died in Armentières on 2 December 1844.

Brunswick
Friedrich Wilhelm, Duke of (1771–1815)

'Brunswick's fated chieftain' (Byron, *Childe Harold*); the son of Karl Wilhelm Ferdinand, overlord of the tiny German dukedom of Braunschweig (Brunswick); field marshal in the Prussian Army. In 1806, the old Duke having been mortally wounded by the French at the Battle of Auerstädt, Friedrich Wilhelm inherited his father's title. But the following year, **Napoleon** – master of Europe after a string of spectacular victories – snatched Brunswick's lands, incorporating them into the Kingdom of Westphalia: newly created for his imperial brother **Jérôme**. Dispossessed of father, home and title, Friedrich Wilhelm fled to Austria, vowing vengeance.

By 1809 Friedrich Wilhelm had reinvented himself as Der Schwarzer Herzog – the Black Duke – raising a corps of troops at his own expense for service with the Austrian Army. As a sign of mourning for his slain father, and an expression of his desire for revenge, Friedrich Wilhelm clothed himself – and his men – entirely in black, adopting a silver death's head for a badge. 'These troops are very remarkable in their appearance,' observed Sir **Walter Scott** (1816), 'their dark and ominous dress sets off to advantage their strong, manly, northern features and white mustachios; and there is something more than commonly impressive about the whole effect.'

Sadly, drastic sartorial statements were not enough to scare Napoleon, and following Austria's disastrous Danube campaign of 1809, the Black Duke fled with his troops to the Baltic and the welcoming arms of the British Royal Navy. A spell in Spain followed: fighting under **Wellington**, the Brunswick troops earning a mixed reputation. But with Napoleon's exile to Elba in 1814 Friedrich Wilhelm returned to his ducal home, there to raise a new national army: the corps of callow youths he would lead in the Waterloo campaign. But the Black Duke only made it as far as Quatre-Bras, where, on 16 June 1815, he emulated his father by sustaining a fatal wound in battle against the French.

Sent to bolster the Netherlanders holding the vital crossroads of Quatre-Bras against Marshal **Ney**, Brunswick proved an inspirtional leader. But Quatre-Bras was a hot action and the Brunswickers lost between 500 and 800 men (sources vary). William Siborne (1848) describes the Duke's demise:

The Brunswickers were, for the most part, young and inexperienced soldiers – in every sense of the word, raw troops: and the numerous casualties which befell their ranks in this exposed situation might have produced a fatal influence upon their discipline, but for the noble example of their prince, whose admirable tact and calm demeanour were most conspicuous on this trying occasion. Quietly smoking his pipe in front of his line, he gave out orders as if at a mere field day . . . and it was in the moment of attempting to rally his soldiers . . . that the Duke of Brunswick was struck from his horse by a shot which terminated the career of this gallant prince.

In fact, Friedrich Wilhelm was hit by a musket ball that entered his body, piercing the liver. He died calling for his second-in-command, Colonel Olfermann.

But the Black Duke's spirit lived on: two days later his 6,000-strong corps was in action at Waterloo, eager to avenge his death. And yet, according to Otto von Pivka (1985), 'There was a general apprehension among the Allied commanders as to how these mainly raw young soldiers would conduct themselves under such a heavy attack, after having suffered quite heavily at Quatre-Bras only two days before.' Apparently, the Brunswickers were divided into three groups during the battle: the hussars and lancers were attached to other Allied cavalry units; the Advance Guard and Life Guard Battalions were deployed near Hougoumont, in support of the garrison; while the remaining infantry and artillery were held in reserve. But by day's end all the Brunswick boys had been in action.

For some, Waterloo was a mind-numbing ordeal, Captain **Mercer** of G Troop, Royal Horse Artillery, describing (Mercer 1927) how:

The Brunswickers were falling fast – the shot every moment making great gaps in their squares, which the officers and sergeants were actively employed in filling up by pushing their men together, and sometimes thumping them ere they could make them move. These were the very young boys whom I had but yesterday seen throwing away their arms, and fleeing, panic-stricken, from the very sound of our horses' feet. Today they fled not bodily, to be sure, but spiritually, for their senses seemed to have left them.

Yet for others, the battle was a chance for revenge. Ensign **Gronow** tells (Gronow 1900) how he and his comrades of the 1st Foot Guards:

observed the red hussars [*sic*] of the Garde Impériale charging a square of Brunswick riflemen, who were about 50 yards from us. This charge was brilliantly executed but the well-sustained fire from the square baffled the enemy, who were obliged to retire after suffering a severe loss in killed and wounded. The ground was completely covered with those brave men, who lay in various positions, mutilated in every conceivable way. Among the fallen we perceived the gallant Colonel of the hussars lying under his horse, which had been killed. All of a sudden two riflemen of the Brunswickers left their battalion and after taking from their hapless victim his purse, watch, and other articles of value, they deliberately put the Colonel's pistols to the poor fellow's head and blew out his brains. 'Shame! Shame!' was heard from our ranks and a feeling of indignation ran through the whole line, but the deed was done: this brave soldier lay a lifeless corpse in sight of his cruel foes, whose only excuse – perhaps – was that their sovereign, the Duke of Brunswick, had been killed two days before by the French.

But whatever the comments of British veterans, or the doubts of Allied commanders, the Brunswickers saved Wellington's bacon at his moment of crisis. Some time around 6.30 p.m. the key outpost of La Haie Sainte fell to the French. As the farmhouse was but a short distance from Wellington's firing line, straddling the Brussels road, it was an ideal vantage point for the attackers. Soon French skirmishers were massing for an assault, supported by some surviving cavalry. A counter-attack by **Alten**'s Hanoverians stalled the French advance, but losses were so high a gaping hole appeared in Wellington's line, the open road to Brussels inviting a renewed French offensive. The only reinforcements left to Wellington were **Chassé**'s Netherlanders and five battalions of Brunswick infantry. The Duke personally led the Brunswickers forward into line between the brigades of **Halkett** and Kruse. But they were hardly in position when, according to **Cotton** (1895):

they were received by such a stinging fire from the French skirmishers, and crashing fire of grape from their artillery, and became so enveloped in smoke, that they could not get into order until they were in close contact with the enemy. The vigorous attack caused the part of Alten's division on Halkett's left, with the Nassau men and Brunswickers, to give way, and fall back under the crest

of the ridge. Now came really the tug of war, the poise of balance
of the battle . . . At this critical moment Wellington galloped to the
spot, and addressing himself to the Brunswickers succeeded by
the electrifying influence of his voice and presence in rallying the
discomfited columns.

Back in line, the Brunswickers stood firm. Then, writes David
Howarth (1968): 'Everyone waited for the skirmishers' fire to die
away, and for the drumbeats of the pas de charge, which would
herald a new French column marching through the smoke.' But the
expected onslaught did not come. For across the battlefield, far away
on Napoleon's right flank, the Prussians were attacking Plancenoit,
obliging the Emperor to commit precious reserves. Thus the French
assault on Mont St Jean stalled for want of men, Wellington's line
held, and the crisis was weathered.

Later, a grateful Wellington praised the Black Duke's boys in his
Waterloo Dispatch: 'The troops of the 5th Division, and those of the
Brunswick Corps, were long and severely engaged, and conducted
themselves with the utmost gallantry.' Total Brunswick casualties
were between 500 and 660 (sources vary). Meanwhile, the Black
Duke's corpse had apparently found its way to an Antwerp inn and
the bed recently vacated by Lady **De Lancey**. The latter had quit the
inn for private rooms, recording in her journal: 'I sent my maid from
the lodging to get some wine, when wandering in the passage of the
inn to find someone who understood English, she opened the door of
the room I had been in and saw the body of the Duke of Brunswick
on the very bed!'

Bull
Major Robert (1778–1835)

Commander of I Troop, Royal Horse Artillery. This unit consisted
of six 5.5-inch howitzers: short-barrelled guns used for high-angle
firing. Most British batteries were equipped with one howitzer, but
Bull's troop was entirely composed of them. The weapon had an

effective range of between 430 and 880 yards, and crews could fire at least one shot a minute. British howitzers fired spherical case (i.e. shrapnel), a British invention not possessed by other armies. The shell – a spherical iron ball – operated on a fuse. Packed with bullets, it was designed to explode over the heads of enemy troops, killing or maiming men within a wide radius. Needless to say, timing the fuse accurately was crucial to the success of the weapon.

Bull's battery began the battle in reserve, near the farm of Mont St Jean, but was soon moved across the field to **Wellington**'s right flank, into position on the ridge above Hougoumont. Around 11.30 a.m. the first French attack on the château had pushed the Hanoverians and Nassauers of the garrison out of the adjoining wood and orchard. Within minutes, Bull was instructed to fire over the heads of the defenders and on to those of the advancing French. It was a tricky operation but perfectly performed, earning Bull a mention in Wellington's dispatches: 'this service, which considering the proximity of the Allied troops in the coppice, was of a very delicate nature, executed with admirable skill and attended with the desired effect'. According to a French survivor, Bull's first salvo killed 17 men from Baudin's brigade.

And yet it seems that later in the battle Bull saw fit to disobey the Duke's instructions. Most histories agree Wellington forbade his gunners from indulging in counter-battery fire, in order to preserve ammunition. This order was famously ignored by Captain **Mercer** of G Troop – and it seems Major Bull too. For when, some time after 4 p.m., I Troop came under from French guns to the right, Bull claimed: 'I directed Lieutenant Louis to turn his two guns towards them, and we shortly succeeded in silencing them, which, as they enfiladed our position from the right, was of considerable advantage to us during the remainder of the day.' According to historian Charles Dalton (1904), Bull's troop continued to provide 'the greatest possible service throughout the early part of the battle; but owing to the loss sustained both in men and horses, together with the disabled condition of the guns (through incessant firing) it was obliged to retire before the close'. Bull himself was wounded in the arm towards the close of the battle.

Bülow
General Friedrich Wilhelm, Baron von (1755–1816)

Soldier-musician, aristocratic patron of the arts, and commander of
Blücher's IV Corps at Waterloo.
Following an excellent education,
the young Bülow came to the attention of the flute-playing King
Frederick William II of Prussia as
an able musician. But although the
adolescent Bülow moved in Court
circles and was lionised by fashionable society, he did not give up the

General Bülow (1755–1816)

day job: that of junior regimental officer in the Prussian Army. Bülow
joined the army in 1768, climbing the steps from ensign to major
with relative ease. By 1803 Bülow was a lieutenant colonel, married
with two children. Then his world turned upside down. First, both
his children died. Then his wife died. And in 1806 **Napoleon** destroyed
the Prussian Army in a single day at the battle of Jena–Auerstädt.

Escaping the fallout from this military fiasco, Bülow served
under Lestocq in the 'Polish' campaign of 1806–7, earning
praise and recognition. In 1808 he married his 18-year-old
sister-in-law, became a major general, and threw himself into the
study of military theory. Soon, Bülow was one of Prussia's leading
architects of military recovery, helping to hone an army eager for
revenge on the French. In 1813 the Prussians gained their chance,
unleashing a War of Liberation following Napoleon's reverses in
Russia. As a lieutenant general, Bülow played a prominent part
in the campaign: on 23 August he defeated General Reynier at
Grossbeeren; and on 6 September he defeated **Ney** at Dennewitz.
The following year Bülow participated in the victorious invasion of
France, which toppled Napoleon from his imperial perch for the first
time. The erstwhile musical protégé was now a full general, ennobled
with the title 'Count Bülow von Dennewitz'.

In the Waterloo campaign of 1815 Bülow commanded Blücher's
IV Corps, consisting of the 13th Infantry Brigade under Hake; the

14th Infantry Brigade under Ryssel; the 15th Infantry Brigade under Losthin; the 16th Infantry Brigade under Hiller von Gartringen; the 1st Cavalry Brigade under Count von Schwerin; the 2nd Cavalry Brigade under Watzdorff; the 3rd Cavalry Brigade under Sydow; and the 4th Artillery Reserve under Braun. A total of perhaps 30,000 men and over 80 guns.

Bülow's corps missed the mauling at Ligny on 16 June, reaching Wavre intact, where, at 7 a.m. on 18 June, it spearheaded Blücher's epic march to **Wellington**'s salvation. It would be the only Prussian corps to fight in its entirety at Waterloo. Hindered by frustrating delays, including a fire that broke out in Wavre and a collision with **Ziethen**'s I Corps, en route for Papelotte via the Ohain road, as well as atrocious conditions – there were no roads as such, only country lanes and tracks, waterlogged by the recent rains – Bülow was still approaching the south-eastern edge of the Waterloo battlefield at noon. An hour or so later, having reached St Lambert on the banks of the River Lasne, Bülow's advance guard halted, in order to let the rest of the column catch up. Before it stood the Bois de Paris, and beyond that the villages of Frischermont and Plancenoit, planted in the French right-rear.

Meanwhile, at his command post at Rossomme, Napoleon spotted the Prussian columns through his telescope. Alerted, the Emperor sent cavalry under **Domon** and Subervie to investigate, while keeping **Lobau**'s VI Corps and the Imperial Guard in reserve, instead of committing them to the newborn battle with Wellington. As historian E.F. Henderson (1911) states:

> It was to be hours . . . before the Prussians could reach the field of battle . . . But their coming was nevertheless of immediate advantage; for at a time when he most needed all his forces to hurl them against the enemy's centre, Napoleon was forced to detach 10,000 soldiers – 2,300 cavalry under Domon and 7,000 infantry under Lobau – to guard at least the exits from the forest.

By 3 p.m. Bülow's leading troops were across the Lasne, having yomped through the muddy valley along a single road. Within the hour they were skirmishing with French cavalry pickets and the outposts of Lobau's VI Corps. Henderson continues:

The head of the column emerged from the woods at Frischermont and the cannonading began. As an objective point the farm of Belle Alliance had been designated and towards it a regular and steady advance was made. The enemy retreated at first, but finally made a stand at the village of Plancenoit where, and on the heights beyond, Lobau had stationed his brigades.

Blücher caught up with Bülow about 4.30 p.m. Observing Wellington's lines in the distance, the Prussian Field Marshal ordered Bülow to launch an immediate attack. General **Gnesienau**, Blücher's chief of staff, records the sequel (Gnesienau 1815):

> The excessive difficulties of the passage by the defile of St Lambert had greatly retarded the march of the Prussian columns, so that only two brigades of the 4th Corps had arrived at the covered position, which was assigned them. The decisive moment was come; there was not a moment to be lost. The Generals did not suffer it to escape. They resolved immediately to begin the attack with the troops which they had at hand. General Count Bülow, therefore, with two brigades and a corps of cavalry, advanced rapidly along the rear of the enemy's right wing.

Having pushed Lobau back on Plancenoit – a village of some 520 souls – Bülow was unable to pierce his adversary's front. The village itself was the key to Lobau's sector, and it was defended by one of his infantry brigades – perhaps 2,000 men supported by eight guns. Lobau's remaining three brigades were strung out on high ground north of the village, so as to link with Napoleon's right flank near Papelotte, on the Waterloo battlefield. By 5.30 p.m. Blücher was calling for the capture of Plancenoit and Bülow sent in his 16th Infantry Brigade, consisting of some 6,000 men supported by 24 guns. Meanwhile, his 13th and 15th Brigades were launched at the bulk of Lobau's command, north of the village. In a ferocious assault, the Prussians pushed Lobau's defenders out of Plancenoit. Reacting immediately, Napoleon sent General **Duhesme** and 5,000 reserves from the Young Guard to retrieve the situation. This was achieved in a single assault, which drove Bülow's attackers out of the village. Meanwhile, to the north, Lobau's infantry cordon – abutting the right wing of Napoleon's Waterloo front at an angle of 90 degrees

– continued to hold. At 6 p.m. Bülow returned to the attack at Plancenoit, but the offensive was repulsed by Duhesme's guardsmen.

With the body count rising, Bülow requested support from approaching Prussian columns and prepared for a third attack. This was heralded by an intense artillery bombardment, prior to an all-out assault by five battalions: Duhesme's Young Guard was scattered. But the see-saw battle for Plancenoit continued, as Napoleon sent yet more troops into the meat-grinder: two battalions of Old Guard under Generals Morand and Pelet. These veteran troops – grenadiers and chasseurs à pied – reputedly cleared Plancenoit of Prussians in 20 minutes, without firing a shot. Legend has it that the 3,000 Prussian casualties these guardsmen caused were reaped with the bayonet alone. Meanwhile, Duhesme's Young Guard rallied and resumed their positions in Plancenoit.

But with more Prussian troops arriving at the front, Napoleon's success at Plancenoit could only be temporary. Meanwhile, victory against Wellington was slipping through his fingers, as E.F. Henderson (1911) explains: 'Napoleon had already perceived that were Plancenoit to be lost the Prussians would be directly in the rear of his reserves at Belle Alliance, and that the danger must be averted at all costs. More and more troops, therefore, were diverted from the attack on Wellington.'

By 7 p.m. Ziethen's I Corps arrived at Papelotte, adding to the weight of Prussian numbers rolling against Napoleon's right flank. Over 40,000 Prussians were now committed to the fight and, once again, Bülow stormed Plancenoit. And once again the Prussians were repulsed, in an orgy of street fighting and savage hand-to-hand combat. According Madame **Dupuis**, a local woman quoted by Dalton (1904), 'At Plancenoit . . . they tell me that the brave French were so beaten down by bayonet charges that the river ran with blood.' And yet it was not until 9 p.m. that Bülow finally secured Plancenoit. Meanwhile, on the Waterloo battlefield, Napoleon's army had ceased to exist. A general collapse had occurred, followed by a wholesale flight up the Charleroi road.

But the victory Bülow won at Plancenoit was a costly affair. Much of the fighting had taken place in the narrow, cobbled streets surrounding the village church. The place had changed hands several times and the slaughter had been appalling. Plancenoit was the scene of the heaviest fighting on 18 June, worse even than Hougoumont or La Haie Sainte. In the words of Waterloo veteran **Edward Cotton** (1895):

> Plancenoit had been the scene of a most dreadful struggle. The French in the churchyard held out, and the Prussians, finding it of no avail to continue the attack in front, turned the village on both flanks, driving the Imperial Guards before them. The latter, finding that they should be cut off from all retreat, fell into disorder, and mixed with the general mass of fugitives, who were flying in all directions towards Rossomme and La Maison-du-Roi, followed by the Prussians.

Gneisenau put it more grimly: 'no prisoners were made, and no quarter was given'.

Despite his victor's laurels, Bülow has been criticised by historians for his performance on 18 June 1815. Some British writers have highlighted his late arrival: though Bülow made every effort to get his men into action quickly, even attacking before his whole force had concentrated. Other pundits claim he blundered at Plancenoit, wasting lives in costly street battles instead of turning the position: and yet, his orders were to take Plancenoit. And in the fighting that took place outside the village, casualties were still high. In fact, no matter which plan Bülow adopted, his men were facing veteran troops in good defensive positions. Finally, Bülow has been accused of providing a mere sideshow, which made no direct impact on the outcome of Waterloo: and yet, even his very appearance on Napoleon's eastern horizon at 1 p.m. caused the Emperor to divert troops from the frontal assault on Wellington at Mont St Jean. And as the ferocity of Prussian attacks on Plancenoit grew, so did the number of French troops committed to its defence.

Thus, although the spirited British veteran **Kincaid** (1847) states: 'I will ever maintain that Lord Wellington's last advance would have made it the same victory had a Prussian never been seen there.' But perhaps A.F. Becke (1914) is nearer the mark in his observation that:

> Before launching his Guard against Wellington, Napoleon decided to beat back Bülow, although the battle was already raging with Wellington and had hardly begun with Bülow . . . At this supreme

moment he was not true to himself. He did not throw for complete success; though had he done so he might have seen the battle turn in his favour. He was undone by adopting a half-measure.

As for Wellington, he recorded in his Waterloo Dispatch that: 'The operation of General Bülow upon the enemy's flank was a most decisive one.'

After Waterloo, Bülow took part in the victorious march on Paris, and was a witness of Napoleon's final fall from grace. He died suddenly on 25 February 1816 – a month after his return to Prussia.

Burney
(married name d'Arblay) Frances or 'Fanny' (1752–1840)

Novelist and diarist, residing in Brussels during the Waterloo campaign. At a time when women were not supposed to take writing seriously, Fanny Burney was something of a phenomenon: churning out novels, plays, and poems – as well as letters and journals, describing everything from the mental health of George III to the aftermath of Waterloo. She was married to General Alexandre d'Arblay, who had fled Revolutionary France for England in the 1790s. In 1802 d'Arblay took advantage of the Peace of Amiens to return to France, hopeful of reclaiming property lost in the dark days of the Terror. Fanny went with him, but war broke out again while the couple were abroad, effectively stranding them on the Continent for the next 10 years.

Spring 1815 saw d'Arblay fighting for French Royalists against the recently reinstalled **Napoleon**, while Fanny remained in the comparative safety of Brussels. The French invasion of 15 June failed to dislodge Fanny, who was determined to remain as close as possible to d'Arblay. Even when rumours swept through the city of a French victory at Waterloo, Fanny stayed put. In the event, Brussels was deluged with broken soldiers rather than conquering ones, as the wounded of all sides flowed into the city following battle. Fanny helped nurse the English wounded, recording her experiences in a

'Waterloo Journal'. This document was eventually published in 1823, possibly inspiring scenes in Thackeray's 1848 novel, *Vanity Fair*.

Fanny also found time to write to d'Arblay. The following extract (Burney 2001) is from a letter dated 1 July 1815, describing the aftermath of Waterloo on Brussels and its citizens:

> The numbers of dead, whether of conquerors or conquered, have not yet been counted! – nor even all the wounded – some are still on the field of Battle, where they are dressed, their wounds, I mean! – while waiting for carriages, which are constantly on the road . . . Brussels is a walking hospital! Maimed and wounded unhappy men of War are met at every step, either entering, carried in Casts, from the Fields of Battle, or the adjoining villages, to be placed in Infirmaries, Work houses, Churches, and also at private houses. Everybody is ordered to receive all their Dwelling can hold. It is even written on the doors of most houses how many are already refuged in them. The Belgians behave with the utmost humanity to the miserable objects of fallen Ambition, or contentious struggles on either side. Almost all the Natives prepare to run from the City, in apprehension of some Contagious fever, from the Multitude of sick!

And in a letter to Georgiana Waddington, dated 3 July 1815, Fanny discusses the vexed question of Belgian loyalty:

> The Belgians have for so many Centuries been accustomed to sanguinary conflicts, and violent, or mercenary, change of masters, that I really thought, from the placid state in which, when seeking here an asylum, I found them, that they were utterly indifferent to the result of the neighbouring struggle, and would just as willingly have fallen again into the hands of Buonaparte as not. They never, of their own accord, opened upon the subject, nor considered nor treated us poor fugitives but as common visitors. I imagined they had gone through too many political changes, to deem one, or two, more or less an addition worth ruffling their serenity. And Buonaparte, whether from hearing of this passive philosophy, or whether from motives yet unknown, certainly expected not alone that they would not oppose, but that, on the contrary, they would join him. This idea, with respect to the Belgian troops, was indeed, spread, and most alarmingly, here. The Duke of **Wellington** was warned by several persons not to trust them: and it is generally understood that

he determined they should neither be trusted in front, lest they should join the Enemy, nor in the Rear, lest they should run away from their friends. Nevertheless, when the day of the most bloody battle that ever Rival Warriors fought, arrived, I found I had taken the calm of their Natures for indifference to their fate; for when a cry was shouted through the streets that the French were come! That Buonaparte et les Français étoient à la porte de la Ville! [Bonaparte and the French are at the city gate!] the consternation that ensued, the horrour [*sic*] that was depicted on every Countenance, shewed they were alive at least to the evils that menaced themselves.

Butterworth
John (?–1815)

First fatal casualty sustained by G Troop, Royal Horse Artillery. (For the Troop's first non-fatal casualty, see **Philip Hunt**.) According to Captain **Mercer** (1927), Gunner Butterworth was:

> one of the greatest pickles in the troop, but at the same time a most daring, active soldier; he was No. 7 (the man who sponged, etc.) at his gun. He had just finished ramming down the shot and was stepping back outside the wheel, when his foot stuck in the miry soil, pulling him forward at the moment the gun was fired. As a man naturally does when falling, he threw both his arms before him and they were blown off at the elbows.

Despite the proximity of Assistant-Surgeon **Hitchens** – presumably busy with other casualties – Butterworth apparently received little or no assistance. His body was later found, according to Mercer, 'lying by the roadside near the farm of Mont St Jean, bled to death!'

Cambronne
General Pierre Jacques (1770–1842)

Commander of the 1st Chasseurs
à Pied of **Napoleon**'s Imperial
Guard. Waterloo made him a
celebrity for something he probably
never said. Cambronne was a hard-
fighting, hard-talking warrior from
an impoverished background. Once
described by Colonel Campbell
(quoted in Cohen 1925) as 'a
desperate uneducated ruffian who
was a drummer in Egypt', Cam-
bronne was a veteran campaigner, a soldier's soldier.

General Cambronne (1770–1842)

Wounded at Ligny on 16 June 1815, Cambronne remained with
the colours, insisting on fighting at Waterloo two days later. His
command, consisting of two battalions, was perhaps 1,200-strong,
and held in reserve at Napoleon's command post at the farm of
Le Caillou the whole day. Legend has it that at battle's close,
Cambronne's command – reduced to a single battalion – was
arranged in a triangle, two ranks deep, and commenced a fighting

retreat, while the rest of the army fled. Invited to surrender by the British, Cambronne allegedly replied: 'La Garde meurt et ne se rend pas!' (The Guard dies but does not surrender!) He was then apparently shot down but miraculously survived. This version is endorsed by Victor Hugo in *Les Misérables* (1862): 'Now, then, among those giants there was one Titan: Cambronne. To make that reply and then perish, what could be grander? For being willing to die is the same as to die; and it was not this man's fault if he survived after he was shot.'

But wounded or not, Cambronne was captured, as noted by Gronow (1900):

> The famous General Cambronne was taken prisoner fighting hand-to-hand with the gallant Sir **Colin Halkett**, who was shortly after shot through the cheeks by a grapeshot. Cambronne's supposed answer of 'La Garde ne se rend pas' was an invention of aftertimes and he himself always denied having used such an expression.

According to **Wellington**, 'Never, certainly, was anything so absurd as ascribing that saying to Cambronne.' So what did Cambronne say? Some say the whole episode was a fabrication, the brainchild of a French journalist looking for a story to soothe dented national pride. Others claim that when asked to surrender, the General shouted 'Merde!' (Shit!) and this expletive subsequently became known in France as 'le mot Cambronne'.

Cambronne, at least initially, endorsed this version. Indeed, he became convinced his expression of defiance had turned him into a national hero, immune from Royalist reprisals. He was wrong. The Bourbons had him arrested and court-martialled in 1816. His life was saved not by 'le mot Cambronne' but by Berryer, his brilliant defence counsel. Cambronne later married a high-born English lady and began moving in refined circles. This obliged him to play down the 'Merde!' story and accept the apocryphally poetic 'The Guard dies but does not surrender!' version. And this is what graces his tombstone.

Campbell
Lieutenant Robert Preston (?–1825)

Aide-de-camp to Major General **Adam**, reputed to have fired the last gun at Waterloo. According to Charles Dalton (1904):

> Robert Preston Campbell fired the last gun at Waterloo, and the gun was a French one! It was one of the guns captured by the 71st Regiment in the *sauve qui peut* of the French, and was turned against their retreating masses by some men of the 71st under Lieutenant Torriano and discharged by Campbell.

Dalton's source is historian William Siborne (1848), who describes how, after the repulse of **Napoleon**'s Imperial Guard some time after 8 p.m., the 71st found themselves at the forefront of Wellington's general advance. It seems that a party of men under Lieutenant William Torriano captured a French battery, and as Siborne states:

> some men of the flank company . . . immediately turned round one of the guns, which was then discharged into the retiring columns of the Imperial Guard by Captain [*sic*] Campbell, ADC to Major General Adam, and was, there is reason to believe, the last French gun fired that day.

The incident was immortalised in a painting entitled *The Last Gun At Waterloo*, which remains in the possession of the 71st Regiment's present incarnation, the Royal Regiment of Scotland. (For more on the 71st at Waterloo, see '**T.S.**') Just for the record, the aide-de-camp Campbell was not a member of the 71st but an officer of the 7th Foot, a regiment not present at Waterloo. Campbell was placed on half-pay in the aftermath of Waterloo, but obtained a captain's commisison in the Ceylon Rifles in 1823, dying only two years later.

Capel
Caroline (1773–1847)

Daughter of the first Earl of Uxbridge; married the Hon. John Thomas Capel (1769–1819), second son of the fourth Earl of Essex, in 1792. The union was a happy one, but Capel was an inveterate gambler, losing heavily and quickly sinking into debt. Eager to escape his creditors, Capel whisked the family off to Brussels in June 1814, as the exiled **Napoleon** headed for Elba. The Capels were still there 12 months later, when the reinstated Napoleon – accompanied by over 100,000 troops – headed for Belgium.

On Waterloo Day, the Capels – including daughters Harriet, Georgiana ('Georgy'), Maria ('Muzzy') and Louisa ('Loui') – occupied the Château de Walcheuse, just outside Brussels – Caroline being pregnant for the thirteenth time. In an atmosphere of uncertainty and alarm, Caroline spent that fateful Sunday writing to her mother in England. In her letter, Caroline tells old Lady Uxbridge how Napoleon caught the Allied generals off guard, crossing the border 'like a Thief in the Night'. She mentions (Capel and Uxbridge 1955) the Duchess of Richmond's ball of 15 June (attended by her husband with daughters Georgy and Muzzy), where news of the French drive on Brussels broke:

> In the midst of the dancing an express arrived to the Duke with an account of the Prussians having been beat and the French having advanced within 14 Miles of Bruxelles – You may imagine the Electrical Shocks of such intelligence – Most of the Women in Floods of tears and all the Military in an instant collected round their respective leaders and in less than 20 minutes the room was cleared.

And she brings matters up to date by describing **Wellington**'s retreat to Waterloo, following the Battles of Ligny and Quatre-Bras, adding that 'in case of a Defeat it was thought advisable for the English to retire from Bruxelles'. At this point Caroline pauses, waiting for news from the battlefield: 'not daring to finish my letter or think of sending it till I knew the result of the Events then passing'.

When Caroline receives news of Napoleon's defeat she returns to her letter, finishing it with a summary of the previous 24 hours' anxieties:

The Horrors of that night [17–18] are not to be forgot – The very Elements conspired to make it gloomy – For the rain and darkness and wind were frightful and our courtyard was filled during the night with poor wounded drenched soldiers and horses seeking for refuge and assistance which you may imagine we administered as well as we were able . . . The next day [18 June] was passed in various alarming reports. Capel obliged to leave us and spend it in Bruxelles, trying every means to get a conveyance for us in case Ld W. was defeated, the report of which reached us, and that the French were in the Town. Two hours before Capel's return, I had the horror of fancying the Gates were shut and he was detained – At last however he appeared, not a Horse to be had for any sum. The Mayor had put them all in requisition for the Military – one man had paid guineas for a pair of Horses to go the first stage to Antwerp, the same difficulty in obtaining a barge; by the greatest interest and acquaintance with the Mayor he got the promise of an order for one, for which we were to pay 20 guineas; 25 was all we could procure anywhere for all the Banks were shut up – In this situation, uncertain about the Barge, or the means of getting to it except on Foot, and without any of our baggage, we determined, if everything failed, to get back into Bruxelles anyhow – For a House in a Wood, without any neighbours or means of assistance in the case of a party of French stragglers coming up, was not to be borne – Heaven however averted any of these evils – for the news reached us early of the total defeat and retreat of the French.

But Waterloo represented a family tragedy for Caroline, for her eldest brother, Henry William Paget – who succeeded his father as second Earl of **Uxbridge** – was wounded at the close of the battle. Paget – or Uxbridge as he is better known – was Wellington's cavalry commander. He was hit in the leg by one of the last rounds fired by the French artillery, as described by his aide-de-camp, Captain Thomas Wildman (Capel and Uxbridge 1955):

Lord Uxbridge was struck by a grape shot on the right knee which shattered the joint all to pieces. I did not see him fall & went on to the charge, but soon missed him and perceived **Seymour** [another aide-de-camp] taking him to the rear. He told me immediately he must lose his leg.

Paget bore the amputation without anaesthetic and without complaint. On 26 June Caroline wrote: 'Paget is dressed and sitting up in his chair as if nothing had happened . . . he is the wonder of everyone.'

Chassé
Lieutenant General David Hendrik, Baron (1765–1849)

Dutch commander of **Wellington**'s 3rd Netherlands Infantry Division at Waterloo. Born of bourgeois parents, Chassé entered the army of the United Provinces as a cadet in 1775. Later, when his Dutch homeland fell under French influence – becoming first the pro-Revolutionary Batavian Republic and then the Bonapartist Kingdom of Holland – Chassé's career took off, thanks to his new masters. And when **Napoleon** annexed Holland in 1810, Chassé transferred to French service as a general of brigade, earning the sobriquet 'General Bayonet', due to his brutal – but effective – methods. Chassé continued in the Emperor's service until 1814, fighting against the Austrians and the British, and earning the title 'baron of the Empire'. But following Napoleon's first abdication in April 1814, and the subsequent redrawing of the European map, Chassé entered the army of the newly created United Kingdom of the Netherlands.

Thus, when the Waterloo campaign opened in June 1815, Chassé found himself in command of Wellington's 3rd Netherlands Infantry Division and facing former friends. Chassé's command consisted of 12 battalions (nine Dutch and three Belgian) grouped into two infantry brigades: the 1st Brigade, under Colonel **Detmers**, and the 2nd Brigade, under Major General d'Aubremé – perhaps 7,000 troops in all. But in general, Wellington was uncertain as to the quality and loyalty of the Netherlanders; while according to some sources, Chassé was actually viewed as anti-British (unlike fellow countrymen **Constant de Rebecque**, **Perponcher** and **van Bijlandt**, who had previously fought *against* Napoleon, not *with* him). Unsurprisingly then, Chassé and his 7,000 Dutch–Belgian troops were initially posted in reserve at Braine l'Alleud, a village of some 2,770 souls, a couple of miles in rear of the Duke's right wing. And there they remained till the early afternoon, untroubled by combat, and liberally supplied with beer by local villagers.

At around 2 p.m., however, Wellington ordered Chassé to advance in support of Lord **Hill**'s II Corps, constituting the army's right wing. Chassé's division arrived in place about an hour later, forming up behind the Nivelles road, still in rear of the firing line on the ridge of Mont St Jean. Here, Chassé's Netherlanders spent the next four hours kicking their heels and occasionally forming battalion squares, when French cavalry swept through the intervals of the red-coated formations in front. Around 6.30 p.m., however, the vital outpost of La Haie Sainte fell to the French, throwing Wellington's line into confusion. This bastion, at the heart of the battlefield, commanded the approaches to Wellington's centre: now it was in **Ney**'s hands, and under the cover it afforded, the French marshal was wheeling cannon up close to the fragile Allied line. For the Duke's battalions were exhausted, having weathered sustained artillery bombardments and massed cavalry attacks for more than five long hours.

Elizabeth Longford (1969) refers to the period as 'the Dreadful Pause'. And 'dread' probably summed up the feelings of many Allied soldiers on Mont St Jean, as they anticipated the storm of iron, lead and steel that must surely come. According to **Edward Cotton** (1895):

Wellington at Waterloo

Numerous applications reached the Duke for support and reinforcements, or to be relieved by the second line, as divisions, brigades and regiments had dwindled away to skeletons and handfuls of men. The only reply was: 'They must hold their ground to the last man.' Sir Guy Campbell delivered that answer to the gallant remains of Pack's brigade, and the Duke told Sir **Colin Halkett** that there must not be the least symptom of falling back, as everything depended on the steadiness of the front troops. Frequently, as the Duke passed the men, he heard murmurs, such as, 'Are we to be massacred here? Let us go at them, let us give them *Brummagum!*' – i.e. the bayonet. And he would calmly reply, 'Wait a little longer, my lads: you shall have at them presently.' . . . It was indeed high time to strain every nerve and strengthen and defend the point where the fiercest storm of battle was about to burst, and repel the last and most desperate struggle, now ready to be made.

Maitland's and Halkett's right was advanced: the Brunswick battalions on the right were to move into the space between Halkett's British and Kruse's Nassau brigades. Chassé's Dutch-Belgian division was to cross the Nivelles road and form, on the left, in rear of **Adam**'s, Maitland's and Halkett's brigades. The remains of the Allied cavalry, except Merle's brigade, were in rear of the position on the right of the Genappe road, and most of our infantry were deployed into four deep lines, and for shelter lay recumbent on the ground behind the crest of the ridge. About this time a French officer of carabiniers rode into the right of the 52nd Regiment, and announced to Major Blair and Colonel Sir A. Fraser that Napoleon was about to attack us at the head of the Imperial Guard: this being made known to the Duke.

Around 7.30 p.m. Napoleon decided to make a last-ditch attempt to punch a hole through Wellington's line and secure the Brussels road. Consequently, the Emperor ordered a general advance of all available units, to be spearheaded by several battalions of the Imperial Guard. But the attack would not be the monumental blow anticipated by the Allied commanders and their troops: for Napoleon had already committed his reserves to beating off **Bülow**'s Prussians at Plancenoit in his right-rear. Nevertheless, five battalions of Imperial Guard infantry led the assault, with a further three some way behind, in support. These leading battalions split into two bodies as they toiled up the slopes of Mont St Jean: three battalions of chasseurs à pied peeled off to hit Wellington's right-centre, held by the brigades of Adam and Maitland; while two battalions of grenadiers marched straight for the centre, held by the remains of Colin Halkett's brigade.

Meanwhile, Chassé had discovered that the British guns were short of ammunition. Anticipating the fatal results of this, he sent forward one of his own horse artillery troops. He also advanced Detmers' brigade, consisting of the 2nd Dutch Line Regiment, the 35th Belgian Chasseurs, and four battalions of Dutch militia, in support of Halkett's 33rd, 2/69th, 2/30th and 2/73rd Regiments of Foot. And so, while the chasseurs of the Guard walked into the murderous volleys of Adam's and Maitland's battalions, the grenadiers on their right collided with Halkett and Chassé.

According to Mark Adkin (2001): 'as the Imperial Guard reached the ridge, he launched Detmers' men in a furious counter-stroke that chased away what was left of the 1/3 and 4th Grenadiers'. Minutes later, with the Imperial Guard bouncing back down the ridge at the point of the bayonet (the three supporting battalions never climbed the slopes, only making it as far as La Haie Sainte), Wellington ordered a general advance. Once again, Chassé – General Bayonet – ordered a charge, leading his men forward in person, shouting 'Vive le Roi!' and 'Vive la Patrie!' Chassé himself describes the sequel, in a passage quoted by Demetrius C. Boulger (1901):

> Seeing the enemy's cuirassiers making an advance on my left, I hastened to the point threatened, and found there Captain de Haan, of the 19th Battalion of National Militia, with a few men. There was not a moment to lose, the enemy being ready to form up. I ordered him at once to profit by this favourable moment to attack them. He promptly jumped over a hedge, re-formed his peleton [i.e. platoon] of about fifty men on the other side, and with a well-sustained fire carried death and confusion into the enemy's ranks. Then, profiting by the disorder, he charged them with the bayonet, and I had the supreme joy of seeing nearly 300 cuirassiers flee before fifty men of the Netherlands army.

In his official report of the battle, Chassé, again quoted by Boulger, expressed pleasure and pride in the performance of his much-maligned Netherlanders:

I am in the highest degree satisfied with the conduct of the whole of my division, particularly with those soldiers who were only a few months in our ranks, and whom we could only look upon as recruits. They gave us the best proof that the blood of their ancestors flows strongly in their veins.

But Chassé was virtually alone in his appreciation of the Netherlanders' efforts, and when Wellington's Waterloo Dispatch failed to pay due homage, the Dutch general felt snubbed. And perhaps with some justification, for Wellington barely mentions his Dutch–Belgian allies in the Waterloo Dispatch. Curiously, a 'General Van Hope' is mentioned by Wellington as commanding 'a Brigade of infantry in the service of the King of the Netherlands', but no such officer existed. In the event, Chassé wrote a letter to Lord **Hill**, registering his dissatisfaction. Historian Demetrius C. Boulger (1901) quotes the correspondence between Chassé and Hill, which, as he puts it, 'English writers have studiously ignored':

Bourget, 5 July 1815
Your Excellency,
It was only yesterday that I read the report which H.E. the Duke of Wellington has made on the subject of the battle of the 18th ult.
On that day I had the honour to serve with my division under the orders of your Excellency. As no mention is made in the report of that division, I must presume that its conduct entirely escaped the attention of your Excellency when making your report to the Duke of Wellington. I find myself under the hard necessity of stating myself to your Excellency the facts as they took place, and the part which I believe my division had in the success of the day. Towards evening, seeing that the fire of the artillery on the right slackened, I proceeded there to learn the cause. I was informed that ammunition was wanting. I saw very distinctly that the French Guard was advancing towards these guns; foreseeing the consequences, I caused my artillery to advance to the crest, and ordered it to keep up the liveliest fire possible. At the same time, leaving the second brigade, commanded by Major-General d'Aubremé, in reserve, and in the formation of two squares in échelon, I formed the first brigade, commanded by Colonel Detmers, in close column, and charged the French Guard. I had the happiness to see it give way before me. Through delicacy I did not make a report of this fact, being entirely

persuaded that your Excellency would mention it in your report, and that with so much the more confidence that your Excellency honoured me two days after the battle (being then at Nivelles) with the expression of your contentment with the conduct of my artillery as well as with that of my infantry. But seeing my error, I should deem myself wanting in my duty towards the brave men that I had the satisfaction of commanding, and even towards the whole of my nation, if I did not make it my task to remedy this omission by begging your Excellency to be so good as to render the justice to these brave troops which I am persuaded that they deserved. They attach the greatest value to the matter, and are deeply sensible of the honour of having contributed to so glorious a victory, etc., etc.

Paris, 11 July 1815
Your Excellency,
I have the honour to acknowledge the receipt of your letter of the 5th inst., which only reached me yesterday. In the report that I had the honour to make to H.E. the Duke of Wellington on the battle of June 18, I made special mention of the conduct of your Division during that day, and I did not omit to mention that it advanced to repulse the attack of the French Imperial Guard. Unfortunately, the report of H.E. the Duke of Wellington was already sent to London before the arrival of my own report. Nevertheless, I am well assured that His Excellency is informed of the fine conduct of the troops under your orders on that glorious day, and I beg your Excellency to feel convinced that it will always afford me great pleasure to show how sensible I am of it. Accept the assurance of the high consideration with which I have the honour to be your very obedient servant, Hill (General).

Boulger adds the following postscript to this exchange, clearly indicating his support for Chassé's case:

It may be added that Lord Hill, in his report of 20 June, is said to have referred to 'the steady conduct of the third division of the troops of the Netherlands under the command of Major General Chassé,' but the report itself has never been found. It has not been discovered either among the Wellington papers at Apsley House or the Hill papers in the British Museum. It also appears quite clear that Lord Hill could himself have known little or nothing of the Chassé charge, because at the moment of its being made he was dismounted and momentarily unconscious. Sir Digby Mackworth, cited in Sydney's *Life of Lord Hill*, is the authority for the fact that at the very moment of the attack by the French Guard, Lord Hill's horse was shot and rolled over, severely bruising the General. It was not known what had become of him for half an hour, or until after the repulse of the French Guard.

After Waterloo, Chassé retained high office in the Netherlands Army and in 1819 became commandant of the fortress of Antwerp. When the Kingdom of the United Netherlands fell apart in 1830, with Belgium's break from Holland, Chassé successfully defended Antwerp against rebel Belgian troops. But two years later, in a sharp twist of fate, Chassé was obliged to surrender the town to French forces under Marshal **Gérard**, commander of Napoleon's IV Corps in June 1815.

Chastel
General Louis Pierre Aimé, Baron (1774–1826)

Commander of the 10th Cavalry Division in **Exelmans**' II Cavalry Corps, consisting of the 4th, 12th, 14th and 17th Dragoons plus two horse artillery batteries. After **Napoleon**'s victory at Ligny on 16 June, he despatched the cavalry corps of Pajol and Exelmans to pursue the defeated Prussians: the former scouting south-east towards Namur, the latter – spearheaded by Chastel's dragoons – heading north-east towards Gembloux. But the dark night and difficult terrain hampered the horsemen and for a while contact was lost. On the morning of 17 June, however, Chastel came upon the rearguard of **Thielemann**'s Prussian III Corps. But instead of calling up reinforcements to bring the bone-weary Prussians to battle, Chastel contented himself with shadowing them as they headed – not east to Liège or Namur as Napoleon expected – but north. Although he reported his discovery to Exelmans, the corps commander saw no urgency in passing the news back to Napoleon:

thus Thielemann was suffered to escape unmolested, joining the rest of **Blücher**'s columns converging on Wavre.

Failure to prosecute the Prussian pursuit more vigorously arguably cost Napoleon the campaign. Had the Prussians been caught and engaged before concentrating at Wavre, Blücher's legendary march to **Wellington**'s aid might never have happened: 'Such an event', as Tony Linck (1993) observes, 'would have had a decisive impact on the outcome of the campaign.' On 18 June, Chastel, with the rest of **Grouchy**'s command, was entangled in the Battle of Wavre, some 10 miles east of Waterloo. But when news of Napoleon's defeat arrived, Grouchy disengaged Thielemann's obstinate Prussian rearguard and retired on Namur, Chastel securing the bridges over the Sambre and the line of retreat. His division then covered Grouchy's withdrawal to Paris, besting Blücher's cavalry several times on the way. But defeat was imminent. On 22 June Napoleon abdicated for the final time: two weeks later the Allies were in Paris – with Louis XVIII in tow – and the remains of the Emperor's Waterloo Army behind the River Loire, far to the south.

The return of Louis unleashed a Bourbon backlash against Bonapartists and Republicans. Known as the White Terror, it constituted a brutal round of officially sanctioned arrests, executions and mob violence. For the 'Brigands of the Loire', as Napoleon's Waterloo veterans were dubbed by their Royalist countrymen, the outlook was bleak: at best, an uncertain future on half-pay; at worst, arrest and possible execution. Many officers slipped away into voluntary exile, usually to Germany: though some, like **Lefebvre-Desnouëttes** and **Vandamme**, fled as far as America. Chastel opted for Switzerland, quitting France on 1 August 1815. Six days later, Napoleon set sail for St Helena aboard HMS *Northumberland*. Chastel returned to France three years later, when the political climate had cooled, but found 'Sacrés Bonapartistes' like himself still out of favour. He remained unemployed until his retirement from public life in 1825, returning to Geneva, where he died the following year.

Clark
Captain Alexander Kennedy (1782–1864)

Commander of No. 8 or G Troop, 1st (Royal) Dragoons, who, by his own account, captured the Eagle of the 105th Regiment. This officer's name appears in a variety of guises in the literature but, according to the *Waterloo Medal Roll* (Buckland 2001), he fought as Captain A.K. Clark on 18 June 1815. Clark added the surname 'Kennedy' at a later date, making him 'Alexander Kennedy Clark-Kennedy' – presumably to confound future historians.

A descendant of the Kennedys of Knockgray, Clark was a Peninsular War veteran. At Waterloo he captained the centre squadron of his regiment, which, as part of the 2nd British (Union) Cavalry Brigade, charged the attacking French columns about 2 p.m. Sergeant **Ewart** of the Scots Greys had already taken the Eagle of the French 45th Regiment, when the 1st Dragoons slammed into the 105th. This regiment, over 900-strong, belonged to General Bourgeois' 2nd Brigade. The 430 or so British riders wreaked havoc among the infantry, slaughtering many and capturing many more. Clark, however, spotted the 105th's regimental Eagle and decided to attack the standard-bearer. Fixed on flagpoles bearing regimental colours, French Eagles were precious objects. Awarded by **Napoleon** himself to the 1st battalion of all infantry regiments, they were to be defended unto death.

Clark picks up the story in a memorandum dated 14 July 1839, quoted in Siborne (1891):

> I did not see the Eagle and Colour (for there were two Colours, but only one with an Eagle) until we had been probably five or six minutes engaged. It must, I should think, have been originally about the centre of the column, and got uncovered from the change of direction. When I first saw it, it was perhaps about forty yards to my left and a little in my front . . . I gave the order to my Squadron, 'Right shoulders forward, attack the Colour,' leading direct on the point myself. On reaching it, I ran my sword into the Officer's right side a little above the hip joint. He was a little to my left side, and he fell to that side with the Eagle across my horse's head. I tried to catch it with my left hand, but could only touch the fringe of the flag, and it is probable it would have fallen to the ground,

had it not been prevented by the neck of Corporal **Styles**' horse, who came up close on my left at the instant, and against which it fell. Corporal Styles was Standard Coverer; his post was immediately behind me, and his duty to follow wherever I led. When I first saw the Eagle I gave the order, 'Right shoulders forward, attack the Colour,' and on running the Officer through the body I called out twice together, 'Secure the Colour, secure the Colour, it belongs to me.' This order was addressed to some men close to me, of whom Corporal Styles was one. On taking up the Eagle, I endeavoured to break the Eagle from off the pole with the intention of putting it into the breast of my coat; but I could not break it. Corporal Styles said, 'Pray, sir, do not break it,' on which I replied, 'Very well, carry it to the rear as fast as you can, it belongs to me.'

And so Corporal Styles ('Stiles' in some accounts) carried the Eagle to safety, while Clark fought on.

Clark remained on the field till about 6 p.m., when, having received his second wound of the battle, he was obliged to go to the rear. It was at this point that Clark remembered the Eagle and claimed its capture. But Styles, having handed the trophy to an officer in the rear, was initially given sole credit. Clark soon put matters right, and to this day most sources state that Clark took the Eagle of the 105th, while Styles, at best, played a supporting role. And yet, Styles makes no mention of Clark in his account of the action, recorded in a letter dated 31 January 1816 and quoted by Dalton (1904). This letter seems to indicate that Styles took the Eagle under orders from Lieutenant George Gunning of Captain C.L. Methuen's No. 7 or D Troop.

Nevertheless, both Styles and Clark were rewarded. According to William Siborne (1848), Clark was made a Companion of the Order of the Bath, while Styles received an ensign's commission in the 6th West India Regiment. In later years, Clark – now calling himself Clark-Kennedy – became colonel of the 6th Dragoon Guards and then the 2nd Dragoons. He was also appointed aide-de-camp to Queen Victoria.

Clay
Private Matthew (1795–1872)

Soldier of the Light Company, 3rd Foot Guards, and one of the heroes of Hougoumont. Born near Mansfield in Nottinghamshire, Clay volunteered for the 3rd Foot Guards at the age of 18, joining the Light Company of the 2nd Battalion. Clay found himself among the defenders of Hougoumont on 18 June 1815, the vital outpost that anchored Wellington's right flank. The château was repeatedly assaulted by **Jérôme** Bonaparte's division, but over the course of some nine hours of savage fighting remained in Allied hands. Clay survived this battle-within-a-battle to leave an account of his experiences, first published in 1853. He is often quoted by historians, especially with regard to the celebrated incident in which the great north gate was shut in the face of a determined French attack.

The accepted story, reprinted countless times, runs as follows: some time around noon the French were milling round Hougoumont's north gate, trying to get in. A latter-day Goliath called

*NCOs of the British
3rd Foot Guards*

Lieutenant Legros – nicknamed 'L'Enfonceur' or 'The Smasher' – grabbed a pioneer's axe and either broke open the gate or broke through it (accounts vary). Legros led a party of men into the courtyard – perhaps 30 or 40 – and a savage hand-to-hand battle broke out. Meanwhile, **Macdonell**, the garrison commander, helped by several others, rushed to the gate before more Frenchmen could enter. According to Elizabeth Longford (1969), Macdonell's group 'threw themselves bodily against the huge door and slowly, slowly, by main force pushed it back against the pressure outside'. And as for Legros and his storming party, 'not a single Frenchman remained alive except for a drummer boy'. To support this version, much is made of Clay's reference to seeing Macdonell carrying 'a large piece of wood or trunk of a tree in his arms . . . with which he was hastening to secure the gates'; and of his comment that no French intruders were left inside the compound except 'a drummer boy without his drum'.

But a careful reading of Clay's narrative reveals a different story, as highlighted by historian Gareth Glover (2006). Clay began the battle outside the château in the kitchen garden, kneeling behind a hedge, waiting to receive the advancing French skirmishers. When they came, Clay and his comrades were caught in 'a most galling fire', the enemy's bullets striking their knapsacks, accoutrements and even the heels of their shoes as they were kneeling. In the firefight and melee that followed, Clay and a comrade named Gann – 'a very steady and undaunted old soldier' – became separated from their company, which, overwhelmed by superior numbers, had retired into the château via the north gate. Clay and Gann remained outside, taking cover behind a large haystack and trading shots with the enemy, while a number of Frenchmen made an unsuccessful bid to storm the château. Clay's situation appeared critical:

> My comrade now from his position by the stack, apprized me of the enemy's advances to renew the attack, and supposing ourselves shut out from the farm, we were for a moment or two quite at a loss how to act, but on turning my eyes towards the lower gates I saw that they were open, and at the same time apprizing my comrade of so favourable an opportunity, we hastened towards that way.

And so Clay and Gann made for the north gate *after* the failed French attempt to enter, and when it apparently stood *open*:

> On entering the courtyard I saw the doors or rather gates were riddled with shot-holes, and it was also very wet and dirty; in its entrance lay many dead bodies of the enemy . . . on gaining the interior I saw Lieutenant-Colonel MacDonnell carrying a large piece of wood or trunk of a tree in his arms, . . . with which he was hastening to secure the gates against the renewed attack of the enemy.

Interestingly, Clay describes the gate as being 'riddled with shot-holes' but does not mention that it had been hacked through by Legros's axe. Furthermore, Macdonell appears to be barricading the gate *after* a fight with the intruders, not *during* it.

But what of Clay's drummer boy? As Gareth Glover observes, Clay seems to be referring to a separate incident altogether. Once inside the château, Clay was posted in an upper room to fire down on the skirmishers outside. But some time around 3 p.m. French shells set Hougoumont ablaze and Clay was obliged to quit his post and return to the courtyard. It was here that Clay observed the following: 'The enemy's artillery having forced the upper [i.e. south] gates, a party of them rushed in who were as quickly driven back, no one being left inside but a drummer boy without his drum, whom I lodged in a stable or outhouse.' From this it is clear that the French forced their way into the château some time after 3 p.m. via the south gate, and that the drummer boy belonged to this storming party, not the earlier one led by Legros. Clay goes on to say that after this incursion the south gate was closed and he took post under its archway:

> The enemy's artillery still continuing their fire, at length a round shot burst them open; stumps intended for firewood, laying within, were speedily scattered in all directions, the enemy not having succeeded in gaining an entry, the gates were again secured although much shattered.

Thus Clay's narrative has led Gareth Glover to conclude:

> Much criticism has been made that the French did not attempt to breach the defences of Hougoumont by artillery fire; however we are

aware that **Saltoun** had failed in an attempt to neutralise a French howitzer . . . Clay makes it clear that the French artillery did break the gates and that the French infantry actually broke in.

With the arrival of the Prussians on **Napoleon**'s right flank and **Wellington**'s repulse of the Emperor's Imperial Guard, French resistance collapsed at Waterloo. Thus, shortly after 8 p.m., attacks on Hougoumont ceased. Clay and his comrades were marched out of the smouldering château and up the slope of Mont St Jean, where, laying on the ground wrapped in their blankets, they fell into sleep.

Awoken next morning by the accidental discharge of a musket, Clay sat up and surveyed the scene:

Being on a hill, we had an extensive view of the field of action, a just description of which, would baffle the skill of the cleverest writer or most proficient artist. Having now with others, received orders to accompany a corporal to the burning ruins of Hougoumont, which we found to be a more complete picture of destruction than we could have anticipated (the fire having continued its ravages during the night); here we saw numbers of soldiers of different regiments, all surrounding the only well of water known to us on the premises, eagerly striving to obtain a drink of it, which had by this time become a mere puddle, and seeing no chance of obtaining any, we separated in the yard. I proceeded up the yard, where on the heap of ruins lay the body of a comrade of the Coldstreams, from whose mess-tin I took some biscuit; and turning to my left, entered the large garden, where I partook of some unripe fruit from a tree by the wall; on proceeding up the shaded avenue or garden walk, by the dead body of a Frenchman, I found a small portion of butter in a single-stick basket, which having partaken of, with my biscuit, and being refreshed, returned again to the yard . . . The heaps of the enemy's slain laying about the exterior of the farm, showed the deadly effect of our fire from within, and on passing near to the site of the circular stack [where Clay and Gann had taken cover the day before] I found that it had been totally destroyed by the enemy's fire and also that many of our comrades had fallen near the spot, and apparently entire, but on touching them, found them completely dried up by the heat. On passing down by the side of the garden we first entered, amongst the numerous bodies of the slain, was a wounded

Frenchman in a sitting posture (having no doubt fallen on the spot the previous evening) being unable to rise, we offered him our assistance, which he refused, and leaving him to his fate, we returned up the hill to our company.

Clay was promoted to corporal a couple of years after Waterloo and then to sergeant. He quit the regular army in 1833 on a pension of 1 shilling 8 pennies a day (about £2.75 in modern reckoning), settling in Bedfordshire as a sergeant major in the local militia. But hard times were coming. Clay had married in 1823 but only three of the couple's 12 children survived infancy. Then, after years of hard labour as a laundrywoman, Clay's wife was struck with paralysis and could no longer work. Clay still received an army pension of 2 shillings 5 pennies a day (£5.25 in modern reckoning) but was eventually reduced to selling off furniture in order to survive. Clay died in 1873 after a period of ill health: he was buried with military honours, courtesy of the Bedfordshire Militia, his Waterloo Medal on the coffin. Three volleys were fired over Clay's grave as the drums rolled . . .

Coignet
Captain Jean-Roch (1776–1850)

Imperial guardsman who witnessed the collapse and rout of the French Army at Waterloo. A veteran of **Napoleon**'s Italian campaigns, having enlisted in 1797, Coignet became a sergeant, and later captain, in the Imperial Guard. Illiterate until the age of 33, his *Note-Books of Captain Coignet* (1928) remains a classic testament to the courage and fortitude of Napoleonic soldiers.

It was probably about 7 p.m. when, by Coignet's account:

An officer came up from our right wing. He told the Emperor that our men were retiring there. 'You are mistaken,' said he, 'it is **Grouchy** coming.' He sent off immediately in that direction to assure himself of the fact. The officer returned, and confirmed the report that a column of Prussians was rapidly advancing on us, and that our troops were retiring.

The column in question was the advanced guard of **Ziethen**'s Prussian I Corps, approaching **Wellington**'s left wing from the direction of Papelotte. Historian Russell F. Weigley (1993) describes the sequel: 'Ziethen's troops . . . soon tore into the north-east corner of the French line. This unexpected threat touched off cries of treason.' Why should this be so? Because Napoleon and his aide **Labédoyère** had been confidently telling everyone the blue-clad newcomers on the horizon were Grouchy's troops: so when Ziethen's guns opened up, many Frenchmen assumed they were being assailed by their own side. Ziethen's appearance was followed by a general Allied advance, which in turn was followed by **Bülow**'s sudden emergence in the French right-rear.

Thus by 9 p.m. Napoleon's army had buckled into a state of collapse. Napoleon – accompanied by **Soult**, **Drouot**, Bertrand and Gourgaud – found a French battalion in square and sheltered behind its human walls. The Emperor ordered the battalion's guns to fire, in order to drive off approaching cavalry (it was one of these shots that shattered Lord **Uxbridge**'s leg). Acutely aware of the coming catastrophe, Napoleon apparently decided – for a moment – to make a final charge with this little battalion, crying: 'Il faut mourir ici, il faut mourir sur le champ de bataille' (It is necessary to die here, it is necessary to die on the battlefield). According to Coignet:

All his generals surrounded him. 'What are you doing?' they cried. 'Is it not enough for them to have gained the victory?' His design was to have himself killed. Why did they not allow him to accomplish it? They would have spared him much suffering, and at least we should have died at his side; but the great dignitaries who surrounded him were not anxious to make such a sacrifice. However, I ought to say that we all surrounded him, and compelled him to retire.

Napoleon quit the Waterloo battlefield almost unnoticed. He withdrew with a few senior officers, protected by a small cavalry escort. Behind the Emperor, the grenadiers of the Old Guard, formed into two battalion squares, effected a coordinated, stately retreat: stopping occasionally to fend off Prussian attacks. Ahead of the Emperor, a rabble of deserters and fugitives made for Genappe, a few miles up the high road leading back to Charleroi and the French border. At the farmstead of Le Caillou, Napoleon's party – including Soult, Drouot, Bertrand and **Lobau** – picked up a battalion of chasseurs à pied of the Old Guard, custodians of the imperial baggage. Then, riding beside the column, Napoleon also hit the road to Genappe, his grenadiers still in rear, keeping the Prussian cavalry at bay. About a mile from Genappe, Napoleon rode ahead of the column to explore the possibility of rallying the army there. But on entering the village – a normally tranquil place of some 1,000 souls – Napoleon discovered bedlam. Coignet describes the scene thus:

> We could not make way through the panic-stricken multitude . . .
> The Emperor tried to re-establish some kind of order among the
> retreating troops, but his efforts were in vain. Men of all units from
> every corps struggled and fought their way along the streets of the
> little town, with no one in command of them, panic-stricken, flying
> before the Prussian cavalry, which hurrah'd continually in rear of
> them. The one thought uppermost in the minds of all was to get
> across the little bridge which had been thrown over the Dyle.
> Nothing could stand in the way of them.

Genappe's single street was choked with abandoned vehicles, while crowds of quitters fought a running battle for possession of the bridge over the Dyle beyond: falsely perceived in these moments of panic as the only means of salvation (when the foot chasseurs and grenadiers of the Imperial Guard reached the banks of the Dyle, a mere 8 feet wide and 3 feet deep, they simply splashed across and on towards Charleroi).

Having survived the slaughter at Waterloo, these renegades were now prepared to kill for a crossing, blinded by night and terror to the fact the Dyle was shallow enough to ford. Coignet continues:

> It was nearly midnight. No voice could make itself heard above the
> tumult; the Emperor, recognizing his impotence, gave way and let
> the torrent flow, being convinced that he would be able to stem it
> next morning; he sent a party of officers to inform Marshal Grouchy
> of the loss of the battle. The confusion lasted a considerable length
> of time. Nothing could calm them; they would listen to no one;
> the mounted men blew out their horses' brains; the foot-soldiers

blew out their own to avoid falling into the hands of the enemy; everything went pell-mell. I found myself taking part in another rout as complete as that of Moscow. 'We are betrayed,' they cried. This great blow came upon us on account of our right wing being broken in.

It took Napoleon's little party an hour to force a passage down the main street at Genappe. At the bottom of the hill Napoleon found his carriage in the crush of vehicles waiting to cross the bridge over the Dyle. The Emperor climbed in: but before horses could be harnessed, the Prussians arrived and he was obliged to jump again. Scrambling upon a steed, Napoleon then galloped across the bridge and into the night. Meanwhile, the Prussian pursuit – described by **Gneisenau** as 'a hunt by moonlight' – had reached its climax at Genappe and a massacre ensued, crowned by **Major von Keller**'s capture of Napoleon's abandoned coach. According to historian Charles Chesney (1868): 'Napoleon, flying through the darkness from his enemies, hurried on with an escort of twenty chance horsemen.' According to Coignet the Emperor arrived at Charleroi between four and five o'clock next morning:

> The Emperor dismounted at the foot of the city; there he had a long conference with his generals; some wanted him to stay with the army, others wanted him to go on to Paris without more ado. To these last he said: 'How can you advise such a thing? My place is here.' . . . After he had given his orders, and made out his bulletin for Paris, an officer arrived who announced the approach of a column. The Emperor sent to reconnoitre it. It was the Old Guard returning in good order from the battlefield. When the Emperor heard this news, he was no longer willing to start for Paris; but he was compelled to do so by the majority of his generals. An old open carriage had been got ready for him, and some carts for his staff . . . At last the Emperor came out into the great court where we were all together in the greatest state of anxiety. He asked for a glass of wine; it was handed to him on a large tray; he drank it, then saluted us, and started off. We were never to see him again.

Colbert-Chabanais
General Édouard de (1774–1853)

Commander of **Napoleon**'s famous Red Lancers at Waterloo. One of three famous brothers, all of them cavalry generals (the others were Alphonse and Auguste), Colbert had been closely linked with Napoleon's bodyguard since the Egyptian campaign of the late 1790s. A former aide-de-camp on the staffs of Junot and Berthier, Colbert was promoted to general and ennobled in 1809. In 1812 he was given command of the 2nd Chevaux-Légers Lanciers of the Imperial Guard – better known as the Dutch or Red Lancers. Rallying to Napoleon in the spring of 1815, Colbert led his regiment – over 900-strong – into Belgium as part of **Lefebvre-Desnouëttes'** Imperial Guard Light Cavalry Division. Colbert's command also included a Polish Squadron, consisting of Napoleon's personal bodyguard, led by Colonel **Jerzmanowski**.

Wounded at Quatre-Bras on 16 June, Colbert was present at Waterloo, leading his lancers with his arm in a sling. Initially placed in reserve with the rest of Lefebvre-Desnouëttes' division, Colbert became embroiled in the massed cavalry attacks on **Wellington**'s centre, late in the afternoon. It appears that **Ney**, mistaking movements in Wellington's line for signs of a general retreat, ordered **Milhaud**'s cuirassiers to attack: but for reasons that remain unclear, the cavalry of the Imperial Guard joined in. Colbert has been blamed for launching the Red Lancers into a series of suicidal attacks, but de **Brack**, a captain in the regiment, later admitted some responsibility. Convinced that Wellington's line was breaking, de Brack called loudly for an immediate attack. The officers behind pushed forward for a better view, and as de Brack states (1876): 'all of a sudden the brigade of Dragoons and Grenadiers thought that the order to charge had been given . . . it set off and we followed'.

In truth, the whole affair remains foggy and obscure, but historian Ronald Pawly (1998) sums up the sequel: 'What is clear, is that the French cavalry went on to smash themselves, repeatedly, on the rocks of Wellington's unbroken lines of infantry squares.' Colbert charged at least four times and in the words of General Thoumas, writing in 1888:

In this Homeric combat our cavalry was overcome by exhaustion. The Red Lancers distinguished themselves by the strength of their blows. Colbert, wounded in the battle of the 16th, fought till the last moment with his arm in a scarf, and when the battle was definitely lost, covered the retreat with the remaining debris of the cavalry of the Guard.

According to some sources, Colbert received a further wound at Waterloo. Nevertheless, he remained in the saddle, his regiment furnishing Napoleon's final escort, as the Emperor quit the field in the evening.

Having lost almost half his men in the short campaign, Colbert was obliged to see the regiment disbanded on the return of Louis XVIII. Imprisoned briefly during the White Terror – Royalist reprisals on Jacobins and Bonapartists – Colbert quit France for a few months, till the heat died down and it was safe to return. But as a Sacré Bonapartiste, Colbert spent the next few years kicking his heels. In 1830, however, the July Revolution deposed the ultra-conservative Charles X – who had succeeded his brother, Louis XVIII, in 1824 – replacing him with his liberal cousin, Louis-Philippe. Suddenly, 'Damned Bonapartists' were back in fashion and Colbert was made a peer and inspector-general of cavalry.

On 28 July 1835 Colbert was present at the assassination attempt on Louis-Philippe, orchestrated by the Corsican terrorist Fieschi. The incident occurred during a review of the National Guard, when Fieschi and two Republican compatriots from the Society of Human Rights detonated an 'infernal machine' consisting of 20 musket barrels strapped together. Several people were killed – including Marshal Mortier, Napoleon's famous lieutenant – though Louis-Philippe, Fieschi's target, escaped with a grazed forehead. Many received more serious injuries, including – somewhat ironically – Fieschi himself, who was carefully nursed until strong enough to stand trial and face the guillotine. Colbert was also wounded but survived the attack, as well as the Republican Revolution of 1848 and Napoleon III's *coup d'état* of 1851. He died in Paris in 1853, at the ripe old age of 79.

Cole
General Sir Galbraith Lowry (1772–1842)

One of **Wellington**'s ablest generals, Cole was intended for the command of Wellington's 6th British Infantry Division, and is often listed as its leader in published orders of battle. But on 15 June 1815 Cole married Lady Frances Harris and was on honeymoon when the battle raged, Sir John Lambert commanding in his place. On 15 August Cole caught up with the army, commanding a division until the evacuation of France in November 1818.

Colville
General Sir Charles (1770–1843)

Commander of the 4th British Infantry Division, part of Lord **Hill**'s II Corps. Third son of the eighth Lord of Culcross, Colville entered the British Army in 1787, seeing service in the Irish Rebellion of 1798 and Abercromby's Egyptian campaign of 1801. By 1810 Colville was a brigade commander in **Wellington**'s Peninsular Army, losing a finger during the Siege of Badajoz (1812).

In 1815 Colville was given command of the 4th British Infantry Division, a mixed British and Hanoverian outfit. In the event, only his 4th Brigade (under Lieutenant Colonel H. Mitchell) saw action at Waterloo, Colville and the rest of his command being posted 8 miles west of the battlefield at Hal, a settlement of some 4,000 souls. Although Wellington later admitted he sent a 'small detachment' to Hal, Colville's division was joined by the Netherlands Corps of Prince Frederick (younger brother to the Prince of **Orange**), a Hanoverian cavalry brigade (under Baron Estorff) and an artillery park of 22 guns: a total of perhaps 17,000 men. Some sources state that Colville exercised command of this combined force, others that he shared command with Prince Frederick: either way, both men were answerable to their corps commander, Lord Hill – posted on the periphery of the Waterloo battlefield with the remaining 10,000 troops of II Corps.

Over the years Wellington has been severely criticised for keeping such a large number of troops kicking their heels while his army fought 'a near run thing' at Waterloo. Wellington's supporters claim the Duke was right to bolster his right wing, in order to protect three strategically vital points: Ostend (his embarkation port should things go pear-shaped), Ghent (the location of Louis XVIII's court in exile) and Brussels (capital of the Netherlands). They also point out that **Napoleon** was famous for doing the unexpected, so Wellington cannot be blamed for fearing an outflanking manoeuvre on his far right. The detachment at Hal was therefore a sensible precaution. But historians like Christopher Hibbert (1967) refer to this insurance policy as 'a strategical mistake that nearly all military historians have condemned'. Hibbert observes that had Napoleon attempted to turn Wellington's right flank, the result would have been the speedy junction of the Anglo-Netherlands and Prussian armies: the very thing the Emperor wanted to avoid. It's a fair point, and one made as early as 1914 by historian A.F. Becke, who dismissed the threat of a French march on Hal as an 'imaginary danger', censuring Wellington for not summoning Colville to Waterloo once battle was joined.

Nevertheless, Wellington's champions – including historian Jac Weller (1967) – maintain the Hal detachment was a necessary evil, serving not only as a blocking force for a surprise French sortie, but also a strategic reserve in case of catastrophe. More recently, Peter Hofschroer (1999) has declared the true purpose of the Hal detachment to be political rather than military. Emphasising the fact that Colville's force covered the road to Louis XVIII's sanctuary at Ghent, Hofschroer concludes that: 'If the battle went badly the troops at Hal would have served to delay a French advance sufficiently to allow the King's escape.'

Whatever the truth, the troops at Hal fired not a shot all day. And curiously, although Colville was posted a mere 8 miles from Waterloo, he always maintained the 500 guns in action there could not be heard.

Constant de Rebecque
Jean Victor (1773–1850)

Constant de Rebecque (1773–1850)

Chief of Staff to the Prince of **Orange** during the Waterloo campaign. Of Swiss origin, Constant de Rebecque joined the Dutch Army two years before the French takeover in 1794–5. Like other Netherlands officers – including **Perponcher** and **van Bijlandt** – Constant de Rebecque fled to Britain to join members of the exiled House of Orange-Nassau. There he entered British service as a lieutenant colonel, and was appointed military tutor to William, the future Prince of Orange. By the summer of 1814, however, Constant de Rebecque and his young charge were back in the Netherlands. For in the aftermath of **Napoleon**'s abdication of April 1814, the victorious Allies had decided to knock Protestant Holland and Catholic Belgium together, thus forming the United Kingdom of the Netherlands. The Prince's father was proclaimed King William I in March the following year.

But William of Orange was not the only homecoming monarch in spring 1815. On 1 March 1815 Napoleon landed in the south of France, having escaped exile on the Mediterranean island of Elba. By 20 March – four days after William I settled into his new capital at Brussels – Napoleon reclaimed his imperial throne at Paris. The Allies, who had been busy redrawing the map of Europe in their favour at the Congress of Vienna, immediately agreed on a new invasion of France. The plan was simple: Russia and Austria would mobilise forces to invade France from the east, while Prussian, British and Netherlands forces – concentrated between the Rivers Scheldt and Sambre – would await their arrival before invading from the north. Napoleon's pleas for peace were ignored. Left with no option but war to preserve his throne, Napoleon conceived his plan for what would become the Waterloo campaign: a pre-emptive strike across the Sambre into Belgian territory, with a view to removing the northern threat before the more serious eastern menace appeared.

Meanwhile, in Brussels, William's first act was to announce the creation of a new national army. His son, the 23-year-old Prince of Orange, was named commander-in-chief, with Constant de Rebecque as chief of staff. It would be the latter's job to hone the new Netherlands Army into an effective fighting force. This was not a simple matter, however, for both Holland and Belgium had been French satellites for 10 years, their sons marching across Europe under the Eagles of Napoleon's Grand Army. Loyalties were further divided along a religious fault line, separating the Protestant Dutch and the Catholic Belgians. Thus, Constant de Rebecque's new army was founded on a shaky alliance between separate Dutch and Belgian units (referred to as North Netherlanders and South Netherlanders respectively), the latter obliged to adopt the orange cockade of their Dutch rulers. Within a matter of weeks, Constant de Rebecque scratched together an army of some 30,000 men, most of them Dutch. Only half these troops were regulars, however (including some veterans of Napoleon's Grand Army), the rest being raw militiamen who were destined to receive but a few weeks' training before being thrust into battle.

In May 1815 **Wellington** took over operational control of all Allied units in the Low Countries, the Prince of Orange retaining nominal command of Netherlands units, as a sop to his father the King. Despite Constant de Rebecque's efforts, the Duke thought the Belgian units of the Netherlands Army 'bad' and untrustworthy. He even wanted experienced Belgian officers like **Chassé** dismissed. Fearing mass desertions – or worse, mass defections – Wellington opted to mix the Netherlanders with his British and Hanoverian units. And yet, these very same Netherlanders saved Wellington's skin at Quatre-Bras on 16 June, fending off a superior French force under Marshal **Ney** for several hours, until Wellington arrived with reinforcements.

Napoleon crossed into Belgium on 15 June, his aim being to split Allied forces, defeat each in turn, and seize Brussels. Marshal Ney commanded Napoleon's left wing (consisting of the corps of **Reille** and **d'Erlon**), and he was sent to secure the crossroads at Quatre-Bras. By this manoeuvre, Napoleon hoped to secure the approaches to Brussels from the direction of Charleroi, while severing the road link between Anglo-Netherlands and Prussian forces. Meanwhile, the Emperor hoped to slip between Wellington and **Blücher**.

Wellington later admitted to being 'humbugged' by Napoleon's movements, apparently expecting a French strike further west, via Mons. For this reason, the Duke had overlooked the importance of Quatre-Bras, ordering his army to concentrate on Nivelles if attacked.

But Constant de Rebecque, in his capacity of chief of staff to the Prince of Orange, disobeyed Wellington's instructions when news of Napoleon's invasion broke. Instead, he dispatched Netherlands units to Quatre-Bras, a movement supported by Perponcher, who also disregarded the Duke's orders. And so, from the evening of 15 June to the afternoon of 16 June, a force of several thousand Netherlanders held up the left wing of Napoleon's army, while Wellington galvanised himself and marched to their aid. According to historian Demetrius C. Boulger (1901):

> The fact of a stubborn resistance being even possible at Quatre-Bras was entirely due, not to Wellington, but to the action in the evening of the 15th of certain Netherlands officers in high command . . . One brigade of Perponcher's division, under Prince Bernard of Saxe-Weimar, was stationed between Genappe and Frasnes and about Quatre-Bras, the cross-roads where the Nivelles–Namur route cuts the chaussée from Brussels to Charleroi. The brigade was composed of four battalions, with one battery and no cavalry. The bulk of the brigade was on the slopes below Quatre-Bras, holding the wood of Bossu and the farm of Grand Pierrepont . . . At 6.30 in the evening of 15 June, the advanced battalion, with the guns in support, was attacked by the French cavalry. It slowly retired on Quatre-Bras in perfect order and without suffering any material loss. At nine in the same evening, Prince Bernard wrote the following letter to his divisional commander, General de Perponcher, at Nivelles: 'I must confess to your Excellency that I am too weak to hold out here long. The two Orange-Nassau battalions have French guns, and each man has only ten cartridges. The Volunteer Chasseurs have carbines of four different calibres and only ten cartridges per carbine. I will defend as well and as long as possible the posts entrusted to me. I expect an attack by the enemy at daybreak. The troops are animated by the best spirit. The battery has no infantry cartridges.'
> Those were the conditions under which the important position of Quatre-Bras was to be held against the corps of Ney, who at daybreak on the 16th had sixteen infantry battalions, five cavalry

regiments, and fifty guns at his immediate disposal. Fortunately, he had no knowledge of the weakness of the force in front of him.

Orders had been given by the Prince of Orange, by command of the Duke of Wellington, to concentrate the division at Nivelles – that was to guard the Mons road and to leave the Charleroi road uncovered. Baron Constant de Rebecque, chief of the Prince's staff, is entitled to the credit of altering the point of concentration from Nivelles to Quatre-Bras, and General de Perponcher to that of ignoring the original order, and, in response to Prince Bernard's letter, of moving in person with his remaining brigade, that of De Bylandt [i.e. van Bijlandt], to Quatre-Bras.

Fighting ceased at 9 p.m. on 16 June, with the Allies still in control of Quatre-Bras. Both sides had lost over 4,000 casualties. Ney continued to hesitate, and the following day waited till afternoon before advancing to the attack, by which time Wellington was already on his way to Mont St Jean, south of Waterloo. And so Constant de Rebecque's initiative saved the Allies. A report on Quatre-Bras, by *London Star* of 21 June 1815, says of Netherlands Troops: 'the brave soldiers of the Low Countries were not slow to prove otherwise than by words that they were resolved to conquer or die for their country and their Sovereign'.

On Waterloo Day, Constant de Rebecque saved Wellington again by rallying van Bijlandt's Belgians and Kruse's Nassauers at the height of the battle, ensuring that Wellington's line remained intact. At the end of the battle, as the Allied line advanced, Constant de Rebecque brushed with death, as a cannonball took off his horse's head, narrowly missing his own (Boulger 1911):

> At this moment a cannon-ball ricocheted under the belly of my horse, covering me with earth and stones and I was bruised on the flesh of my left leg. Immediately afterwards, while I still had my sword in my hand following the final cavalry charge, a canister shot struck the sheath of my sword against my leg . . . I was advancing with Lord Wellington in a hail of canister and my eyes were anxiously fixed on him but the happiness of victory shined in his. A canister shot passed through my horse's head; a fountain of blood came from its nostrils, covering me entirely, and it fell dead on the spot.

Cooke
Major General Sir George (1768–1837)

Commander of the 1st British Infantry (Guards) Division, part of the Prince of **Orange**'s I Corps. Son and heir of George John Cooke of Harefield, Middlesex, Cooke was educated at Harrow School, joining the 1st Foot Guards as an ensign in 1784. By 1792 Cooke had advanced to lieutenant (with the corresponding Line rank of captain – the 'gentlemen's sons' of the Guards enjoying a higher status than their comrades in the rest of the British Army) and in 1794 he went to war in Flanders as aide-de-camp to Major General Samuel Hulse. The following year Cooke was appointed to the staff of Major General Edmund Stevens, and in 1798 he attained the rank of Guards captain. In August 1799 Cooke was back in action, serving in the Netherlands campaign, where he was severely wounded. Back in Britain, Cooke served as adjutant-general of the North West District between 1803 and 1805, prior to a stint of soldiering in Sicily. In 1808 he took part in the expedition to the Scheldt, returning home sick shortly after. In 1811 he was sent to Cadiz, where, with the rank of major general, he commanded the British garrison until 1813.

At Waterloo, Cooke was just one of 240 generals present on the field of battle (164 French, 46 Anglo-Allied, and 30 Prussian). Nevertheless, he was the only British major general to command a division (the rest being senior lieutenant generals). The corps in question was the 1st British Infantry (Guards) Division, numbering perhaps 4,000 British guardsmen. The division consisted of four battalions, split into two brigades: the 1st Brigade under Major General **Maitland** (2/1st Foot Guards and 3/1st Foot Guards), and the 2nd Brigade under Major General Sir John Byng (2/2nd Foot Guards and 2/3rd Foot Guards). Cooke's division was deployed on Wellington's right, on that sector of the Allied position above the bastion of Hougoumont. The 2nd Brigade and the Light Companies of the 1st Brigade took part in the defence of the château, while the remainder of the 1st Brigade remained on the ridge to help repulse **Napoleon**'s Imperial Guard about 8 p.m. According to historian Mark Adkin (2001), at Waterloo, 'rank was no protector

British infantryman, 1815
– print after Genty

of person'. That being the case, Cooke was among the many wounded brass hats on the field, being struck by a round shot and losing his right arm as a consequence. Command of the division then passed to Byng, who relinquished control of the 2nd Brigade to Colonel Hepburn.

After Waterloo, Cooke was appointed KCB and colonel of the 77th Foot. He also received the order of St George of Russia (third class) and the order of Wilhelm of the Netherlands (third class). In 1819 Cooke became Lieutenant Governor of Portsmouth, and in 1821 he attained the rank of lieutenant general. By the 1830s, however, Cooke's health was severely compromised by a demanding military career and he died of flu. Cook's second sister, Penelope Anne – who married Robert Brudenell, sixth earl of Cardigan – was the mother of James Thomas Brudenell, the seventh earl of Charge of the Light Brigade fame.

Cotton
Edward (1792–1849)

One of the first Waterloo guides, the founder of a battlefield museum, and author of a celebrated account of the battle, *A Voice from Waterloo*. Cotton served in the 7th Hussars, under Lieutenant Colonel Sir Edward Kerrison. The regiment – part of Colquhoun Grant's 5th British Cavalry Brigade – was some 362-strong at Waterloo, and sustained over 150 casualties. Frequently described by Waterloo historians as a sergeant major on 18 June 1815, it seems Cotton achieved this rank much later. According to Dalton's *Waterloo Roll Call* (1904) – compiled from regimental muster rolls – Cotton was a private soldier on the day of battle. He was, however, an intelligent man, being both observant and literate. He was also brave. For when Private Edward Gilmore (a regimental comrade) lay trapped beneath his wounded horse in the path of advancing French cavalry, Cotton dashed forward to drag him to safety. Cotton survived the battle, though his own horse was shot under him.

In 1835 Cotton retired from the army, returning to Belgium to settle at Mont St Jean. He purchased property on the edge of the battlefield, establishing Le Grand Hôtel du Musée de Waterloo. The building was of considerable size, being subsequently described as comprising: '[an] English Bar, four rooms for restaurant, one of which is capable of seating 100 people, 24 sitting and bedrooms, stabling for 40 horses and vast coach-houses and outhouses'. Catering for a healthy tourist trade – Waterloo was already an obligatory stop on the European Grand Tour – Cotton added to the appeal of his hotel by displaying relics found on the battlefield. He augmented his income by offering his services as a 'Guide and Describer of the Battle'.

In 1846 Cotton published *A Voice From Waterloo*, produced in Brussels and originally intended as a guidebook for visitors: but demand was so great that London publishing houses were soon fighting over it. According to S. Monick, editor of the 2001 edition: '*A Voice from Waterloo* must undoubtedly rank as one of the most popular histories of the Waterloo campaign produced during the 19th century.' Indeed it must: for between 1846 and 1913 the book went through an astounding 13 editions.

Chiefly a history of the Waterloo campaign and a guide to the terrain, *A Voice From Waterloo* is careful to pay tribute to all. Of the British foot soldiers, Cotton says: 'No other troops in the world would have endured, for so long a period, so terrible a struggle.' And of the French, Cotton is no less complimentary:

> Their bearing throughout the day was of gallant soldiers; their attacks were conducted with a chivalric impetuosity and admirably sustained vigour which left no shadow of doubt upon our minds of their entire devotedness to the cause of **Napoleon**, of their expectation of victory, and the determination of many of them not to survive defeat. The best and bravest of them fell: but not till they had inflicted almost equal loss upon their conquerors. To deny them the tribute of respect and admiration which their bravery and misfortunes claim would tarnish the lustre of our martial glory.

In 1849 Cotton died, having lived on the battlefield for 14 years, during which time he reputedly amassed over 1 million signatures in his museum visitors' book. He was buried, at his own request, in the orchard of the château of Hougoumont. His body was placed beside that of Captain Robert Blackwood of the 69th Foot, who fell in the battle. But Cotton's remains were later exhumed and placed in a vault at Evere Cemetery in Brussels. He was in good company, for the remains of 14 other British heroes – including Sir **William De Lancey** and Sir **Alexander Gordon** – were also transported to Evere, where a monument to the nation's Waterloo dead was unveiled by the Duke of Cambridge (Commander-in-Chief of the British Army) on 26 August 1890. This event produced such a wave of emotion in Britain, the Belgian Mail Steam Packet, running from Ostend to Dover, offered special facilities for Britons wishing to attend the service.

On his death, Cotton handed the Grand Museum Hotel to his family for safe keeping. For 60 years the business continued, the hotel being developed at the expense of the museum. But in autumn 1909 Cotton's great-niece, a certain Mrs Browne, sold up. The hotel plus the museum and its 3,000 battlefield relics were auctioned off at 38 rue du Fossé-aux-Loups, Brussels, in two sessions: a preliminary bidding on Friday 3 September, and a final bidding on Tuesday 5 October. According to the catalogue accompanying the sale, Cotton's museum was easily reached from Brussels by rail or motor car: 'the Museum Hotel is always made the terminus and the halting place for dinner and refreshments'. At the time of writing, the building – opposite the Waterloo visitors' centre – houses a wax-works museum.

Crawford
Donald (dates unknown)

Orphan allegedly found on the field of Waterloo by a soldier of the 1st Foot or Royal Scots Regiment. The June 1895 edition of *The Thistle*, penned anonymously by 'An Old Milestone' features the following Waterloo anecdote:

> At the time I write of, it was customary for soldiers' wives to follow and accompany their husbands' regiments on active service, many of them being present at every engagement in the Peninsula from Corunna to Waterloo . . . Donald Crawford was rescued on the field of Waterloo while nestling as a child in the bosom of his mother who was killed in action. It may be asked what she was doing there, but the poor woman knew of nowhere else to go, and naturally followed the regiment in whose ranks her husband fought and fell on the same day as her. Fortunately for wee Donald he was seen by a private who was fighting in the ranks and picked him up out of his inanimate mother's arms, laying him lengthways across his back on the top of his knapsack lodged between his rolled greatcoat and the nape of his neck, and immediately resumed his place in the front rank of the fighting line, where the little boy was as happy as a sand boy. I regret, at the distance of time, I cannot recall the good man's name. Donald revered the man's memory with all the affection of a son for his

father, and was brought up in the regiment by his guardian, and later attained the rank of sergeant. The incident of his having been picked up on the field of Waterloo, having been brought to the notice of the Duke of **Wellington**, he ordered him to be granted the Waterloo Medal . . . as he was under fire during the whole three day engagement. He wore the medal on his left breast, until he was discharged to pension in the year 1851, at Halifax, Nova Scotia, where he elected to settle, like so many other time-expired men of his regiment.

A good story, but is it true? A scan through those pages relating to the Royal Scots Regiment in the *Waterloo Medal Roll* (Buckland 2001) does not produce the name Donald Crawford: but then, as the book was complied from British Army muster rolls, perhaps this is to be expected. Sadly, the author of the anecdote does not provide the name of Donald's protector: saying only that he raised the child 'in the regiment', acting as a guardian, while being revered as a father. Yet in these circumstances it seems reasonable to suppose the man might have given the orphan his own surname: especially as, seemingly, no other relative stepped forward to claim him.

Interestingly, the surname Crawford crops up several times in the Waterloo muster rolls of the Royal Scots: a Private Robert Crawford is mentioned in Captain MacLachland's company; a Corporal Alexander Crawford in Captain Brereton's company; and a Sergeant William Crawford in Captain MacRa's company. Could one of these men be Donald's saviour and surrogate father? Certainly, none could have been the child's real parent, as all survived the battle, whereas, as the author of the anecdote states, Donald's father 'fought and fell'.

Creevey
Thomas (1768–1838)

British MP best remembered for journals and letters recording the great personalities and events of the time. Creevey and his wife were living in Brussels in June 1815. They were there – like the **Capels** and a whole colony of British émigrés – because they were heavily in debt back home, and wanted to avoid their creditors. It was in Brussels that Creevey got to know **Wellington**, who arrived on 4 April 1815 to take command of the British garrison. Apparently, the two met in the Parc de Bruxelles a few weeks before the battle. Creevey asked Wellington if he and **Blücher** could 'do the business' and defeat **Napoleon**. His answer came as a British foot soldier crunched along the gravel path, gawping at the ornamental statues: 'There, it depends all upon that article whether we do the business or not!'

The two met again in Brussels on 19 June, as Wellington was finishing his Waterloo Dispatch: 'It has been a damned serious business. Blücher and I have lost 30,000 men. It has been a damned nice thing – the nearest run thing you ever saw in your life.' Next day, Creevey (1904) visited the battlefield:

> My great surprise was at not being more horrified at the sight of such a mass of dead bodies. On the left of the road going from Waterloo to Mont St Jean, and close up to within a yard or two of a small ragged hedge which was our own line, the French lay as if they had been mowed down in a row without any interval. It was a distressing sight, no doubt, to see every now and then a man alive amongst them, and calling out to Lord Arthur for something to drink . . . I rode home with Hume, the physician at headquarters, who said there were 14,000 dead on the field; and upon my expressing regret at the wounded people being still out, he replied: 'the two nights they have been out is all in their favour provided they are now got into hospitals. They will have a better chance of escaping fever than our own people who have been carried into hospitals first.' This of course was probably a fallacy, although a great number of men who had been carried to a nearby spa died from infected wounds, suspected at the time as having been caused by the mineral waters used to wash their wounds.

Decoster

Jean (dates unknown)

Flemish innkeeper pressed into service as **Napoleon**'s guide. According to historian Harold T. Parker (1944), Decoster (whom he mistakenly refers to as 'Lacoste')

> was a man in the early fifties who kept a small, obscure tavern on the high road between the farm of Rossome and Belle-Alliance. On the day of the battle he was used by Napoleon as a native guide, and was by the side of the Emperor from about eight o'clock in the morning unil late at night.

Writer Louis Cohen (1925), however, states that Decoster was seized at 5 a.m. on 18 June (his inn being some 500 yards in rear of French lines) and brought before Napoleon, who being dissatisfied with his maps, required a local guide. Decoster was hoisted on to a horse, whose saddle was attached by a long strap to the saddle bow of a chasseur of the Emperor's escort. When the bullets began to fly, the reluctant guide began ducking and wriggling to such an extent that Napoleon, exasperated by his antics, declared: 'Now, my friend, do not be so restless. A musket shot may kill you just as well from behind as from the front, and will make a much worse wound.'

But Decoster survived the battle to become something of a local celebrity, regaling visitors to his tavern with tales of his adventures. An English tourist, anxious to picture the scene at Napoleon's command post, eagerly questioned Decoster (Fraser 1912):

'What was going on?' 'His orders were always "Advance!"'
'Did he eat or drink during the day?' 'No!' 'Did he take snuff?'
'In abundance.' 'Did he talk much?' 'Never, except when he gave orders.' 'Did he say "Sauve qui peut"?' [Every man for himself]
'No! When he saw the English infantry rush forward, and the cavalry in the intermediate spaces coming down the hill, he said: "A présent il est fini. Sauvons-nous!"' [And now it is finished. We must escape!]

Napoleon tried to recruit at least one other guide on 18 June: a farmer named Joseph Bourgeois from the hamlet of Odeghien. Confused with Decoster in some accounts, Bourgeois was immediately dismissed by the Emperor as useless, being so terrified he could hardly speak. When asked about Napoleon after the battle, Bourgeois allegedly replied: 'If his face had been the face of a clock, nobody would have dared to look at it to tell the time.'

De Lancey
Lady Magdalen (1793–1822)

Wife of **Wellington**'s Adjutant-Quartermaster-General, Sir **William De Lancey**. Following Napoleon's return to power, Sir William was summoned to Brussels to join Wellington's assembling army. Newly married, Magdalen insisted on accompanying her husband, and the young couple spent their evenings 'in tranquil enjoyment' with no idea of the coming French attack. When,

Lady Magdalen De Lancey (1793–1822) – print after Engleheart

on 15 June 1815, news came of Napoleon's offensive, Magdalen wrote in her journal (De Lancey 1906):

> The reveille was beat all night, and the troops actively prepared for their march. I stood with my husband at a window of the house, which overlooked a gate of the city, and saw the whole army go out. Regiment after regiment passed through and melted away in the mist of the morning. At length my husband was summoned. He had ordered everything ready for my removal to Antwerp, thinking Bruxelles too near the probable field of battle, and he charged me to remain as much as possible alone, to hear no reports nor to move till he sent for me.

On the morning of 18 June Magdalen heard the guns of Waterloo as she sat at her hotel window in Antwerp, 50 miles north of the battlefield: a noise 'like the distant roaring of the sea'. She believed her husband would be safe because his post was near Wellington, but in fact there was no more dangerous place to be. Magdalen's journal informs us that Sir William was hit by a cannonball

> as he rode by the Duke's side; the ball was a spent one, yet the shock was so violent, that he was thrown a considerable distance, and fell with such a force that he rebounded from the ground again. There was no visible contusion, but the internal injury was too great to be surmounted . . . when the Duke took his hand and asked how he felt, he begged to be taken from the crowd that he might die in peace, and gave a message to me.

After the battle, Sir William's name was left off the casualty list to spare Magdalen's pain, so at first she thought he was safe. When she eventually received the news she 'became almost distracted' and left Antwerp for Waterloo:

> The journey was dreadful; the roads were filled with waggons, carts, and litters bringing the wounded; with detachments of troops; with crowds of people; it seemed impossible to get on. The people were brutal in the extreme, particularly the Prussian soldiers. I had the greatest difficulty to prevent my servant who was on the box from

losing his temper. I spoke to him from the carriage, begging him not to return the abusive language they gave us, and to remember we were unable to oblige them to let us pass. Once a Prussian rode up to the carriage with his sword drawn and refused to let it proceed, and even cut at the servant's legs. I had kept the blinds down, but I then drew them up, and implored him with my gestures to let us go on. He drew back, and the look of pity on his before fierce countenance proved what effect the appearance of real distress will have on even the most hardened.

The journey took a full day and Magdalen did not reach Sir William until 20 June. She found him in a 'wretched' hovel, in great pain, and unable even to move his head. Magdalen continues:

> It was scarcely possible to procure food or necessaries, but all that could be found was brought to us. My maid proved an excellent nurse, and prepared everything that Sir William ate, but he could take but little. The cottage had two rooms, in one we cooked his food, and I had the inexpressible comfort of knowing that he had all that he wished for . . . I passed the greatest part of the days his life lasted sitting by him and holding his hand; he could not speak much, but all he said was kind, soothing, and perfectly resigned. He often desired me to go and lie down in the other room; but if I returned in a few moments he forgot to send me away again. I fear he concealed his sufferings out of consideration for me, for sometimes, when I was out of sight, I heard him groan deeply . . . I think I slept but once during the ten days, and that was when he had fallen into a doze, and I leaned my head on his pillow; when I awoke he was looking at me and said it had done him good to see me sleep . . . I can scarcely recall the circumstances of the last twenty-four hours. He suffered much at times from oppression of the breath, and the advances of death, though slow, were very visible. He sunk into a lethargy and expired without a struggle . . . Sir William was buried near Bruxelles, in the same place with many other officers. I wished to have attended, but was advised not to do so . . . As I sat alone on the day of the funeral, reflecting on what had passed, I remembered it was three months that very day since my wedding.

De Lancey
Sir William Howe (c. 1781–1815)

Wellington's Adjutant-Quartermaster-General at Waterloo. Charming and handsome, De Lancey was born in New York, the son of American loyalists who sent him to England for schooling and a career in the British Army. After two years or so at Harrow, De Lancey was commissioned as a cornet (the lowest rank for a cavalry officer) in the 16th Light Dragoons. Most sources agree that De Lancey entered the army as a boy – probably aged 16 – but as the year of his birth is not known for sure, this cannot be verified. But whatever his age, De Lancey was a captain in the 80th Regiment by 1794, experiencing his first taste of war against the French in Holland.

If **Rees Howell Gronow** of the foot guards is to be believed, most young officers at that time received little or no training, learning their trade at the cannon's mouth – if they survived long enough. According to Gronow (1900):

> I . . . cannot but recollect with astonishment how limited and imperfect was the instruction which an officer received at that time: he absolutely entered the army without any military education whatever. We were so defective in our drill, even after we had passed out of the hands of the sergeant, that the excellence of our non-commissioned officers alone prevented us from meeting with the most fatal disasters in the face of enemy.

But De Lancey appears to have enrolled as a student at the Royal Military College, eventually becoming a staff officer in Wellington's Peninsular Army. Attractive, ambitious and able, De Lancey rose to become one of the Duke's favourite aides, serving with great distinction in Spain and Portugal.

On 4 April 1815 – the day Wellington arrived at Brussels to take charge of the assembling Allied army destined to fight at Waterloo – De Lancey married Scottish beauty Magdalen Hall in Edinburgh. But within days De Lancey was on his way to Belgium, Wellington having insisted he join him as Adjutant-Quartermaster-General in preference to the hated Sir Hudson Lowe (**Napoleon**'s future gaoler on St Helena). On 8 June De Lancey was joined at Brussels by his new wife, and over the following week the couple snatched what little time they could, as the army geared up for war. On 15 June Napoleon invaded Belgium, De Lancey marched for the front, and Magdalen was sent to Antwerp out of harm's way.

Following the battles of Quatre-Bras and Ligny on 16 June, both **Blücher** and Wellington were on the retreat, the latter to a position astride the Brussels high road near the villages of Mont St Jean and Waterloo. Wellington sent De Lancey ahead to reconnoitre the position, armed with a map on which the farmhouse of La Haie Sainte had been marked as the location for a possible stand against the pursuing French. When De Lancey arrived in the vicinity of La Haie Sainte he found himself in a shallow valley between two ridges. The southernmost ridge was dominated by the inn and farmstead of La Belle Alliance, owned by Nicolas Delpierre of nearby Plancenoit; the lower northernmost ridge (a mere 100 feet above the valley floor), close to the farm of Mont St Jean, was protected by two nearby bastions: the château of Hougoumont on its right flank and the farmhouse of La Haie Sainte at its centre. Furthermore, this ridge had a gentle reverse slope – dead ground ideal for concealing troops. Having considered the merits of both ridges, De Lancey chose the

La Belle Alliance – Napoleon's forward command post

northernmost for the Allied stand. Wellington apparently preferred the southernmost ridge but deferred to De Lancey, opting to defend the Mont St Jean position. When Napoleon arrived on the battlefield about 6.30 p.m. on 17 June, he occupied the southern ridge, converting La Belle Alliance into a makeshift command post and field hospital. Thus the two armies were configured for battle, which erupted late the following morning.

At the height of the battle, while talking to Wellington, De Lancey was struck in the back by a spent cannonball, which bounced up from the ground – the dragoon orderly who accompanied him was killed instantly by a second shot. Horrifically wounded – the cannonball smashed eight of De Lancey's ribs, splinters of bone puncturing his lungs – he was immediately attended to, but simply said: 'Pray tell them to leave me and let me die in peace.' But De Lancey's cousin – De Lancey Barclay – saw the incident and insisted he be removed from the field. And so De Lancey was carried off in a blanket by four soldiers, who took him to a barn at Mont St Jean, Wellington's map still in his pocket (this bloodstained item is currently held in the Royal Engineers' Museum at Chatham). De Lancey asked his cousin to write to Magdalen at Antwerp telling her of what had happened. Meanwhile, as Barclay feared the farm of Mont St Jean might fall to the French, he had De Lancey moved to a peasant's cottage at the village of Waterloo. There he was left and given up for dead.

On 20 June – having initially been told her husband had survived the battle unharmed – Magdalen arrived from Antwerp to nurse De Lancey. Forgoing food and sleep, she tended him for almost a week, but in vain: De Lancey died on 26 June. Magdalen later wrote of her husband's last day:

> At 5 in the morning I arose; he was very anxious to have his wound dressed – It had never been looked at – he said there was a little pain, merely a trifle, but it teazed him – Mr Powel objected; he said it would fatigue him too much that day – he consented to delay.
>
> I then washed his face and hands, and brushed his hair, after which I gave him his breakfast – he again wished to rise, but I persuaded him not to do it – he said he would not do anything I was averse to, and he said, 'See what control your poor husband is under;' he smiled and drew me close to him, so that he could

touch my face, and continued stroking it with his hand for some time – Towards 11 he grew more uneasy – he was restless and uncomfortable, his breathing was like choking – and as I sat gazing at him, I could distinctly hear the water rattling in his throat – I opened the door and window to make a thorough draft – I desired the people to leave the outer room, so that his might be as quiet as usual, and then I sat down to watch the melancholy progress of the water in his chest, which I saw would soon be fatal.

About 3 Dr H— and Mr Powel came; I must do the former the justice to say he was grave enough now. Sir William repeated his request to have the wound dressed. Dr H— consented, and they went away to prepare something to wash it with; they remained away about half an hour – I sat down by my husband, and took his hand; he said he wished I would not look so unhappy – I wept – and he spoke to me with so much affection. He repeated every endearing expression – he bid me kiss him – he called me his dear Wife.

The Surgeons returned – my husband turned on his side with great difficulty – it seemed to give much pain. After I had brought every thing the Surgeons wanted, I went into another room; I could not bear to see him suffering.

Mr Powel saw a change in his countenance – he looked out and desired Emma to call me – to tell me instantly Sir William wanted me; I hastened to him. I stood near my husband – he looked up to me and said, 'Magdalen, my love, the spirits' – I stooped down close to him, and held the bottle of lavender to him – I also sprinkled some near him and he looked pleased.

He gave a little gulp, as if something was in his throat – the Doctor said 'Ah, poor De Lancey, he is gone' – I pressed my lips to his and left the room.

De Lancey was first buried on 28 June in the Protestant cemetery of St Joost-ten-Node. But in 1889 his remains were exhumed and reintered in the vault of Evere cemetery, in a north-eastern suburb of Brussels, alongside 14 other British heroes, including ex-hussar and battlefield guide **Edward Cotton** and Wellington's aide-de-camp **Alexander Gordon**.

Delort
General Jacques Antoine (1773–1846)

Commander of **Napoleon**'s 14th Cavalry Division who attempted to stop the suicidal French cavalry charges at Waterloo. A veteran of the Peninsular War, which left him with a healthy respect for British infantry, Delort was a true professional, devoted to his men rather than any political cause. Interestingly, it was Delort's cuirassiers that unhorsed **Blücher**, while charging at Ligny on 16 June. Failing to recognise the Prussian commander, Delort's troopers left the septuagenarian bruised but at liberty: an oversight that arguably cost Napoleon the campaign.

At Waterloo, Delort's division was posted in reserve, left of the Brussels–Charleroi high road. The unit comprised two brigades of steel-clad cuirassiers – some 1,700 sabres in all – and formed part of **Milhaud**'s IV Reserve Cavalry Corps. Having successfully supported **Jacquinot**'s counter-charge against Sir **William Ponsonby**'s Union Brigade in the early afternoon, Delort became an unwilling participant in **Ney**'s grand cavalry attacks, which began about 4 p.m. It was around this time that Ney apparently mistook a retrograde movement in **Wellington**'s lines for a general retreat. Some claim the movement was a partial retreat in the face of heavy and prolonged bombardment from Napoleon's grand battery; others that it was an exodus of casualties to the rear, augmented by a mass of deserters. Either way, it seemed to Ney that Wellington's line was evaporating: an opportunity to be seized at once. The quickest way to exploit the situation was with cavalry and Ney sent word to IV Cavalry Corps, urging a brigade of cuirassiers to attack.

The order should have been carried to General Milhaud but it ended up with one of Delort's brigade commanders. This officer, a certain General Farine, immediately set the 5th and 10th Cuirassiers in motion as Delort, his divisional commander, looked on aghast. From Delort's viewpoint Wellington's line looked solid enough, and his Peninsular War experience told him that British infantry was virtually impregnable in defence. In Delort's eyes, Farine was behaving like a madman, sending unsupported cavalry against unbroken infantry. He galloped up and demanded to know what

Farine was about. Farine explained he was simply obeying Ney's orders, but Delort cancelled the manoeuvre and launched into a lecture on cavalry tactics. At that moment Ney arrived, demanding to know why the cuirassiers were not advancing. According to Delort (Stouff 1905):

> I pointed out that heavy cavalry should not attack infantry which was posted on heights, had not been shaken and was well placed to defend itself. The Marshal shouted 'Forwards, the salvation of France is at stake!' I obeyed reluctantly.

Ney was furious with Delort and, in a fit of pique, ordered Milhaud's whole corps to the attack. A.F. Becke (1914) describes the sequel:

> Ney promptly repeated the order and included the whole corps of cuirassiers, whom he then led forward to carry out his premature and reckless enterprise . . . Unfortunately, **Lefebvre-Desnouëttes** (who was behind Milhaud) saw the cuirassiers move off, and on his own initiative he determined to support Milhaud. Ney, riding at the head of the cuirassiers, could not see the strength of the cavalry following him; and, until the attack was fairly launched, the convexity of the ground prevented Napoleon from noticing what was going on . . . It was 4 p.m. when Ney led the cavalry forward, keeping well to the west of La Haye Sainte. When the intrepid horsemen closed they were received by a hurricane of fire, and the leading squadrons were blown to pieces.

Not that this deterred Ney. Between 4 p.m. and 6 p.m. a number of cavalry assaults were made on Mont St Jean. The French horsemen advanced over muddy ground, pressing together into a solid mass to avoid flanking fire from Hougoumont and La Haie Sainte. Some say that eventually 10,000 riders were committed to these fruitless attacks – welcomed by Wellington's infantry as a respite from Napoleon's cannonade. And according to some sources, Ney's horsemen charged 23 times: though as historian Jac Weller (1967) points out, there was time enough only for perhaps eight separate attacks. Certainly the final assault was made at a trot, over sticky, slippery ground churned into a bog and cluttered with corpses. Few made it as far as Wellington's guns. Delort led his cuirassiers to the charge at least four times. Struck in the leg by a bullet, and on the arm by a sabre-cut, he rallied his survivors, marching them off the field in good order at the close of the battle.

D'Erlon
General Jean-Baptiste Drouet, Count (1765–1844)

Commander of **Napoleon**'s I Corps during the Waterloo campaign. According to Louis Cohen (1925), d'Erlon was

> quite unsuited to a military career, and so universal was the opinion of his incompetency [*sic*] as a general, that the officers spoke of him as Count d'Erlon, never as *General*

General Count d'Erlon (1765–1844)

d'Erlon. Through false manoeuvring at Ligny, d'Erlon saved the Prussians from annihilation, and he contributed much to the French disaster at Waterloo.

Born at Rheims, d'Erlon was a staunch Bonapartist who, prior to the Waterloo campaign, served the Emperor well in the Austerlitz, Friedland and Spanish campaigns. After Napoleon's first abdication of 6 April 1814, d'Erlon pledged loyalty to the Bourbon monarchy. But when the erstwhile Emperor landed in the South of France on 1 March 1815, having sprung himself from exile on the Mediterranean isle of Elba, d'Erlon immediately rallied to his cause. Louis Cohen's colourful account of d'Erlon's efforts at Lille on behalf of Bonaparte is worth repeating for entertainment value:

> After the landing of Napoleon at Cannes, but before the army had declared in his favour, d'Erlon was stationed at Lille, where Marshal Mortier was Governor under the Legitimists. Mortier detected d'Erlon tampering with the soldiery, and had him promptly tried by

court martial. He was condemned to death, and without delay was led to the square of the citadel, with eyes bandaged. A file of soldiers were drawn up before him, their pieces were presented, and the fatal signal was momentarily expected, but the troops rose suddenly against Mortier, and declared d'Erlon commander of the place. The wheel of fortune having thus turned, d'Erlon generously released Mortier, and sent him in safety to Paris, where he soon declared in favour of the Emperor, and would have commanded the Imperial Guard at Waterloo if he had not been laid up at Beaumont with acute sciatica.

Most accounts, however, simply state that d'Erlon made an abortive attempt to call out the Lille garrison on 8 March, only to be arrested the following day by Marshal Mortier. Released 12 days later – by which time Napoleon had triumphantly entered Paris to take up the reins of power – d'Erlon had little trouble persuading the Lille garrison to support the Emperor's cause. D'Erlon was rewarded with command of I Corps, consisting of four infantry divisions and a cavalry division, almost 20,000 troops in all. But in a bizarre series of misadventures, d'Erlon failed to employ this powerful asset effectively. On 16 June, while Napoleon fought **Blücher** at Ligny, and Marshal **Ney** fought the Prince of **Orange** and **Wellington** at Quatre-Bras, d'Erlon marched and counter-marched between the two battles, fighting at neither.

The fiasco has never been satisfactorily resolved. D'Erlon, however, claimed he was diverted from Quatre-Bras to Ligny by an imperial aide, bearing a scribbled pencil note from Napoleon – only to be urgently recalled by Marshal Ney. Strange to say, Napoleon denied sending the pencil note – no record of which exists – while Ney refuted the suggestion that he recalled d'Erlon. This has led some to accuse d'Erlon of incompetence, or even treachery. Others, however, blame Marshal **Soult** for poor staff work, or General **Labédoyère**, Napoleon's aide-de-camp, for meddling with I Corp's marching orders. But whatever the explanation behind it, d'Erlon's failure to fight on 16 June probably cost Napoleon the campaign.

Despite the debacle on 16 June, two days later d'Erlon was given the honour of launching the first serious attack at Waterloo. Aimed at Wellington's left-centre, this opening assault was designed to smash through the Duke's line and open the road to Brussels. Napoleon had originally planned to bolster d'Erlon's advance with **Lobau**'s VI Corps, but having spotted **Bülow**'s Prussians approaching his extreme right flank, thought better of it. Keeping Lobau in reserve, the Emperor made d'Erlon go it alone. Historian Hilaire Belloc (1931) sets the scene:

> That assault was to be preceded . . . by artillery preparation from the great battery of eighty guns which lay along the spur to the north and in front of the French line. For half an hour those guns filled the shallow valley with their smoke; at half-past one they ceased, and d'Erlon's First Corps d'Armée, fresh to the combat, because it had so unfortunately missed both Ligny and Quatre Bras, began to descend from its position, to cross the bottom, and to climb the opposite slope, while over the heads of the assaulting columns the French and English cannon answered each other from height to height. The advance across the valley . . . had upon its right the village of Papelotte, upon its left the farm of La Haie Sainte, and for its objective that highway which runs along the top of the ridge, and of which the most part was in those days a sunken road, as effective for defence as a regular trench.

According to Georges Blond (1979), d'Erlon's divisional generals – with the exception of **Durutte**, who apparently disobeyed orders – chose to deploy their infantry in dense masses, difficult to manoeuvre and lacking offensive firepower. Richard Holmes (2002) suggests the divisions of **Quiot**, Donzelot and Marcognet were deployed in columns one battalion wide, and 12 battalions deep: a formation that brought the muskets of the leading battalion to bear, while providing the necessary weight for successful shock tactics. The disadvantage of this system, however, was that a single cannonball could kill up to 24 men as it ploughed through the column.

Nevertheless, d'Erlon's monster columns moved off, each battalion a mere five paces from its neighbour, drums beating and officers yelling. Soon the French foot soldiers were struggling across the soggy plain – their feet becoming entangled in the long rye stalks – and then up the shallow but slippery slope of Mont St Jean. According to Uffindell and Corum (1996), however, the divisional columns did not advance in a single tight formation, but as separate, staggered slabs of sweating soldiery. 'Because of this staggering of the columns,' they write, 'the action on the crest of Wellington's ridge was far longer and slower and fragmented than is usually realised.' Nevertheless, the skirmishers of **van Bijlandt**'s 2nd Netherlands Infantry Division were pushed back, as were a party of British riflemen under Lieutenant **George Simmons**: 'They moved steadily towards us. We formed a sort of line and commenced a terrible fire upon them, which was returned very spiritedly, they advancing at the same time within a few yards' (Simmons 1899).

But as the French reached the crest, shot slammed into them at close range. Redcoats from **Picton**'s division, covered by hedges lining the Ohain road running atop the ridge, poured in several volleys before charging with the bayonet. Moments later, Lord **Uxbridge** launched the heavy cavalry of brigades of **Somerset** and Sir **William Ponsonby**. Captain Duthilt, a Frenchman caught up in the drama, describes the sequel (Duthilt 1909):

> A terrible firing exploded. In an instant musketballs, roundshot, grape had killed a third of our brigade's men. The ravine made us make a left turn and for several hundred paces forced us to present our right flank as we moved along it. Cavalry moved swiftly to the opening we were making for, made a left turn and fell unexpectedly on our column. We hadn't time to form square. Bursting in through our intervals, it sabred everything the bullets, grape, roundshot had spared. The brigade began to retreat, pierced through at every point by this cavalry. The ground was heaped with dead and wounded.

Meanwhile, Durutte's column, which had captured the village of Papelotte during the advance, was caught up in the general retreat and obliged to give ground.

And so d'Erlon's attack ended in failure, costing perhaps 5,000 men killed, wounded or taken prisoner. Furthermore, two regimental Eagles were taken (that of the 45th Line was captured by Sergeant **Ewart** of the Scots Greys, that of the 105th Line by Captain **Clark** and/or Corporal **Styles** of the Royals) and several cannon wrecked. Although d'Erlon's corps fought on – taking the bastion of La Haie Sainte about 6.30 p.m., when its garrison, under Major **Baring**, ran out of ammunition – by the end of the battle it was a spent force, and its survivors fled following **Ziethen**'s arrival, the Imperial Guard's repulse, and Wellington's subsequent advance.

D'Erlon was one of the last French brass hats to quit the field. As he made for Napoleon's command post at La Belle Alliance, d'Erlon passed Marshal Ney, who was attempting to stem the flood of fugitives. His face black with powder, his uniform in shreds, a broken sword in his hand, Ney cut a tragic figure. As d'Erlon passed by, Ney threw the following words after him: 'D'Erlon, if you and I escape from this we shall be hanged!' As it happened, Ney was shot – executed by a Bourbon firing squad, which he had the composure to command himself – while d'Erlon fled abroad. Sentenced to death *in absentia* (by vengeful Royalists), d'Erlon settled in Bayreuth, where, by all accounts, he became an innkeeper. D'Erlon returned home 10 years later, however, and was eventually rehabilitated, becoming a Marshal of France in 1843.

Detmers
Colonel H. (dates unknown)

Occasionally referred to as 'Ditmer' in English sources, he commanded the 1st Brigade of **Chassé**'s 3rd Netherlands Infantry Division, comprising 35th Belgian Jäger, 2nd Dutch Line, and the 4th, 6th, 17th and 19th Dutch Militia: some 3,000 men in total. Like **van Bijlandt**, Detmers was an experienced officer who had previously served in the British Army. It was his Netherlanders that – with the Brunswick infantry – plugged the yawning gap in **Wellington**'s centre around 7 p.m. on 18 June 1815. Half an hour later, **Napoleon** attacked, launching some 3,500 foot soldiers of his Imperial Guard against Wellington's position. The young, inexperienced Brunswickers near La Haie Sainte were put to flight, but Sir **Colin Halkett**'s 5th British Brigade stood firm, buying time for Chassé (positioned behind the Brunswickers) to order the brigades of d'Aubremé and Detmers into line. They were accompanied by Smissen's Dutch Battery, which poured shot into the approaching French, causing devastating loss.

Detmers' Netherlanders had spent most of the day guarding Wellington's right flank at Braine l'Alleud, where they had been well supplied with beer by the locals. And so, while d'Aubremé's troops – a mixed force of Dutch–Belgians some 3,800-strong – fled, Detmers' men held firm beside the shattered ranks of Halkett's 30th and 73rd Regiments. When the Imperial Guard broke, Detmers' troops pursued as far as the high ground south of Hougoumont, reputedly yelling 'Long live the House of Orange! Long live the King!' Wellington then ordered his general advance as the French Army crumbled. According to Boulger (1901): 'the Detmers brigade charged, taking a prominent part in the final overthrow of the remaining battalions of the Old Guard'. A sentiment emphasised in the following colourful account by a sergeant major in Detmers' 35th Chasseurs, given to a Bruges newspaper, and quoted by Boulger:

> It was we Belgian Chasseurs who in the evening after seven o'clock attacked a square and pursued it to Charleroi. This square was composed of vieilles moustaches of the Guard. We commenced firing square against square, but that irritated us Chasseurs, and we called out for an attack with cold steel. This order we were happy enough to obtain from our General. It was then that you should have seen how that fine Guard fled at full speed. Never in my life shall I see again such a carnage . . . All perished by the bayonet.

D'Hoogvoorst
Baron Joseph van der Linden (dates unknown)

Mayor or *Burgomaster* of Brussels at the time of Waterloo. One of Belgium's principal aristocrats, the diminutive and good-natured Baron d'Hoogvoorst was appointed *maire de Bruxelles* in February 1814 and held the post for three years. He attended the celebrated Richmond Ball on 15 June, and when warned of the possibility of a large battle near Brussels, issued a notice declaring that the city was to become the 'Grand Hospital of the Allied army'.

But what of d'Hoogvoorst's Brussels and its history? Following the War of the Spanish Succession (1701–14) Belgium came under

Habsburg protection, being ruled from Vienna. In 1794 the armies of Revolutionary France evicted the Austrians, declaring Belgium 'French' and promptly annexing it. The French remained in control until February 1814, when Brussels, the capital city, was 'liberated' by the Prussians. Following **Napoleon**'s first abdication, the victorious Allied Powers decided to unite Catholic Belgium and Protestant Holland under the rule of the Dutch House of Orange. Thus, on 24 February 1815, the Sovereign Prince of Orange was proclaimed William I of the Kingdom of the United Netherlands. But on 26 February 1815 Napoleon escaped from Elba, making a dramatic return to Paris and imperial power. British troops were dispatched to Belgium to protect the new state, while Europe prepared for war. As David Miller (2005) states: 'Suddenly Brussels would no longer be a political backwater . . . indeed, it would shortly become the first target of the dictator seeking to restore his empire and thus one of the most important strategic places in Europe.'

In June 1815 Brussels was still a walled city with a population not exceeding 75,000. The town was garrisoned by British troops (**Wellington**'s headquarters was in the Rue Royale), exciting a small community of English émigrés, including **Fanny Burney**, **Caroline Capel** and **Charlotte Eaton**. Fashionable society was headed by the 23-year-old hereditary Prince of **Orange**, son of the new king, who held the honorary rank of lieutenant general in the British Army. Even with the shadow of war looming, life for the elite revolved around parties, picnics, and balls: set against the backdrop of Laecken Palace, the Hôtel de Ville, and the picturesque Parc de Bruxelles in the city centre. But the daydream was shattered when, at 3 p.m. on 15 June, Napoleon crossed the Sambre onto Belgian soil. The Emperor's pre-emptive strike raised howls of discouragement and dismay in Brussels. So much so, Wellington's military commandant refused to issue passports to Britons wanting to quit: 'It is not for us, the English, to spread alarm or prepare for an overthrow.'

Following initial clashes at Quatre-Bras and Ligny, on 16 June, it became clear that Brussels would see a cataclysmic battle on its doorstep. D'Hoogvoorst prepared for an influx of wounded into the city by making a public appeal for lint, bandages and mattresses. He also announced that wealthy citizens must be prepared to receive wounded soldiers into their houses. On 18 June, when the guns of Waterloo were heard, d'Hoogvoorst ordered brewers' waggons laden with water to be sent down the high road to meet the first wounded. The brewers of Brussels complied, but instead of water they took beer. In return, the wounded (not to mention the deserters) brought news of disaster and defeat, throwing Brussels into a panic. According to **James Anton** (1841) of the 42nd Highlanders:

> The approach of the fugitives, and the confused appearance of our light baggage, struck Brussels with alarm: the living tide rolled in at its gates, and the early fugitives of the day declared that all was lost; while every succeeding runaway confirmed the unwelcome tidings, to cover his own cowardly flight. The walls were crowded with the anxious inhabitants of the city, as well as with the deeply interested peasantry, who had fled from the scene of action, listening to the hostile report of the guns. Imagination brought the sound at times louder, and as if approaching nearer to the gates; but now when the stream of fugitives poured in, all was confusion and despair. Some fled for safety towards Ghent, Ostend, or Antwerp, while others withdrew to their houses and trusted to the simple security of their bolted doors.

By nightfall, however, the hysteria had subsided, as the *Bruxellois* were obliged to acknowledge victory – and its horrendous human cost.

In total, perhaps 20,000 wounded were treated in Brussels, largely thanks to d'Hoogvoorst's foresight and organisational ability. And yet the numbers were so great they overwhelmed the city. Although many casualties received care in hospitals and private houses, many more were simply laid on straw beneath the city walls, between the Louvain and Namur gates (still in existence in 1815), to await treatment. On 26 June – almost a week after the battle – Miss 'Georgy' Capel, sister of Caroline, wrote to her grandmother:

> How can I describe all the horrors of a Hospital Station – which Brussels is – the streets crowded with wounded wretches and with waggons filled with dead and dying – the atmosphere is so much affected by it that many English are thinking of quitting Brussels in fear of pestilence . . . We are all constantly employed in making lint for the unfortunate wounded; it is impossible to shew more humanity than the Belgians do for them, all the shopkeepers spend much of

their time in their service. Brussels looks very dismal indeed to us who have seen it in such gaiety, the Parc is quite deserted, nothing but wounded men wandering about. Hundreds of dead horses lying also, having been shot since they came into town. Upon the ramparts not far from us, 3,000 dead bodies are exposed, there not being room to bury them.

Domon
General Jean Simon (1774–1830)

Commander of **Napoleon**'s 3rd Cavalry Division, comprising the 4th, 9th, and 12th Chasseurs à Cheval: some 1,000 sabres. Part of **Vandamme**'s III Army Corps at the start of the campaign, Domon's division was detached to harry **Wellington**'s troops as they retreated from Quatre-Bras to Mont St Jean on 17 June. Arrived at Waterloo, Domon's command was added to **Lobau**'s VI Corps, which formed part of Napoleon's reserve.

About 1 p.m. Napoleon, at his command post at Rossomme, spotted troops far away to the east, on his right flank. According to William Siborne (1848):

> All the staff directed their telescopes upon the point indicated; and, as the atmosphere was not very clear, different opinions were entertained: some asserting that what had been taken for troops were trees; others that they were columns in position; whilst several agreed with Soult, that they were troops on the march. In this state of uncertainty and suspense, the Emperor sent for General Domon, and desired him to proceed instantly with a strong reconnoitring party to the right, and procure intelligence.

But Domon made a serious error: for instead of advancing beyond the Bois de Paris and deploying along the line of the River Lasne – compromising any hostile troops and holding up their advance indefinitely – he stopped before the exits of the wood and simply waited.

This passivity is even more curious when one considers that a captured Prussian hussar was brought before Napoleon shortly after

1 p.m., confirming the distant column to be **Bülow**'s IV Corps. According to Napoleon's biographer, Bourrienne (1905):

> The time of the arrival and cooperation of the Prussians has been variously stated . . . French writers make it at an early hour, to account more satisfactorily for their defeat. The Prussians also make it somewhat earlier than was actually the case, in order to participate more largely in the honours of the day.

The Prussians probably debouched from the Bois de Paris around 4 p.m., and although Domon fought hard, aided by another 1,000 men from Subervie's 5th Cavalry Division, the French were overwhelmed and obliged to retire to Plancenoit. The Prussians followed, preparing to stove in Napoleon's right flank as the Emperor continued to launch frontal assaults on Wellington's line at Mont St Jean. Although wounded in the fighting, Domon remained at his post, joining the general retreat up the Charleroi road in the late evening.

Dörnberg
Major General Sir Wilhelm Kaspar Ferdinand von (1768–1850)

Prussian officer (referred to as Sir William de Dornberg in some British sources) who commanded **Wellington**'s 3rd British Cavalry Brigade at Waterloo. When the campaign opened on 15 June 1815, Dörnberg was stationed at Mons. While there, he was responsible for forwarding intelligence from Wellington's 'observing officer', Colquhoun Grant, to the Duke's headquarters in Brussels. A.F. Becke (1914) describes the sequel:

> On the 15th, Grant's agent reported that 'the roads were encumbered with men and vehicles and that officers of all ranks spoke freely of a great battle being fought within three days.' This information Grant immediately sent back for transmission to the Duke. General von Dörnberg, however, arrogated to himself the right to select those messages which he considered worth sending on to the Duke; and the General returned the message to Grant with the remark that, far from convincing him that the Emperor

was advancing to give battle, it assured him the contrary was the case. Grant instantly arranged to send the message straight to the Duke, but it was impossible to get it through in time and it only reached Wellington at 11 a.m. on the 18th at Waterloo, too late to be of the slightest service.

According to Elizabeth Longford (1969), Grant delivered his message to Wellington on 16 June at Quatre-Bras, but Longford still describes Dörnberg as a 'witless Hanoverian cavalry officer' who had deserted to the Allies in 1813 after service with **Jérôme** Bonaparte. But Philip Haythornthwaite (1998) is kinder to Dörnberg. He writes that Dörnberg merely edited Grant's report, toning down the danger before actually sending it on to the Duke: and when subsequent events proved him wrong, galloped to Wellington in person to retrieve the situation. Historian Peter Hofschroer (1999) also defends Dörnberg, claiming he regularly sent reliable reports to Brussels.

But whatever Dörnberg's worth as an intelligence gatherer, at least he made it to Waterloo, where he was wounded leading his brigade. This command consisted of the 23rd Light Dragoons and the 1st and 2nd Light Dragoons of the King's German Legion: some 1,400 sabres in total. According to H.T. Siborne (1891): 'At Waterloo the brigade was first posted in rear of Sir Colin **Halkett**'s infantry in the Allied right-centre, and was engaged during the day in several successful combats with the French cavalry attacking that part of the line.' During the final charge of the day, Dörnberg's brigade joined those of **Vivian** and **Vandeleur** in a series of charges between La Haie Sainte and Hougoumont, which scattered the remnants of **Napoleon**'s cavalry, allowing Wellington's infantry to advance to victory unmolested.

Drouot
General Antoine, Count (1774–1847)

Like the Spaniard, General **Alava**, fought at both Trafalgar and Waterloo: on the former occasion as an officer of marines, and on the latter as commander of **Napoleon**'s Imperial Guard. Drouot found himself in charge of the Guard thanks to Marshal Mortier's sciatica. Mortier normally led Napoleon's 'Immortals' on campaign, but in June 1815 he pleaded sick, command passing to Drouot, his chief of staff. A professional soldier with over 20 years' experience, Drouot was close to Napoleon. He had accompanied the Emperor to Elba in May 1814, hoping to devote his time to the study of philosophy and the Bible. But Napoleon's escape 10 months later put paid to Drouot's dreams of a quiet life.

At Waterloo Drouot commanded some 20,000 troops, including **Duhesme**'s Young Guard, **Friant**'s foot grenadiers, Morand's foot chasseurs, and the cavalry divisions of **Lefebvre-Desnouëttes** and **Guyot**. Batteries of foot and horse artillery, artisans, gendarmes, engineers and marines made up the numbers of Drouot's mini-army. But Waterloo Day dawned wet and cold, following night storms and torrential rain, and Drouot reputedly convinced Napoleon to delay his attack on account of sodden ground. Napoleon had originally planned to attack **Wellington** at 6 a.m. on 18 June: the reason he dallied till after midday has been blamed by generations of historians on boggy conditions, the result of recent downpours. According to David Chandler (1980): 'the postponement of opening battle until late in the forenoon because of the sodden ground proved the most fatal one of the day for the French'. While Houssaye (1900) was convinced that: 'had the battle begun towards 6 or 7 o'clock in the morning . . . the English Army would have been routed before the arrival of the Prussians . . . the state of the ground compelled the Emperor to alter his orders . . . this delay saved the English Army.' Drouot is named as a leading voice among those who advised Napoleon to let the ground dry before doing battle. But the rain had only stopped at 4 a.m., while the sun remained obscured by clouds. Thus, as Mark Adkin (2001) points out, a delay of a few hours would not have made much difference to the state of the ground: a fact surely obvious to everyone at the time.

But, it was not so much the state of the ground that held Napoleon in check as the state of his army. For at 6 a.m. on 18 June many Frenchmen were more concerned with attacking breakfast than Wellington's redcoats. Napoleon's forces were still assembling and many units – including the Imperial Guard – had yet to arrive on the field of battle. Strung out for miles on miry tracks or toiling up the only main road, the French Army was in a miserable state: cold, wet, hungry and disorganised. Put simply, the French didn't attack in the early morning because they weren't ready. Napoleon, however, was not unduly worried. He was confident. He was a military genius and knew better than anyone when to begin an attack. And yet generations of historians have him advised by the likes of Drouot on the topic of mud.

Drouot quit the battle with Napoleon when defeat was imminent. According to historian John Naylor (1960), Napoleon and his suite sought refuge among the grenadiers of the Guard, positioned near Jean **Decoster**'s house, some 500 yards in rear of the original French front line:

> Attacked by cannon, and mounting numbers of enemy cavalry and infantry, the Emperor ordered the withdrawal, and the Grenadiers marched slowly away before a running assault, which from time to time they halted to drive off. Ahead of them rode the Emperor, **Soult**, Drouot, Bertrand and **Lobau**, and a handful of cavalry.

Drouot survived the battle but was tried for treason by the incoming Bourbon monarchy. He defended himself so skilfully, however, he was acquitted, retiring from the army on a handsome pension. Having overseen the disbanding of the Imperial Guard, Drouot spent his remaining years caring for the welfare of Napoleon's old warriors.

Duhesme
General Philibert Guillaume, Count (1766–1815)

Commander of **Napoleon**'s Young Guard Division at Waterloo. 'A thoroughly unpleasant individual' according to historian Mark Adkin (2001), Duhesme was the son of a labourer, and his military career was kick-started by the Revolution of 1789. As a Republican general, Duhesme was no lover of Napoleon's imperial adventure, which he believed betrayed the principles of the Revolution. Nevertheless, General Duhesme prospered in the Grand Army, becoming military governor of Gerona and then Barcelona. But he was dismissed from the latter post in 1810, having been implicated in corruption, brigandage, torture and murder. Three years later, however, Napoleon was in need of experienced officers and Duhesme was recalled. He fought with distinction throughout 1813 and 1814, always a tough, inspirational leader on the battlefield. After Napoleon's first abdication, Duhesme saw fit to serve the Bourbons. When the Emperor returned in March 1815, Duhesme hesitated before throwing in his lot. But when he finally did, Napoleon rewarded him with the Young Guard Division. Duhesme's command comprised two brigades, each one consisting of a battalion of tirailleurs and voltigeurs. Roughly translated, *tirailleur* means skirmisher, while *voltigeur* means vaulter or leaper – referring to a species of light infantry supposedly capable of keeping pace with a trotting horse.

Initially posted in reserve, Duhesme's division was the first Imperial Guard infantry unit to see action at Waterloo, being thrown into the defence of Plancenoit on Napoleon's right flank in the late afternoon of 18 June. It was about 4 p.m. when the Prussians, having marched from Wavre, emerged from the Bois de Paris on Napoleon's far right, threatening the village of Plancenoit and lobbing cannonballs on to the Brussels–Charleroi road in the Emperor's rear. By 5.30 p.m. **Bülow**'s IV Corps had succeeded in shunting **Lobau**'s holding force out of Plancenoit, threatening Napoleon's line of retreat. The Emperor ordered Dushesme to retake the village and a successful counter-attack was launched. But around 6.15 p.m. the Prussians – reorganised and reinforced – attacked again, evicting Duhesme's Guards. Napoleon responded by tossing in two battalions of his Old Guard. Although heavily outnumbered, the Old Guard reputedly cleared Plancenoit in 20 minutes and Duhesme's men, having rallied, returned to the village. But Bülow, receiving a steady stream of reinforcements, kept up the pressure. By 9 p.m. the French defenders – outnumbered five to one – could hold no longer and were evicted from Plancenoit for the final time.

It had been a bitter battle: a savage fight for each street, indeed each house. Soon flames consumed all and the French survivors beat a retreat. The Young Guard retired in good order, the mortally wounded Duhesme – hit in the head by a musket ball – was still in the saddle, held in place by his aide-de-camp. But the retreat became a rout as Bülow stoved in Napoleon's right flank and **Wellington** – who had successfully repulsed the Middle Guard – advanced to his front. Napoleon quit the field about 9.30 p.m., his army ebbing away up the Charleroi road. Duhesme struggled on for 5 or 6 miles, making it as far as the Roi d'Espagne inn at Genappe. There he was abandoned, to be discovered by some officers of Marshal **Blücher**'s staff in the early hours of 19 June. Despite their care, Duhesme died next day: his remains still lie in the graveyard of Saint Martin at the nearby village of Ways.

Dupuis
Madame Thérèse (1802–c.1904)

Local peasant from the tiny village of Chapelle and possibly the last eyewitness of the battle to die. Thérèse was 13 years old in 1815 and witnessed incidents from the battle she could still clearly recall almost 90 years later. The following is taken from the *Pall Mall Gazette* of 18 June 1904, quoted by Dalton (1904):

> As a little girl, stirred and fascinated by the long lines of horsemen, guns, and tired foot regiments passing our cottage, I stood at our door and served out water to the beaux soldats. Afterwards I followed them to Waterloo. In the evening we heard the booming of great cannon, and from the windows I could see the clouds of smoke rising into the air like trees. I was in the mill and the windows rattled. All night long we heard the tramp of silent men and the creaking, stumbling guns passing our doors. When I looked out next morning, I saw wounded men lying by the roadside . . . Not far away soldiers were digging trenches in our fields to bury the dead. There were so many of them, so many of them.

Dupuy
Major Victor (1777–?)

Commanded a squadron of the French 7th Hussars at Waterloo. Dupuy joined the cavalry in 1798, rising to the rank of sergeant by 1802. A veteran of some of the hardest fought battles of the period, Dupuy was a major (*chef d'escadron*) by 1813. The elite 7th Hussars remained loyal in spirit to **Napoleon** after the first abdication, raising the town of Valenciennes to his cause in March 1815. For the Waterloo campaign, the regiment – led by Colonel **Marbot**, who later produced a set of celebrated reminiscences – was brigaded with the 3rd Chasseurs à Cheval: part of **Jacquinot**'s 1st Cavalry Division of **d'Erlon**'s I Corps.

Dupuy – commanding one of the regiment's three squadrons – spent the night before Waterloo in the saddle, soaked to the skin, observing **Wellington**'s lines on Mont St Jean. Diverted only by the occasional British artillery rocket streaking across the murky sky, he recalled (Dupuy 1892) the night of 17/18 June as: 'A dreadful time – the rain fell in torrents.' At dawn the following day, having been on horseback over eight hours, the 7th Hussars – mustering just over 400 sabres – were posted on Napoleon's extreme right. According to Dupuy:

> The combat was joined on our left, all along the line. Around midday, panic seized some regiments of infantry belonging to the I Corps and a stampede broke out. These troops fled in the greatest disorder. I galloped up with a platoon of hussars to stop them. Seeing among the runaways a standard-bearer with his Eagle, I told him to give it to me. He had already stepped forward to hand it over when a thought came to me: 'I do not want to dishonour you, sir,' I said to him, 'unfurl your flag and carry it forward by shouting with me Vive l'Empereur!' He did it at once, the good man! Soon the soldiers stopped and in a moment – thanks to the Eagle and our efforts – nearly three thousand men were rallied and turned around.

After stemming the tide of fleeing foot soldiers – presumably the survivors of d'Erlon's ill-fated attack on **Picton**'s division – Dupuy and his troopers 'remained peaceful witnesses of the battle' for some four hours. Then, in the late afternoon, General **Domon** arrived, telling Dupuy that the enemy had ceased firing; that the battle was almost won; and that any moment Marshal **Grouchy** would arrive to seal Wellington's fate. But instead of French reinforcements, the 7th Hussars were faced with the lances of a regiment of Prussian Ulans – the leading elements of **Bülow**'s advancing IV Corps:

> We pushed them back vigorously, giving chase: but they withdrew behind a battery of six guns, which forced us to retire on account of their grapeshot. Colonel Marbot had been wounded by a lance-blow to the chest . . . during our retreat on the centre, we met Marshal **Soult**, who ordered us to escort a battery of the Guard and support it: the enemy guns did us some harm. A little later we were ordered to the rear to oppose some Prussian riflemen. Until then, we thought that the battle was won on the other parts of the line; but when we arrived on the main road, we saw it jammed with deserters and were undeceived.

Dupuy and his hussars were obliged to join the general retreat, following Wellington's repulse of the Imperial Guard and the appearance of Bülow and **Ziethen** on the French right. But, as Dupuy himself states, 'at least we retired in good order, walking a few hundred paces to the side of the road, until night and the difficulty of the ground forced us to return and go pell-mell with the runaways of all arms'.

Dupuy survived the campaign, convinced that Wellington had been saved only by the arrival of Blücher's Prussians: 'Without that skilful march, Waterloo Bridge on the Thames would have been built on the Seine! Ah, if there was any justice, one should see on this monument a statue of the Prussian General at least!'

Durutte
General Pierre François (1767–1827)

Commander of **Napoleon**'s 4,000-strong 4th Infantry Division, part of **d'Erlon**'s I Corps. A veteran with almost 23 years' military experience, Durutte was sent back and forth between the battles of

Quatre-Bras and Ligny on 16 June, his division playing no effective part in either, thanks to shoddy staffwork. At Waterloo, Durutte's command was intially placed on the extreme right of Napoleon's line. But around 1.30 p.m. Durutte was ordered to advance as part of d'Erlon's attack on **Wellington**'s left-centre. D'Erlon ordered his four infantry divisions forward in dense, ungainly masses. This formation – the so-called *Colonne de Division par bataillon* – required each divisional general to form up his 12 battalions one behind the other before moving off. Donzelot, **Quiot** and Marcognet complied with the order, but Durutte refused. Instead, he divided his command into two brigades, each of six battalions, thus halving its depth and doubling its firepower.

Durutte's initiative paid off: for while his colleagues foundered, he successfully stormed the village of Papelotte, on Wellington's extreme left, around 2 p.m. Obliged to vacate the village shortly after, following the rout of Donzelot's and Marcognet's divisions, Durutte kept his command intact. He advanced again in the late afternoon, retaking Papelotte around 6 p.m. Threatened by the approach of **Ziethen**'s Prussians, approaching from Wavre, Durutte clung on to Papelotte until the repulse of Napoleon's Imperial Guard around 8 p.m.

At this point the morale of the division cracked and Durutte's troops quit, many falling to the sabres of **Vandeleur**'s cavalry. Attempting to rally his men, Durutte was caught in the bloodbath, his right hand being severed at a single stroke of a dragoon's sabre. His head was split open shortly after, disfiguring him for life and leaving him blind in his right eye. Durutte's life was saved by his horse, which, panic-stricken, bolted back to La Belle Alliance and the surgeons' post.

In the aftermath of Waterloo, Durutte quit France for Belgium, settling at Ypres, where he eventually died. The inscription on his tomb reads: 'His military career started at Valmy and ended at Waterloo.'

Eaton
(née Waldie) Charlotte Anne (1788–1859)

Eyewitness to the immediate aftermath of the Battle of Waterloo, and ghostwriter of J. Booth's best-selling account of the battle, published in 1815. According to Elizabeth Longford (1969):

> Among the wise virgins to reach Antwerp before the 'tumult, terror and misery' of a refugee avalanche, was Miss Charlotte Waldie. She arrived with the first crash of the thunder-storm and had to listen at midnight to a sinister hammering in the hotel room next door. The nails were being driven into the Duke of **Brunswick**'s coffin.

And yet the situation might well have appealed to Charlotte, who several years before had begun a novel in the Gothic style. Little is known of Charlotte's early years – save her literary leanings – but June 1815 saw her visiting Brussels with brother John and sister Jane. As Longford states, Charlotte was among those evacuated to the port of Antwerp on 16 June, ahead of **Napoleon**'s lightning strike on Brussels. At Antwerp, some 50 miles north of Waterloo, Charlotte occupied a room in the same crowded hotel as Lady **Magdalen De Lancey**, who like herself, would find fame as a narrator of the battle's tragic sequel.

Despite rumours of a Napoleonic triumph, Charlotte and her companions remained in Antwerp until confirmation of **Wellington**'s victory brought them back to Brussels. On 12 July they made a point of visiting the field of Waterloo before returning to England. Charlotte, exercising her considerable descrpitive powers, wrote:

> The ground was ploughed up in several places with the charge
> of the cavalry, and the whole field was literally covered with soldiers'
> caps, shoes, gloves, belts, and scabbards, broken feathers battered
> into the mud, remnants of tattered scarlet cloth, bits of fur and
> leather, black stocks and haversacks, belonging to the French
> soldiers, buckles, packs of cards, books, and innumerable papers
> of every description . . . The quantities of letters and of blank sheets
> of dirty writing paper were so great that they literally whitened the
> surface of the earth.

Obviously inspired by what she had seen and experienced in Belgium, Charlotte set to work on an account of the battle. And yet, as Sabor and Troide (2001) observe in their introduction to *Frances Burney: Journals and Letters*: 'Contemporary society frowned upon any female who "wasted" her time writing anything other than familiar letters or household memoranda.' Indeed, serious writing was regarded by some as beyond a woman, and the desire to attempt it morally suspect. Better for a woman to stick to household chores and pastimes such as music or sewing: activities that could not possibly compromise a woman's chance of making a good marriage. And so it was that when, in 1815, John Booth published Charlotte's account as *The Battle of Waterloo: Circumstantial Details of the Memorable Event*, the author went uncredited. As did Charlotte's sister Jane, who had provided panoramic sketches of the battlefield.

Available within weeks of the action, Booth's *Battle of Waterloo* sought to capitalise on a new phenomenon: battlefield tourism. For no sooner had the soldiers marched out of the Waterloo area than the sightseers marched in. Although the first civilians on the scene were a curious mixture of scavengers and poets (the former in search of loot, the latter artistic inspiration), they were soon followed by hordes of tourists. Largely drawn from Britain's professional and lower-middle classes, they flooded across the

Channel on specially chartered ferries, eager to view the scene of the nation's greatest triumph. This was Booth's – and Charlotte's – market. And indeed, if Elizabeth Longford is to be believed, most of these patriotic ramblers arrived at Waterloo armed with a copy of their book. Then, fortified with brandy and laden with snuff (to block the battlefield stench), they would set off to make their grisly tour. The fashion was to find a memento: the half-buried hand of a Frenchman, for example, which might be brought home and pickled in spirits.

But macabre keepsakes aside, Charlotte's narrative allowed Britons to make sense of the cataclysm: either as virtual tourists in the comfort of their own homes, or real ones on the slopes of Mont St Jean. Her book was a best-seller, evolving through numerous editions to become, in 1852: *The Battle of Waterloo with those of Quatre Bras and Ligny, described by eye-witnesses and by the series of official accounts published by authority. To which are added memoirs . . . Illustrated by maps, plans and views of the field and 34 etchings from drawings.* According to Victor Sutcliffe (1996):

> The earlier editions were simply a vehicle for carrying the official accounts of the battle. To these were added, as the years went by, 'an account . . . by a near observer', 'other circumstantial details', 'biographical notes', and finally the suite of plates by George Jones.

In 1817 Charlotte published a personal account of her experiences in Belgium, entitled *Narrative of a Residence in Belgium During the Campaign of 1815; and of a visit to the field of Waterloo*, published by John Murray. The book was tactfully credited to 'an Englishwoman'. And yet Charlotte's writing was as good, if not better than her male contemporaries'. Indeed, her account of Waterloo's grisly aftermath – a perfect vehicle for her Gothic tendencies – was acknowledged by contemporaries as the best by a non-military writer: 'the effluvia which arose from [the grave pits], even beneath the open canopy of heaven, was horrible; and the pure west wind of summer, as it passed us, seemed pestiferous, so deadly was the smell that in many places pervaded the field'. Thanks to the great battle Charlotte had 'found' her voice, while 'losing' her identity.

Encouraged by her undoubted success as a writer, Charlotte travelled to Europe once more, and in the process helped establish a new genre: travel writing. In 1820 Charlotte published an anonymous book on Rome, which quickly became the definitive guide to the city – and remained so for the rest of the nineteenth century. Charlotte followed up in 1826 with the anonymous *Continental Adventures*, which, according to Clare L. Taylor's essay for the *Oxford Dictionary of National Biography*, was a piece of straight travel writing augmented by 'a fictitious story and imaginary characters'. In 1831 Charlotte returned to her unfinished Gothic novel, publishing it as *At Home and Abroad*. And following the death of her husband, Stephen Eaton, in 1834 (they had married in 1822), Charlotte revised *Narrative of a Residence in Belgium*, reissuing it in 1852 as *The Days of Battle*.

Charlotte died on 28 April 1859 from breast cancer. A further edition of the *Narrative* was issued in 1888 as *Waterloo Days*.

Evans
Tom (dates unknown)

Trooper in the Royal Regiment of Horse Guards, who saved the life of regimental commander, Lieutenant Colonel Sir Robert Hill, brother of Lord **Hill** (commander of **Wellington**'s II Corps) at Waterloo. Around 2 p.m. the cuirassiers of Wathier's 13th Cavalry Division advanced to the left of the Brussels high road, in support of **d'Erlon**'s infantry columns, toiling ahead on the right. The cuirassiers had pushed beyond La Haie Sainte when they were hit by the charge of the Household Brigade, including Sir Robert Hill's Royal Horse Guards. During the melee that followed, Sir Robert found himself surrounded by five French cuirassiers, his life in imminent danger. The situation was retrieved by the timely intervention of Private Evans from Captain Clayton's Troop, who hacked down four of Hill's assailants, at which point his sword snapped: Evans reputedly laid the fifth Frenchman low with the hilt. Sometimes described as belonging to the 1st Life Guards,

Evans survived the battle to become the landlord of a tavern in Old Windsor. His regiment – numbering some 277 sabres at the start of the battle – lost about one-third of its strength in killed and wounded.

Ewart
Sergeant Charles (1769–1846)

Soldier of the 2nd Royal North British Dragoons (Scots Greys), under Lieutenant Colonel **James Inglis Hamilton**, who captured the Eagle and colour of the French 45th Regiment. Born in Kilmarnock, Scotland, Ewart enlisted in the Greys in 1789. A tall, powerful man, Ewart was an expert swordsman and – perhaps unusually for a common soldier of the time – was reasonably well-educated, being able to read and write. In his 46th year in 1815, Ewart was an experienced veteran and a respected figure in the regiment. The Greys' clash with Marcognet's column of infantry took place around 2 p.m. on 18 June. Ewart recorded his bloody combats for possession of the French regimental Eagle – beginning with its bearer – in a letter dated 16 August 1815, and quoted by Dalton (1904):

> He and I had a hard contest for it. He thrust for my groin;
> I parried it off, and cut him through the head. After which I was
> attacked by one of their lancers, who threw his lance at me, but
> missed the mark by my throwing it off with my sword by my right
> side. Then I cut him from the chin upwards, which went through
> his teeth. Next I was attacked by a foot soldier, who, after firing at
> me, charged me with his bayonet – but he very soon lost the combat
> – for I parried it, and cut him down through the head: so that
> finished the contest for the Eagle.

Having won the trophy, Ewart – a member of Captain Vernor's troop – was ordered to take it to the rear. Unwilling to quit the field, Ewart reluctantly obeyed and set off for Brussels.

In the wave of British euphoria following the battle, Ewart became a celebrity, exhibited at dinners and receptions up and down the country by poet and novelist Sir **Walter Scott**. Encouraged to embellish his story for the benefit of awestruck listeners, Ewart – an honest, simple man – remained uneasy about the manner in which he quit the battle, especially as his comrades had sustained such a cruel casualty rate: perhaps as high as 45 per cent. But Ewart was now public property and expected to tell his tale to order. The Sergeant was lionised in Scotland, his regiment presenting him with a silver cup, which, sadly, was later stolen and lost for ever. In February 1816 Ewart was promoted ensign in the 5th Veteran Battalion. He quit the army in 1821, having been awarded a pension of £100 per annum (around £5,000 in modern terms).

Ewart died at Davyhulme, near Manchester, on 17 March 1846 aged 77. He was buried at Salford and soon forgotten, the graveyard disappearing under a glut of Victorian buildings. Rediscovered in the 1930s, buried beneath a builder's yard, Ewart's remains were reinterred with the decorum befitting a hero, on the esplanade of Edinburgh Castle. His Eagle rests nearby in the castle complex, in the National War Museum of Scotland.

Exelmans
General Rémy Joseph Isidore
(1775–1852)

Commander of **Grouchy**'s II Cavalry Corps in the Waterloo campaign. Possessed of a reckless, even arrogant, streak. **Napoleon** once said of Exelmans: 'I know very well there is no braver man in the army than you.' Enlisting in an artillery company in 1791, Exelmans transferred to the cavalry eight years later. By 1807 he was a general and senior aide to Murat. Captured by

General Exelmans (1775–1852)

the British in Spain, Exelmans broke parole, escaping in time to join Napoleon's Imperial Guard for the Russian adventure of 1812. Ennobled in 1813, and prominent in the campaign of France a year later, Exelmans was one of Napoleon's star cavalry generals. He was also loyal, rallying to Napoleon's cause in March 1815, on the latter's return to French soil. For this, Exelmans was rewarded with the II Cavalry Corps, comprising the dragoon divisions of Strolz and **Chastel**, some 3,000 sabres in all.

Following the victory over **Blücher** at Ligny on 16 June, Napoleon expected the Prussians to retire eastwards on Liège or Namur, along their lines of communication with Germany. During the night of 16–17 June, the Emperor sent Exelmans and Pajol in pursuit. Marshal Grouchy followed some 10 hours later. Having lost the Prussians in the dark, Exelmans' cavalry, led by Chastel's dragoons, picked up the scent at Gembloux, making contact with the rearguard of **Thielemann**'s III Corps in the late morning of 17 June. But Exelmans dallied in passing this news to Grouchy, who only learned of the Prussians' whereabouts and line of march after 3 p.m. The Marshal immediately marched to the scene through heavy downpours, arriving at Gembloux some four hours later with 30,000 men. Exelmans, however, had already pushed north, dogging the Prussians up the road to Wavre. And so Grouchy decided to halt for the night, dashing off a dispatch to Napoleon, who was busy chasing **Wellington** onto the Waterloo battlefield. In the message, Grouchy informed the Emperor of his plan to strike north next day, via Sart-les-Walhain, in order to prevent Blücher from joining the British. But while Grouchy got his head down, Blücher and **Gneisenau** – having gathered their columns at Wavre – determined to march west to Wellington's aid at first light. Only Thielemann's III Corps would remain, holding the line of the River Dyle.

Grouchy arrived at Sart-les-Walhain, the midpoint between Gembloux and Wavre, around 10.30 a.m. on 18 June. According to historian Georges Blond (1979), Grouchy and his staff – apparently with Exelmans in attendance – sheltered from the rain in the summerhouse of the local notary, breakfasting on strawberries. There the party heard the sound of gunfire from Waterloo, as **Jérôme** Bonaparte launched the first of his assaults on the château of Hougoumont. General **Gérard** urged Grouchy to march to the sound of the guns. Grouchy refused. Gérard then begged Grouchy to let him lead his own corps across country to join the battle. Rattled, Grouchy rebuffed Gérard, adding that: 'If the Emperor had wished me to take part, he would not have sent me away at the very moment he was moving on the British.' But Exelmans was as frustrated as Gérard. Some writers even suggest he offered to shoot Grouchy. This theme is pursued by David Johnson (1989), who claims that Exelmans told Gérard: 'You're the senior general; it's you who'll take over if anything happens to Grouchy. Are you ready to rejoin the Emperor? If so, I'll blow Grouchy's brains out.' But Gérard declined the offer of immediate promotion and Exelmans stormed off, shouting: 'Go to the devil! You're all traitors and cowards!' Thus, as Chesney (1868) states:

> In spite of warm remonstrances, the march on Wavre was continued, and a little before 2 p.m. **Vandamme**'s infantry, preceded by Exelmans' horse, reached Baraque, 2 miles south from the town, and became engaged soon after with a considerable force of Prussians.

Ferrior
Lieutenant Colonel Samuel (1772–1815)

Commander of the 1st Life Guards, part of Lord **Edward Somerset**'s 1st British (Household) Brigade, which also included the 2nd Life Guards, the Royal Horse Guards (Blues) and the 1st Dragoon Guards. The Household Brigade was launched, with Sir **William Ponsonby**'s Union Brigade, against **d'Erlon**'s I Corps about 2 p.m. on 18 June 1815. The Union Brigade attacked to the left of the Brussels high road, the Household Brigade to the right. While the former smashed into French infantry, the latter made contact with Dubois' cuirassiers west of La Haie Sainte. According to William Siborne (1848):

> The Household Brigade continued its charge down the slope on the right, and partly on the left, of La Haye Sainte, with the most distinguished gallantry and success; and bringing their right shoulders forward, the 1st Life Guards pressed severely on the rear of the cuirassiers, as a very considerable portion of them rushed tumultuously towards that part of the high road beyond the orchard of La Haye Sainte which lies between high banks, and which was thus completely choked up with the fugitives. Many of those who

found their retreat so seriously impeded, again faced their
opponents, and a desperate hand-to-hand contest ensued.

Ferrior's men – some 255 sabres in all – extricated themselves
successfully from this savage melee, but failing to rally, were badly
mauled in the inevitable counter-attack.

The survivors eventually made it back to their lines and the
remnants of the brigade. Ferrior remained in command of the 1st
Life Guards, but it seems he had been severely wounded in the
fighting. After a lull, **Ney** began his massed cavalry attacks on Mont
St Jean around 4 p.m. **Wellington**'s infantry, formed in battalion
squares, withstood repeated attacks, while his cavalry – only 60 per
cent of which remained functional – made many desperate counter-
charges in support. The result, as noted by Major Knollys (1880),
was 'a murderous struggle', with the French riders harried by the
exhausted British and Allied squadrons. According to Dalton
(1904), Ferrior 'is said to have led his regiment to the charge no less
than eleven times' – adding from an unacknowledged source that
'most of the charges were not made till after his head had been laid
open by the cut of a sabre and his body was pierced with a lance'. In
all, the 1st Life Guards lost some 65 men, including Ferrior, who was
either killed outright or – perhaps more likely – died of his wounds.
Either way, he received his Waterloo Medal posthumously.

Fitzroy Somerset
Colonel James Henry (1788–1855)

Wellington's military secretary during the Waterloo campaign.
The youngest son of the fifth Duke of Beaufort, Fitzroy Somerset
joined the army in 1804, quickly becoming attached to Wellington's
staff. He served the Duke as both aide-de-camp and military
secretary during the Peninsular War, rising to become a colonel in
the 1st Foot Guards. (Wellington apparently thought him not
especially talented, but truthful, obedient and reliable.) After

Napoleon's first abdication in April 1814, Fitzroy Somerset accompanied Wellington to Paris, where the Duke acted as British ambassador. Four months later, he cemented his ties to Wellington by marrying Lady Emily Wellesley-Pole, the Duke's niece. And in January 1815, when Wellington quit Paris to represent Britain at the Congress of Vienna, Fitzroy Somerset was left in charge of the embassy as minister-plenipotentiary. And there he remained, even after Napoleon's escape from Elba in February 1815 and Wellington's arrival in Brussels to take charge of the Allied army assembling there. But on 20 March Napoleon entered Paris in triumph, and six days later Fitzroy was obliged to make his exit, joining Wellington at Brussels. There he resumed duties as the Duke's military secretary, and in May Emily gave birth to their first baby.

At Waterloo, Fitzroy Somerset stuck close to Wellington, who was often in the thick of the action. About 7 p.m. Fitzroy's right elbow was smashed by a French bullet fired from the farmhouse of La Haie Sainte, recently vacated by the survivors of Major **Baring**'s garrison. According to Stanhope (1888): 'The Duke was . . . near Lord Fitzroy Somerset at his wound, which was given from behind by a musket ball proceeding from the wall of La Haie Sainte. It shattered the arm, and Lord Fitzroy fell from his horse.' Later that evening, Somerset's arm was severed above the elbow by the surgeon Dr Gunning. He remained conscious during the operation, which was performed on a blood-soaked kitchen table, and without the benefit of anaesthetic. When a medical orderly carried off Fitzroy's limb he reputedly called out: 'Hallo! Don't carry away that arm until you've taken off my ring!'

After Waterloo, Fitzroy Somerset became Military Secretary at the Horse Guards, Master-General of the Ordnance, and was eventually promoted general in 1854. Ennobled as Baron Raglan, Fitzroy Somerset led the British expedition to the Crimea, where, broken by military failure and dysentery, he died in 1855.

Fleury de Chamboulon
Pierre Alexandre Édouard (1779–1835)

Prefect of Rheims; joined **Napoleon**'s camp during the latter's triumphal return to power in March 1815, and in June accompanied the Emperor to Belgium as a private secretary. In his memoirs – published in 1820 and apparently received unfavourably by the exiled Napoleon – he describes the scene at Rossomme around 7 p.m. on 18 June, when, as he puts it: 'The issue of the battle seemed to be growing dubious.' An account of the sudden collapse of the French Army follows, including Napoleon's flight from the battlefield. Fleury de Chamboulon's version of these events is interesting on two counts. First, he implies Napoleon genuinely mistook the approaching **Ziethen** for **Grouchy**, when it is generally agreed the Emperor deliberately misled his army on this point in an effort to shore up morale. Second, he overestimates Ziethen's strength by about 25,000: only a quarter of the Prussian I Corps saw action at Waterloo – fewer than 5,000 men.

But whether accurate in its details or not, Fleury de Chamboulon's narrative does capture the atmosphere of alarm, desperation and panic in the French camp. His account is worth quoting, as it rarely appears in English sources. As a matter of interest, the closing sentence describes Napoleon and Bertrand driving off in a barouche, but this occurred the day after the battle at Philippeville:

> The issue of the battle seemed to be growing dubious. It was time to strike a great blow by a desperate attack. The Emperor did not waver. Orders were immediately given to Count **Reille** to gather all his forces and hurl himself on the enemy's right, while Napoleon in person would make a frontal attack with his reserves. The Emperor was already marshalling his Guard in column of attack when he heard that our cavalry had just been forced to abandon part of the heights of Mont St Jean. He at once ordered Marshal **Ney** to take four battalions of the Middle Guard and make all speed to the fatal plateau . . . At that moment a burst of rifle-fire was heard. 'There's Grouchy!' cried the Emperor. 'Victory is ours.' **Labédoyère** flew to tell the army this joyful news. He broke through the enemy to the head of our columns: 'Marshal Grouchy is here, the Guards are

being thrown in! Courage! Courage! The English are lost.' Just then Ziethen's 30,000 Prussians, who had been taken for Grouchy's army, carried the village of La Haie by main force, driving us before them. Our cavalry, our infantry, already shaken by the defeat of the Middle Guard, were afraid of being cut off and retired headlong. The English cavalry, taking advantage of the confusion caused by this sudden retreat, made a way through our ranks and brought their disorder and discouragement to a climax. The other troops on the right, who had already done all they could to withstand the Prussian attacks, and had been short of ammunition for more than an hour, on seeing some squadrons in chaos and men of the Guard stampeding, thought all was lost and abandoned their position. This contagious impulse spread to the left in a flash, and the whole army, which had so gallantly carried the best positions of the enemy, became as eager to give them up as it had been zealous in seizing them. The English army, which had been advancing as we fell back, and the Prussians, who had not ceased to pursue us, swooped with one accord on our scattered battalions; darkness increased the turmoil and panic; and soon the whole army was only a chaotic mass, which the English and the Prussians overcame without effort and slaughtered without pity. The Emperor, witness to this appalling defection, could scarcely believe his eyes. Two or three hundred fugitives of all arms were rounded up to escort the Emperor. Along with General Bertrand, he got into a barouche and drove off.

Fouler
General Albert Emmanuel (1769–1831)

Napoleon's Master of the Horse at Waterloo. Son of Louis XVI's stable master, Fouler worked in the royal stables as a boy, before joining the infantry in 1787. Switching to the cavalry in 1799, Fouler was a general by 1806, having served at Austerlitz and Jena. In 1810 he took charge of the imperial stables, becoming responsible for over 1,000 horses. Fouler had no operational command during the Waterloo campaign, but probably saved the Emperor from capture – or worse – by supplying him with a fresh mount when he quit the battlefield in the late evening, amid the confusion of the French collapse. Sadly, we cannot be sure of the identity of this animal, though it may have been Tauris, allegedly one of the Emperor's favourites.

In fact, Napoleon rode several horses at Waterloo: Cerbère was killed by a cannonball, Désirée (named after Désirée Clary, Napoleon's first fiancée) disappeared without a trace, Jaffa survived the battle to be purchased by a certain Mr Green at a Belgian auction, and Marie (named after Napoleon's Polish mistress, Marie Walewska) was bagged as a war trophy by Marshal **Blücher**. But a small Arab stallion, apparently bearing imperial markings, was found in the stables at Le Caillou, wounded by a bullet in the hip. Claimed by Lieutenant **Henry William Petre** of the 6th (Inniskilling) Dragoons, this horse later turned up in London as 'Marengo', the horse reputed to have carried Napoleon 3,000 miles to Moscow and back in 1812 – the skeleton is still on show at the National Army Museum. Interestingly, there is no record of a Marengo in French archives, leading Jill Hamilton (2000) to speculate that the animal in question was actually an imperial mount named Ali.

Perhaps Fouler could have shed light on these issues, but as a member of the fallen Emperor's household he sensibly kept his head down after Waterloo. Opting for a quiet life, Fouler returned to his home at Lillers, where he lived out his remaining 16 years in peace.

Foy
General Maximilien Sebastien
(1775–1825)

Commander of **Napoleon**'s 9th Infantry Division, part of **Reille**'s II Corps, and celebrated author of *Histoire des Guerres de la Péninsule sous Napoleon* (1827). An experienced commander and veteran of battles against the British in Spain, Foy was among those who warned

General Foy (1775–1825)

Napoleon of **Wellington**'s abilities, at breakfast on 18 June 1815. Outraged, Napoleon – who had called a meeting of his generals as a morale-boosting exercise – stormed: 'I tell you he is a bad general, and the English are but poor troops! This, for us, will only be an affair of a picnic!' But Foy continued: 'Wellington never shows his troops, but if he is yonder, I must warn your Majesty that the English infantry, in close combat, is the very devil!' Napoleon promptly broke up the meeting. Within a few hours the battle began and Foy was hit in the shoulder by a musket ball. Badly bruised, Foy was carried from the field, but returned to lead several assaults on Hougoumont during the afternoon. Foy also supported the Imperial Guard's assault on Wellington's lines around 7.30 p.m. At the battle's end, Foy marched off the field with 300 survivors – all that remained of his command. He later wrote (Foy 1900):

> We saw those sons of Albion formed in square battalions in the
> plain between the wood of Hougoumont and the village of Mont
> St Jean . . . The cavalry which supported them were cut to pieces,
> and the fire of their artillery completely silenced. The general
> and staff officers were galloping from one square to another,
> not knowing where to find shelter. Carriages, wounded men,
> parks of reserve and auxiliary troops were all hurrying in disorder
> towards Brussels. Death was before them and in their ranks;
> disgrace in their rear. In this terrible situation, neither the balls
> of the Imperial Guard, discharged at almost point blank, nor the
> victorious cavalry of France could make the least impression on the
> immovable British infantry.

Fraser
Sergeant Ralph (dates unknown)

Soldier of the 3rd Foot Guards and one of the heroes of Hougoumont. At noon on 18 June 1815 the French returned to the assault at Hougoumont, attacking from the west. The attack, led by the brigades of Soye and Baudin from **Jérôme** Bonaparte's 6th Infantry Division, caught the 100 light troops of Dashwood's 3rd

Foot Guards – including Sergeant Ralph Fraser – out in the open at the south-west corner of the compound. A fierce firefight erupted, Dashwood's men being shunted along Hougoumont's west wall. Eventually rounding the corner of the great barn, the British foot guards dashed to safety through the open north gates, the French hot on their heels. It was at this point that Fraser – a hard-bitten veteran of the Peninsular War – noticed Colonel Despans de Cubières of the 1st Light Regiment, mounted on his horse, waving his troops to the attack. Without a moment's thought, Fraser leaped back through the open gates, dragged the astonished Cubières from his horse, mounted the steed himself, and rode it into the courtyard. The story goes that the gates closed behind Fraser, only to be forced open again by the attackers: a desperate battle ensued, in which the French were killed, wounded or expelled, and the gates barricaded shut by Lieutenant Colonel **Macdonell**, with the help of several others, including Fraser.

In most British accounts of Fraser's startling feat, the intrepid Sergeant fights with the mounted Cubières, parrying the Frenchman's sabre-thrusts with a pike or halberd. But according to **Jean-Baptiste Jolyet**, an officer of the 1st Light Regiment, Cubières showed conspicuous gallantry at Waterloo by going into action with his wounded arm in a sling. Attacked by Fraser and falling to the ground, Jolyet states that: 'he showed such bravery that the English officers threw themselves in front of their soldiers to prevent them from killing him' (Jolyet 1903). Be that as it may, Cubières remained forever grateful to Fraser for taking only his horse and not his life. Interestingly, Dalton (1904) claims it was Sergeant Brice MacGregor, of Lieutenant Colonel Master's company, who galloped into Hougoumont on a captured mount. According to Dalton, MacGregor 'shot a cuirassier dead who attacked him, and rode into the courtyard on the Frenchman's horse'. It is Fraser, however, who is generally remembered for this act of bravura, and who was rewarded with a medal for it.

Frazer
Lieutenant Colonel Sir Augustus Simon (1776–1835)

Commander of **Wellington**'s Royal Horse Artillery at Waterloo. The son of an officer in the Royal Engineers, Frazer attended the Royal Military Academy at Woolwich, before joining the Royal Artillery as a second lieutenant in 1793. Three months later, he was fighting the French in Flanders. In 1795 Frazer transferred to the Royal Horse Artillery (RHA) and in 1803 he was promoted captain, gaining command of his first troop. After taking part in an expedition to Buenos Aires in 1807, Frazer joined Wellington's Peninsular Army, seeing service at Salamanca, Vitoria, San Sebastian, Bayonne and Toulouse. During the Waterloo campaign, Frazer – now a lieutenant colonel and one of Wellington's firm favourites – was appointed commander of the Duke's horse artillery. And it was in this role that Frazer made a major contribution to Wellington's victory, by insisting on the inclusion of powerful 9-pounder guns for the RHA – a significant factor in repelling French assaults on Waterloo Day.

Frazer commanded eight troops of Royal Horse Artillery at the battle, each of six guns. Three troops deployed 9-pounders, three 6-pounders, one 5.5-inch howitzer only, and one 6-pounder plus rockets. Created in 1793, the RHA was usually tasked with giving fire support to cavalry, but at Waterloo Frazer's gunners were charged with defending the Duke's line at Mont St Jean. The basic RHA unit was a six-gun troop, consisting of a senior captain, a second captain, 3 subalterns, 2 staff sergeants, 3 sergeants, 2 corporals, 6 bombardiers, 80 gunners, 60 drivers, a farrier, a carriage-smith, 2 shoeing-smiths, 2 collar makers, a wheelwright, plus 56 saddle horses and 108 draught horses.

According to Charles Dalton (1904), Frazer was 'a modest and unassuming man, possessing a heart that could feel for others' woes'. This is borne out by the following letter, dated 18 June, 11 p.m., which Frazer (1859) wrote to his wife:

> How shall I describe the scenes through which I have passed since morning? I am now so tired that I can hardly hold my pen. We have gained a glorious victory, and against **Napoleon** himself. I know

not yet the amount of killed, wounded, or prisoners, but all must be great. Never was there a more bloody affair, never so hot a fire. Bonaparte put in practice every device of war. He tried us with artillery, with cavalry, and last of all with infantry. The efforts of each were gigantic, but the admirable talents of our Duke, seconded by such troops as he commands, baffled every attempt. For some hours the action was chiefly of artillery. We had 114 British, and some 16 Belgian guns, 6- and 9-pounders; the enemy upwards of 300, 8- and 12-pounders: never were guns better served on both sides. After seven hours' cannonading, the French cavalry made some of the boldest charges I ever saw: they sounded the whole extent of our line, which was thrown into squares. Never did cavalry behave so nobly, or was received by infantry so firmly. Our guns were taken and retaken repeatedly. They were in masses, especially the horse artillery, which I placed and manoeuvred as I chose. Poor fellows! Many of them – alas, how many! – lie on the bed of honour. Failing in his repeated attacks of cannonading and movements of cavalry, Napoleon at length pierced the left of our centre with the infantry of the Imperial Guard: the contest was severe beyond what I have seen, or could have fancied. I cannot describe the scene of carnage. The struggle lasted even by moonlight. I know not the losses of other corps, nor hardly of our own; but Bean, Cairnes, and Ramsay, are among the horse artillery dead. **Whinyates**, **Bull**, Macdonald (junior), Webber, Strangways, Parker, Day, and, I am sorry to say, many others, including Robe, are among our wounded. Many of my troops are almost without officers, and almost all the guns were repeatedly in the enemy's hands; but we retired from them only to shelter ourselves under our squares of infantry, and instantly resumed our posts, the moment the cavalry were repulsed. I have escaped very well.

Maxwell's horse, on which I rode at first, received a ball in the neck, and I was afterwards rolled over by a round of case shot, which wounded my mare in several places, a ball grazing my right arm, just above the elbow, but without the slightest pain; and I now write without any inconvenience. In a momentary lull of the fire I buried my friend Ramsay, from whose body I took the portrait of his wife, which he always carried next his heart. Not a man assisted at the funeral who did not shed tears. Hardly had I cut from his head the hair which I enclose, and laid his yet warm body in the grave, when our convulsive sobs were stifled by the necessity of returning to renew the struggle.

Pray get me two mourning rings made; but I will describe them when I can write next. All now with me is confused recollection of scenes yet passing before me in idea: the noise, the groans of the dying, and all the horrid realities of the field are yet before me. In this very house are poor Lloyd (leg shot off but not yet amputated), Durnaresque (General Byng's aide-de-camp) shot through the lungs and dying; Macdonald, Robe, Whinyates, Strangways and Baynes, wounded. Sir **Thomas Picton** and Sir **William Ponsonby** are killed. So many wounded, that I dare not enumerate their names. Bolton of ours is killed, so is young Spearman. What a strange letter is this, what a strange day has occasioned it! Today is Sunday! How often have I observed that actions are fought on Sundays. Alas! what three days have I passed, what days of glory, falsely so called; and what days of misery to thousands. The field of battle today is strewn with dead! I see so many. But let me turn from all that is distressing, even in description, and lay me down, which I shall do with a grateful sense of mercies vouchsafed. I might have got a decoration for you, but the officer of the Imperial Guard who wore it, and who offered it as a prisoner, looked so wistfully at the reward of many a gallant day, that I could not think of taking it. I made an acquaintance in the field with a French lieutenant colonel of the 7th Dragoons, poor fellow, sadly wounded and prisoner. How misery makes friends of all. My friend Lord **Saltoun** is well. I hear he alone escaped of two companies of the Guards under his command. Lord **Fitzroy Somerset** has lost an arm. Lord **Uxbridge** has a ball in the knee. **De Lancey** severely wounded. Adieu: I will send you a more connected account of the battle when I am able.

Fremantle
Lieutenant Colonel John (dates unknown)

One of **Wellington**'s aides-de-camp at Waterloo. An officer of the 2nd Foot Guards, Fremantle had served on the Duke's staff during the Peninsular War. At Waterloo – with others such as Lieutenant Colonel Sir **Alexander Gordon** and Major the Honourable **Henry**

Percy – Fremantle galloped about the battlefield delivering orders and running messages for his chief. Perhaps Fremantle's most important mission occurred in the early evening of 18 June, when Wellington sent him to hurry along the Prussians marching to the Duke's aid. According to William Siborne (1848):

> Wellington . . . having satisfied himself that his position was destined shortly to be again assailed by a formidable force, became anxious for the arrival of the Prussian troops expected on his extreme left. He desired his aide-de-camp, Lieutenant Colonel John Fremantle, to proceed immediately in that direction, to hasten the advance of any corps he might fall in with, and to represent to its commander that if he would supply him with the means of strengthening those points along his line which had been so seriously weakened by repeated attacks, he entertained no doubt of not only maintaining his ground, but of also gaining the victory.

Fremantle describes the sequel in a letter dated 20 November 1842, quoted by H.T. Siborne (1891):

> Towards six o'clock Sir **Horace Seymour** came and reported to the Duke of Wellington that he had seen the Prussian column. The Duke called upon me to go to the head of their column, and ask for the 3,000 men to supply our losses. **Blücher** had not arrived, but Generals **Ziethen** and **Bülow** were at the head of the column, who gave me for answer – that the whole army was coming up, and that they could not make a detachment.

In other words, Ziethen refused to march on Wellington's left wing until his column had closed up and concentrated somewhat. Although the Duke's position was perilous, and he was only asking for 3,000 troops, Ziethen insisted on going by the book and only committing his force when it was fully assembled.

According to David Howarth (1968) in his classic account of the battle, Fremantle announced that he *could not* (my emphasis) go back to Wellington with such an answer. (As a matter of fact, Fremantle's letter, as quoted by Siborne (1891), runs 'I said I could [would?] return to the Duke with such a message.' Nevertheless, Howarth's account has become the accepted version.) Howarth continues:

But von Ziethen kept him waiting while he sent one of his own officers forward to reconnoitre. And that officer . . . saw the crowds of wounded, deserters and prisoners making their way for the forest, and came back to report that Wellington was in full retreat. The upshot was that Ziethen turned his troops about and set off south to support Bülow at Plancenoit: a movement spotted by Baron von **Müffling**, Wellington's Prussian liaison officer, who would soon gallop after Ziethen to put matters right.

Meanwhile, Fremantle had no choice but to return to Wellington's lines. On his way back to Mont St Jean, Fremantle stumbled upon an instance of friendly fire involving a Prussian battery. Once again, the Englishman failed to persuade the Prussians to help, rather than hinder, Wellington's troops. Fremantle's letter continues:

> On my way back I found a Prussian battery of eight guns firing between our first and second lines, and desired the officer to cease firing. I returned . . . and begged the generals to send orders for the battery to cease fire.

But presumably to little effect. For, back on the battlefield, Captain **Mercer**'s G Troop, Royal Horse Artillery, found itself plastered with incoming fire from the distant Prussian battery: one shot narrowly missing the Captain and killing one of his troop horses. Mercer ordered his guns to return fire, and in his account of the battle recalled that:

> A tall man in the black Brunswick uniform came galloping up to me from the rear, exclaiming, 'Ah! Mine Gott! Mine Gott! Vat is it you doos, sare? Dat is your friends de Proosiens; an you kills dem! Ah, mine Gott! Mine Gott! Vill you no stop? Ah! Mine Gott! Vat for is dis? De Inglish kills dere friends de Proosiens! Vere is de Dook von Vellington? Oh, mine Gott! Mine Gott!' etc., etc. And so he went on raving like one demented. I observed that if these were our friends the Prussians they were treating us very uncivilly; and that it was not without sufficient provocation we had turned our guns on them, pointing out to him at the same time the bloody proofs of my assertion.

Friant
General Louis, Count (1758–1829)

Commander of the foot grenadiers of **Napoleon**'s Imperial Guard. Entering the Garde Française in 1781, Friant switched to the Paris National Guard in 1789. Six years later he was serving in the French Revolutionary Wars as a general of brigade. A veteran of Austerlitz (1805), Auerstädt (1806) and Eylau (1807), he was ennobled by Napoleon in 1808. After further service in the Danube campaign of 1809 and the Russian campaign of 1812, Friant was given command of the veteran foot soldiers of the Imperial Guard. A brave and capable commander (and the brother-in-law to Marshal Davout, one of Napoleon's principal lieutenants), Friant remained loyal to the Emperor until the first abdication of 6 April 1814, whereupon he accepted Bourbon rule and command of the *Grenadiers de France* – as the *grognards* (i.e. grumblers) of Napoleon's Guard had become. But when Napoleon returned to power in March 1815 the clock was turned back and Friant found himself leading the legendary grenadiers of the Imperial Guard once more.

Napoleon's Imperial Guard was the most celebrated corps of its day. Its origin lay in the bodyguard formed to protect members of the French Revolutionary government. When Napoleon seized power in 1799 he transformed this unit into the Consular Guard, dedicated to preserving his own person. Following the establishment of the Empire in 1804, the Consular Guard became the Imperial Guard. But the corps was not simply a latter-day Praetorian Guard. Napoleon turned it into a powerful reserve for the Grand Army, consisting of infantry, cavalry, artillery, marines and engineers. In effect, the Imperial Guard was an army-within-an-army.

In 1812 the distinction was made between Old and Young guardsmen, according to length of service. And yet many accounts of Waterloo speak of a Middle Guard. But what did this Middle Guard consist of? Napoleon had three Imperial Guard infantry divisions at Waterloo: the Young Guard Division under **Duhesme**, the foot chasseurs under Morand and the foot grenadiers under Friant. Each division consisted of four regiments (numbered 1 to 4), and each regiment consisted of two battalions some 600 men strong. It would seem that the 1st and 2nd Regiments from Friant's and Morand's commands were classed as Old Guard, while the 3rd and 4th Regiments were designated Middle Guard. As to the difference between foot grenadiers and foot chasseurs, it would appear to have been negligible. Although grenadiers were supposed to act as shock troops and chasseurs as skirmishing 'light' troops, in reality they took on any tactical role the Emperor saw fit to throw at them. And the appearance of the two corps was almost identical. Both wore fur bonnets, but while grenadiers had a red plume, chasseurs sported a red-over-green plume (and green epaulettes instead of red).

On 10 June 1815 the 'grumblers' of the Guard quit Paris and marched to war one last time, joining Napoleon's Army of the North for its passage of the River Sambre on 15 June – the Emperor's opening move of the Waterloo campaign. At 7.30 the following evening, Friant led them in a ferocious assault on the Prussian centre at Ligny, which delivered victory to Napoleon and hurled **Blücher** and **Gneisenau** into headlong retreat. Exactly 48 hours later, Napoleon expected a repeat performance at Waterloo.

By 7.30 p.m. on 18 June Napoleon's position was critical. Contrary to the Emperor's expectations, **Wellington** had stood firm on the ridge of Mont St Jean, defying every attempt to dislodge him. Meanwhile, Prussian forces under **Bülow**, **Pirch** and **Ziethen** had appeared on the French Army's right, threatening its line of retreat. As for the Imperial Guard – Napoleon's only reserve – its units were scattered all over the place: at Plancenoit, Rossomme and La Belle Alliance. Nevertheless, Napoleon scratched together some eight battalions of Guard infantry to spearhead a general advance against Wellington's centre before the Prussian *coup de grâce* materialised. In a bid to shore up shaky French morale, Napoleon apparently sent General **Labédoyère** to spread the false news that **Grouchy** was arriving; then the Emperor led the foot soldiers of his Guard into the shallow valley before handing them over to Marshal **Ney** and General Friant.

But for some reason, three of the Guard battalions (2/1st Chasseurs, 2/2nd Chasseurs and 2/2nd Grenadiers) halted south of La Haie Sainte, leaving the remaining five to go it alone. These attacking battalions – perhaps 3,000 men in all – moved off in echelon from the right, muskets shouldered and drummers beating the *pas de charge*. But instead of marching straight ahead, the five battalions – formed in squares as protection against cavalry – careered left across the battlefield, towards strong Allied units hidden behind the crest of the looming ridge. As they toiled forward – following the route of **Milhaud**'s and Kellermann's earlier cavalry attacks – they split into two distinct groups: on the right, the 4th Grenadiers and 1/3rd Grenadiers; and following on the left, the 1/3rd Chasseurs, 2/3rd Chasseurs and 4th Chasseurs. In the intervals between the columns, the Guard's divisional guns advanced for fire support. At some point during the advance Ney's horse was shot under him (the fifth that day), but the Marshal disentangled himself and continued on foot, sword in hand. Then Friant was shot in the hand. Badly wounded but in good spirits, the General quit the field and returned to Napoleon, announcing that victory was in the offing.

Meanwhile, Wellington was waiting. He had already been informed of the attack by a French deserter. Apparently, an officer of carabiniers had galloped up to the Allied line shouting 'Vive le Roi!' (Long live the King!), adding: 'That son of a bitch Napoleon is down there with his Guard. You will be attacked within half an hour.' Wellington lost no time strengthening his centre with **Chassé**'s Netherlands Division. The cavalry brigades of **Vivian** and **Vandeleur** had already been pulled in from the left wing, though on whose orders it is hard to say (Wellington's Prussian liaison officer, **Müffling** later claimed a hand in this).

The five columns – or squares – of the Imperial Guard breasted the Allied ridge in a staggered line. On their right, Donzelot's infantry (from **d'Erlon**'s I Corps) had issued from the cover of La Haie Sainte to engage the remains of **Alten**'s division, bolstered by Kruse's Nassauers and troops from the Duke of **Brunswick**'s corps. Things were going well for Donzelot when, according to Henry Lachouque and Anne S.K. Brown (1978), the fog of war descended to frustrate the French initiative. As the French attack developed, Ziethen's Prussians began arriving on Wellington's extreme left wing (the French right). Mistaking the Prince of Saxe-Weimar's Netherlanders for French (they were wearing blue uniforms and French-style shakos), Ziethen's Prussians opened fire on them. Donzelot's troops then made the same mistake. Believing Grouchy had arrived at last they tried to support the Netherlanders, receiving a volley for their trouble. This unleashed a howl of anguish from the French, who apparently fled in panic, crying 'Treason!' Thus the Guard was left alone on the ridge.

Fifteen minutes later it was all over. The foot grenadiers – after a fleeting moment of triumph when several Allied battalions fell back in disorder – were felled by Chassé's artillery then charged with the bayonet. On their left, the foot chasseurs walked into the red wall of **Maitland**'s foot guards, which was shored up by the battalions of **Adam**'s brigade – notably Colborne's 52nd, which took the 4th Foot Chasseurs in flank. After a brief firefight the Frenchmen broke and fled. Prior to the close-quarter fighting the Imperial Guard had suffered heavily at the hands of Allied gunners. In the end – as Ney himself later admitted – there simply were not enough men to ram home Napoleon's projected *Schwerpunkt*.

The repulse of the Imperial Guard was Wellington's cue to launch his own general advance: an unstoppable wave that washed over the valley, lapping up the opposite slope as far as La Belle Alliance, Napoleon's forward command post. If this wasn't enough, the appearance of Prussian troops in their right rear convinced most French troops it was time to quit. According to Napoleon's Bulletin, published in the *Paris Moniteur* of 21 June 1815:

> In an instant the whole army was nothing but a mass of confusion; all the soldiers of all arms were mixed pell-mell, and it was utterly impossible to rally a single corps . . . all was lost by one moment of panic . . . there was nothing to do but follow the torrent.

This image of a general French meltdown is taken up by Lachouque and Brown (1978), who state:

> Much has been written about mass hysteria. These men gone berserk, drunk with fear, rage, enthusiasm, blood; killing one another regardless of nationality; shouting with joy, cursing, crying for vengeance in five languages, were victims of an emotion neatly summed up in the imprecation attributed to **Cambronne** on the evening of 18 June 1815 [i.e. 'Merde!' or 'Shit!'].

And yet, historian Harold T. Parker, writing in 1944, paints a slightly different picture, maintaining that **Reille**'s II Corps, **Lobau**'s VI Corps, and most Imperial Guard units – both infantry and cavalry –

retired in good order. Parker's version of events is as follows: As the French line retreated, Wellington halted his infantry in the valley to dress his line. Meanwhile, Vivian's cavalry bypassed the redcoats, galloping up the French slope to unleash havoc. Napoleon counterattacked Vivian with the 400 sabres of his personal headquarters staff, but the British hussars made short work of this gallant little corps, then set about sabreing French artillery teams. By this time Wellington had sorted out his infantry, sending them up the French slope as Ziethen's Prussians surged forward from Papelotte. At this point, Reille's II Corps and the heavy cavalry of the Imperial Guard – in effect, Napoleon's left wing – retired in good order; as did Lobau's corps and many Imperial Guard units on the right. But the French centre – caught between a frontal and lateral advance by Allied and Prussian forces – degenerated into a rabble and fled up the Charleroi road. 'In this manner,' writes Parker, 'by the dissolution of the French centre and right an immense gap – over a mile wide – was opened in the French position.'

The Allied advance continued as far as La Belle Alliance, engulfing the remaining squares of the Imperial Guard, which Napoleon had deployed as rallying points. But south of La Belle Alliance, the two battalions of General Jean-Martin Petit's 1st Foot Grenadiers stood firm, firing on friend and foe alike – anyone who threatened their cohesion. Nearby, the engineers and marines of the Guard also remained steady, supported by a battery of guns. It was here – in the square of Petit's 1/1st Foot Grenadiers – that Napoleon and his staff found sanctuary. They were joined by General Friant. The brass hats remained inside Petit's square as it cautiously crawled back to Rossomme. Then Napoleon and his entourage galloped ahead to Le Caillou, where the 1/1st Foot Chasseurs were guarding the imperial baggage. Napoleon ordered the battalion to escort him to Genappe, and in this manner quit the battle.

Within hours the Emperor was speeding back to Paris, having left the wreck of the army in the hands of Marshal **Soult**. As for Friant, he collected his survivors together at Laon on 21 June, before marching them back to Paris. Only one-third of his original command remained with the colours. Next day Napoleon abdicated, offering his services as a general to the French government. The offer was refused and the erstwhile Emperor was obliged to go to ground.

On 3 July French forces surrendered to the Allies: consequently, the survivors of Napoleon's Waterloo army were ordered to retire behind the River Loire. On 7 July Allied troops entered Paris, dragging Louis XVIII and his court in their wake. The following week Napoleon surrendered to Captain Maitland of HMS *Bellerophon*. And on 3 August Louis XVIII announced the dissolution of the Imperial Guard.

But Friant survived the round of dismissals, arrests and executions that followed the second Bourbon restoration. True, he had answered Napoleon's call to arms prior to Waterloo, but Friant had not rushed to betray the Bourbons on Bonaparte's return from Elba: so he was left in peace. Apparently unhappy at this turn of events, Friant resigned on 4 September 1815 in a blush of embarrassment.

Gérard
General Maurice Étienne
(1773–1852)

General Gérard (1773–1852) by Delpech

Officer in charge of **Napoleon**'s IV Corps, later attached to **Grouchy**'s command. One of Napoleon's ablest corps commanders, Gérard entered the army in 1791 as a private, working his way up to general by 1806. A veteran of titanic battles like Austerlitz, Eylau, Wagram, and Leipzig, Gérard was loyal to France rather than a particular political master. Nevertheless, he rallied to Napoleon's cause in the spring of 1815, becoming the youngest corps commander in the Emperor's Army of the North. But the Waterloo campaign constituted a series of disasters for Gérard. The first setback occurred on 15 June when, having spearheaded Napoleon's advance into Belgium, Gérard's advance guard commander, General **Bourmont**, defected to the Prussians. To make matters worse, Bourmont took his whole staff and a copy of Napoleon's plan of operations with him. Gérard was obliged to halt his IV Corps while a replacement was found for Bourmont and a report filed to Napoleon. Even more embarrassing for Gérard was the fact that he had personally recommended Bourmont – a known Royalist – for high command: the result was a scolding from the Emperor.

Bourmont's defection caused Gérard to arrive late on the battlefield of Ligny, where on 16 June, Napoleon faced **Blücher**'s Prussians. According to Sir Evelyn Wood (1895), Gérard

> ordered his men to fall out and rest, while he himself went forward to reconnoitre the enemy's position, accompanied by Staff officers and a few Hussars of the 6th Regiment. When near the Prussian line of front, a body of cavalry advanced against him, and the General and his escort retreated at full speed. During the flight, the General's horse fell in a ditch which was hidden from view by the high standing wheat crops, and the whole of his escort, seeing the General down, turned back to defend him. His Aide-de-camp, Lafontaine, having killed two Prussian Lancers, and broken his sword on the head of a third, was struck in the side by a bullet fired from a pistol close to his body. The Chief of the Staff, Saint-Remy, was dangerously wounded by seven lance thrusts. Another aide-de-camp, Captain Duperron, dismounted and tried to put Count Gérard up on his horse, but in the hand-to-hand fighting then being waged this became impossible, and the General must have been killed, or taken, had not a cavalry regiment, led by Grouchy's son, who was attracted by the sound of the firing, galloped up and driven off the Prussian horsemen.

Napoleon began the battle proper around 2.30 p.m. and this late start cost the Emperor dear: for although Napoleon gained the victory, Blücher extricated his army under cover of darkness and slipped away unmolested. Two days later, the Prussian Field Marshal would avenge Ligny by smashing into Napoleon's right flank at Waterloo.

Gérard's corps was attached to Grouchy's command in the wake of Ligny, detailed with dogging the retiring Prussians and preventing them from joining **Wellington**. No love was lost between Gérard and Grouchy: as far as Gérard was concerned, he should have been the marshal, not Grouchy. On Waterloo Day, the two men clashed in dramatic fashion, over an issue that still has historians arguing to this day. Late in the morning of 18 June (accounts vary) Grouchy and his lieutenants were some 15 miles east of Napoleon, marching north to Wavre on the banks of the River Dyle. Grouchy was breakfasting at Sart-les-Walhain when, according to historian J.F.C. Fuller (1954):

> the roar of cannon was heard in the direction of Mont St Jean. At once Gérard exclaimed: 'I think we ought to march on the cannon.' This Grouchy refused to consider . . . A violent altercation followed, in which finally Gérard urged that he and his corps be sent off alone. Grouchy would not hear of this, but said that he must obey the Emperor's orders.

Much has been made of this incident over the years, many pundits claiming that Grouchy should have listened to Gérard's advice (although by all accounts it was presented in a tactless manner), which was apparently endorsed by Generals **Exelmans** and **Vandamme**. Historian David Chandler (1966) states: 'Gérard was right; had he only moved westward – even at midday – Grouchy would have caught up with the Prussians over the River Dyle. The moment passed, however, and with it the chance of intercepting **Bülow** and **Pirch**.' But this outcome has not received universal support from historians. For example, General Sir James Shaw Kennedy, writing in 1865, observed:

> Had Grouchy acted upon the principle of directing his march by the sound of the artillery, his doing so would in all probability have produced little or no effect in favour of Napoleon on the field of Waterloo, from the following causes: the length of the march, the state of the roads, the extreme intricacy of the country, and the opposition that **Thielemann**'s corps would have offered. But the idea that Grouchy was entirely wrong, that the fault was entirely his, that his bungling or treason caused the loss of the action, cannot be admitted as a portion of authentic history: it has soothed French susceptibilities, and has been employed to give a more favourable view of Napoleon's combinations.

Rightly or wrongly, Grouchy ordered his generals – Gérard included – to continue the march on Wavre. By mid-afternoon they were contesting the crossings over the Dyle with Blücher's rearguard, commanded by General Thielemann. During the course of the battle Gérard led an assault on a bridge at the mill of Bierges. Grouchy described the sequel in his dispatch to Napoleon, quoted by Christopher Kelly (1818): 'General Gérard was wounded by a ball in the breast, while endeavouring to carry the mill of Bielge, in order to pass the river, but in which he did not succeed.' Hit in the chest by a musket ball, Gérard's life had been saved by one of his medals, which deflected the projectile. Carried from the field sporting a severe bruise, Gérard could at last claim a little good luck. Despite numerical superiority, Grouchy failed to force a passage of the Dyle on 18 June. Next day he would get troops across, but by then it was too late, Napoleon's defeat at Waterloo plunging Grouchy and Gérard into headlong retreat.

Like so many of Napoleon's generals after Waterloo, Gérard quit France rather than risk imprisonment or worse. But after two years' exile in Brussels, Gérard returned to France to resume his career, the succeeding years seeing him elevated to a number of important posts, including Marshal of France, Commander of the National Guard, Minister of War and Senator.

Gneisenau
August Wilhelm Anton, Count von
(1760–1831)

Chief of Staff of Marshal **Blücher**'s Army of the Lower Rhine at Waterloo. Son of a Saxon officer, Gneisenau obtained a commission in the Prussian Army in 1786. He came to prominence for his successful defence of the Baltic port of Kolberg (present-day Kołobrzeg in Poland), against **Napoleon**'s forces in 1807. Following Prussia's defeat at the hands of the French,

General Gneisenau (1760–1831) by George Dawes

Gneisenau studied Napoleon's methods, becoming a force for military regeneration and reform. His association with the fiery Blücher founded a successful partnership: Gneisenau effectively running Blücher's army as chief of staff, leaving the old hussar to get on with what he did best – lead from the front.

According to historian J.F.C. Fuller (1954), it was Gneisenau who conceived the Seventh Coalition's grand design to crush Napoleon by weight of numbers: **Wellington** and Blücher would invade France from Belgium, but in addition, some 200,000 Austrians under Schwarzenberg would advance on the Upper Rhine, 150,000 Russians under Barclay de Tolly would advance on the Middle Rhine, and 75,00 Austro-Italians under Frimont would advance on northern Italy. The five armies would enter France simultaneously between 27 June and 1 July. Napoleon was aware of the plan, however, and decided to strike first: but the only Allied armies within reach were those of Wellington and Blücher in Belgium. As is well known, Napoleon's plan was to keep Wellington and Blücher apart and defeat each one in turn. On 16 June 1815, while Marshal **Ney** kept Wellington occupied at Quatre-Bras, Napoleon defeated Blücher at Ligny. It was a hard-fought battle, which lasted till sundown, when the Prussians were obliged to quit the field.

But Blücher had suffered a fall from his horse, and in his temporary absence, command passed to Gneisenau. According to historian A.F. Becke (1914):

> It was clear that neither Wellington nor **Bülow** [commander of the Prussian IV Corps] would reach Ligny during the night, and the only course open to Gneisenau was to order an immediate retreat. The pregnant question was, in which direction to retire?

Colonel Charles Chesney, writing in 1868, provides the answer:

> Gneisenau, coming into temporary command after the fall of Blücher at the end of the battle, and finding the struggle for the present hopelessly decided, chose at all risk of inconvenience to abstain from the notion of a retreat to the east, and to keep as near as might be to the English army.

Wellington later referred to Gneisenau's order to march north on Wavre, rather than east on Liège as: 'the decisive moment of the century'. According to E.F. Henderson (1911), however, Gneisenau did not take the decision alone: 'Blücher and Gneisenau had met unexpectedly in a little village along the route and had laid all their plans.' Becke, meanwhile, claims the decision to retreat on Wavre

> appears to have been decided on before Blücher became a casualty; as a little later when Gneisenau, seated on his horse . . . with his map spread out in front of him, was surrounded by officers who came to him asking for orders, he merely glanced at his map in the moonlight and uttered the historic words, 'Retreat on Tilly and Wavre!' ('Rückzug nach Tilly und Wavre!') These five words led to the great Allied victory at Waterloo.

In a more prosaic version of events, historian Albert Nofi (1993) has the Prussians marching on Wavre because it was the only identifiable place on the map. Be that as it may, the fact remains that after suffering a knockout blow courtesy of the French, the Prussians stayed in the ring. And in so doing, they wrong-footed Napoleon, who assumed the only logical course open to the Prussians was withdrawal in an easterly direction, along their lines of communication.

Over the years, Napoleon's assessment has generally become accepted as correct: the Prussians *should* have marched east, but defying military logic they marched north instead, thus thwarting the Emperor's genius. But A.F. Becke (1914) – while admitting that a withdrawal east was probably desirable – concludes the Prussians had no option but to march north:

> The most prudent course was to withdraw down the communications in the direction of Liege. But this withdrawal would mean the abandonment of all idea of concentrating with Wellington and bringing the campaign in Belgium to an end, by delivering a pitched battle in which the two allies would combine to ensure Napoleon's overthrow. Even to attempt this eastward retreat might prove dangerous, since the defeated Prussian Army had been driven off the Nivelles–Namur highway and it would have to draw off across the front of the Armée du Nord . . . As matters stood the

Prussians could have retired to Quatre-Bras . . . although this would necessarily entail abandoning Bülow. This westward retreat, however, could only have been considered if the Prussian Staff was certain that Wellington was victorious at Quatre-Bras; but this was just what Gneisenau did not know . . . there was another course to adopt which met the needs of the emergency. The Prussian Army having been driven to the north of the main road, the easiest and safest way to open the retirement was undoubtedly northward. Principally for this reason the Staff selected this line of retreat.

And retreat on Wavre they did. Next day a bruised Blücher was back in command and promising Wellington Prussian aid. And on the strength of this, the Duke announced his decision to make a stand at Waterloo.

Not that Gneisenau was entirely happy about this. For it seems Gneisenau did not trust Wellington. Some pundits even suggest the Prussian chief of staff wanted to cut Wellington adrift but was overruled by the indefatigable Blücher – old Marshal 'Vorwarts'. In essence, Gneisenau blamed Wellington for not supporting the Prussians at Ligny – although the Duke had only promised Blücher support if his own forces were not attacked, which they were, at Quatre-Bras. Nevertheless, Gneisenau was not satisfied, and suspected Wellington of using the Prussians as a decoy to cover his own retreat to the port of Antwerp and the arms of the Royal Navy. As historian Peter Hofschroer (1999) explains:

> Despite the repeated assurances of support he had received from Wellington, not one of the promised 20,000 men had reached the battlefield of Ligny. As the French forces there had overwhelmed the Prussian Army, Gneisenau believed that the Duke could not have had more than 10,000 Frenchmen against him, which he should have been able to drive off with ease. . .

In the event, over twice as many French troops menaced Wellington's army at Quatre-Bras, which only gained numerical superiority late in the day, as reinforcements arrived. But seeds of doubt had been planted in Gneisenau's mind, which, once they had taken root, could not be extirpated. At dawn on 18 June the

Prussians began an arduous march from Wavre to Waterloo, via waterlogged lanes and sodden open ground. Historian Jac Weller (1967) suggests that Gneisenau – still fretting over Wellington's 'real' intentions – deliberately caused delays, requiring another rocket from Blücher to get him moving.

And so the Prussian troops arrived piecemeal throughout the afternoon (the only corps to fight in its entirety was Bülow's), most being tossed into the meat-grinding battle for Plancenoit on Napoleon's right flank. This intervention diverted French troops from the frontal battle against Wellington and sealed Napoleon's defeat. Gneisenau, quoted by Christopher Kelly (1818), paid homage to the Duke's redcoats: 'The English army fought with a valour which it is impossible to surpass,' but added, 'Napoleon continually brought forward considerable masses, and with whatever firmness the English troops maintained themselves in their position, it was not possible but that such heroic exertions must have a limit.' The message is clear: Wellington would have been beaten without Prussian aid. And to illustrate his point, Gneisenau gives the strength of Wellington's army as 'about 80,000' and Napoleon's as 'above 130,000'. This was something of an overestimate – modern analysts suggest Wellington had around 73,000 men on the field of battle and Napoleon no more than 78,000 – but to be fair, both the Prussians and the British exaggerated Napoleon's strength at Waterloo, thus magnifying their achievement.

After the collapse of the French Army, perhaps around 10 p.m. (accounts vary), Wellington and Blücher met at, or near, Napoleon's former command post at the farm of La Belle Alliance. According to **Gronow** (Gronow 1900) of the 1st Foot Guards, an eyewitness of the event,

> The two victorious generals shook hands in the most cordial and hearty manner. After a short conversation our chief rode off . . . while Blücher and the Prussians joined their own army, which under General Gneisenau, was already in hot pursuit of the French.

According to Gneisenau, in his *Life and Campaigns of Field-Marshal Prince Blücher* (1815):

The French army, pursued without intermission, was absolutely disorganised. The causeway presented the appearance of an immense shipwreck; it was covered with an innumerable quantity of cannon, caissons, carriages, baggage, arms, and wrecks of every kind. Those of the enemy who had attempted to repose for a time, and had not expected to be so quickly pursued, were driven from more than nine bivouacks. In some villages they attempted to maintain themselves; but as soon as they heard the beating of the Prussian drums, or the sound of the trumpet, they either fled or threw themselves into the houses, where they were cut down or made prisoners. It was moonlight, which greatly favoured the pursuit; for the whole march was but a continued chase, either in cornfields or the houses.

At Genappe the enemy had intrenched himself with cannon and overturned carriages, at the approach of the Prussians. Suddenly they heard in the town a great noise and a motion of carriages; at the entrance they were exposed to a brisk fire of musketry, which was replied to by some cannon-shot, followed by a *hurrah*; and an instant after the town was theirs. Thus the affair continued till break of day. About 40,000 men in the most complete disorder, the remains of the whole army, saved themselves by retreating through Charleroi, partly without arms, and carrying with them only twenty-seven pieces of their numerous artillery.

By morning, however, the Prussians had lost contact with the fleeing French. According to historian John Naylor (1960): 'It was not until he had passed Frasnes that Gneisenau called off the chase; he had with him fewer than 2,000 men and horses who had been in the field for over twenty hours.' But Gneisenau was euphoric, describing his nocturnal pursuit of French fugitives as 'the most glorious night of my life'. And with some justification: for by preventing the French from rallying, Gneisenau forestalled a further battle, effectively opening the gates of Paris to the Allies and sealing Napoleon's fate. And to cap it all, at Genappe, troops under Major von **Keller** had seized Napoleon's abandoned carriage: soon after, a Prussian officer observed that the Emperor's seal-ring 'now blazes on the hand of the hero, Gneisenau'.

But Gneisenau's euphoria was shortlived. In less than two months he was complaining bitterly about Wellington in letters to colleagues: accusing the Duke of breaking his promise to aid the Prussians on

16 June at Ligny, and of 'the most contemptuous ingratitude' for Prussian assistance at Waterloo and on the march to Paris. This breakdown in Anglo-Prussian relations following Napoleon's abdication and the subsequent occupation of Paris is noted by E.F. Henderson (1911), Blücher's biographer: 'A spirit of opposition . . . was developing between Blücher and Wellington.' In short, Prussian grievances against Wellington were as follows: first, the Duke had apparently marginalised their contribution to victory by naming the struggle on 18 June after his own headquarters at Waterloo; second, he had not supported their calls for Napoleon's execution; and third, he had prevented them from destroying Parisian monuments – especially the Pont de Jéna, built to celebrate victory over Prussia in 1806.

With regard to the naming of the great battle, Gneisenau clarified the Prussian position in an official report, quoted by Henderson:

In the middle of the position occupied by the French army, and exactly upon the height, is a farm called La Belle Alliance. The march of all the Prussian columns was directed towards this farm, which was visible from every side. It was there that Napoleon was during the battle; it was thence that he gave his orders, that he flattered himself with the hopes of victory; and it was there that his ruin was decided. There, too, it was, that, by a happy chance, Field Marshal Blücher and Lord Wellington met in the dark and mutually saluted each other as victors. In commemoration of the alliance which now subsists between the English and Prussian nations, of the union of the two armies, and their reciprocal confidence, the Field Marshal desired that this battle should bear the name of La Belle Alliance. That Wellington chose and adhered to the name of Waterloo – the Prussians, as we know, still adhere to the name of Belle Alliance – can only be taken as a sign that he wished the preponderance of credit for the victory to be on the English side.

With regard to Napoleon's fate, Gneisenau wrote the following lines to Baron von **Müffling**, again quoted by Henderson:

The Field Marshal [Blücher] also commissions me to have you inform the Duke of Wellington that it had been the Field Marshal's intention to have Bonaparte executed on the same spot where the Duke of Enghien [a Bourbon prince kidnapped, tried and executed on Napoleon's orders in March 1804] was shot, but that out of regard for the Duke's wishes he would omit the execution; but that the Duke must bear the responsibility of said omission.

Gneisenau himself was strongly in favour of executing Napoleon, and wrote:

> Should we not regard ourselves as the instruments of Providence, which had given us such a victory to the end that we should exercise eternal justice? Does not the death of the Duke of Enghien alone demand such vengeance? Shall we not expose ourselves to the reproaches of the Prussian, Russian, Spanish, and Portuguese peoples if we neglect to do justice?

As for the despoliation of Paris and the destruction of the Pont de Jéna, the following extract is taken from the memoirs of British guardsman Rees Howell Gronow (1900):

> At that period there were rumours – and reliable ones too – that Blücher and the Duke of Wellington were at loggerheads. The Prussians wanted to blow up the Bridge of Jena, but the Duke sent a battalion of our regiment to prevent it, and the Prussian engineers who were mining the bridge were civilly sent away: this circumstance created some ill-will between the chiefs.

Indeed there was, and Gronow continues:

> A sort of congress of the Emperors of Austria and Russia and the King of Prussia (with Blücher and Wellington) met at the Hotel of Foreign Affairs, on the Boulevard, when, after much ado, the Duke of Wellington emphatically declared that if any of the monuments were destroyed he would take the British Army from Paris: this threat had the desired effect. Nevertheless, Blücher levied contributions on the poor Parisians and his army was newly clothed. The Bank of France was called upon to furnish him with several thousand pounds, which, it was said, were to reimburse him for the money lost at play [i.e. the gambling table]. This, with many other instances of extortion and tyranny, was the cause of Blücher's removal, and he took his departure by order of the King.

And so Blücher quit Paris under a cloud, declaring 'I cannot and will not remain here any longer'. Gneisenau followed, and, pleading ill health, retired from public life to publish a biography of his illustrious chief, which appeared in English as *The Life and Campaigns of Field-Marshal Prince Blücher*. But within three years Gneisenau was back, this time as Governor of Berlin, and by 1825 he had been made a field marshal. He died of cholera in 1831 while commanding the Army of Observation on the Polish frontier.

Gordon
Lieutenant Colonel Sir Alexander (1768–1815)

Wellington's favourite aide-de-camp, who died soon after the battle, following the amputation of a leg. Third son of George Gordon (Lord Haddo), Gordon was educated at Eton College, before entering the 3rd Foot Guards as an ensign in 1803. Thanks to the British purchase system, which allowed officers to buy commissions, Gordon was lieutenant colonel of the regiment within 10 years. A veteran of campaigns in South America and the Iberian Peninsula, Gordon picked up 10 medals for general actions plus a knighthood. From 1810 he served on Wellington's staff.

In the British Army of the day, a commander-in-chief like Wellington was permitted four official aides-de-camp (ADCs). But in practice, most generals paid for extra aides out of their own purse. In an era before electronic communications, the importance of this role can well be imagined, for an ADC was nothing less than the eyes, ears and voice of his master: the job basically involving the delivery of orders, messages and dispatches. At Waterloo, Wellington employed eight ADCs. Apart from Gordon, these were Lieutenant Colonel **Fremantle**, Lieutenant Colonel Canning, Lieutenant Colonel Lennox, Major the Honourable **Henry Percy**, Captain Lord Arthur Hill, Lieutenant Lord George Cathcart and the Prince of Nassau-Usingen. All except Percy were either killed or wounded. Indeed, some 33 per cent of all ADCs employed in the British Army at Waterloo became casualties.

Gordon received his wound at the height of the battle, while rallying a battalion of Brunswickers, near La Haie Sainte.

A cannon-ball smashed his thigh and the leg was amputated by Wellington's personal physician, Dr John Hume. He died a few hours later – in those days, about a third of all amputees died during, or soon after, surgery. The story goes that Gordon died at Wellington's head-quarters at the village of Waterloo, in the Duke's own bed. Most accounts have Wellington sleeping on the floor, either in the same room or one nearby. Yet Hume gives the following version, as quoted by historian Brett-James (1970):

> I came back from the field of Waterloo with Sir Alexander Gordon, whose leg I was obliged to amputate on the field in the late evening. He died unexpectedly in my arms about half-past three in the morning of the nineteenth. I was hesitating about disturbing the Duke, when Sir Charles Broke-Vere came. He wished to take his orders about the movement of the troops. I went upstairs and tapped gently at the door, when he [Wellington] told me to come in . . . As I entered, he sat up in bed, his face covered with the dust and sweat of the previous day, and extended his hand to me, which I took and held in mine, whilst I told him of Gordon's death, and of such of the casualties as had come to my knowledge. He was much affected. I felt the tears dropping fast upon my hand, and looking towards him, saw them chasing one another in furrows over his dusty cheeks. He brushed them suddenly away with his left hand, and said to me in a voice tremulous with emotion: 'Well, Thank God, I don't know what it is to lose a battle; but certainly nothing can be more painful than to gain one with the loss of so many of one's friends.'

But according to Earl Stanhope (1888), Wellington rose between 3 a.m. and 4 a.m., having been told that Gordon was dying. Stanhope records Wellington as saying: 'they came to tell me that poor Gordon was dying, and I went immediately to see him; but he was already dead'.

Either way, Wellington lamented Gordon's loss, describing him as an officer of great promise. But it was Gordon's siblings who erected a column to his memory at Waterloo, with contributions from the great and good of Brussels society.

Graeme
Lieutenant George Drummond (dates unknown)

Scottish officer in the 2nd Light Battalion, King's German Legion, tasked with the defence of La Haie Sainte on Waterloo Day. Like **Edmund Wheatley**, Graeme was a British officer in the King's German Legion (KGL), a corps of Hanoverians in the service of the British Crown. Also like Wheatley, he was temporarily captured by the French and left an account of his experiences. The garrison of La Haie Sainte – a farm complex on the Brussels road, guarding the approach to **Wellington**'s centre on the ridge of Mont St Jean – initially consisted of some 400 riflemen from the 2nd Light Battalion, KGL, under Major **Baring**. But Baring's defence of the bastion was hampered by the fact his pioneers had been sent to fortify the château of Hougoumont on the far right of the battlefield, leaving his riflemen to make loopholes with bare hands and bayonets. Making the best of it, Baring put three companies in the orchard facing the French, two among the farm buildings, and one in the kitchen garden. An abatis or barricade was also placed across the high road outside La Haie Sainte's main gate, to slow any French advance from the south.

The French attack on the farmstead began after midday, when a swarm of skirmishers penetrated the orchard and attacked the farm buildings. Graeme began the battle behind the barricade on the Brussels road, but when the French attacked in earnest, retreated

La Haie Sainte – print by J. Booth, 1815

into the farm complex. For most of the afternoon, Graeme was posted on the roof of a pigsty (which, by his account, contained a calf but no pigs), from which he could fire down on the French attackers outside the main gate. Despite repeated pleas for ammunition, sent to Lieutenant General Sir **Charles Alten**, Baring's divisional commander at Mont St Jean, the garrison had run out of bullets by 6.30 p.m. and was overwhelmed. Baring ordered the evacuation of La Haie Sainte via the farmhouse, sending his men through the narrow corridor and out into the kitchen garden beyond, from where they could climb the slope of Mont St Jean back to Allied lines. Graeme takes up the story in a letter written shortly after the battle, quoted by Siborne (1891):

> We had to pass through a narrow passage. We wanted to halt the men and make one more charge, but it was impossible; the fellows were firing down the passage. An officer of our company called to me, 'Take care,' but I was too busy stopping the men, and answered, 'Never mind, let the blackguard fire.' He was about 5 yards off, and levelling his piece just at me, when this officer stabbed him in the mouth and out through his neck; he fell immediately.
>
> But now they flocked in; this officer got two shots, and ran into a room, where he lay behind a bed all the time they had possession of the house; sometimes the room was full of them, and some wounded soldiers of ours who lay there and cried out 'Pardon' were shot, the monsters saying, 'Take that for the fine defence you have made.'
>
> An officer and four men came first in; the officer got me by the collar, and said to his men, 'C'est ce coquin' [It is this rascal]. Immediately the fellows had their bayonets down, and made a dead stick at me, which I parried off with my sword, the officer always running about and then coming to me again and shaking me by the collar; but they all looked so frightened and pale as ashes, I thought, 'You shan't keep me,' and I bolted off through the lobby; they fired two shots after me, and cried out 'Coquin,' but did not follow me.

The officer who saved Graeme's life was Ensign Frank. While hiding under his bed, Frank heard the French yelling, 'Pas de pardon à ces coquins verts!' (No mercy for the rascals in green!) before murdering those who had surrendered. The testimonies of soldiers like Graeme, Frank, **Wheatley** and the Frenchman Jean-Baptiste **Jolyet** belie the myth of chivalry towards prisoners at Waterloo.

Graham
Corporal (1791–c.1845)

Soldier of the 2nd Foot Guards at Hougoumont, who helped close the château's great north gate. Referred to as James, John or Joseph in secondary sources, and often described as a sergeant, the *Waterloo Medal Roll* (Buckland 2001) lists Corporal James Graham as serving in Lieutenant Colonel the Honourable J. Walpole's Light Company, 2nd Battalion 2nd Foot Guards. Graham's brother was at Hougoumont too, and he is also referred to as James or John in the history books. The *Waterloo Medal Roll* perpetuates the incertitude surrounding the forenames of the brothers by listing a Private James Graham in Lieutenant Colonel Lord **Saltoun**'s Light Company of the 1st Foot Guards. Two brothers named James? Perhaps, although it seems unlikely. Whatever the true forenames of the brothers Graham, the result has been a confusion of identities in published accounts.

And yet some facts are known about the life of Corporal Graham of the 2nd Foot Guards. Born in County Monaghan, Ireland, Graham was a man of great strength. He was one of several soldiers who, under Lieutenant Colonel **Macdonell**'s command, barricaded the north gate of the château in time to thwart a determined French attack. This event, which occurred shortly after midday on 18 June 1815, has gone down in legend as the pivotal moment of the battle, **Wellington** himself observing: 'the outcome of the Battle of Waterloo rested upon the closing of the gates at Hougoumont'. Shortly afterwards – with the fighting in the château's orchard still raging – Corporal Graham asked Macdonell's permission to fall out. The Colonel expressed his surprise but Graham explained that his brother lay wounded in a part of the château then ablaze; that he wished to carry him to safety but would return with all speed. According to regimental historian Mackinnon (1833): 'The request was granted; Graham succeeded in snatching his brother from the terrible fate which menaced him, laid him in a ditch in rear of the enclosure, and true to his word, was again at his post.'

Although some accounts switch the roles, claiming it was Corporal Graham who was saved by his brother, it was the Corporal who was rewarded for acts of bravery at Hougoumont. Promoted to sergeant, Graham also received cash from the patriotic Reverend Norcross, who wished to honour 'the most deserving soldier at Waterloo'. This endowment took the form of an annuity of £10 (about £500 in modern terms) for life. Named the 'Wellington Pension', it was to be paid annually on 18 June, and Graham shared the accolade with Private Joseph Lister of the 3rd Foot Guards. But sadly, Norcross was declared bankrupt within two years and payments ceased. Meanwhile, Graham remained with his regiment and is said to have saved the life of Captain (later Lord Frederick) Fitzclarence during the dramatic arrest of notorious insurrectionist Arthur Thistlewood and his Cato Street conspirators, in 1820. Graham eventually quit the Guards but re-enlisted in a cavalry regiment, serving as a private for over nine years. In 1830, aged 39, Graham was discharged from the army with a Chelsea pension of 9 pennies a day.

Some sources claim Graham received a substantial sum following Norcross's death in 1837. The story goes that Norcross made provision in his will for 'the bravest man in England' as named by Wellington. The Duke apparently chose Macdonell, who gallantly insisted the money be shared with Graham. If true, Graham did not have long to enjoy the windfall, as he was admitted to the Royal Hospital, Kilmainham, Dublin, in 1841. His health broken by long and arduous military service – he was described as having 'an injured chest' and being 'worn out'. Graham died there some years later: on 23 April 1843 according to some sources, on 28 April 1845 according to others.

Gronow
Rees Howell (1794–1865)

Ensign in the 1st Foot Guards and author of the four-volume *Recollections and Reminiscences of Captain Gronow*, first published between 1861 and 1866. According to his entry in the *Oxford Dictionary of National Biography*, Gronow was 'a remarkably handsome man, always faultlessly dressed, and was very popular in society'. He was also a celebrated dandy, duellist and courtier. The eldest son of William Gronow, a wealthy Welsh landowner, Gronow was educated at Eton College, where he counted P.B. Shelley, the future poet, among his friends, and where the tyrannical headmaster, Dr John Keate ('a sort of pocket Hercules'), ruled by terror. Having survived Keate's brutal regime, Gronow received an ensign's commission in the 1st Foot Guards on 24 December 1812. Somewhat small and slight in stature (his friends nicknamed him 'No-Grow'), the young officer's time was initially taken up in mounting guard at St James's Palace and learning how to powder his hair:

> I remember, when on guard, incurring the heavy displeasure of the late Duke of Cambridge for not having a sufficient quantity of powder on my head, and therefore presenting a somewhat piebald appearance. I received a strong reprimand from H.R.H., and he threatened even to place me under arrest should I ever appear again on guard in what he was pleased to call so slovenly and disgraceful a condition.

Within a few short months, and having received little or no military training, Gronow was packed off to Spain, where he joined **Wellington**'s army, and participated in the closing stages of the Peninsular War. By the summer of 1814 Gronow was back in London, where he became a dandy and one of the few guards officers admitted to Almack's assembly rooms, where quadrilles and waltzes were the order of the day. And so, as a member of fashionable society, Gronow danced out the year, making new acquaintances, and observing that: 'It appears to be a law of natural history that every generation produces and throws out from the mob of society a few conspicuous men that pass under the general appellation of "men about town".' A suitable sobriquet, in fact, for Gronow himself: for soon he would become a noted dandy and deadly duellist, his portrait hanging in shop windows, alongside those of the Prince Regent and 'Beau' Brummell.

Despite his later claim to have belonged to the 2nd Battalion of the 1st Foot Guards, he actually belonged to the 1st, which was stationed in London at the start of the Waterloo campaign. Eager for action, Gronow crossed the Channel unofficially, hoping to take part in the coming battle and return to London before being missed. He funded his adventure with £600 (approximately £30,000 in modern reckoning) won at a gambling 'hell'. After a stint on **Picton**'s staff, Gronow joined the 3rd Battalion of his regiment on the morning of the battle:

> I was now greeted by many of my old friends with loud cries of 'How are you, old fellow? Take a glass of wine and a bit of ham? It will be perhaps your last breakfast.' Then Burges called out, 'Come here Gronow and tell us some London news!'

Privates of the British 1st Foot Guards

The 2nd and 3rd Battalions of the 1st Foot Guards formed **Maitland**'s 1st Brigade, which, with Byng's 2nd Brigade (2/2nd Foot Guards and 2/3rd Foot Guards), formed the 1st British Infantry (Guards) Division, under Major General **George Cooke**. Maitland's brigade was situated on Wellington's right flank, approximately halfway between the bastions of La Haie Sainte and Hougoumont. According to Gronow, the guards had

> a hot corner of it . . . I confess that I am to this day astonished that any of us remained alive . . . During the battle our squares presented a shocking sight. Inside we were nearly suffocated by the smoke and smell from burnt cartridges. It was impossible to move a yard without treading upon a wounded comrade or upon the bodies of the dead; and the loud groans of the wounded and dying were most appalling.

About 4 p.m. Wellington sheltered in Gronow's square, the dandy recalling that:

> Our Commander-in-Chief, as far as I could judge, appeared perfectly composed; but looked very thoughtful and pale. He was dressed in a grey greatcoat with a cape, white cravat, leather pantaloons, Hessian boots, and a large cocked hat *à la Russe*. The Duke sat unmoved, mounted on his favourite charger. I recollect his asking Colonel Stanhope what o'clock it was, upon which Stanhope took out his watch and said it was twenty minutes past four. The Duke replied, 'The battle is mine; and if the Prussians arrive soon there will be an end of the war.'

In fact, the Prussian IV Corps under **Bülow** was already debouching from the Bois de Paris on **Napoleon**'s right flank and **Ziethen**'s I Corps would link with Wellington's army shortly after 7 p.m. Thanks to this intervention on the part of **Blücher**'s Army of the Lower Rhine, there was indeed an end to the war, and Gronow entered Paris on 7 July with his regiment.

Looking back on the battle, Gronow later wrote:

> When I call to mind how ill rewarded our noble soldiers were for their heroic deeds, my heart bleeds for them. 'Under the cold shade

of aristocracy', men who in France would have been promoted for their valour to the highest grades of the army, lived and died, twenty or thirty years after the battle, with the rank of lieutenant or captain.

Gronow might well have included himself in this category: for though he was promoted Guards lieutenant 10 days after Waterloo (with the equivalent Line rank of captain, which, needless to say, he adopted on retirement), he progressed no further, presumably lacking the £8,300 necessary to buy a majority. After spending some time with the Army of Occupation in Paris, Gronow finally quit the army on 24 October 1821 for a life of pleasure and idleness. After stints in debtors' prison and the Houses of Parliament (as MP for Stafford), Gronow decamped to Paris to write his scandalous – though frequently amusing and entertaining – memoirs.

Grouchy
Marshal Emmanuel, Marquis de (1766–1847)

Commanded the right wing of **Napoleon**'s Army of the North in the Waterloo campaign, detached to pursue **Blücher**'s defeated Prussians after the Battle of Ligny on 16 June 1815. The last of Napoleon's marshals to receive his baton, Grouchy was one of the few genuine aristocrats among the Emperor's lieutenants (most, like **Ney**, duc d'Elchingen and prince de la Moskowa, who was the son of a barrel-maker, received their titles as rewards for hard-fought victories). He had served as an officer in the Royalist Army of Louis XVI, but was thrown out by Revolutionaries on the grounds of class. Undeterred from pursuing a military career, and smitten with Revolutionary fervour, the blue-blooded Grouchy joined France's Republican Army as a private citizen, rising to the rank of general on merit. But Grouchy's career suffered a further setback with Napoleon's coup of 1799: failing to display sufficient enthusiasm for the Corsican's takeover, the General was marginalised and consistently passed over for promotion in favour of vocal Bonapartists. A talented cavalry commander, Grouchy continued to serve in France's major campaigns, but by 1809 had opted for semi-retirement.

Summoned from the shadows for the Russian campaign of 1812, Grouchy displayed courage and ability at the head of the III Cavalry Corps, and even commanded Napoleon's celebrated 'Sacred Squadron' on the infamous retreat. After Napoleon's first abdication of April 1814, Grouchy became a Royalist again, serving in the army of Louis XVIII. But with Napoleon's escape from exile and triumphant return to power 12 months later, he returned to the Emperor's fold. Although historian A.G. MacDonell (1934) comments that Grouchy's conscience was 'singularly elastic', it was no more so than most French career officers' of the period. As for Napoleon, who lacked experienced leaders for his new army, Grouchy was a godsend and the Emperor finally made him a Marshal of the Empire.

In the Waterloo campaign Grouchy commanded the right wing of Napoleon's Army of the North, consisting of **Vandamme**'s III Corps and **Gérard**'s IV Corps, plus Pajol's I Cavalry Corps and **Exelmans**' II Cavalry Corps – perhaps 30,000 troops in all. These troops took part in the opening battle of the campaign at Ligny on 16 June 1815. A victory for Napoleon over Blücher's Prussians, Gérard's late arrival robbed the Emperor of a knockout blow, darkness lending cover to the Prussian withdrawal. Even so, Napoleon assumed Blücher was out of the ring and would retreat east along his line of communication with Germany. Although the operational picture was far from clear – obscured by night, difficult terrain, and thousands of Prussian deserters filling all available roads – Napoleon sent Exelmans north-east to Gembloux and Pajol south-east to Namur, not realising that Blücher and **Gneisenau** had opted to retire north on Wavre.

Next day around noon, Grouchy headed east from Ligny with the rest of his command, charged with dogging the Prussians and preventing them from re-entering the fray. About 3 p.m. on 17 June Grouchy received word from Exelmans that **Thielemann**'s Prussian rearguard had been located near Gembloux. Hindered by heavy downpours and violent thunderstorms, Grouchy marched through the mud in pursuit. Arriving at Gembloux about 7 p.m., he found the place deserted, Exelmans having followed the Prussians north.

At Namur, Pajol fared no better: no Prussians to be seen, though intelligence reports suggested at least one of their columns was heading north.

Napoleon was also heading north, having spent the day trudging after **Wellington**, obliged to decamp from Quatre-Bras in the wake of Blücher's defeat. Thus, as Grouchy reached Gembloux, advanced elements of the Emperor's army reached the southern edge of the Waterloo battlefield. An hour or so later, Napoleon received a report from a staff officer telling of Blücher's retirement on Wavre: the Emperor did not see fit to alter Grouchy's orders. But this left Grouchy in the dark. Piecing together evidence from scouts and informers, the Marshal speculated the Prussians had split in two: one column marching east to Liège, another north to Wavre. Believing his principal task to be pursuit of a beaten foe, he sent word to Napoleon about 10 p.m., advising the Emperor of his decision to march on Wavre at daybreak. In the meantime, Blücher's army was concentrating in preparation for a strike west to Waterloo. For despite his defeat at Ligny, the septuagenarian Prussian was not interested in sloping back to Germany: instead, Blücher would seize the initiative and march on Napoleon's right flank. To this end, Blücher ordered **Bülow**'s corps to quit Wavre at dawn, to be followed by those of **Pirch** and **Ziethen**: that of Thielemann would linger at Wavre as a rearguard against Grouchy, with orders to stand fast on the banks of the River Dyle.

And so at daybreak on 18 June the first Prussian units began their cross-country hike from Wavre to Waterloo, as Napoleon received Grouchy's dispatch, telling of his intention to strike north. Satisfied that Grouchy was dealing with Blücher, and apparently confident of beating Wellington unaided, the Emperor did nothing to change Grouchy's game plan. But on the morning of 18 June Grouchy made a late start from Gembloux. He should have hit the road north at first light, but did not get moving till around 7.30 a.m. Some historians blame Grouchy's generals for the delay, claiming Vandamme or Gérard, or both, acted without energy. Most simply blame Grouchy for a lack of 'grip'. But all generals, of all armies, suffered setbacks and delays that morning in trying to move large numbers of men via a handful of tracks and lanes turned to quagmire by the recent rains. Furthermore, the troops were far from fresh, having spent a wretched night in the open, the rain falling in torrents – and this after fighting battles on 16 June and marching throughout 17 June. Consequently, Grouchy's operations – like Bülow's, and for that matter, Napoleon's – were hampered by circumstantial factors. Indeed, Napoleon was obliged to postpone his initial attack on Wellington several times, while his sodden soldiers sorted themselves out.

As for Grouchy, he marched his bedraggled column up a single road from Gembloux, covering a mere 5 miles in three hours, and reaching Sart-les-Walhain some time after 10 a.m. Having been informed by an aide-de-camp that no Prussians obstructed his march on Wavre, the Marshal stopped for a breakfast of straw-berries at the summerhouse of Walhain's notary, M. Hollert. Meanwhile, 15 miles or so to the west, Napoleon dictated an order (Becke 1914) apparently confirming the Marshal's stated plan of marching on Wavre:

> The Emperor is about to attack the English, who have taken up
> position at Waterloo. Therefore His Majesty desires you to direct
> your movements upon Wavre, in order to come near to us, and
> connect yourself with our operations, pushing before you the
> Prussian corps which have taken this direction, and which
> may have stopped at Wavre, where you are to arrive as soon
> as possible.

Much has been made of the wording of this document, some historians claiming that Napoleon bamboozled Grouchy with contra-dictory instructions, but the sense seems pretty clear: the Emperor wanted Grouchy to reach Wavre 'as soon as possible'.

An hour or so later, the Emperor's Waterloo guns announced battle as Prince **Jérôme** attacked the château of Hougoumont. Grouchy was still breakfasting at Walhain when the sound reached his ears, and those of his generals. A heated discussion arose, in which some officers suggested marching to the sound of the guns, while others opted for the strike on Wavre. According to historian Charles Chesney (1868):

> Gérard with much warmth urged the former view . . . The Marshal,
> however, decided against this suggestion. The arrival of his troops,
> as he judged, over the fourteen miles of difficult ground, and with

an uncertain river-passage to make, could not be counted on to be of service to Napoleon that day; and his own business was to press the Prussians.

Pleas and protestations followed, during which Grouchy became increasingly irritated by Gérard's insubordinate manner. According to historian Georges Blond (1979), Grouchy cut matters short with:

> The Emperor told me last night that he intended to attack . . . if Wellington accepted battle. I am therefore in no way surprised at the engagement which is now taking place. If the Emperor had wished me to take part, he would not have sent me away at the very moment he was moving on the British. Besides, in taking bad roads cross country, flooded by yesterday's rain, I would not arrive in time on the battlefield. My duty is to carry out the Emperor's orders which require me to pursue the Prussians. To follow your advice would be to disregard his orders.

With this display of faultless logic, Grouchy put an end to the discussion. A courier from Exelmans, confirming strong Prussian forces holding the Dyle, only stiffened Grouchy's resolve to march on Wavre, and he ordered an immediate advance.

But the 'strong Prussian forces' defending the River Dyle belonged to Thielemann's understrength III Corps only: the rest of Blücher's army was already marching to Waterloo. Indeed, by 1 p.m. Napoleon had spotted the lead elements of Bülow's corps gathering on the eastern horizon. And the Emperor was obliged to take a further reality check when, minutes later, he was presented with a captured Prussian hussar, confirming Bülow's approach. Napoleon dictated another dispatch to Grouchy, quoted by A.F. Becke (1914):

> It is for you to see where we are, and to regulate yourself accordingly, so as to connect our communications, and to be always prepared to fall upon any of the enemy's troops which may endeavour to annoy our right, and crush them . . . battle is engaged on the line before Waterloo. The enemy's centre is at Mont St Jean. Manoeuvre therefore to join our right.

Emphasising the danger, Napoleon added a postscript:

A letter, which has just been intercepted, tells that General Bülow is about to attack our flank; we believe we see this corps on the heights of St Lambert. So lose not an instant in drawing near and joining us, in order to crush Bülow, whom you will catch in the very act of concentrating [with Wellington].

These orders were sent to Grouchy as **d'Erlon** prepared his grand attack on Wellington's line. But Grouchy was 15 miles from Napoleon as the crow flies – many more by the sodden tracks and lanes the Emperor's courier would have to take – and he would not receive the message in time to act upon it. This is made plain by historian Hilaire Belloc (1931), who observes:

Hard riding could not get Napoleon's note to Grouchy's quarters within much less than an hour and a half. When it got there Grouchy himself must be found, and that done his 33,000 must be got together in order to take the new direction. Further, the Emperor could not know in what state Grouchy's forces might be, nor what direction they might already have taken.

As a matter of fact, Grouchy had still not received Napoleon's message of 10 a.m., and would not do so until around 4 p.m., suggesting a delivery time of almost six hours for imperial dispatches (according to some accounts, Napoleon's messengers did not cut across country to reach Grouchy, but took a long, circuitous route via Quatre-Bras and Gembloux). But Napoleon could not know this, and anyway, he was not unduly worried, as Belloc explains:

It should be mentioned . . . to explain Napoleon's evident hope . . . of things going well, that the prisoner had told the Emperor it was commonly believed in the Prussian lines that Grouchy was actually marching to join him, Napoleon, at that moment.

In other words, Napoleon could at least entertain the possibility that Grouchy was already on his way (some suggest Napoleon genuinely mistook the appearance of Ziethen's troops at 7 p.m. for those of Grouchy, others that he deliberately misinformed his soldiers to boost flagging morale).

By 4 p.m., with Bülow finally emerging on Napoleon's right flank at Waterloo, Grouchy reached Wavre. It was around this time he received Napoleon's orders of 10 a.m., instructing him to 'direct his movements on Wavre'. Naturally, the Marshal concluded he had done the right thing after all, and promptly launched an attack on Thielemann's 15,000 Prussians, strung out along the marshy banks of the Dyle. Three hours later, with victory at Waterloo slipping through Napoleon's fingers, Grouchy received the Emperor's message of 1 p.m., requesting him to 'join our right'. But it was too late. Unable to affect the outcome at Waterloo, Grouchy fought on at Wavre, finally overcoming the Prussians by sheer weight of numbers as darkness fell.

Grouchy's report to Napoleon, detailing the affair at Wavre, is quoted at length by Christopher Kelly (1818):

It was not till after seven in the evening of the 18th of June that I received the letter of the Duke of Dalmatia, which directed me to march on St Lambert, and attack General Bülow. I fell in with the enemy as I was marching on Wavre. He was immediately driven into Wavre; and General Vandamme's corps attacked that town, and was warmly engaged. The portion of Wavre on the right of the Dyle was carried; but much difficulty was experienced in debouching on the other side. General Gérard was wounded by a ball in the breast, while endeavouring to carry the mill of Bielge, in order to pass the river, but in which he did not succeed, and Lieutenant General Aix had been killed in the attack on the town. In this state of things, being impatient to cooperate with your majesty's army on that important day, I detached several corps to force the passage of the Dyle, and march against Bülow.

The corps of Vandamme, in the meantime, maintained the attack on Wavre, and on the mill, whence the enemy showed an intention to debouch, but which I did not conceive he was capable of effecting. I arrived at Limale, passed the river, and the heights were carried by the division of Vichery and the cavalry. Night did not permit us to advance further, and I no longer heard the cannon on the side where your majesty was engaged. I halted in this situation until daylight.

At 10.30 am on 19 June Grouchy heard the news from Waterloo:

I was in front of Rozierne, preparing to march on Brussels when I received the sad intelligence of the loss of the Battle of Waterloo. The officer who brought it informed me, that your majesty was retreating on the Sambre, without being able to indicate any particular point on which I should direct my march. I ceased to pursue, and began my retrograde movement.

Grouchy conducted a skilful retreat upon Paris following Napoleon's defeat. Then, fearing for his life in the inevitable Bourbon reprisals, he fled to the USA. According to David G. Chandler (1979), Grouchy 'lived for some years in Philadelphia, Pennsylvania, until allowed to return to France in 1820. Louis-Philippe restored his marshal's bâton in 1831 and he became a peer of France the next year.'

Grouchy may have been forgiven by the monarchy, but not by the Bonapartists, who blamed him for the defeat at Waterloo. Recriminations began with Napoleon's attempts to rewrite history and exonerate his own failings while in exile on St Helena. The chorus of criticism was taken up by other veterans, including Gérard, who never let Grouchy forget his decision to ignore the Emperor's guns and march on Wavre. At best, Grouchy was accused of incompetence, at worst, of treachery. Haunted by the events of June 1815, Grouchy could not put the past behind him, and as historian James D. Hunt observes (Chandler 1987), he

> spent most of the rest of his life in a battle of polemics to justify his conduct at Waterloo. Napoleon's biased account was published by General Gourgaud in 1818. It was contested in a pamphlet by Grouchy . . . but the facts are hard to avoid, placing the blame, as they do, for all that went wrong with Grouchy's right wing fairly and squarely on Napoleon himself.

Guyot
General Charles, Claude-Étienne, Count (1768–1837)

Commanded **Napoleon**'s Imperial Guard Heavy Cavalry Division at Waterloo. Having enlisted in 1791 as a cavalry trooper, by 1805 Guyot was second in command of the elite Chasseurs à Cheval of the Imperial Guard. A veteran of the Peninsular War, Guyot took command of the Grenadiers à Cheval of the Imperial Guard in 1813. But Napoleon was unimpressed by Guyot's ability to organise and lead large formations, removing him from command and attaching him to his personal escort. Loyal to the Emperor, Guyot returned to Napoleon's colours in 1815 and was rewarded with command of the Imperial Guard Heavy Cavalry Division, consisting of the Grenadiers à Cheval and the Empress's dragoons.

At Waterloo, Guyot's command – just over 2,000 sabres strong – was kept in reserve most of the day, in expectation of a break-through at Mont St Jean. But when, at about 4 p.m., **Ney** ordered **Milhaud**'s cuirassiers into action, Guyot followed as a matter of course, as described by Captain de **Brack** of the Red Lancers (Brack 1876): 'all of a sudden the brigade of Dragoons and Grenadiers thought the order to charge had been given . . . it set off and we followed'. Without specific orders from Napoleon, Guyot's imperial troopers became embroiled in the desperate charges against **Wellington**'s infantry squares, advancing to the attack at least five times. They achieved little, however, as confirmed by de Brack: 'It was said the Dragoons and Grenadiers to our left forced their way into certain squares; I did not see this.' Guyot, meanwhile, had two horses shot under him during the assaults. He survived the battle however, and with the bulk of the French Army – including Napoleon – in flight, led his men from the field in perfect order, as recalled by Captain Barton of the 12th Light Dragoons in a letter quoted by Siborne (1891):

> We saw to our left front, at no great distance, a strong Regiment of Cavalry, which we soon ascertained to be the Grenadiers à Cheval of the Imperial Guard; they were formed in a dense column, and appeared to take but little notice of our advance, when opposite their flank they fired a few pistol or carbine shots. We were some distance in front of our Brigade, and being too weak to make an impression [on them], they literally walked from the field in a most majestic manner.

Halkett
Major General Sir Colin (1774–1856)

Commander of the 5th British Brigade, part of **Alten**'s 3rd British Infantry Division. Born in the Netherlands, Colin Halkett was the eldest son of a major in the Scots Brigade. His elder brother, Hew, found fame at Waterloo as the captor of General **Cambronne**. Entering the Dutch Foot Guards in 1792, Colin Halkett transferred to British service in 1803 as lieutenant colonel of the 2nd Light Battalion of the King's German Legion – the unit destined to defend La Haie Sainte at Waterloo, under the command of Major **George Baring**. In the years leading up to the great battle, Halkett led this battalion through tough campaigns in North Germany, Scandinavia and the Iberian peninsula. By 1811 Halkett was leading the Light Brigade of the King's German Legion, and was subsequently promoted to major general and knighted.

In the Waterloo campaign, Halkett commanded the 5th British Brigade, which consisted of four battalions (2/30th Foot, 33rd Foot, 2/69th Foot and 2/73rd Foot), numbering over 2,000 men in all. The brigade was heavily engaged at Quatre-Bras and played a part in the repulse of the Imperial Guard at Waterloo. According to historian David Chandler (1980), the Imperial Guard's assault on **Wellington**'s right-centre about 7.30 p.m. was 'One of the most celebrated engagements in military history'. Constituting **Napoleon**'s final desperate throw for victory, the attack was intended to be a general advance merely spearheaded by the Guard. In the event, however, five battalions of guardsmen found themselves out in front, toiling up the slope of Mont St Jean with little in the way of support. By the time these battalions were closing on the crest of Wellington's position, they had split into two distinct groups: on the left, three battalions of chasseurs à pied advanced on the infantry of **Maitland** and **Adam**; and on the right, two battalions of grenadiers headed for Halkett's brigade, having already overthrown some troops of the Duke of **Brunswick**'s Corps.

According to some sources, Halkett was ordered to retire behind the crest of the ridge, a manoeuvre that apparently caused some confusion among his troops, especially when the Imperial Guard's divisional artillery began slamming shot into them. But within minutes Halkett had restored order, and when the grenadiers of the Guard breasted the ridge they were given a hot reception. Despite sorely depleted numbers, Halkett's battalions – formed four ranks deep – stood their ground long enough for **Chassé**'s Netherlanders (**Detmers**' infantry plus supporting artillery) to deploy. Within moments, the Imperial Guard wavered, broke and fled – pursued by blue-coated Netherlanders, yelling and hoisting their shakos high in the air on their bayonets.

Needless to say, Chassé and Detmers – with some justification, no doubt – claimed a share of the glory, but Halkett's men later claimed they finished off the Guard unaided, and were piling their muskets when the Netherlanders charged. Either way, Halkett became a casualty of the firefight. According to **Gronow** of the 1st Foot Guards (Gronow 1900):

> Sir Colin Halkett's wound, which was . . . from a musket ball
> through the jaws, was not so dangerous; for it was said by Forbes the
> surgeon, that the General must have been in the act of ordering his
> men to charge, with his mouth open when he was struck. Wellington
> paid tribute to Halkett's bravery and professionalism in his Dispatch,
> dubbing him 'a very gallant and deserving officer'.

After Waterloo, Halkett remained in the British Army and went on to greater things. Apart from a succession of British and foreign honours, Halkett became Lieutenant Governor of Jersey (1821), Commander-in-Chief at Bombay (1831) and Governor of the Royal Hospital, Chelsea (1849). Halkett also rose to the rank of full general in the British Army, as well as being made an honorary general in the Hanoverian service.

Halkett
Colonel Hew, Baron von (1783–1863)

Commander of the 3rd Hanoverian Brigade, part of Clinton's 2nd British Infantry Division. Born at Musselburgh near Edinburgh, Hew Halkett was the diminutive but cheerful second son of Major General Frederick Godar Halkett. His older brother was **Colin Halkett**, commander of a brigade in **Alten**'s 3rd British Infantry Division at Waterloo. Hew Halkett joined the army as an ensign in 1794, serving in India between 1798 and 1801. He later became a captain, and then a major, in what was to become the 2nd Light Battalion of the King's German Legion (commanded by his brother Colin) – reputedly speaking bad German with a heavy English accent. A veteran of the siege of Stralsund, the expedition to Copenhagen, the retreat from Corunna and the doomed invasion of Walcheren, Halkett was a soldier of courage and initiative. In 1811 he joined **Wellington**'s Peninsular Army, commanding his battalion at the Battle of Albuera. In 1813 he was sent to Germany to organise Hanoverian recruits and distinguished himself in clashes with French forces at Göhrde, and with Danish forces at Schestedt. The following year he was present at the Sieges of Glückstadt and Harburg.

At Waterloo, Halkett's brigade consisted of four battalions of Hanoverian militia or *Landwehr*, numbering perhaps 2,500 men in all. Posted near the château of Hougoumont, Halkett's moment of glory came at the close of the battle, when he galloped up to a disintegrating French column and collared General **Cambronne**, commander of the 1st Chasseurs à Pied of the Imperial Guard. Halkett describes the incident in a letter dated 20 December 1837, quoted by H.T. Siborne (1891):

187

During our advance we were in constant contact with the French
Guards, and I often called them to surrender. For some time I had
my eye upon, as I supposed, the General Officer in command of
the Guards (being in full uniform) trying to animate his men to
stand . . . After having received our fire with much effect, the
column left their General with two officers behind, when I ordered
the sharpshooters to dash on, and I made a gallop for the General.
When about cutting him down he called out he would surrender,
upon which he preceded me [to the rear], but I had not gone many
paces before my horse got a shot through his body and fell to the
ground. In a few seconds I got him on his legs again, and found my
friend, Cambronne, had taken French leave in the direction from
where he came. I instantly overtook him, laid hold of him by the
aiguillette, and brought him in safety and gave him in charge to a
sergeant of the Osnabruckers to deliver to the Duke.

Halkett's feat is also given an airing in *The Life of Baron Hugh
von Halkett* by E. von dem Knesebeck (1865), which features an eyewitness report by an officer of the Osnabruck Battalion:

A French general, accompanied by two other officers on horseback
were attempting to bring the Old Guard back to a standing position.
They tried very hard. One could see the General riding back and
forth encouraging his men, especially to shoot towards the enemy
rider (Halkett). Finally the General's horse was felled by a bullet.
The General lay under his horse and could not immediately free
himself. We called out to Colonel Halkett, who was in the first rows,
about this General – marked by his uniform as such and whom we
had been watching for a long time – who had now fallen from his
horse. As soon as the Colonel saw this he drew his sword, gave his
horse the spur, and raced in a gallop toward the fallen officer. He
passed among individual enemy soldiers causing them to flee and
thereby was actually right in the middle of the enemy. As the Colonel
came up to the fallen rider, the rider had been able to free himself
from his horse and was standing upright. I believed I saw the Colonel
take a stab at him. All of the gun crew from the vicinity and I myself
raced up to the scene because the Colonel obviously seemed to be in
very great danger. He could be killed from all sides – by shot or by a
bayonet. No Frenchman appeared to have time to come to the
rescue of his General as evidenced by the fact that both officers
accompanying the General had run away. The General was at this

moment the prisoner of the Colonel. The Colonel had taken hold of him by the collar and dragged him alongside his horse. I was 3–4 steps away and the first to come that close. Others followed. The Colonel, who was holding on to his prisoner, let him loose and asked who he was. The General was bleeding a lot from a head wound; the blood flowed over his entire face. He wiped away the blood from his mouth with his hand and answered 'Je suis le General Cambronne' – I am General Cambronne. Whether the wound Cambronne had was from the sword of Colonel Halkett or due to a shot I cannot say. We had only a few moments here because all of a sudden we had to go forward at the urging of the Colonel. Late in the evening as the battalion finally came to halt I heard that sergeant Fuhring and three men had escorted General Cambronne to Brussels.

After Waterloo the King's German Legion was disbanded and Halkett was put on British half-pay. He soldiered on as a major general in the Hanoverian Army until 1858, when, upon his retirement, the authorities made him a baron with a pension for life. Sadly, this act of gratitude and recognition came a little late in the day for the old Waterloo warrior, who was already a sick old man – he died in Hanover five years later.

Hamilton
Lieutenant Colonel James Inglis (1777–1815)

Commander of the 2nd Royal North British Dragoons (Scots Greys). Born in an army camp at Tayantroga during the American War of Independence, Hamilton was the second son of William Anderson, a Scottish sergeant major in the 21st Fusiliers. After the American campaign Anderson returned to Glasgow, apparently entrusting the care of his new son to General James Inglis Hamilton, his former regimental colonel. General Hamilton funded the boy's education and in 1792 secured him a cornet's commission in the Scots Greys. By this time Anderson junior was known by the name of his benefactor, entering the army as James Inglis Hamilton. With his patron's backing, Hamilton advanced rapidly up the career ladder, becoming lieutenant colonel of the Scots Greys in 1807, at the tender age of 30.

At Waterloo Hamilton's regiment – numbering over 400 sabres – formed part of the 2nd British (Union) Cavalry Brigade under Sir **William Ponsonby**. At the start of the battle the Union Brigade was held in reserve, posted behind **Picton**'s 5th British Infantry Division, left of the great Brussels high road. About 2 p.m., however, Lord **Uxbridge** – **Wellington**'s cavalry supremo – sent Ponsonby's Union Brigade and **Somerset**'s Household Brigade (posted to the right of the high road) into action against **d'Erlon**'s advancing I Corps. According to Corporal Dickson of F Troop, the Scots Greys, Lieutenant Colonel Hamilton waved his sabre aloft and shouted, 'Now the Scots Greys, charge!' before spurring his horse over a hedge, 'which he took in grand style' (Maughan, n.d.).

And so began the legendary 'charge' of the Scots Greys, immortalised in Lady Butler's 1881 painting *Scotland Forever* and the celebrated slow-motion sequence of Sergei Bondarchuk's 1970 movie, *Waterloo*. But it wasn't so much a charge as a canter: for no sooner had the Greys (apparently supporting **Muter**'s 6th Dragoons and Clifton's 1st Dragoons) ascended the reverse slope of Mont St Jean and crossed the lane that snaked along its crest, when they found themselves among the ranks of Picton's redcoats – in particular the Scottish troops of the 92nd Regiment – with the oncoming

The Scots Greys and Highland Infantry *by George Jones*

French a mere 30 yards beyond. According to General Sir Evelyn Wood (1895): 'As the Scots Greys passed through the 92nd Regiment, each corps mutually cheered the other, and many of the Highlanders, by holding on to the stirrups, passed on with the horsemen.'

As for Corporal Dickson, tagging after Hamilton with the rest of the Greys, he later recalled that:

> As we tightened our grip to descend the hillside among the corn, we could make out the feather bonnets of the Highlanders, and heard the officers crying out to them to wheel back by sections. A moment more and we were among them. Poor fellows! some of them had not time to get clear of us, and were knocked down. I remember one lad crying out, 'Eh! but I didna think ye wad ha'e hurt me sae.' They were all Gordons [i.e. the 92nd], and as we passed through them they shouted, 'Go at them, the Greys! Scotland for ever!' My blood thrilled at this, and I clutched my sabre tighter. Many of the Highlanders grasped our stirrups, and in the fiercest excitement dashed with us into the fight.

The head of the leading French column – that of General Marcognet – was composed of the 45th Line, not an elite formation as is sometimes reported but regular troops. According to an article by W.A. Thorburn (1998), late curator of the National War Museum of Scotland, 'the Greys simply *walked* into the 1/45th Infantry of the Line. There was no gallop and no "charge".' Nevertheless, the effect was devastating. Dickson continues:

> The French were uttering loud, discordant yells. Just then I saw the first Frenchman. A young officer of Fusiliers made a slash at me with his sword, but I parried it and broke his arm; the next second we were in the thick of them. We could not see five yards ahead for the smoke . . . The French were fighting like tigers. Some of the wounded were firing at us as we passed; and poor Kinchant, who had spared one of these rascals, was himself shot by the officer he had spared. As we were sweeping down a steep slope on the top of them, they had to give way. Then those in front began to cry out for 'quarter', throwing down their muskets and taking off their belts . . . I was now in the front rank, for many of ours had fallen. It was here that Lieutenant Trotter, from Morton Hall, was killed by a French officer after the first rush on the French. We now came to an open

space covered with bushes, and then I saw **Ewart** [a sergeant in Dickson's Troop], with five or six infantry men about him, slashing right and left at them. Armour [a comrade] and I dashed up to these half-dozen Frenchmen, who were trying to escape with one of their standards. I cried to Armour to 'Come on!' and we rode at them. Ewart had finished two of them, and was in the act of striking a third man who held the Eagle; next moment I saw Ewart cut him down, and he fell dead. I was just in time to thwart a bayonet-thrust that was aimed at the gallant sergeant's neck. Armour finished another of them. We cried out, 'Well done, my boy!' and as others had come up, we spurred on in search of a like success.

But the Greys bagged only one of two captured Eagles at Waterloo: that of the 105th Line being taken by Captain **Alexander Kennedy Clark** and/or Corporal **Styles** of the 1st (Royal) Dragoons.

Meanwhile, the infantry columns of Marcognet, **Quiot** and Donzelot – perhaps over 12,000 troops in all – had been completely overthrown by Ponsonby's dragoons, losing many men killed, wounded and taken prisoner; and away to the right, Somerset's troopers had trounced the French cavalry. Now, flushed with success and possessed by battle-fury, the two brigades mingled: as a result, all cohesion was lost, the dragoons failed to rally, and a madcap career across the battlefield ensued. According to Lieutenant Archibald Hamilton of Captain Payne's Troop, Scots Greys:

> After passing through and killing, wounding and making prisoners the whole of the advanced column of the French, we ought to have stopped and reformed the brigade: but our men were not contented with what they had done: they still went on.

But what about James Inglis Hamilton? Could he not have rallied his men? Corporal Dickson's account suggests that far from holding his men back, Hamilton urged them on: 'At this moment Colonel Hamilton rode up to us crying, "Charge! charge the guns!!" and went off like the wind up the hill towards the terrible battery.' And so, in the words of historians Grant and Youens (1972): 'Totally incapable of rallying or re-forming, they went galloping wildly up towards the French guns. Many artillerymen fell beneath their sabres as not only men but officers were caught up in the frenzy.'

Corporal Dickson was among the first to reach the guns of **Napoleon**'s grand battery – over 80 in number – positioned on the heights near La Belle Alliance:

> We sabred the gunners, lamed the horses, and cut their traces and harness. I can hear the Frenchmen yet crying 'Diable!' when I struck at them, and the long-drawn hiss through their teeth as my sword went home. Fifteen of their guns could not be fired again that day. The artillery drivers sat on their horses weeping aloud as we went among them; they were mere boys, we thought.

But Napoleon's revenge was swift. The Emperor had observed Hamilton's killing spree, commenting: 'Look at those grey horses! Who are these fine cavaliers? They are brave troops, but in half an hour I will cut them to pieces.' And he was as good as his word: for **Milhaud**'s cuirassiers and **Jacquinot**'s lancers were sent to scatter the exhausted British dragoons, the Greys alone losing over 200 casualties in the ensuing melee. Thus, as Grant and Youens (1972) describe:

> Napoleon . . . flung strong forces of light and heavy cavalry against the Greys and the rest of the brigade. Ponsonby fell and many more of his men were mercilessly slaughtered as they straggled back towards the Mont St Jean position.

Later, the French concluded that Hamilton and his men had been drunk: for the regiment's name – the Scots Greys – translates into French as *Écossais Gris*, and *gris* can mean also mean drunk.

As for Hamilton, he had taken his last ride, for according to Corporal Dickson:

> It was the last we saw of our Colonel, poor fellow! His body was found with both arms cut off. His pockets had been rifled. I once heard Major Clarke tell how he saw him wounded among the guns of the great battery, going at full speed, with the bridle-reins between his teeth, after he had lost his hands.

And according to historian Charles Dalton:

> Hamilton's body was found on the field – shot through the heart in addition to other wounds, and rifled. His trusty sword was gone, but

the scabbard and silken sash remained. These relics were transmitted to Lieutenant Jno. Anderson, the Colonel's brother.

Hill
General Rowland (1772–1842)

Commander of **Wellington**'s II Corps. One of the 16 children of Sir John Hill's (third baronet of Hawkstone, Shropshire), Rowland Hill entered the army in 1790. Four years later – thanks to the British system of purchasing army commissions – Hill was a lieutenant colonel at the tender age of 22. A veteran of Abercromby's Egyptian campaign of 1801, he was a major general by 1805. But it was during the Peninsular War of 1808–14 that Hill found fame. Present at Vimeiro (1808) and Corunna (1809), Hill led a victorious force at the Battle of Arroyo dos Molinos in 1811. The following year he was knighted and made a lieutenant general. From this point, Hill became Wellington's principal lieutenant, commanding the right wing of the Duke's army. Distinguishing himself in the latter battles of the Peninsular War, especially the Nivelle and Nive (both 1813), Hill displayed sound tactical judgement, while loyally operating under Wellington's guiding hand.

The great historian of the Peninsular War, Sir Charles Oman (1913), pays tribute to the General, describing him as 'a zealous Christian'; and adding that he was one of the very few officers 'to whom Wellington ever condescended in his correspondence to give the why and wherefore of a command that he issued: the others simply received orders without any commentary'. Indeed, Oman's character sketch of Hill is worth quoting in full:

> There can be no stronger contrast than that between the impression which the Iron Duke left on his old followers and that produced by his trusted and most responsible lieutenant, Sir Rowland Hill. Hill was blessed and kindly remembered wherever he went. He was a man brimming over with the milk of human kindness, and the mention of him in any diary is generally accompanied by some anecdote of an act of thoughtful consideration, some friendly word,

or piece of unpremeditated, often homely charity. A wounded officer from Albuera, who is dragging himself painfully back to Lisbon, reports himself to Hill as he passes his headquarters. Next morning 'the General himself attended me out on my road, to give me at parting a basket with tea, sugar, bread, butter, and a large venison pasty.' A grateful sergeant, who bore a letter to Hill in 1813, remembers how he expected nothing but a nod and an answer from such a great man, and was surprised to find that the General ordered his servant to give the messenger a supper, arranged for his billet that night, and next morn had his haversack stuffed with bread and meat, presented him with a dollar, and advised him where to sleep on his return journey. He would give an exhausted private a drink from the can that had just been brought for his personal use, or find time to bestow a piece of friendly advice on an unknown subaltern. This simple, pious, considerate old officer, whose later portraits show a decided resemblance to Mr Pickwick, was known everywhere among the rank and file as 'Daddy Hill'.

After **Napoleon**'s escape from Elba, on 26 February 1815, the British Cabinet sent Wellington to Belgium to organise forces for a projected invasion of France. Hill duly followed, arriving in Brussels on 2 April to take command of II Corps. He was also tasked with keeping a watchful eye on the 'Young Frog' – the 23-year-old Hereditary Prince of **Orange**, who, as a concession to his father, King William I of the Netherlands, had been given command of the Duke's I Corps. Hill's corps consisted of the 2nd British Infantry Division (under Lieutenant General Sir Henry Clinton), the 4th British Infantry Division (under Lieutenant General Sir **Charles Colville**) and a Netherlands Corps under Prince Frederick (younger brother of the Prince of Orange). But of these 27,000 troops only some 10,000 were deployed at Waterloo, the bulk of Colville's command and the whole of Prince Frederick's being sent to Hal, 8 miles west of the battlefield, for reasons best known to Wellington and debated by historians ever since (for some the Hal detachment was insurance against a Napoleonic outflanking manoeuvre, for others a strategic reserve in case of defeat). Thus, Hill's Waterloo brigade commanders were **Adam**, Mitchell, Plat and **Hew Halkett**. They were deployed on the far right of the Duke's line, covering the Nivelles road west of Hougoumont.

Private William Wheeler of the 51st Foot – one of Mitchell's battalions – describes the hail of iron and lead Allied troops were subjected to for much of the afternoon (Wheeler 1951):

> On the hill behind us . . . was posted some 20 or 30 guns blazing away over our heads at the enemy. The enemy on their side with a battery of much the same force were returning the compliment, grape and shells were dupping about like hail, this was devilish annoying. As we could not see the enemy, although they were giving us a pretty good sprinkling of musketry, our buglers sounded to lie down. At this moment a man near me was struck and as I was rising to render assistance I was struck by a spent ball on the inside of my right knee . . . A shell now fell into the column of the 15th Hussars and bursted. I saw a sword and scabbard fly out from the column. It was now time to shift our ground to a place of shelter, the Hussars moved to the left and we advanced again to the crossroad under a sharp shower of shells. One of the shells pitched on the breast of a man some little distance on my right, he was knocked to atoms.

By the late afternoon, however, it became clear to Hill that Wellington's right flank was not seriously menaced, and he began filtering units into the fight for Hougoumont. Hill arrived on the scene about 7.30 p.m., just as the French were advancing to their final, fatal assault on Mont St Jean, spearheaded by five battalions of the Imperial Guard. It was then that Hill's horse was shot (apparently sustaining five separate injuries) and as it fell, the General took a tumble and was badly concussed. For the next 30 minutes or so Hill was out of action. At first he was thought to have been killed, but eventually surfaced with nothing more serious than a few bruises. Meantime the fate of the fight had been decided: the Imperial Guard had been repulsed by cannon, musket and bayonet, and Wellington's hard-pressed troops unleashed for a victorious romp across the battlefield. In a letter to his sister, dated 24 July 1815, Hill declared: 'I verily believe there never was so tremendous a battle fought as that at Waterloo.'

On 7 July the Allies entered Paris to put Louis XVIII back on his throne. Bonaparte, having abdicated after defeat at Waterloo, surrendered to the captain of HMS *Bellerophon* (who happened to be the brother of Major General **Peregrine Maitland**, scourge of the Emperor's Imperial Guard at Waterloo) a week later. Hill accompanied the army to Paris, later becoming second-in-command of Wellington's Army of Occupation, which remained on French turf till 1818. Having received his share of awards, medals and honours, Hill replaced Wellington as Commander-in-Chief of the British Army in 1828 (the Duke having become Prime Minister). During his tenure, Hill sought to improve the lot of the British soldier: combatting drunkenness, providing educational facilities like regimental libraries, and curbing the practice of flogging. His kindness to the common soldier earned him the sobriquet of 'the soldier's friend'. In September 1842 – three months before his death – 'Daddy Hill' became Viscount Hill. He was buried at the village church of Hadnall, in Shropshire.

Hitchens
Richard (dates unknown)

Assistant-surgeon attached to G Troop, Royal Horse Artillery. According to Dr Martin Howard (2002), almost half of **Wellington**'s medical officers at Waterloo had no previous experience of battle. Howard goes on to say that: 'With so many rookie doctors at Waterloo, it is not surprising that at least one or two became visibly alarmed as the fighting intensified.' And such was the case with Hitchens. Having assisted G Troop's first casualty, **Philip Hunt**, Hitchens accompanied the guns when they were moved up to the front line in the afternoon. There, amid the roar of cannon and crackle of musketry, the medic was immediately overawed. Captain **Mercer**, G Troop's commander, records (Mercer 1927) that Hitchens:

> began staring round in the wildest and most comic manner imaginable, twisting himself from side to side, exclaiming, 'My God, Mercer, what is that? What is all this noise? How curious! How very curious!' And when a cannon-shot rushed hissing past, 'There!

There! What is it all?' It was with great difficulty that I persuaded him to retire.

Hunt
Philip (dates unknown)

First casualty of G Troop, Royal Horse Artillery. (For the Troop's first fatality, see **John Butterworth**.) When the battle began, G Troop's commander, **Mercer** (1927) – 'being impatient of standing idle' – disobeyed Wellington's order not to engage in counter-battery fire. Instead, Mercer flung shells at a distant French battery sited on the Nivelles road. Moments later, shot poured in from powerful enemy guns, firing unseen and with great precision. Alarmed, Mercer tried to mask his position by ordering a ceasefire, but it was too late for Gunner Hunt:

> I shall never forget the scream the poor lad gave when struck. It was one of the last they fired, and shattered his left arm to pieces as he stood between the waggons. That scream went to my very soul, for I accused myself as having caused his misfortune. I was, however, obliged to conceal emotion from the men, who had turned to look at him; so, bidding them 'stand to their front' I continued my walk up and down, whilst **Hitchins** ran to his assistance.

Hunt survived his wounds and on 10 December 1815 received his discharge.

Jacquinot
Charles Claude, Baron (1772–1848)

Commander of the 1st Cavalry Division of **d'Erlon**'s I Corps at Waterloo. A graduate of military academy, Jacquinot joined the French Army in 1791 as an infantry lieutenant. Two years later he switched to the cavalry, becoming a *sous lieutenant* (i.e. second lieutenant) in the 1st Chasseurs à Cheval. A veteran of the Revolutionary Wars, Jacquinot went on to serve in **Napoleon**'s Grand Army, distinguishing himself at the Battles of Austerlitz, Jena, Eylau and Wagram. A career soldier who regarded himself loyal to the army, as opposed to a particular leader of doctrine, Jacquinot's talents as a cavalry commander were rewarded with steady steps up the promotion ladder. In 1812 he was given command of a brigade in Bruyère's 1st Light Cavalry Division (alongside **Marie-Guillaume Piré**, who would lead the 2nd Cavalry Division of **Reille**'s II Corps at Waterloo) during the campaign against Russia, and was present at the Battles of Smolensk, Borodino and Vinkovo. The following year Jacquinot attained the rank of divisional general, having fought through the German War of Liberation and received a severe wound at Dennewitz (5 September 1813) during **Ney**'s drive on Berlin. In 1814 Jacquinot took command of the 6th Light

Cavalry Division during the campaign of France, seeing action at Bar-sur-Aube under Kellermann (27 February 1814), and at Saint Dizier 23 March 1814).

Following Napoleon's first abdication of 6 April 1814, Jacquinot was initially retained in office by the Bourbons, but was nudged into retirement on half-pay several months later, thanks to Royalist paranoia concerning ex-Bonapartist officers. Despite this setback, Jacquinot kept a low profile when Napoleon jumped exile and returned to France in the spring of 1815. Never a rabid Bonapartist, he preferred to wait on events before making his move. Eventually, however, Jacquinot was obliged to declare his colours, and on 1 June 1815 accepted command of the 1st Cavalry Division of d'Erlon's I Corps. The division consisted of two brigades: the 1st Brigade, under Baron Bruno, was composed of the 7th Hussars (led by Colonel **Marbot**, who would become a celebrated memoirist) and the 3rd Chasseurs à Cheval; the 2nd Brigade, under Baron Gobrecht, was composed of the 3rd and 4th Lancers (led by Colonel **Brô**, another chronicler).

On 16 June 1815, while Ney battled with the Prince of **Orange** and **Wellington** at Quatre-Bras, and Napoleon engaged **Blücher** at Ligny, the soldiers of I Corps – including Jacquinot's division – fired not a shot. This was due to the wanderings of d'Erlon, the corps commander, who spent the day marching and counter-marching between the two battles and fighting at neither (apart from d'Erlon himself, blame for this fiasco has been laid at the feet of **Soult**, Ney and **Labédoyère**). But on 17 June, amid a torrential downpour that culminated in a ferocious thunderstorm, Jacquinot dogged Wellington north from Quatre-Bras to Waterloo, his horsemen skirmishing with Allied cavalry under Lord **Uxbridge**.

At Waterloo, Jacquinot's division – approximately 1,500 sabres-strong – was posted on Napoleon's far right. Elements of the division (notably Brô's 4th Lancers), successfully counter-charged British cavalry brigades under **Somerset** and Sir **William Ponsonby**, badly mauling blown dragoons who failed to rally after upsetting d'Erlon's infantry columns. A couple of hours later, Jacquinot was ordered to take post on the heights above Frischermont, there to block the approach of **Bülow**'s Prussians, already seen advancing on the French right flank. Jacquinot stood his ground till about

4.30 p.m., when Prussian cavalry, emerging from the Bois de Paris, shunted his troopers back to the Waterloo battlefield. When the order to retreat came, Jacquinot conducted an orderly withdrawal, and was not 'routed' as some accounts suggest.

After Waterloo, Jacquinot was again retained by the Bourbons, leading some to question his loyalty to Bonaparte. But as before, he soon found himself out of a job and on half-pay. He was recalled in 1816, however, and made an inspector general of cavalry. Two years later Jacquinot joined the General Staff, and was later reappointed to the command of a cavalry division. He retired from the army on 12 April 1848 and died 12 days later.

Jardin
père or *aîné* (father or the elder) (dates unkonwn)

Napoleon's celebrated horse-breaker, present at Waterloo as a member of the Emperor's personal staff. Unlike the athletic **Wellington**, Napoleon was considered an awkward rider, and yet, as Matthew Morgan (2004) states, the Emperor was also considered 'both fast and fearless' – an observation supported by the fact that some 18 horses were killed under him during his career. A small man (though not unusually so, for the period), Napoleon preferred small horses – much to the disdain of his entourage – and as Jill Hamilton (2000) informs us: 'Arabs were the horses on which he was most at ease and his horse-buyers were usually advised not to purchase any large horses for him.' And it was these sensitive, spirited animals Jardin was employed to tame.

According to Barry O'Meara (1822), Napoleon once commented that 'A horse has memory, knowledge, and love.' Jardin capitalised on the former attribute by putting the Emperor's horses through a punishing training course designed to prepare them for active service. Jardin's methods were brutal but effective. First, he accustomed new mounts to pain by beating them with whips. Then he inured them to noise by beating drums in their ears. He prepared them for sudden distractions by waving flags in their eyes and rolling live sheep or pigs under their hooves. And he hardened them to the experience of battle by letting off pistols, muskets – even cannon and rockets – nearby. And so, if not the kindest horse-breaker in Europe, Jardin was probably the best: the Emperor's horses remaining calm on parade ground or battlefield.

At Waterloo, Jardin remained close to Napoleon – holding the reins of his horse according to some accounts – and this proximity gave him chance to observe the Emperor's moods. Later, this material formed the basis of a narrative quoted by Mackenzie Macbride (1911) in *With Napoleon at Waterloo*. During the morning of 18 June, Jardin tells us that Napoleon: 'showed extreme depression; however, everything was going on as well as could be expected with the French'. At 2 p.m., with the fighting 'desperate', Jardin observed that:

> Napoleon rode through the lines and gave orders to make certain that every detail was executed with promptitude; he returned often to the spot where in the morning he had started, there he dismounted and, seating himself in a chair which was brought to him, he placed his head between his hands and rested his elbows on his knees. He remained thus absorbed sometimes for half an hour, and then rising up suddenly would peer through his glasses on all sides to see what was happening.

At 3 p.m., according to Jardin, Napoleon ordered **d'Erlon** to reinforce I Corps, 'suffering so heavily' on the French right wing: Napoleon's face showing 'a look of disquietude'. At 6 p.m. Jardin observed an officer of the Chasseurs à Cheval of the Imperial Guard gallop up to Napoleon, raise his hat, and declare the battle won. Napoleon then 'rode off at a gallop close to the ranks encouraging the soldiers'. But the report was false and by 9 p.m. all was lost – Napoleon's earlier hopes of victory dashed on the slopes of Mont St Jean and in the corpse-strewn streets of Plancenoit:

> He remained on the battlefield until half-past nine when it was absolutely necessary to leave. Assured of a good guide, we passed to the right of Genappes and through the fields; we marched all the night without knowing too well where we were going until the morning. Towards four o'clock in the morning we came to Charleroi, where Napoleon, owing to the onrush of the army in

beating a retreat, had much difficulty in proceeding. At last after he had left the town, he found in a little meadow on the right a small bivouac fire made by some soldiers. He stopped by it to warm himself and said to General Corbineau, 'Et bien Monsieur, we have done a fine thing.' General Corbineau saluted him and replied, 'Sire, it is the utter ruin of France.' Napoleon turned round, shrugged his shoulders and remained absorbed for some moments. He was at this time extremely pale and haggard and much changed. He took a small glass of wine and a morsel of bread which one of his equerries had in his pocket, and some moments later mounted, asking if the horse galloped well. He went as far as Philippeville where he arrived at midday and took some wine to revive himself. He again set out at two o'clock in a mail carriage towards Paris, where he arrived on the 21st at 7 a.m.

Jérôme
Prince (1784–1860)

Jérôme Bonaparte (1784–1860)

Napoleon's brother and commander of the 6th Infantry Division at Waterloo. The youngest – and in Philip Haythornthwaite's words (1998) 'perhaps least talented' – of Napoleon's brothers, Jérôme began his military career with a stint in the Consular Guard. But big brother had big plans for the stripling, transferring him to the navy with the rank of admiral. Lacking the experience and maturity such a post demands, playboy Jérôme jumped ship in America, got involved with Baltimore beauty Elizabeth Patterson, and promptly married her. Napoleon was furious, and when the happy couple returned to France, refused to let Elizabeth ashore. Pregnant with a baby Bonaparte boy, she was sent packing by the Emperor, who annulled the marriage. (Elizabeth gave birth to Jérôme Napoleon in London, in 1805, before returning to Baltimore with a pension of 60,000 francs a year courtesy of Napoleon.) Jérôme was then shackled to Princess Catherina of Württemberg and given the newly created kingdom of Westphalia to play with.

But Napoleon was disgusted by Jérôme's behaviour, referring to him as a 'prodigal' and a 'libertine'. According to Saxon soldier-diplomat Ferdinand von Funck (1931), Jérôme's

> rapid rise in rank had fostered all the self-confidence of one born in the purple with the hotheadedness of an undisciplined, wealthy youngster. Because he had grown up to be the brother of the most powerful monarch in the world, he regarded nothing as impossible; everything had, in his opinion, to give way to his mere wishes, his whims, and even every naughtiness whereby he meant no harm had to be permitted him. He was therefore capable of committing acts of great harshness and injustice, not of any evil intent, but from sheer irresponsibility. Human beings did not count at all in his eyes. They were only there to submit to every whim of the Bonaparte family, called by destiny to rule over them.

No wonder the Westphalians were glad to see the back of Jérôme when, in 1812, Napoleon gave him command of his VIII Corps for the coming invasion of Russia. But Jérôme's absence was short-lived: he quarrelled with his imperial brother two weeks into the campaign, and in a fit of pique, packed his bags and headed home. The following year, having reduced Westphalia to near-bankruptcy (despite an income in excess of 10 million francs per annum from foreign revenue, plus taxes levied on his own subjects), Jérôme was thrown out of his tiny kingdom. First he went to Switzerland, and then to Italy: finally, in spring 1815, Jérôme rejoined Napoleon in France, following the Emperor's return to power. He was rewarded with command of an infantry division for the Waterloo campaign.

Part of **Reille**'s II Corps, Jérôme's 6th Infantry Division was Napoleon's biggest and best, containing 13 battalions of crack troops from the 1st and 2nd Light and 1st and 2nd Line Regiments (for more on the 1st Light Regiment, see **Jean-Baptiste Jolyet**). Although Jérôme was in charge, Napoleon appointed General Armand Charles Guilleminot – an acknowledged master of tactics – to keep an eye on his wayward brother, and, as Tony Linck (1993) puts it, 'curb any rash ideas the young Bonaparte might have'. At first this arrangement worked well, Jérôme taking note of Guilleminot's advice. The division fought at Quatre-Bras on 16 June, aiding in the capture of Piraumont and Gemioncourt farms and the clearing of Bossu Wood. Next day, with **Wellington** retreating north to Waterloo, Jérôme followed, but found time to stop off at the Roi d'Espagne inn at Genappe. It was here that a waiter – who had served Wellington breakfast that morning – reported a conversation overheard at the Duke's table. According to the waiter, one of Wellington's aides had spoken of a junction with **Blücher**'s Prussians near the Forest of Soignies. Even the route of Blücher's march was given – via Wavre. Jérôme passed the intelligence to Napoleon, but the Emperor was dismissive: he had crushed Blücher at Ligny and **Grouchy** was in pursuit. According to historian Christopher Hibbert (1967), Napoleon quashed Jérôme's news with: 'the junction between the English and the Prussians is impossible for at least two days'.

On the morning of Waterloo Day, 18 June, Jérôme's division took post on the left of Napoleon's line with the rest of Reille's corps. Before them, nestling behind a small wood, stood the château of Hougoumont, which guarded Wellington's right flank and dominated the approaches to the Allied line atop the ridge of Mont St Jean. According to historian Hilaire Belloc (1931):

> The plan in the Emperor's mind was perfectly simple. There was to be no turning of the right nor of the left flank of the enemy, which would only have the effect of throwing back that enemy east or west. His line was to be pierced, the village of Mont St Jean, which lay on the ridge of Wellington's position and which overlooks the plateau on every side, was to be carried, and this done, Napoleon would be free to decide upon his next action, according to the nature and extent of the disorder into which he had thrown the enemy's broken line.

But first Napoleon ordered an assault on Hougoumont. The idea was to weaken Wellington's centre by forcing the Duke to reinforce this vital outpost. Consequently, Napoleon ordered Reille to advance on Hougoumont and occupy the château's wood, orchard and gardens: the first gun announcing this manoeuvre was thus the first gun fired at Waterloo. After a brief artillery exchange, the French infantry marched down to Hougoumont Wood facing them. The foot soldiers concerned were Jérôme's. At this point, Guilleminot's influence over Jérôme evaporated and things went badly wrong. Belloc continues:

> Napoleon had no other intention that history can discover in pressing the attack against Hougomont so early. It was almost in the nature of a 'feint'. But when, towards half-past twelve, his brother's division had cleared the wood and come up against the high garden wall of the farm, for some reason which cannot be determined, whether the eagerness of the troops, the impulsiveness of Jérôme himself, or whatever cause, instead of being contented with holding the wood according to orders, the French furiously attacked the loopholed and defended wall. They attempted to break in the great door, which was recessed, and therefore protected by a murderous cross-fire. They were beaten back into the wood, leaving a heap of dead. At this point Reille, according to his own account (which may well enough be accurate), sent orders for the division to remain in the wood, and not to waste itself against so strong an outpost. But Jérôme and his men were not to be denied. They marched round the chateau, under a heavy artillery fire from the English batteries above, and attempted to carry the north wall. As they were so doing, four companies of the Coldstreams, the sole reinforcement which Wellington could be tempted to part with from his main line, came in reinforcement to the defence, and, after a sharp struggle, the French were thrust back once more.

According to historian A.F. Becke (1914):

> Jérôme had entirely misinterpreted Napoleon's project. The Emperor only intended a thrust to be delivered at Hougoumont, so as to draw the Duke's attention to a secondary part of his line and induce him to weaken his centre in order to reinforce his right. Unhappily for the French, Jérôme engaged in a murderous struggle which went in favour of the resolute garrison of Hougoumont, who kept fully employed around the château a very superior number of assailants, as well as the numerous reinforcements who were drawn into the vortex of strife which raged all day for the possession of the buildings.

And so Jérôme turned Napoleon's feint against Hougoumont into a battle-within-a battle, lasting all day, and soaking up some 15,000 French troops better employed elsewhere. Several separate assaults were made against the bastion, but the garrison under **Macdonell** held firm.

Thousands of Frenchmen lost their lives at Hougoumont, leading Victor Hugo (1862) to pronounce the place 'a funereal spot'. In the late afternoon, the 'impossible' junction between Blücher and Wellington took place, just as Jérôme's waiter said it would. Caught between two fires, Napoleon launched a last-minute bid to break Wellington's line with his Imperial Guard. With the band playing *La Marche des Bonnets à Poil*, Napoleon led his 'Immortals' forward around 7.30 p.m. But when the columns reached the bottom of the valley, Napoleon stood aside and waved his warriors on. Jérôme – who had assumed his brother would command this final assault in person – exclaimed: 'Can it be possible he will not seek death here? He will never find a more glorious grave!' He had a point and Napoleon knew it. Years later, in exile on St Helena and dying of stomach cancer, the fallen Emperor ruefully observed: 'to be killed at Waterloo would have been a good death'. (According to **Coignet** (1928) of the Imperial Guard, Napoleon expressed a desire to seek death on the battlefield but was dissuaded by his generals.)

But if the historians are to be believed, Napoleon was half dead at Waterloo anyway, plagued by a bewildering number of maladies including (from A to Z): acromegaly (a rare disease involving overproduction of growth hormone by the pituitary gland, resulting in abnormal enlargement of the hands, feet and face); arsenic poisoning; constipation; cystitis (inflammation of the bladder and urinary tract, resulting in severe pain in passing water and accompanied by fever); obesity; stomach ulcers; thrombosed internal piles (swollen veins at or near the anus, also called haemorrhoids); urinary stones; and venereal disease. And yet Napoleon never complained of being ill at Waterloo, merely 'fatigued'. It is generally recognised, however, that the Emperor was unwell on 18 June, spending most of the day in an old armchair at Rossomme, more than a mile from the front (some reports have him sitting on a stool before a collapsible card table, others sitting in his bulletproof coach). Historian Russell F. Weigley (1993) explains the Emperor's demeanour thus: 'Napoleon was only forty-six but the accumulated strain of his years of ambition and responsibility had left him with the deteriorated constitution of a much older man.' And yet, according to noted military historian J.F.C. Fuller (1954), Napoleon was 'no better or worse than he had been at Marengo, Austerlitz, Jena, and Leipzig; a man so mastered by his genius that at times he lived in a land of illusions'.

But confirmation of Napoleon's physical suffering and distress at Waterloo was given by Jérôme, in what may be seen as an act of meanness (in revealing a previously well-kept secret) or an act of generosity (in revealing an important historical fact). For according to Jérôme, his imperial brother did indeed suffer from one of the ailments listed above while at Waterloo: piles. Napoleon always kept this embarrassing problem hidden – confiding only in Marchand, his valet, **Larrey**, his doctor, and Jérôme, his brother. But it was the latter – once told by Napoleon that 'Honour is the best currency' – who saw fit to uncover the truth. As author David Howarth (1968) states:

> to suffer from piles was not a dignified mishap . . . and it was only
> Jérôme who revealed the secret, years after the Emperor's death . . .
> His own remedy was to apply leeches to the affected parts, but
> Larrey had a lotion that he recommended. In an acute attack, the
> piles would no doubt have prolapsed and become extremely painful.

This, then, goes some way to explaining Napoleon's lethargy at Waterloo and his unwillingness to observe and direct events from the saddle of his horse, as he had in previous battles.

Napoleon once complained to Jérôme: 'You think and talk of nothing but trifles.' Nevertheless, in the autumn of his life, the 'prodigal' Bonaparte ended up as Governor of Les Invalides, a Marshal of France and President of the Senate. Perhaps big brother would have been proud, having written the following lines to kid brother in 1802: 'Die young and I shall accept your death – but not if you have lived without glory, without being useful to your country, without leaving a trace of your existence: for that is not to have lived at all.'

Jerzmanowski
Lieutenant Colonel Jan Pawel, Baron (1779–1862)

Commander of **Napoleon**'s celebrated Polish lancers at Waterloo. Born in Poland at Mniewo, Jerzmanowski joined the Légion Polonaise of the French Army in 1800, rising to the rank of lieutenant within a year. By 1807 Jerzmanowski had become a captain in the elite Chevaux-Légers Lanciers Polonais of the Imperial Guard, via staff appointments with Generals Ordener and Duroc. Further distinctions followed: in 1809 Jerzmanowski was wounded at Wagram; in 1813 he received the Legion of Honour and was made a baron of the Empire; in 1814 he was wounded at Craonne and promoted to major. But Jerzmanowski's finest hour was yet to come. For when Napoleon embarked on his first stint of exile in May 1814, Jerzmanowski followed with 118 Polish veterans: volunteers who wished to form part of the fallen Emperor's bodyguard on the tiny island of Elba. And although only 22 of these loyal Poles had horses, they formed the nucleus of the legendary Elba Squadron, destined to charge with the Imperial Guard at Waterloo.

The island of Elba, off the west coast of Italy, had been chosen by Tsar Alexander as Napoleon's open prison. There, he was to be nominal sovereign over some 112,000 subjects – primarily Tuscans, Spaniards and Neapolitans. Meanwhile, Allied commissioners would keep a watchful eye over the erstwhile Emperor, who was promised an income of 2 million francs a year by Louis XVIII, the Bourbon monarch who replaced him at the Tuileries.

Napoleon set up home in an eighteenth-century house, originally built to accommodate the governor of Elba's gardener. A tiny army of less than 1,000 Imperial Guardsmen – including Jerzmanowski's Poles – remained at his command. But after a promising start to life as a castaway king, Napoleon grew restless. For a start, he soon got bored with his Lilliputian kingdom, and with being a tourist attraction: registering his dissatisfaction with interminable parties of sightseers by staying indoors and playing cards. Meanwhile, the new Royalist French government had seen fit to renege on its promise to provide Napoleon with cash, leaving the ex-Emperor financially embarassed. And finally, rumours that the Bourbons were secretly plotting to remove him from Europe – or even to assassinate him – began reaching Bonaparte's ears.

Fully aware of the disenchantment growing in France over Bourbon rule, Napoleon decided it was time to stage a comeback: after all, he had nothing to lose. His chance came when Campbell, the British Commissioner on Elba, departed for a 10-day sojourn on the Italian mainland (to consult his doctor according to some accounts, to see his mistress according to others). The Emperor ordered seven small ships to be prepared in secret, and on 26 February 1815, under cover of darkness, he slipped away with 1,000 men and 800,000 francs in gold to conquer a new country: France. Thus, as the Polish historian Dr Maryan Kukiel (1912) states:

> Napoleon's conquest of France began. A conquest that did not shed a drop of blood. The old campaigners following the Emperor did not have to shoot; and the Polish light cavalrymen did not have to lower their lances. The sight of the Emperor was enough for the Army that had been sent to fight him: after a moment of inner conflict, these soldiers broke their lines, crying out 'Vive l'Empereur!' White cockades – the symbol of betrayal – were trampled, tricolores and imperial Eagles appeared from hiding, and the handful of companions surrounding Napoleon became an avalanche. The Bourbon government fell apart, the King and his court fled to Belgium, followed by his ministers and a few generals . . . The [Polish] light cavalrymen entered Paris in triumph, some of them mounted . . . others on foot, stooping under the weight of their saddles and equipment. Soon, the whole of Napoleon's 'Elba Squadron' would be mounted, following the resurrected Emperor.

The last week of March 1815 saw Napoleon back on his throne and Jerzmanowski's Poles back in their Parisian barracks. In fact, the men of the Elba Squadron were packed into 12 rooms, bare of beds or even a stick of furniture: so Jerzmanowski's men slept on the floor.

Napoleon, meanwhile, sought to tighten his tenuous grip on the reins of power. His situation was certainly a precarious one: France divided in its support for him, Europe united in its oppostion. Kukiel relates the outcome:

The Emperor hoped in vain to make peace with Europe. Faced with Napoleon's return, the world powers . . . now united. The Seventh Coalition was born in a single moment. The Austrians would march slowly from the east. **Wellington**'s English Army and **Blücher**'s Prussian Army were in Belgium, preparing to march. The Emperor and his excellent Army would throw themselves among them. Before the two Allied armies could concentrate, he would smash them with two great blows. Then he would return to France to hit the flank of the main coalition partner, if the coalition survived the defeat in Belgium.

And so the conceptual framework of Napoleon's Waterloo campaign was born.

Meanwhile, Jerzmanowski – now a lieutenant colonel – prepared his lancers for war. But while the Poles of the Elba Squadron had been languishing in exile, their homeland had fallen under Russian influence, and a new Polish Army was being raised for service with the Tsar. Consequently, Jerzmanowski received orders from Konstanty Pawtowicz, commander-in-chief of the Tsar's Polish forces, recalling the men of the Elba Squadron 'on pain of the highest punishment'. The order was ignored. As Kukiel comments: 'the Poles of the Elba Squadron would perform their final fatal service for Napoleon'. But there were not enough Poles under Jerzmanowski's command to form an independent unit. In the event, the Elba Squadron was absorbed into **Colbert**'s 2nd Chevaux-Légers Lanciers of the Imperial Guard (the famous Dutch or Red Lancers), becoming the regiment's 1st Squadron. Meanwhile, Jerzmanowski became Colbert's deputy, handing over tactical command of the Elba Squadron to Major Balinski.

As to the campaign itself, Kukiel summarises the part played by Jerzmanowski's lancers:

> The Polish cavalrymen fought the Prussians at Ligny. Next day they took part in the impetuous chase after Wellington to La Belle Alliance. Finally, on 18 June, they halted at Mont St Jean to join the Battle of Waterloo . . . The Polish cavalrymen took part in **Ney**'s mad, untimely attacks, which exhausted all Napoleon's cavalry.

The cuirassiers were supposed to break through the enemy's lines, the light cavalry widening the gap with lances and swords. The Elba Squadron charged ahead of the other squadrons of cavalry. General Colbert and Jerzmanowski led that heroic regiment to meet the English cavalry, to face batteries belching fire, or iron squares of infantry . . . The cavalry attack, which was not supported by infantry, was defeated. But Napoleon's cavalry reformed and charged again, galloping over the enemy's guns. From 3 p.m. till . . . 7 p.m. the Elba Squadron charged again and again, obstinately, desperately.

But ultimately in vain. Defeat at Waterloo heralded Napoleon's second and final abdication on 22 June 1815. The Allies occupied Paris, Louis XVIII returned, and the Imperial Guard was disbanded. As for Jerzmanowski – who had been wounded in the great battle – he was instructed to lead his Polish troops back to Warsaw and service with the Russians. But Jerzmanowski – a staunch Bonapartist and political exile – returned to France in 1819, where he remained till the end of his days. In 1831 Jerzmanowski found employment as a cavalry colonel; and on 5 December 1840 he was among those who welcomed the return of Napoleon's remains from St Helena. Jerzmanowski died in Paris aged 83.

According to Ferdinand von Funck (1931), a Saxon courtier, 'Napoleon had got to know the Poles in his Italian wars and to value them for fine soldiers.' And indeed, Bonaparte could count himself lucky that Polish émigrés had marched to France when their own country was gobbled up by Russia, Prussia and Austria in the late eighteenth century. For the dismemberment of Poland, coinciding as it did with the French Revolutionary Wars, gave Poles the chance to hit back at their own oppressors while serving under the tricolour. Later, Napoleon harnessed the fighting qualities and patriotic zeal of the Poles by hinting at a reconstitution of their kingdom. In 1807 a step towards this goal was taken with the creation of the Grand Duchy of Warsaw, a French satellite whose soldiers marched with Napoleon's Grand Army. But full freedom for the Poles never materialised under Napoleon, and after the Emperor's final defeat at Waterloo, Polish nationalism was forced underground. The country did not re-emerge as a national entity until 1918.

According to historian Frank McLynn (1997), Napoleon 'was clearly a man fated to be betrayed by all those he had helped and protected'. But this charge cannot be levelled at the Poles, who, if anything, were more devoted to the Emperor than the French. Sadly, Jerzmanowski's Poles did not gain a kingdom at Waterloo, but in 1990 they did gain a stone, erected on the battlefield and inscribed: 'To the officers, NCOs and soldiers of the Polish Squadron who fell at Mont St Jean, 18 June 1815'.

Jolyet
Major Jean-Baptiste (1785–1863)

Fought at Waterloo as *chef de battaillon* (major) in the 1st Regiment of Light Infantry, led by Colonel Cubières. A distant cousin of Marshal Moncey, Jolyet began his military career as a *sous lieutenant* (1st lieutenant) in the 42nd Regiment in 1805, and was a veteran of the Peninsular War and the Battles of Bautzen and Leipzig in 1813. At Waterloo, caught up in the meat-grinding battle for Hougoumont, Jolyet's regiment had sustained over 60 per cent casualties by the early evening, including Colonel Cubières, who was seriously wounded. The survivors were rallied by General Guilleminot, who sent his aide-de-camp to Prince **Jérôme** for news. It was about 7 p.m. when the messenger returned, carrying word from Jérôme that Marshal **Grouchy** was approaching and the battle was as good as won. But within moments Jolyet and his men were showered with roundshot, while gawping at the novel sight of the Imperial Guard in full retreat down the slopes of Mont St Jean. Jolyet was in the act of forming his survivors into column when he was struck in the stomach by a musket ball and thrown from his horse.

Jolyet describes what happened next in an astonishing narrative, quoted by Teissedre (2000) (my translation):

> Two chasseurs from my battalion supported me under the arms and led me a little way to the rear. Despite the pain, I forced myself to walk, as balls and shells fell in great profusion. A shell smashed the

musket of one of my chasseurs without injuring the man at all. When we came to the fields beyond the road, I urged our troops to escape at all costs . . . hoping the chaos would abate at the first favourable position. Alas! The more I walked, the plainer I could see that the rout was gaining momentum.

And so I arrived at Genappe. Carts, carriages, caissons were piled so high, one upon the other, that any man who ventured into the brawl was very likely to be crushed. My guides, who, in spite of my orders and exhortations, refused to abandon me, entered a backstreet. Exhausted by fatigue and loss of blood, I collapsed in a house, the door of which was open. There I found not a few other wounded soldiers, and a medical orderly hurriedly dressed my wound without any preparation. He gave me a crumb of bread and a drop of beer, which helped revive me, and I lay on the straw – glad to rest and hoping our troops would rally on the heights of Genappe and take their revenge next day.

Suddenly, when we least expected it, we heard Prussian bugles sounding in the street. I will never forget the sensation I experienced on hearing these triumphal blasts. We whispered to each other: 'Poor France! Poor Army!' and we thought – with rage and shame – that nothing could save us from capture. Even so, though we believed that all those burdened with such sorrow must lose their freedom, one of us extinguished the candle and closed the door. All night we expected to be delivered up to the Prussian troops, but no one entered the house . . .

It was hardly light when someone banged at the door with numerous blows. Left no choice but to open the door, a Prussian officer and NCO entered, and I was obliged to give them my watch and a portion of my money (the rest was hidden in one of my shoes). They also took my epaulettes and anything that had any value. They seemed to suggest that I was lucky to have been stripped of my possessions and not my life. Hardly had they left when others of their kind arrived, also requiring money, turning us over in all directions and searching everywhere. I must say that some, seeing my bloody clothing and my carelessly bandaged wound, refrained from touching me. But a Prussian drummer wanted my boots, and twice pursued me round the room, trying to pull them off. His comrades indignantly threw him out of the door.

I remained until midday in this state – hustled and threatened with death by the soldiers of every regiment that passed. One took my straps, another my neckcloth, another my belt, another my shirt: but one was magnanimous enough to leave me my hat and my breeches.

But my faithful chasseurs told me that someone had set up an ambulance post in the house opposite. Taking me by the arms once more, they led me there, dishevelled, blood-stained, my breeches slipping over my loins and my head covered by a black silk bonnet! It was necessary to cross the Prussian columns in this state, whose soldiers treated us as fools. I finally arrived at the ambulance, the surgeon quickly made me a bandage, and I lay down on the floor.

The ambulance post was established at an inn, where **Blücher** had slept the previous night [presumably Le Roi d'Espagne]. An aide-de-camp, who had remained behind, took pity on me and gave me a glass of wine. Then we were informed that a Prussian convoy would soon arrive, and the place must be emptied of all wounded. I left via the courtyard, where I found a captain of the Dragoons of the Guard, who cut as sad a figure as me. His name was Monsieur de Gasc, if I remember correctly.

Obliged to seek a lodging, we arrived at a smart house, in front of which were two French officers – aides-de-camp of General **Duhesme**. They told us the General was mortally wounded in the head, and we must let him die in peace. They pointed out a small building where we could find a room at the top of a steep staircase. At the cost of great suffering, I climbed the stairs and retired to a small room, where I found a bed. The Captain of Dragoons, who could not lie down because of his wound, took the mattress, which he spread on the floor and sat upon, his back against the wall . . . We could hear the groans and blasphemies of other wounded men, stretched out in the filth below our window. Some of them joined us and we remained five days without receiving food, medicine, nor care of any kind.

A young lieutenant, who had received two sabre cuts but could still walk, went every morning to find food for us. Finally, on 25 June, we were informed that we would be taken to Brussels, and they put me, with seven other wounded, into a wretched cart led by a Belgian peasant. At first, because the road was paved and the horse went gently, we were not troubled much by our wounds. But a Prussian soldier, who was watching, decided we were not going fast enough for his liking and hurried the peasant along with a few blows of his sabre. The poor peasant put his horse into a trot and for 15 minutes the bumps of the cart caused us excruciating pain . . .

While traversing the Forest of Soignies we saw masses of upturned carts, broken gun limbers, dead horses, and unburied English corpses. These remains, and the signs of disorder, convinced us that without the arrival of Blücher and his Prussians, the English Army would have been completely crushed on 18 June. But for us it was small consolation. Upon leaving the Forest of Soignies we were met by a delegation from the Brussels Guild of Hat-Makers, who offered us bread and wine, expressing their pity for us. This warm greeting was a pleasant surprise. Soon our cart arrived at Brussels, making its way through the middle of a crowd of curious onlookers. Some threw insults at us, but the majority – very sympathetic spirits – gave us bandages, dressings, tobacco and refreshments.

Hardly were we installed in the attic of a little château, when the ladies of Brussels, in great numbers, brought us food, wine, cordial, broth, linen, etc. All day long there was a procession of these good and charitable ladies, who also brought encouragement and consolation. It was the same routine the following day. But the English looked upon us with a certain amount of jealousy, and the ladies were not allowed to see us for more than a few moments each day. Certainly, all those, who like me were wounded and discouraged by seven days of suffering, were comforted by these visits, and will keep for the rest of their lives a warm and sincere regard for the ladies of Brussels.

Jolyet survived the Waterloo campaign, ending his service as lieutenant colonel of the 35th Regiment, and retiring a few months short of the Revolution of 1830.

Keller

Major von (dates unknown)

Commander of the 15th Fusilier Regiment, part of the 16th Infantry Brigade of **Bülow**'s Prussian IV Corps at Waterloo. After the collapse of the French Army at Waterloo, its fugitives were pursued by a Prussian force under **Gneisenau**, which included Keller's regiment of Fusiliers. About 5 miles up the Charleroi road the Prussians encountered French resistance at the entrance to the village of Genappe. Ordered to carry the place, Keller advanced, his way blocked by a barricade of overturned waggons and guns. Nevertheless, the Prussians pushed forward, and as they fought their way into Genappe a cry of panic went up from the French horde fleeing down the main street and across the bridge over the Dyle. But in the bedlam that greeted his senses, Keller picked out a singular sight: **Napoleon**, fearful of capture, leaping out his carriage – losing his hat in the process – and dashing off into the night. Shaken to his senses by gunfire and a crescendo of anguished cries, Keller threw his men into the attack. Moments later, with the dregs of French soldiery in flight, he found himself beside the Emperor's abandoned carriage. Unsure what to do next, Keller placed a guard around the vehicle and waited on events. Gneisenau arrived soon after, and bidding Keller's battalion form up, made them sing the hymn *Herr Gott dich loben wir* (Lord God, we Praise thee). Then, breaking into three hearty cheers, the Prussians continued their pursuit – Gneisenau's 'hunt by moonlight'. Half an hour later, having bagged 78 abandoned guns and some 2,000 stragglers, Keller's Fusiliers were laying their hands on Napoleon's treasury and baggage waggons.

Keller, meanwhile, laid claim to the imperial carriage ditched at Genappe. According to Gneisenau, the vehicle contained the Emperor's hat, sword, imperial mantle, the whole of his private and secret correspondence, and a cache of diamonds worth over 1 million francs. But Keller did not keep his prize. Instead, he handed it over to the Prussian top brass, who raided it for keepsakes (Gneisenau allegedly took Napoleon's ring of state). As for the diamonds, a number were presented to King Frederick William III, who decided to incorporate them into Prussia's crown jewels. The carriage itself passed into the hands of Marshal **Blücher**, who, as a *beau geste*, presented it to George, the British Prince of Wales. Keller got a medal.

Built by the coachmaker Goeting in April 1815, Napoleon's *dormeuse* or 'sleeper' was a bulletproof home on wheels, drawn by four stout horses. It boasted a spring suspension capable of bearing a half-ton load, and was painted dark blue. The interior could be converted for a variety of uses: bedroom, bathroom, dressing room, kitchen, dining room and office. Apart from books, bedding, pistols and maps, the carriage contained a huge watch, some 4 pounds in weight, by which all Napoleon's officers had to set their own timepieces.

George was delighted by this windfall and immediately sold it to William Bullock, a Sheffield silversmith, for £2,500 (approximately £125,000 in modern terms) to pay off a gambling debt. Bullock, a keen antiquary, owned the Egyptian Hall, which once stood at 22 Piccadilly, London. A shrewd businessman, Bullock made room among his 15,000 relics to exhibit the carriage in 1816, charging a shilling for admittance. The response was spectacular: an avalanche of Brits descended on Bullock's museum to feast their eyes on Bonaparte's carriage. It is estimated that on a single day as many as 10,000 people queued for admittance, and the crush and chaos were so pronounced the celebrated cartoonist Thomas Rowlandson

*'A Swarm of British Bees Hiving in the Imperial Carriage' – cartoon
by Thomas Rowlandson*

could not resist satirising the scene as: 'A Swarm of British Bees
Hiving in the Imperial Carriage' (Napoleon's adopted the bee as his
symbol). Lord Byron was particularly taken with the imperial
dormeuse and instructed Charles Baxter, the famous coachmaker, to
build him an exact replica. A few months later, Bullock closed his
exhibition at the Egyptian Hall and took the carriage on tour. In
all, perhaps as many as 800,000 people paid to see Napoleon's
carriage, making Bullock a fortune of some £40,000 (over £2 million
in modern terms). Bullock then sold the carriage to a London
coachmaker for £168 (around £8,400 in modern terms).

In the early 1840s the carriage was acquired by Madame Tussaud's,
where it took pride of place in 'the Napoleon Room', much beloved
by the Duke of **Wellington**. But on 18 March 1925 a fire destroyed
Tussaud's museum and with it, Napoleon's Waterloo carriage. In
1976 the only remaining artefact from the vehicle – a fire-damaged
axle – was presented to the Napoleonic museum at Malmaison.

Kelly
Captain Edward (1771–1828)

Officer of the 1st Life Guards who charged with the Household Brigade. Kelly's regiment – which, fielding two squadrons, totalled some 255 sabres – was brigaded with the 2nd Life Guards, the Royal Horse Guards and the 1st Dragoon Guards. This unit, the 1st British or 'Household' Brigade, numbered some 1,300 sabres in total. It was commanded by Lord **Edward Somerset**. Around 2 p.m. on 18 June 1815 **Wellington**'s cavalry supremo, Lord **Uxbridge**, launched both Household and Union Brigades against **d'Erlon**'s I Corps, advancing on Wellington's left-centre. The Household Brigade, making their charge to the right of the Brussels high road, crashed into the 4,000 infantrymen of **Quiot**'s Division, supported by 1,000 horsemen from the 1st and 4th Cuirassiers. It was with these steel-clad horsemen the 1st and 2nd Life Guards principally had to contend. Kelly apparently had three horses shot from under him during the ensuing melee. And yet, according to Dalton (1904), Kelly killed Colonel Dubois of the French 1st Cuirassiers, coolly dismounting in the thick of the action to remove the Frenchman's epaulettes for souvenirs. This story is echoed by **Gronow** (1900), who states Kelly slew Dubois after the latter had mortally wounded Corporal **John Shaw** of the 2nd Life Guards:

> Kelly was seen cutting his way through a host of enemies. Shaw . . . came to his assistance, and these two heroes fought side by side, killing or disabling many of their antagonists, till poor Shaw, after receiving several wounds, was killed from a thrust through the body by a French colonel of cuirassiers, who in his turn received a blow from Kelly's sword, which cut through his helmet and stretched him lifeless upon the ground.

Kelly, too, was wounded: hit in the leg by a round shot, which tore away part of the flesh. But he survived the battle, writing a letter to his wife bemoaning the loss of so many gallant comrades: 'All my fine troopers knocked to pieces'. The regiment sustained a total of 65 casualties.

Kempt
Major General Sir James (1764–1855)

Commander of **Wellington**'s 8th British Brigade at Waterloo. Born in Edinburgh, Kempt entered the army as an ensign in the 101st Foot in 1783. By 1799, having attained the rank of major, Kempt was serving as aide-de-camp to Sir Ralph Abercromby, the first of a long string of staff appointments. Kempt saw service in Holland, the Mediterranean, Egypt, British North America, Spain and France before taking command of Wellington's 8th British Brigade for the Waterloo campaign. The brigade consisted of the 28th Foot, 32nd Foot, 79th Foot and six companies of the 1st Battalion 95th (Rifle) Regiment: a total of almost 2,000 men.

Part of **Picton**'s 5th British Infantry Division at Waterloo, Kempt's brigade was thinly spread across a wide sector of Wellington's line, left of the Brussels high road. To Kempt's left was Pack's brigade, to his right was **Ompteda**'s. Some distance behind stood Sir **William Ponsonby**'s 2nd British (Union) Cavalry Brigade. When the firing started, Picton's division – and Kempt's brigade in particular – became the target for **Napoleon**'s gunners and **d'Erlon**'s infantry columns. The latter, attacking across the shallow valley about 1.30 p.m. on 18 June, made straight for Kempt, drums beating and tongues yelling 'Vive l'Empereur! En avant!' According to historian William Siborne (1848):

> The left central column was advancing in a direction which would have brought it in immediate contact with the right of the 28th British regiment and the left of the 79th Highlanders, and had arrived within about forty yards of the hedge lining the edge of the Wavre road [an alternative name for the Ohain road, running atop Mont St Jean], when Picton moved forward Kempt's brigade close to the hedge . . . Suddenly the column halted and commenced a deployment to its right, the rear battalions moving out rapidly to disengage their front. Picton, seizing upon the favourable moment, ordered the brigade to fire a volley into the deploying mass, and its brief but full and condensed report had scarcely died away, when his voice was heard loudly calling 'Charge! Charge! Hurrah!' Answering with a tremendous shout, his devoted followers burst through the nearest of the two hedges that lined the Wavre road.

But Picton went down almost immediately, shot in the head by a musket ball. Now command of the division devolved upon Kempt. In a letter to Sir **Hussey Vivian**, quoted by H.T. Siborne (1891), Kempt describes the sequel:

> My Brigade consisted of the 28th, 32nd, 79th, and 1st Battalion 95th Regiments, and on poor Picton's fall the command of the 5th Division, with the 6th that had just come up to our support, and all the troops, in short, on the left of the Great Brussels road, devolved upon me throughout the day . . . the 95th Regiment was in front of the other regiments of my brigade, occupying a knoll and some broken ground as light troops, and in a line with a considerable corps of Belgian and Nassau Infantry. All these retired as the head of the enemy's mass of infantry approached them, at which critical moment, and just as the French infantry were gaining the road and hedgerow which runs all along the crest of the position, I met it at the charge with the 28th, 32nd, and 79th Regiments in line, and completely repulsed the enemy's column, driving it in a state of the greatest confusion down the slope of the position . . . I was in the act of restraining the men from the pursuit (having no support whatever), when General Ponsonby's Brigade of cavalry charged a separate column that had come up to our left where Pack's brigade was stationed. The enemy made three different attempts to carry the position immediately on the left of the road where my brigade was posted, and were invariably repulsed in the same manner.

Although Kempt's troops continued to see off Napoleon's attacks, they could do little to avoid the unwelcome attention of the Emperor's gunners and suffered accordingly. By early evening the rate of attrition was beginning to tell, Wellington himself observing that 'night or the Prussians must come'. By the end of the battle, Kempt's brigade had suffered around 660 casualties, perhaps 34 per cent of its starting strength. Kempt was among the wounded, but survived the campaign to be heaped with honours, prestigious appointments and promotions. He received the KCB and GCB after Waterloo, and the GCH the following year. He went on to serve as Governor of Nova Scotia, Governor General of Canada, Master-General of the Ordnance and the colonel of several regiments. He was promoted lieutenant general in 1825 and full general in 1841.

Kennedy
Ensign James Grant (1799–1815)

Sixteen-year-old junior officer in the 3rd Battalion 1st Foot (Royal Scots), who died carrying the King's colour. A tale is to be found in several sources that Kennedy – son of an Inverness physician – was killed at Waterloo while advancing at the head of his battalion. The story goes that when Kennedy fell, a colour sergeant tried to take the colour from him, but he would not let go. The onlooking French were apparently so impressed, they held their fire till the colour sergeant returned to the safety of his battalion square. But according to Dalton (1904), Ensign Kennedy was killed at Quatre-Bras on 16 June. Credence is lent to Dalton's version by the absence of Kennedy's name from the *Waterloo Medal Roll* (Buckland 2001). Dalton does confirm, however, that Kennedy died 'whilst carrying the colours. Aged 16'. Quoting from Mudford's *Historical Account of the Campaign in the Netherlands in 1815* (1817), Dalton goes on to state that:

> The 3rd Batt. of the Royal Scots . . . distinguished itself in a
> particular manner at Quatre Bras. 'Being removed from the centre
> of the 5th Division, it charged and routed a column of the enemy.
> It was then formed to receive the cavalry, and though repeated
> attacks were made, not the slightest impression was produced.
> Wherever the lancers and cuirassiers presented themselves they
> found a stern and undismayed front which they vainly endeavoured
> to penetrate.

Having suffered over 200 casualties at Quatre-Bras – including, it seems, Ensign Kennedy – the 3rd Battalion 1st Foot marched to Waterloo with less than 500 men. On 18 June the battalion formed part of the 9th British Brigade under Major General Sir Denis Pack, entering the front line left of the crossroads above La Haie Sainte.

223

In the early afternoon the 1st Foot – or Royal Scots – were embroiled in the battle with **d'Erlon**'s infantry divisions. Afterwards, they were pounded by **Napoleon**'s grand battery and charged by **Ney**'s massed cavalry. At the end of the day the battalion had sustained around 140 casualties, including their commander, Lieutenant Colonel Colin Campbell. According to Ian Fletcher (1994), 'Four officers and a sergeant major in turn fell carrying the King's Colour.' But if Dalton is to be believed, Kennedy was not one of them.

In the British Army, the practice of carrying colours dates from the English Civil War, when the colour of a unit's flag corresponded to its title: the 'Red' Regiment carrying a red flag, etc. These flags – designed to serve as rallying points in the confusion of battle – came to embody the 'spirit' of the regiment, bearing its battle honours. A second flag – the Sovereign's colour – might be awarded as a sign of especial esteem or honour. A regiment's colours were usually carried by an ensign, who was protected by a number of colour sergeants. This group was collectively known as the colour party. Although it was a great honour to carry the colours, the death rate among ensigns was high, for these flags were the most prized of all battle trophies: indeed, the extent of a victory was gauged by the number of enemy colours captured. The British Army ceased carrying colours into battle some 65 years after Waterloo: after defeat at Isandlwana (1879) according to some, after the Battle of Laing's Nek (1881) according to others.

Kincaid
Lieutenant John (1787–1862)

'I had never yet heard of a battle in which everybody was killed,' wrote Kincaid of Waterloo, 'but this seemed likely to be an exception, as all were going by turns.' Author of *Adventures in the Rifle Brigade* (first published in 1830) and *Random Shots From a Rifleman* (first published in 1835); Kincaid was adjutant of the 1st Battalion 95th (Rifle) Regiment at Waterloo. Born and educated in Stirlingshire, Scotland, Kincaid grew into 'a lean lank fellow' over 6 feet tall. Initially serving as a lieutenant in the North York Militia, he volunteered for the 95th on 27 April 1809. The regiment was a relatively new entity, having been spawned by the Experimental Corps of Riflemen on 25 December 1802. Almost immediately, the riflemen of the 95th – sporting distinctive dark green uniforms – were bathed in glamour: highly professional light infantrymen, trained to go anywhere and do anything, they were Britain's first 'modern' soldiers. Furthermore, they were armed with a new weapon: the Baker rifle. Invented by London gunsmith Ezekiel Baker, this weapon was more accurate than a standard musket, having a grooved or rifled barrel, but required considerable expertise to deploy it quickly and effectively in the field. Consequently, British riflemen received intensive training in its use, becoming superb marksmen in the process. During an advance, soldiers from the 95th were at the forefront as skirmishers, sharpshooters or shock troops. During a retreat they formed the rearguard, keeping the enemy at bay, while the army made good its escape. The regiment was the cream of **Wellington**'s army and considered itself an elite unit. By the time Kincaid joined the 95th – led by Sir Andrew Barnard – it was one of the most celebrated fighting forces in Europe.

On 21 July 1814 Kincaid became adjutant of the regiment's 1st Battalion, and was recalled from a shooting leave in Scotland to fight at Quatre-Bras and Waterloo. An astute observer with an eye for the ridiculous, Kincaid (1847) wrote of Quatre-Bras:

> While our battalion reserve occupied the front of the wood, our skirmishers lined the side of the road, which was the Prussian line of communication. The road itself, however, was crossed by such a shower of balls, that none but a desperate traveller would have undertaken a journey on it. We were presently reinforced by a small battalion of foreign light troops, with whose assistance we were in hopes to have driven the enemy a little further from it; but they were a raw body of men, who had never before been under fire; and, as they could not be prevailed upon to join our skirmishers, we could make no use of them whatever . . . Sir Andrew Barnard repeatedly pointed out to them which was the French and which our side; and, after explaining that they were not to fire a shot until they joined our skirmishers, the word 'March!' was given; but 'march', to them, was always the signal to fire, for they stood fast, and began blazing away,

chiefly at our skirmishers too; the officers commanding whom were every time sending back to say that we were shooting them; until we were, at last, obliged to be satisfied with whatever advantages their appearance could give, as even that was of some consequence, where troops were so scarce.

After Quatre-Bras, Wellington retreated to Waterloo, dogged by the French and an almighty thunderstorm. The Duke's army took up positions on the ridge of Mont St Jean during the filthy night of 17 June. Thus, as dawn broke on 18 June, Kincaid recalled:

> I found myself drenched with rain. I had slept so long and so soundly that I had, at first, but a very confused notion of my situation; but having a bright idea that my horse had been my companion when I went to sleep, I was rather startled at finding that I was now alone; nor could I rub my eyes clear enough to procure a sight of him, which was vexatious enough; for, independent of his value as a horse, his services were indispensable; and an adjutant might as well think of going into action without his arms as without such a supporter. But whatever my feelings might have been towards him, it was evident that he had none for me, from having drawn his sword and marched off. The chances of finding him again, amid ten thousand others, were about equal to the odds against a needle in a bundle of hay; but for once the single chance was gained, as, after a diligent search of an hour, he was discovered between two artillery horses, about half a mile from where he broke loose.

Having located his horse – which would be killed under him in due course – Kincaid sought refreshment:

> We made a fire against the wall of Sir Andrew Barnard's cottage, and boiled a huge camp-kettle full of tea, mixed up with a suitable quantity of milk and sugar, for breakfast; and, as it stood on the edge of the high-road, where all the bigwigs of the army had occasion to pass, in the early part of the morning, I believe almost every one of them, from the Duke downwards, claimed a cupful.

Troops from the 1st, 2nd and 3rd Battalions of the 95th fought at Waterloo. Kincaid's battalion was part of **Kempt**'s Brigade (**Picton**'s 5th Division), posted near Wellington's centre, about

100 yards in rear of La Haie Sainte. As a consequence, it became heavily involved in the fighting around the farmhouse and the Brussels high road. Kincaid describes this sector as being 'tolerably quiet' in the early afternoon, but 'one continued blaze of musketry' after 4 p.m. This firestorm broke out in response to **Ney**'s intensifying attacks on Wellington's line, as the Marshal tried to break through before **Ziethen**'s I Corps could intervene: 'The smoke hung so thick about us that, although not more than eighty yards asunder, we could only distinguish each other by the flashes of the pieces . . . [we were] so many hours enveloped in darkness'. Finally, with the repulse of **Napoleon**'s Imperial Guard about 8.15 p.m., Kincaid joined Wellington's general advance:

> A cheer, which we knew to be British, commenced far to the right, and made everyone prick up his ears; it was Lord Wellington's long-wished-for orders to advance; it gradually approached, growing louder as it grew near; we took it up by instinct, charged through the hedge . . . sending our adversaries flying at the point of the bayonet. Lord Wellington galloped up to us at the instant, and our men began to cheer him; but he called out, 'No cheering, my lads, but forward, and complete your victory!'

But Waterloo was also Wellington's victory: under his leadership the British Army had been transformed from battle-losers into battle-winners – more than that, into war-winners and giant-killers. Thus the successful conclusion of the Napoleonic Wars saw an upturn in status for the humble redcoat, a wave of national euphoria erasing from memory the defeats and disgraces of the 1790s and early 1800s. And although the years following Waterloo were marked by social unrest in Britain, with jumpy magistrates relying on troops to keep the peace – with tragic and lethal consequences – the glory and glamour surrounding the battle remained untarnished. Fifteen years after Waterloo the British belly still rumbled for tales for soldier exploits. A circumstance exploited by Kincaid, who, in 1830 published *Adventures in the Rifle Brigade*, followed by *Random Shots From A Rifleman* five years later. Kincaid's pithy memoirs of warfare under Wellington were just what the doctor ordered for the British psyche: a mixture of humour (often self-deprecatory), drama, observational detail and mild xenophobia. His books sold out almost immediately and were quickly reissued. Rarely out of print since, Kincaid helped establish the genre of the 'popular' military memoir in Britain, still going strong today. A final tribute to Kincaid is the following Waterloo soundbite: 'The usual salutation on meeting an acquaintance of another regiment after an action was to ask who had been hit? But on this occasion it was "Who's alive?"'

Labédoyère
General Charles-Angélique-François-Huchet, Count (1786–1815)

Aide-de-camp to **Napoleon** during the Waterloo campaign. Labédoyère is one of those French officers – like **d'Erlon**, **Grouchy** or **Bailly de Monthion** – accused by historians of losing the Waterloo campaign for Napoleon. The scion of an ancient aristocratic family, Labédoyère was a rabid Bonapartist who hero-worshipped the Emperor. **Marbot**, the celebrated French memoirist and Waterloo veteran, described Labédoyère as 'a tall and handsome man, brave, cultivated, and witty; a good talker, though with a slight stammer'. A veteran of the Polish, Danube and Russian campaigns, he displayed great courage but little military tact. Perhaps for this reason, Labédoyère was employed as an aide-de-camp, serving on the staffs of brass hats like Marshal Lannes, Marshal Mortier and Napoleon's stepson Prince Eugène. Following Napoleon's first abdication in April 1814, Labédoyère pledged allegiance to the restored Bourbon monarchy, and was rewarded with command of the 7th Line Regiment, stationed at Grenoble. But when Napoleon 'returned with the violets' in spring the following year, Labédoyère immediately defected with his whole regiment, setting off an avalanche of support for the fugitive Emperor. Within weeks,

Napoleon's band of rebels had swelled from hundreds to thousands, Paris opened its gates, and the Bourbons fled to Belgium. Labédoyère's act earned him promotion to general, appointment to the Emperor's staff as aide-de-camp, and the undying hatred of the Royalists.

During the subsequent Waterloo campaign, Labédoyère's name has become linked to a series of tragic blunders: the first resulted in the escape of both **Wellington** and **Blücher** from Napoleon's clutches on 16–17 June 1815; the second in the complete collapse of French morale at Waterloo; and the third in Labédoyère's own death. Historian David Chandler (1966) writes: 'All too often the Battles of Quatre-Bras and Ligny are treated as mere preliminary skirmishes preceding the Battle of Waterloo two days later. This is very much to underrate their importance.' Chandler maintains that Napoleon might have successfully concluded his campaign against Blücher and Wellington on 16 June 1815, had a bizarre series of events not put **d'Erlon**'s I Corps *hors de combat*. For d'Erlon – who might have played a decisive role at Ligny or Quatre-Bras – spent the day marching between the two battles, fighting at neither. As we will see, Labédoyère has been blamed for this fiasco, which undoubtedly compromised Napoleon's chances of ultimate strategic success.

At midday on 16 June Napoleon faced a strong Prussian force under Blücher at Ligny, while 7 miles to the north-west, Marshal **Ney** faced a weak Anglo-Netherlands force under the Prince of **Orange** at Quatre-Bras. Both Napoleon and Ney believed themselves committed to major battles, and both expected to be reinforced by the other. In the days before radio and satellite links, effective cooperation between commanders was dependent on efficient staff work. But the Emperor's chief of staff, Marshal **Soult**, was better suited to field command and failed to get a grip on this vital aspect of operations. Thus, messages were badly worded, or delayed, or never delivered at all. Suffice to say that in June 1815, communication was not the French forte. And so time passed on 16 June as Ney waited for Napoleon, and Napoleon waited for Ney. By mid-afternoon, however, both commanders were obliged to press home their attacks, hopeful that reinforcements were on the way. Napoleon – outnumbered at Ligny – was still pinning his hopes on

Ney's support, when, about 3.30 p.m., the Marshal sent word from Quatre-Bras, informing the Emperor that he was embattled with Wellington (who by this time had reinforced the Prince of Orange).

What happened next is open to discussion. According to some, Napoleon sent a message to Ney, hastily scribbled with a pencil, demanding that d'Erlon's I Corps – then tramping north to Quatre-Bras – be diverted to Ligny. And yet, as Vincent Esposito and John Elting (1999) state:

> No trace of this order remains; Napoleon apparently knew nothing of it . . . It is possible that some staff officer, knowing Napoleon's plan and seeing d'Erlon unexpectedly available, acted on his own initiative.

Historian A.F. Becke (1914), writing 100 years after the event, believed that staff officer to be Labédoyère. According to Becke, Labédoyère was on his way to Quatre-Bras with dispatches for Ney when he fell in with d'Erlon, marching to reinforce the Marshal. Aware of Napoleon's urgent need for troops at Ligny, Labédoyère forged the pencil note that turned d'Erlon around and sent him marching to the Emperor. Becke writes:

> No trace of this 'pencil note' exists, nor is this note recorded in Soult's register. It did exist, however, on the 16th, since it was shown, certainly to d'Erlon and possibly to Ney. It was left, however, in no one's hands. Is it not probable that it was a fabrication? The General ADC [Labédoyère], bearing a duplicate of one of the earlier authentic orders and being fully conversant with the Emperor's plan and the situation at Ligny, overtook the I Corps. Here, and available, was the needed reinforcement; but it marched north and not eastward. How could he turn it? Two lines scrawled in pencil and substituted for the duplicate which he carried, and the curt command: 'Order of the Emperor' and the deed was done.

D'Erlon arrived within sight of Ligny about 5.30 p.m. For some reason he did not send advance notification of his arrival, as was common practice, so the sight of his columns put the fear of God into Napoleon's hard-pressed troops, who mistook them for Prussians. As a result, the Emperor's operations against Blücher were suspended until the identity of the newcomers was established. An hour or so later, Napoleon was informed that the approaching host belonged to d'Erlon's corps. But no sooner had these welcome reinforcements been identified, when they turned tail and marched back west to Quatre-Bras – apparently recalled by a furious Marshal Ney (at least, that is what d'Erlon later claimed, although Ney denied it, maintaining that I Corps marched back from Ligny on Napoleon's orders). Deserted in his hour of need, Napoleon fought on at Ligny, his Imperial Guard succeeding in pushing the Prussians off the battlefield as dusk fell. D'Erlon arrived at Quatre-Bras about the same time – too late to assist Ney, who had failed to crush Wellington. And so, by shuttling between Ney and Napoleon, d'Erlon deprived both of badly needed manpower.

Arguably, the debacle cost Napoleon the campaign: for Blücher's mauled Prussians slipped away under cover of night to fight another day; as did Wellington's Anglo-Netherlanders. But was Labédoyère to blame? Becke thinks so, claiming the imperial aide-de-camp, 'risked all to gain all', adding that: 'd'Erlon's fruitless counter-march and Napoleon's failure to destroy Blücher at Ligny were directly due to this thoughtless, but well-intentioned, fabrication'.

If some doubt hangs over Labédoyère's involvement in the d'Erlon disaster, his part in the following debacle is firmly established. By 7 p.m. on 18 June the tide of battle had turned against Napoleon at Waterloo: **Bülow**'s Prussians were banging at the doors of Plancenoit in the Emperor's right rear; the Allied garrison at Hougoumont was still beating off **Jérôme**'s attacks; and Wellington's line, though shaky, was still intact. Completing this picture of doom was **Ziethen**'s Prussian corps, marching into position on Wellington's extreme left. The Emperor had noted Ziethen's approach, but believed he still had a chance to snatch victory. Placing his hopes on a final throw of the dice, Napoleon ordered an assault on Wellington by the grenadiers and chasseurs of his Imperial Guard. Their job was to smash through Wellington's flimsy line and open the road to Brussels. But what about Ziethen? Aware that he had to buy time for the Guard to deploy, Napoleon decided on a *ruse de guerre* to disguise the threat posed by the Prussians, while putting fresh heart into his flagging soldiers. To this end, the Emperor sent Labédoyère riding along the front, announcing the arrival of Marshal Grouchy. Even when the Prussian guns opened up, the lie was upheld, as noted by Waterloo veteran **Edward Cotton** (1895):

> The firing was distinctly heard by Napoleon and his troops, and being apprehensive that it might damp their courage, he sent General Labédoyère through the line, with the false report that it was Grouchy's guns that had fallen upon the Prussian rear, and it only required a little firmness to complete the victory to which they were advancing.

But the French soldiers – already shaken by the defection of General **Bourmont** on the eve of the campaign – simply assumed Grouchy had also turned his coat, and was training his guns on them. Within minutes the ruse had backfired and French morale was crumbling. Wellington's repulse of the Imperial Guard completed this collapse and a general rout ensued. Labédoyère, distraught at the panic and terror he had unleashed, is said to have sought death on the battlefield, or at the very least, to have been among the last to quit.

Nevertheless, Labédoyère was one of the first to enter Paris, where he made his final faux pas. Apparently arriving ahead of the news from Waterloo, Labédoyère attempted to rally support for Napoleon by announcing a great victory at Waterloo. This performance was punctured by the arrival of Marshal Ney, who calmly proclaimed the truth. On 22 June Napoleon abdicated for the final time. Two weeks later, Louis XVIII returned to Paris. At this point, Labédoyère should have sloped away, quietly disappearing into exile like **Lefebvre-Desnouëttes**, **Vandamme**, **Gérard** and others. But, fearing for the welfare of his wife and child, Labédoyère stayed put. This was a fatal mistake, for France was sliding into a period of internecine violence known as the White Terror, as Royalists howled for the blood of Bonapartists and Jacobins. And at the top of the Bourbon's hit list were those officers who had betrayed them, when Napoleon returned from Elba. Historian Gregor Dallas (1996) describes the sequel: 'General Labédoyère made the mistake of returning to Paris to say farewell to his wife; he was recognised, court martialled, and on 19 August shot in front of a firing squad.'

Larrey
Dominique-Jean, Baron (1766–1842)

Surgeon to **Napoleon**'s Imperial Guard. Son of a shoemaker, Larrey joined the French Army as a medic in 1792, his talent and dedication quickly earning him promotion and recognition. Napoleon was impressed by Larrey's skill as a surgeon and his insistence on treating friend and foe alike. A humanitarian determined to improve medical care for soldiers, Larrey was the inventor of the original 'ambulance', a vehicle designed for speedy evacuation of battlefield casualties. Larrey's so-called 'flying ambulance' was a two or four-wheeled waggon, well sprung and drawn by a pair of horses. A veteran of many hard fought campaigns, including Austerlitz, Jena, Wagram and Russia, Larrey was Napoleon's chief medical officer at Waterloo. According to L.A.H. Leroy-Dupré (1862), in his *Memoirs of Baron Larrey*:

> Larrey's conduct throughout the whole of that eventful day towards the wounded was most zealous and humane. His efforts, however, were rendered most difficult by the charges of the enemy's cavalry, which almost scoured the country. At length, when the sun had set on the field of Waterloo, and on the fortunes of the great Napoleon, Larrey was enjoined to obey the same order, *sauve qui peut*; but this order was not in unison with the humane feelings of the medical officer.
>
> The pursuit, commenced by **Blücher**'s 30,000 fresh troops [misleading – the Prussians had been on their feet since 4 a.m. that morning] at the close of the day, was sweeping and rapid, merciless and sanguinary. It swept before it the remains of the French Army as forcibly as the angry wave of the ocean dashes against the wreck of some noble vessel. Night came and Larrey was far away from his countrymen, except some medical officers and also French soldiers who lay weltering on the field of Waterloo. He was wandering about

with some French surgeons when suddenly they were overtaken by a squadron of Prussian lancers. Larrey, who expected no quarter from Prussians, discharged his pistols at them and galloped away, hoping that the darkness of the night would enable him to elude pursuit. The enemy discharged their carbines, wounding the horse of Larrey, which upset the rider. As Larrey was lying on the ground he received two sabre-cuts, which rendered him insensible. The Prussians, who believed him dead, then left him, and galloped off after fresh victims.

As soon as Larrey recovered his senses and perceived that the enemy had gone away he endeavoured, though in pain, to make his escape into [sic] French soil by some cross paths. Unfortunately, upon arriving at the banks of the Sambre, he met another detachment of Prussian cavalry and was then taken prisoner. They not only deprived him of his arms, but even robbed him of his watch, his ring, and part of his clothes. Nor did they stop with these indignities but they led him before a superior officer who sentenced him to be shot. Thus the good and charitable Larrey, who during so many campaigns had never recognised any distinction between friend and foe where the rights of humanity were involved, and who had so often devoted his mental and physical energies to the preservation of the lives of the sick and wounded, although those sick and wounded might be the enemies of France and his own beloved Emperor, seemed doomed to death the day after the Battle of Waterloo. Yet at that critical moment the memory of his good and able deeds stepped in between Baron Larrey and an untimely death. A surgeon-major, about a quarter of an hour before the moment at which the sentence was to be executed against Napoleon's medical chief, recognised the lecturer at Berlin in the person of Larrey. This Prussian doctor had attended with deep interest and much advantage those lectures which Larrey had delivered in the Prussian capital about six years previously, and now he succeeded in obtaining a reprieve for the accomplished medical officer of Napoleon's army. Larrey was conducted before **Bülow**, Grand Prévôt of the Allied armies and finally presented to Field Marshal Blücher. That introduction was, indeed, all the more fortunate, because in the campaign of Austria the son of the Marshal had been badly wounded and had fallen into the hands of the French, on which occasion his life had been saved through the exertions of Larrey. So in grateful recollection of his Samaritan benevolence, Blücher not only cancelled the sentence of death against Larrey, but granted him an escort to Brussels. Here the wounds of Larrey were healed. Yet while only convalescent, this worthy member of a profession which, in its blended stoicism and sensibility, in its fortitude and humanity, is inferior to no other, passed much of his time in the hospitals, suggesting measures for the relief of the large number of wounded men who had been carried to Brussels from the field of Waterloo.

According to Georges Blond (1979), **Wellington** spotted Larrey through his telescope during the battle, and was impressed by the man's energy and courage. He asked an aide who the man was, and when the reply came that it was Larrey, the Duke ordered his guns not to fire in the medic's direction. Then, raising his hat, Wellington added: 'I salute honour and loyalty which are passing by.'

After Waterloo, Larrey held a number of prestigious medical posts, retaining the love and gratitude of Napoleon's old warriors. The Emperor himself said of Larrey: 'he looked upon all the wounded as belonging to his family,' adding that the surgeon was 'the most virtuous man that I have known'.

Lawrence
Sergeant William (1791–1867)

Soldier of the 1st Battalion 40th Foot, whose autobiography was first published in 1886. Lawrence's battalion formed part of Lambert's 10th British Brigade, which had marched to Waterloo straight from disembarkation at Ostend, arriving on the field about 10.30 a.m. on 18 June 1815. Initially posted on **Wellington**'s left flank, between the villages of Merbe Braine and Mont St Jean, the battalion was later moved to the centre of the firing line. Here it was pounded by artillery and charged by cavalry for several hours, sustaining a casualty rate of over 26 per cent. Many officers were wounded and several killed, including the battalion commander, Major Arthur Rowley Heyland. According to Lawrence, a member of Captain J.H. Barnett's company:

About 4 o'clock I was ordered to the colours . . . That day alone fourteen sergeants and officers in proportion, had been killed or wounded in the duty and the staff and colours were almost cut to pieces. Nevertheless, I went to work as boldly as I could. That task will never be blotted from my memory. I am an old man now but I remember it as if it were yesterday. I was with a captain and he was so close to me that his right side was touching my left. Within a quarter of an hour, a cannon-shot came and took his head clean off, spattering me all over with his blood. A man from his company – Marten was his name – witnessed his end: 'There goes my best friend,' he commented. 'Never mind,' said the lieutenant, quickly stepping forward to take his place: 'I will be as good a friend to you as the captain.' 'I hope not, sir!' said Marten. The lieutenant had misunderstood, for Marten was a notorious character in the regiment on account of the dirtiness of his person. He had been in my company but because of his poor hygiene had been transferred to the 5th Company, where his poor captain had tried, and failed, to reform him by giving him extra duty and suchlike punishment. For all that, Marten was an excellent soldier in the field.

The name of the unfortunate captain was William Fisher, while the credulous lieutenant may have been Fisher's understudy, Hugh Boyd Wray. As to Marten – a man apparently blessed with a sense of humour as black as his person – the muster rolls reveal no one of that surname in Fisher's company, although a Private Carty Martin is recorded.

Lawrence quit the army in 1819 with a pension of 9 pennies a day, returning to his native Dorset to become an innkeeper at Studland. Here he entertained guests with tales of his military adventures. Urged to record his reminiscences, the illiterate Lawrence dictated them to a friend. The work appeared in print in 1886, 19 years after Lawrence's death, as *The Autobiography of Sergeant William Lawrence*, edited by G.N. Banks.

Leach
Captain Jonathan (1785–1855)

Officer of the 1st Battalion 95th (Rifle) Regiment and celebrated memoirist. Obtaining a commission in the 70th Foot at the age of 16, Leach soon discarded his red coat: desiring 'most ardently to wear a green jacket', he joined the 95th Rifles in 1806. Like fellow riflemen **John Kincaid**, **Henry Smith** and **George Simmons**, Leach saw tough service in Spain and Portugal as part of **Wellington**'s legendary Peninsular Army.

Perhaps the most celebrated British fighting unit of the Napoleonic wars, the 95th (Rifle) Regiment had sprung from the Experimental Corps of Riflemen, formed in 1800 to provide the British Army with a pool of highly trained light infantrymen. These troops were taught to fight both as regular infantry and as skirmishers. A high value was placed on intelligence and initiative among its members, a code of mutual loyalty and respect binding officers and men into a kind of extended military family. Furthermore, they were armed with a new weapon: the Baker rifle. With its grooved or rifled barrel to impart spin to the bullet, this weapon possessed greater range and accuracy than a musket. But the Baker rifle required considerable expertise in the field, so British riflemen received intensive training in its use, becoming superb marksmen in the process. Indeed, it was common practice for men to *hold* targets for their comrades to shoot at, standing some 200 yards distant. Finally, riflemen were issued with a rudimentary form of camouflage: drab rifle-green uniforms with black belts and facings. Thus the 95th was considered a highly exotic outfit by the redcoats of the Line regiments, while the French, constantly annoyed by their sharp shooting tactics, dubbed them 'grasshoppers' or 'the rascals in green'.

At Waterloo, the 95th fielded plenty of 'rascals', elements of the regiment's 1st, 2nd and 3rd Battalions being dotted about the field. Leach's belonged to the 1st Battalion, commanded by Lieutenant Colonel Sir Andrew Barnard, seconded by Major Alexander Cameron: a total of some 400 men. As for Leach, he began the battle halfway between Wellington's front line and the outpost of La Haie Sainte. Holding rough ground left of the Brussels high road – an area excavated for gravel and known to history as 'the sandpit' – Leach commanded two companies of riflemen, supported by a third a little to the rear. Thrust forward from the main line, Leach's men were to act as skirmishers, slowing down any French advance. It was a somewhat exposed position: to Leach's immediate front, a mere 500 yards distant, gaped the muzzles of **Napoleon**'s grand battery; to his right-front stood the walled farm of La Haie Sainte, garrisoned by the riflemen of the 2nd Light Battalion, King's German Legion, under Major **Baring**; to his rear rose the slopes of Mont St Jean rose, concealing **Picton**'s 5th British Infantry Division; while to his left-rear, stood van **Bijlandt**'s stranded Netherlanders – soon to be withdrawn behind the ridge.

About 11.30 a.m. **Jérôme** Bonaparte launched the first of many assaults on the château of Hougoumont, over on Leach's far right and out of his field of vision. But an hour or so later the guns of Napoleon's grand battery began heaving shot at Wellington's ridge, one of the first rounds taking off a rifleman's head. Leach (1831) recalled:

> Under cover of this cannonade several large columns of infantry, supported by heavy bodies of cavalry, and preceded by a multitude of light infantry, descended at a trot into the plain, with shouts and cries of 'Vive l'Empereur!' some of them throwing up their caps in the air, and advancing to the attack with such confidence and impetuosity, as if the bare possibility of our being able to withstand the shock was out of the question, fighting as they were under the immediate eye of their Emperor.

Leach ordered his men forward, fanning them out into loose, skirmisher order. Within minutes they were embroiled in a sharp firefight with the French. Unable to arrest the momentum of **d'Erlon**'s infantry, the riflemen fell back on the main position, scuttling up the slope to take cover behind hedges lining the Ohain road, running atop the hill. Having rejoined Picton's redcoats, Leach describes how the French:

> pressed boldly and resolutely on, until met by our first line, which delivered such a fire, when they approached the thorn hedge, as

shattered their ranks and threw them into disorder; and this was increased by the cheers, and an attempt of our line to close with them.

Seizing the moment, Picton ordered a bayonet charge and the French attack stalled. Moments later, Sir **William Ponsonby**'s 2nd British (Union) Cavalry Brigade appeared from behind the ridge. Crashing through the hedges of the Ohain road, the dragoons rolled up the French infantry, Leach's riflemen hugging the ground to avoid being trampled to death. And so d'Erlon's attack was repulsed, though Picton was killed in the affair: shot in the head by a bullet. Most histories of the battle have Picton falling at the head of his bayonet charge, but Leach says the hero fell afterwards, having advanced to the crest of the ridge to watch the retreating French: 'an unlucky straggling musket-shot put a period to his existence'.

Leach led his men back to the sandpit to enjoy a short lull in the fighting, as the French returned to the fight for Hougoumont. By 4 p.m., however, the grand battery was in action again, some 80 guns bombarding La Haie Sainte, making life unpleasant for its defenders as well as Leach's men:

> After having endured for a length of time, and with a tolerable degree of patience, this eternal pounding of shot and shells, strong symptoms appeared of a second and equally formidable attack being about to commence on our division and on the farm-house of La Haye Sainte. The second edition of 'Vive l'Empereur!' 'En avant, mes enfans!' and other stimulating cries, burst forth as their masses of infantry and of cavalry again advanced in the most imposing and intrepid style, under cover of a terrible cannonade and of their light troops.

Leach lingered as long as possible, blazing away at the oncoming French. Sadly, Baring's Germans no longer had bullets to blaze away with, and about 6.30 p.m. were driven out of La Haie Sainte. In imminent danger of being outflanked, Leach had little option but to quit too, leading his men back up the ridge:

> The house was instantly filled with the enemy's infantry. For several hours afterwards they kept up a dreadful fire from loop-holes and

windows in the upper part of it, whereby they raked the hillock so as to render it untenable by our battalion. They were also enabled to establish on the knoll, and along the crest of the hill, a strong line of infantry, which knelt down, exposing only their heads and shoulders to our fire.

Leach now found himself in command of the whole battalion, Barnard and Cameron having both been wounded. It was with some relief, then, that around 7 p.m. the Prussian I Corps under **Ziethen** arrived at the village of Papelotte, on Wellington's extreme left:

> The arrival of the Prussians had been long expected; but the only intimation we had of their approach was the smoke of a distant cannon occasionally seen far on the left. About seven o'clock in the evening a party of their Lancers arrived on the field to announce the approach of their army. It was about this time that the last and desperate attack was made by Napoleon with his guard, to annihilate us before the Prussians should arrive to our assistance. That this grand effort entirely failed, and that his Imperial Guard was driven back in irretrievable confusion and with immense slaughter, carrying with it over the field, like the receding waves of the sea, everything on its surface, is universally known.

So, too, is the sequel: a general advance of the whole Allied line. According to Leach:

> The lines moved forward rapidly and in fine order, loudly cheering; and the time only which was required for us to reach the enemy's position, sufficed to complete this most hardly contested, sanguinary, and important of battles.

Sanguinary indeed, for Leach's battalion sustained over 140 losses, the Captain himself among the wounded. In 1831 Leach published his memoirs: *Rough Sketches of the Life of an Old Soldier*. He died at Worthing, aged 70.

Leeke
Ensign William (1798–1877)

Junior officer of the 52nd Foot and author of *The History of Lord Seaton's Regiment (the 52nd Light Infantry) at the Battle of Waterloo*. Born in the Isle of Wight, the son of a Hampshire squire, Leeke was supposed to enter the Church at the age of 17 but opted for the 1/52nd Foot instead (he was eventually ordained in 1829), his father purchasing him an ensign's commission – then the

Ensign William Leeke (1798–1877)

lowliest commissioned rank in the British infantry, since replaced by that of second lieutenant. A month later Leeke was carrying the regimental colour at Waterloo. The 52nd (Oxford Light Infantry) Regiment formed part of **Adam**'s brigade within Clinton's 2nd Division of Lord **Hill**'s II Corps. It was commanded at Waterloo by Sir John Colborne, and was deployed on **Wellington**'s right flank, on the ridge above the château of Hougoumont. Some time after 7 p.m. the 52nd played a significant role in repulsing a column of French Imperial Guardsmen – and it became Leeke's self-appointed mission to let the world know about it.

Napoleon launched the grenadiers and foot chasseurs of the Guard against Wellington about 7.30 p.m. Five battalions of the Imperial Guard – perhaps 3,500 men in all – led the assault, supported by three others, which in the event, did not advance beyond La Haie Sainte. The advance of the Imperial Guard was supposed to herald a general French assault, but when the leading columns were crushed, morale crumbled and the battle fell into Wellington's lap. The question is: how were these leading columns crushed? Formed into squares as a protection against cavalry, the five leading Guard battalions advanced across the shallow valley in echelon, the rightmost column leading. Within 10 minutes they were within musket range as well as cannon range of Wellington's position. Nevertheless, the Frenchmen toiled up the slopes of Mont St Jean with muskets shouldered, marching to the beat of the *pas de* *charge*. But for some reason – never satisfactorily explained – the Guard veered left, switching their line of attack from Wellington's weak left-centre above La Haie Sainte, to his strong right-centre above Hougoumont. It must be stated, however, that the majority of Wellington's infantrymen were stationed on the reverse slope of Mont St Jean, giving the Guard little visual evidence of the Duke's dispositions. By the time the Imperial Guard neared the crest of the ridge, its five battalions had split into two groups: on the right, the 4th and 1/3rd Grenadiers were met by and repulsed by troops under **Colin Halkett** and Baron **Chassé**; while on the left, the 1/3rd, 2/3rd and 4th Foot Chasseurs were met by troops under **Maitland** and Adam – including Leeke and the 52nd.

What happened next divided Waterloo veterans for years afterwards, inducing Leeke to produce his own account, in order to 'put the record straight'. Early English accounts of Waterloo frequently climaxed with the repulse of the Imperial Guard. The scenario typically ran as follows: at the crucial moment when the foot chasseurs (usually dubbed 'grenadiers of the Old Guard' by British contemporaries) breast the ridge, Wellington shouts 'Up, Guards, and at 'em!' – or something similar – and up from the tall rye stalks jump Maitland's 1,400 foot guards to deliver a murderous volley. The astonished French are then bounced back down the ridge at bayonet point as the British Army advances to victory. But one Brit – namely Leeke – was not happy with this version of events and in 1866 published a controversial history of the battle in which he states:

> The story of Maitland's brigade of Guards having attacked and routed the leading column of the Imperial Guard is a mere myth . . . well known to every officer of the 52nd who was present at Waterloo, from Lord Seaton [i.e. Colborne] down to myself the youngest ensign.

According to Leeke, Napoleon sent 10,000 Imperial Guardsmen into action against the redcoats, and they were defeated by Colborne's 52nd:

> As the 52nd moved down towards the enemy it answered the cries of 'Vive l'Empereur' with three tremendous British cheers. When the left of the regiment was in a line with the leading company of the Imperial Guard, it began to mark time, and the men touched in to

their left, everyone seeing the necessity for such a movement, and that, if they proceeded, they would be outflanked by the French column, which was then not quite 200 yards from us. In two or three seconds the word of command, 'Right shoulders forward' came down the line from Sir John Colborne, repeated by the mounted officers, and the officers commanding the front companies; the movement was soon completed, and the 52nd four-deep line became parallel to the left flank of the leading column of the French Guard, there being a slight dip and rise again of the ground between us and the enemy. The 52nd was alone, the other regiments of Adam's brigade having been thrown out by the suddenness and peculiarity of the movement . . . As we closed towards the French Guard they did not wait our charge; but the leading column at first somewhat receded from us, and then broke and fled.

But Leeke's claims were soon countered by Sir William Maynard Gomm, a captain in the 2nd Foot Guards at Waterloo and Assistant Quartermaster-General to Sir **Thomas Picton**. Pointing out Leeke's gross overestimation of the numbers involved in the Imperial Guard's leading attack, Gomm (1881) writes:

> It is . . . hardly within the range of possibility that this column should have gone over to court a flank fire from any portion of Adam's Brigade, posted as it was, below and beyond the right flank of the brigade of Guards, in furtherance of its mission to assail our left centre. Yet this is the mode of proceeding of the French Guard so perniciously contended for by Mr Leeke, for arriving at its end.

But having written Leeke and the 52nd out of the crucial action against the leading battalions of the Imperial Guard, Gomm graciously concedes they engaged those in support, during Wellington's subsequent general advance:

> The 52nd . . . was mainly instrumental in the check and subsequent dispersion of this second heavy column; and it is therefore a matter of regret that no special mention was made in the despatch of the signal services rendered by Adam's Brigade, and especially by the 52nd, in this crowning portion of the great encounter, furnishing occasion for the question said to have been put by Byng (I think) to Colborne, at Paris, 'How will your fellows like our being given all the

credit for what they did?' But to contend, as Mr Leeke persistently does, that the French attack by the Guard was made in one sole column, divided in its centre by an inappreciable interval, and that its overthrow was due to the prowess of the 52nd single-handed, is shown to be an absurdity by reference to authenticated numbers.

Both Leeke and Gomm had their supporters, though Maitland and Colborne refused to be drawn into the debate: but who was right? In a sense they were both right – and then again, they were both wrong. Most, modern accounts of the battle describe events as follows: the Imperial foot chasseurs, marching in echelon with the grenadiers on their right, continued their advance even as the grenadiers were overthrown by Halkett and Chassé (the uniforms of the foot chasseurs and grenadiers were almost identical, making confusion in the heat of battle by British veterans forgivable). When the 1/3rd, 2/3rd Foot Chasseurs breasted the ridge, Maitland's foot guards – lying in the rye grass – rose to deliver a volley that took out one-fifth of the attackers. The British foot guards then closed with the bayonet, sending the two Imperial Guard battalions back down the ridge. But as the British guards charged, the 4th Foot Chasseurs – the final Imperial Guard battalion in echelon – loomed out of the smoke on Maitland's right. Seeing the danger, Maitland ordered a retreat back up the slope, which took place amid some confusion. Meanwhile, Colborne – deployed on Maitland's immediate right in the firing line – had also spotted the approach of the final French column. Realising he could take the French in flank, Colborne swung the 52nd out from the Allied line, bringing his 1,000 muskets parallel to the head of the approaching French. Moments later Colborne ordered a volley, which slammed into the left flank of the 4th Foot Chasseurs, which, after a show of resistance, followed their comrades down the slope.

When the Imperial Guard broke, Wellington famously remarked 'In for a penny, in for a pound' and ordered a general advance. Soon Colborne's 52nd – now supported by the rest of Adam's brigade plus **Hew Halkett**'s Hanoverians – came upon the three supporting Imperial Guard battalions (2/2nd Grenadiers, 2/2nd Chasseurs and 2/1st Chasseurs, the last commanded by the celebrated General **Cambronne**), which as stated above, did not advance beyond La

Haie Sainte. A firefight erupted, but eventually these battalions were also overthrown and the Allied troops advanced to Napoleon's command post at La Belle Alliance and victory. And so elements of Leeke's account were accurate, as indeed were elements of Gomm's.

In 1823 Leeke was finally promoted to lieutenant, but quit the army the following year. In 1829 he was ordained, becoming a curate, and later served as Rural Dean of Duffield: a post he held for 25 years.

Lefebvre-Desnouëttes
General Charles, Count (1773–1822)

General Lefebvre-Desnouëttes (1773–1822)

Commander of **Napoleon**'s Imperial Guard Light Cavalry Division at Waterloo. The son of a Parisian draper, Lefebvre-Desnouëttes was perhaps the most dashing and handsome of Napoleon's generals. Originally enlisting in 1789, Lefebvre-Desnouëttes was bought out by his disapproving parents. By 1792, however, the headstrong youth got his own way, becoming a trooper in a light cavalry regiment. A skilled horseman and natural leader, Lefebvre-Desnouëttes climbed the promotion ladder through merit, becoming a general of division in 1808 at the age of 35. He had already served as aide-de-camp to Napoleon and **Jérôme** Bonaparte, held the post of Grand Equerry – and colonel of the elite Chasseurs à Cheval of the Imperial Guard – been ennobled, and married Stéphanie, Napoleon's second cousin. But on 29 December 1808 Lefebvre-Desnouëttes was captured by the British at Benavente in Spain. He spent the next two years on parole in Cheltenham, where his status, charm and good looks made him something of a star. The General was eventually joined by his wife and son – Napoleon granting them passports – and the family became a popular addition to the Cheltenham social scene.

But in 1811 Lefebvre-Desnouëttes betrayed his British hosts. Posing as a Russian count, he broke parole and made it to the coast with his son and Stéphanie (disguised as a male travelling companion) in tow. Paying for a passage to France with a signet ring given him by Napoleon, Lefebvre-Desnouëttes made good his family's escape. The General rejoined the Grand Army in time for Napoleon's ill-fated Russian campaign.

After Napoleon's first abdication, Lefebvre-Desnouëttes remained loyal, rejoining the Emperor on his return from Elba in March 1815. Rewarded with command of the light cavalry of the Imperial Guard, Lefebvre-Desnouëttes marched into Belgium in June 1815, but not before conceiving his only daughter, Charlotte-Lavinie. His command consisted of Lallemand's Chasseurs à Cheval and **Colbert-Chabanais**' 2nd Chevaux-Légers Lanciers (better known as the Red Lancers). The division totalled almost 2,500 sabres.

Initially deployed as part of Napoleon's cavalry reserve at Waterloo, the Imperial Guard Light Cavalry Division became mysteriously involved in **Ney**'s fatal charges on **Wellington**'s centre in the late afternoon. According to historian Ronald Pawly (1998):

> After perhaps 3.30 p.m., at a period when the distracted Napoleon had handed tactical control of the battle to Ney, a gigantic cavalry movement began to take place. Exact responsibility for this rash gamble has been endlessly argued but never settled.

The story goes that Ney mistook some movement among Wellington's troops – a partial withdrawal, the evacuation of a column of wounded, or the flight of deserters – for a general retreat. As a consequence, Ney ordered a brigade of cuirassiers from **Milhaud**'s IV Cavalry Corps into action.

According to General Charles Thoumas (1888), the light cavalry of the Guard got involved due to a fatal misunderstanding:

> Milhaud's cuirassier regiments were ordered to pass from the right-hand side of the battlefield to the left, to be put at the disposal of Marshal Ney. They crossed with loud cries of 'Vive l'Empereur!' and when Milhaud . . . passed Lefebvre-Desnoëttes, he gripped his hand, saying: 'I will charge, support me.' Lefebvre-Desnoëttes, displaying the same audacity, or rather recklessness, he had shown in Spain,

believed that Milhaud had transmitted a direct order from the Emperor and followed him . . . Ney, seeing the cavalry of the Guard behind the cuirassiers, felt himself obliged to use it.

A.F. Becke (1914), however, blames Lefebvre-Desnouëttes directly, letting both Milhaud and Ney off the hook:

> Lefebvre-Desnouëttes (who was behind Milhaud) saw the cuirassiers move off, and on his own initiative he determined to support Milhaud. Ney, riding at the head of the cuirassiers, could not see the strength of the cavalry following him; and, until the attack was fairly launched, the convexity of the ground prevented Napoleon from noticing what was going on.

Yet another version of the debacle comes from the pen of Captain de **Brack** of the Red Lancers. Writing some twenty years after the event, de Brack claims (1876) that no direct order to charge was ever issued by Lefebvre-Desnouëttes. The attack of the Guard cavalry was, he says, an accident: the front squadrons, which had become disordered, began dressing their lines, and the rear squadrons, mistaking the movement for a general advance, sounded the charge.

Whatever kick-started the cavalry of the Guard, a number of ineffectual charges were made between 4 p.m. and 6 p.m. and Lefebvre-Desnouëttes went down wounded in one of them. According to de Brack, the sun had almost set when the light cavalry of the Guard quit the field, placing the event at perhaps 9.30 p.m.:

> General Lefebvre-Desnouëttes cried out in the greatest excitement that 'it is here that we must all die; that no Frenchman could outlive such a horrible day; that we must look for death among the mass of English facing us'. We tried to calm him down.

According to Raymond Horricks (1995), Lefebvre-Desnouëttes, 'announced his intention to stay in [sic] the battlefield and be killed, but Lallemand, also wounded, persuaded him to join the retreat'. Although badly hurt and almost incapable of riding, Lefebvre-Desnouëttes led his cavalry from Waterloo back to France. Maintaining a position north of Paris, Lefebvre-Desnouëttes remained in action until the city surrendered on 3 July 1815.

After Napoleon's second and final abdication, Lefebvre-Desnouëttes was sentenced to death, *absente reo*, by the Bourbons. Shaving off his cavalryman's moustache, he effected another disappearing act, escaping to the USA in the guise of a travelling salesman. Lefebvre-Desnouëttes lived in America until 1821, when his wife obtained permission for his return. He sailed back to Europe on the *Albion*, but the ship hit bad weather near the coast of Ireland and sank off Kinsale. Lefebvre-Desnouëttes, who had cheated death in so many charges, was among the drowned. He never saw his only daughter, the Waterloo child Charlotte-Lavinie.

Lobau
General Georges Mouton, Count
(1770–1838)

General Lobau (1770–1838)

Commander of **Napoleon**'s VI Corps, during the Waterloo campaign. *Mouton* means sheep in French – hence Napoleon's celebrated quip: 'Mon Mouton est un lion!' (My Sheep is a lion!) The son of a baker, 'Mr Sheep' joined the French Revolutionary Army in 1792, rising to become a general of brigade by 1805. A veteran of Austerlitz, Eylau, Friedland and the Peninsular War, he joined Napoleon's staff in 1809 for the Danube campaign against Austria. It was a lucky appointment, for he shone during the campaign and was rewarded with the title Count Lobau, after the Danubian isle of Lobau, Napoleon's base of operations. Serving in the campaigns of Russia and Germany that foreshadowed Napoleon's fall in 1814, Lobau (as Mouton was now known) reluctantly acknowledged the returning Bourbons, but rejoined the erstwhile Emperor on his return from exile in March 1815. Napoleon rewarded him with command of VI Corps, which, with the Imperial Guard, formed the reserve of the Emperor's Army of the North.

On 15 June 1815 the French lunged across the Sambre at Charleroi, pushing into Belgian territory and apparently 'humbugging' the Duke of **Wellington**. Lobau's corps was in the rear, however, making slow progress to the front, and taking no part in the early clashes with **Ziethen**'s Prussians at Fleurus, Gilly and Gosselies. Next day, 16 June, saw **Ney** squaring up to the Prince of **Orange** and Wellington at Quatre-Bras and Napoleon facing **Blücher** at Ligny. But Lobau was still dawdling. By 2 p.m. VI Corps was still several miles from Ligny, and Lobau, unsure whether to join Ney or Napoleon, halted for three hours to await orders. Eventually summoned to Ligny, he managed to arrive at 7.30 p.m., thus delaying the Emperor's knockout blow against Blücher's centre. This delay had disastrous consequences: for although the French beat the Prussians at Ligny, the latter withdrew under cover of darkness, confounding Marshal **Grouchy**'s pursuit, only to reappear in Napoleon's right-rear two days later at Waterloo. Thus it may be argued that Lobau's tardiness and lack of initiative saved Blücher on 16 June – although most histories make more mileage out of **d'Erlon**'s equally unimpressive performance on that day.

At Waterloo, Lobau's corps – perhaps 10,000-strong – was initially held in reserve. After 1 p.m., however, Lobau – who might otherwise have joined d'Erlon in the assault on Wellington – was sent to deal with **Bülow**'s Prussian corps, seen advancing towards the French right. But again Lobau wasted time: for instead of pushing the cavalry of **Domon** and Subervie beyond the wood to hold the line of the River Dyle, he halted at the exits of the Bois de Paris and spent the next three hours waiting for Bülow to appear. When the Prussians finally emerged from the Bois de Paris about 4 p.m., Lobau temporarily halted their progress with a series of bold attacks. But superior numbers eventually told and Lobau was shunted back on the village of Plancenoit, in Napoleon's right-rear. By 5.30 p.m. Lobau had taken on the job of guarding Napoleon's exposed right flank.

Although reinforced by **Duhesme**'s Young Guard, VI Corps was exhausted by the murderous fight developing in and around Plancenoit. Two hours later, Lobau was clinging on to the wreck of the burning village, desperately trying to buy time for Napoleon to make an orderly withdrawal from the battlefield. But the Emperor threw the Imperial Guard at Wellington instead, in a final throw for victory. When this failed and Wellington launched a general advance, many French units threw in the towel and quit the field, precipitating a wholesale withdrawal. But Lobau stood his ground at Plancenoit, allowing many French units to march or fly from the field. However, when the Prussian tide could no longer be stemmed, he too joined the retreat to Charleroi.

Next day, Lobau was wounded and then captured by Prussian horsemen. Taken to Blücher's headquarters at the Roi d'Espagne inn, Genappe, he was later delivered up to Wellington, who sent him back to England as a prisoner. This probably saved his life, as the returning Bourbons had placed Lobau on the 'most wanted' list of Jacobins and Bonapartists. Others, like Ney and **Labédoyère**, were not so lucky – they were arrested and executed as traitors. Lobau returned to France in 1818, when the political climate had cooled, after several years' exile in Belgium.

Macdonell
Lieutenant Colonel Sir James (c.1781–1857)

Commander of the Light Company, 2nd Battalion, 2nd Foot Guards, and officer commanding all troops within the château of Hougoumont. Third son of Duncan Macdonell (d.1788), chief of clan Macdonell of Glengarry, James entered the army as ensign in 1793, rising to become a captain of the elite 2nd Foot (Coldstream) Guards by 1811. As a guards officer, Macdonell was permitted two ranks: his regimental guards rank and a higher army rank, thus he was both captain and lieutenant colonel. A veteran of campaigns in the Mediterranean, Egypt and the Iberian peninsula, Macdonell was renowned as a capable leader. He was also a powerfully built man, allegedly the model for Fergus MacIvor in **Scott**'s 1814 novel *Waverley*.

But Macdonell would find greater fame at Waterloo as the defender of Hougoumont, the château at the foot of Mont St Jean, which protected **Wellington**'s right flank. According to Waterloo veteran **Edward Cotton** (1895):

> Hougoumont was first occupied on the afternoon of the 17th by the light companies of the 1st Division, composed of four battalions of

Foot Guards: the light troops of the 1st Regiment, under Colonel Lord **Saltoun**, held the orchard and wood; those of the Coldstream and 3rd Guards, under Colonel MacDonell, held the buildings and garden. In the out-grounds and wood there were also a battalion of Nassau troops, a company of Hanoverian field riflemen, and a hundred men of the Lüneberg Battalion. The other companies of the Guards were thrown into the valley on our side of the enclosures, as a support, and to keep up a communication with the main line.

Some time in the early morning of 18 June, Wellington moved the 1st Battalion, 2nd Nassau Regiment, the 1st Lüneberg Battalion and a company of riflemen or 'Jägers' into the wood commanding the southern approaches to the château, and pulled the 'light bobs' of the 1st Guards out of the complex and back to their brigade. Macdonell remained in command of the farm buildings and was ordered to 'defend the post to the last extremity'.

The battle for Hougoumont began around 11.30 a.m. with first French attack, led by Baudin from the south, via the wood. Although guns and howitzers from **Sandham**'s and **Bull**'s batteries opened up on the advancing French, the Nassauers and Hanoverians were driven back through the wood and into the orchard. Saltoun's light infantry were immediately sent back to the château and, after a determined counter-attack, reclaimed the orchard. At noon the

The château of Hougoumont – a contemporary print

French renewed their assault on Hougoumont, attacking from the west. Led by the brigades of Soye and Baudin, this sortie pushed a party of Dashwood's 3rd Foot Guards north along the west wall of Hougoumont. Rounding the corner of the château, the British guardsmen fled to safety through the open gate. The great north gate was closed behind them – but not before Sergeant **Ralph Fraser** had knocked Colonel Cubières, of the pursuing 1st Light Regiment, off his horse, mounted the steed himself, and ridden it into the courtyard in triumph.

But the attackers were determined to break in and according to Waterloo veteran **Rees Howell Gronow** (1900): 'When the French had taken possession of the orchard, they made a rush at the principal door of the château, which had been turned into a fortress.' They were reputedly led by Lieutenant Legros – nicknamed 'L'Enfonceur' or 'The Smasher' – who, according to most English history books, effected entry by means of an axe. The story goes that Legros 'hacked open' the north gate or at the very least stove in one of its panels. At any rate, Legros got into the courtyard, followed by a number of his men (accounts vary from 30 to 100), but all were slaughtered in hand-to-hand fighting (some writers claim a drummer boy survived, but for more on this, see Private **Matthew Clay**). Meanwhile, say the historians, Macdonell dashed to the open (damaged?) gate to prevent more enemies entering. He was joined by several others, and as can be imagined, this list varies with each retelling. But according to A.F. Becke (1914), Macdonell's helpers were Lieutenant Colonel H. Wyndham, Ensigns H. Gooch and J. Hervey, plus several NCOs, including Sergeant Fraser, Corporal **Graham** and Private Lister – perhaps ten men in all. Then the muscular Macdonell, aided by his colleagues, heaved the gate shut in the teeth of the oncoming French – a scene immortalised in the famous painting *Closing the Gates at Hougoumont* by R. Gibb – and secured it by dropping the heavy crossbar (presumably undamaged by Legros's axe).

And yet, shortly after this incident, Private Clay of the 3rd Foot Guards arrived before the north gate, having been separated from his unit in the initial firefight with the advancing French and left outside. Surprisingly – given the version of events outlined above – he found the gate open:

On entering the courtyard I saw the doors or rather gates were riddled with shot-holes, and it was also very wet and dirty; in its entrance lay many dead bodies of the enemy; one I particularly noticed which appeared to have been a French officer, but they were scarcely distinguishable, being to all appearance as though they had been very much trodden upon, and covered with mud; on gaining the interior I saw Lieutenant Colonel MacDonell carrying a large piece of wood or trunk of a tree in his arms (one of his cheeks marked with blood, his charger lay bleeding within a short distance) with which he was hastening to secure the gates against the renewed attack of the enemy.

Clay's testimony (1853) would seem to suggest that a desperate fight took place in the *open* doorway and that Macdonell decided to barricade the gate *after* this had occurred. A scenario supported by Macdonell's fellow Coldstreamer and Waterloo veteran Daniel Mackinnon (1833), who describes how a 'cloud of tirailleurs' menaced the château's 'rear' or north gate, which they succeeded in forcing:

At the critical moment, MacDonell rushed to the spot with the officers and men nearest at hand, and not only expelled the assailants, but reclosed the gate. The enemy from their overwhelming numbers again entered the yard, when the Guards retired to the house, and kept up from the windows such a destructive fire, that the French were driven out, and the gate once more closed.

According to Mackinnon, then, the French entered the courtyard not once but twice: and he does not mention axes, hand-to-hand slaughter, or pushing gates closed against a crush of French soldiery. Instead, Mckinnon suggests the French attackers were 'expelled' and 'driven out' by 'destructive' musket fire, and the gate closed later (presumably after Private Clay had wandered in).

Whatever the details of the incident, however, the result was the same: the French attack was thwarted and the vital bastion of Hougoumont saved – and as a consequence, so was **Wellington**'s skin. As the Duke later remarked: 'The success of the Battle of Waterloo depended on the closing of the gates of Hougoumont.'

(Strange to say, Wellington refers to Macdonell as 'MacDonald' in his Waterloo dispatch.)

Meanwhile, the Allied victory at Waterloo unleashed a wave of patriotic fervour in Britain. Reverend John Norcross (*c.*1762–1837), the loyal and steadfast vicar of Framlingham, Suffolk, offered a pension of £10 per annum (approximately £500 in modern terms) to 'the most deserving soldier at Waterloo'. Norcross repeatedly petitioned Wellington to select a hero – 'any one of my brave countrymen who fought under your grace in the late tremendous but glorious conflict' – but the Duke passed the honour to Sir John Byng, in recognition of the part played by his foot guards in the defence of Hougoumont. Thus, on 18 August 1815, Norcross's prize was split between Corporal **Graham** of the 2nd Foot Guards and Private Joseph Lister of the 3rd Foot Guards. But within two years Norcross was declared bankrupt and the annuity ceased. Norcross died on 10 April 1837 and some sources claim he left £500 (perhaps £25,000 in modern terms) to 'the bravest man in England'. The story goes that Norcross's will stipulated that Wellington should nominate the beneficiary and the Duke chose James Macdonell, in recognition of his heroic feat in securing Hougoumont's north gate. But Macdonell apparently demurred, declaring he was not solely responsible for the deed, and the Norcross bequest was shared with Graham. This story may be true – several versions of the Norcross story have been told over the years – but there is no mention of it in biographical material relating to MacDonell. But after Waterloo, as legend has it, Macdonell – the 'bravest man in England' – could never bear being in a room with an open door.

MacKay
Piper Kenneth (dates unknown)

Bagpipe-playing hero of the 79th Foot (Cameron Highlanders). MacKay's regiment was part of **Kempt**'s Brigade (**Picton**'s 5th Division), situated in **Wellington**'s centre, in advance of the farm of Mont St Jean, and behind the Ohain road. Attacked by French cavalry in the late afternoon of 18 June 1815, the 79th was ordered to form square. The battalion had suffered heavy casualties, including its commander, Lieutenant Colonel Neil Douglas, who was wounded. To boost morale, MacKay bravely strode forward, faced his foes, and launched into the 79th's traditional rallying call, *Cogadh no Sith* (War or Peace, the True Gathering of the Clans). MacKay proceeded to march round the outside of his battalion square, coolly piping his comrades to lift their spirits. This act of courage earned MacKay a handsome reward: for, having survived the battle, he received a magnificent set of silver-mounted bagpipes from the Crown. His regiment was one of only four units selected for especial praise by Wellington in his Waterloo Dispatch.

Maitland
Major General Peregrine (1777–1854)

Commander of the 1st Guards Brigade of **Cooke**'s 1st British Infantry (Guards) Division. Son of Thomas Maitland of Shrubs Hall in the New Forest, Peregrine Maitland joined the elite 1st Foot Guards on 25 June 1792 as a lowly ensign. A veteran of Flanders (1794), Corunna and Walcheren (both 1809), Maitland went on to command his regiment in the latter clashes of the Peninsular War, becoming a major general in 1813.

In the spring of 1815 – following **Napoleon**'s return to power – Maitland arrived at Brussels to take command of a brigade consisting of two battalions of the 1st Foot Guards (the 2nd and 3rd Battalions). As a hero of the Peninsular War and a widower (his wife, Louisa Crofton, having died 10 years before, after only two years of marriage), Maitland proved popular among the ladies of the British community anxious to secure a husband with prospects. But the 38-year-old Maitland embarked on a secret affair with Lady Sarah Lennox, daughter of the Duke of **Richmond**: a woman somewhat above his social station and almost half his age. But the love birds were to be separated – if only temporarily – by Napoleon's invasion of 15 June, which was stopped in its tracks three days later at Waterloo.

For most English writers, the climax of the Battle of Waterloo was the attack and repulse of Napoleon's Imperial Guard between 7.30 p.m. and 8 p.m. on 18 June. Napoleon threw in his Guard as a last roll for victory before Prussian forces under **Bülow** and **Ziethen** smashed through his right flank. Five battalions of the Imperial Guard – perhaps 3,500 men in all – spearheaded what was intended to be a general advance on **Wellington**'s ridge, supported by **d'Erlon** and **Reille**. A further three Guard battalions followed the leading columns as supports: but in the event marched no further than La Haie Sainte. The five Guard battalions in front advanced in echelon, the rightmost leading. Instead of ploughing straight ahead into Wellington's weak centre above La Haie Sainte, the columns – led by **Ney** and **Friant** – veered left, making towards Wellington's stronger right-centre, on the reverse slope of the hill and out of sight. As the Guard marched they broke into two parties. The leading, rightmost party consisted of the 4th and 1/3rd Grenadiers under Friant, which would be repulsed by the guns and muskets of Generals **Colin Halkett** and **David Hendrik Chassé**. The leftmost column consisted of the 1/3rd, 2/3rd and 4th Foot Chasseurs, which toiled up the hill towards Maitland's sector. 'As the leading column of the Imperial Guard began to ascend,' wrote historian William Siborne (1848), 'it became very much exposed to the concentrated fire from nearly all the batteries of the Anglo-Allied right wing, by which the most frightful havoc was dealt amidst its devoted ranks.'

Nevertheless, the foot chasseurs pushed on, driving off the Allied artillery crews. Siborne continues:

> Notwithstanding the terrible havoc made in the ranks of the leading column of the Imperial Guard, it continued its advance in admirable order, and with the greatest enthusiasm . . . They had now topped the summit. To the astonishment of the officers who were at their head, there appeared in their immediate front no direct impediment to their further advance . . . Pressing boldly forward, they had arrived within fifty paces of the spot on which the British guards were lying down, when Wellington gave the talismanic call – 'Up, guards; make ready!' and ordered Maitland to attack. It was a moment of

thrilling excitement. The British guards springing up so suddenly in a most compact four-deep line, appeared to the French as if starting out of the ground. The latter, with their high bonnets, as they crowned the summit of the ridge, appeared to the British, through the smoky haze, like a corps of giants bearing down upon them. The British guards instantly opened their fire with a tremendous volley, thrown in with amazing coolness, deliberation, and precision.

Rees Howell Gronow (1900), a young ensign fighting with the 3rd Battalion of the 1st Foot Guards, describes the sequel:

It was at this moment that the Duke of Wellington gave his famous order for our bayonet charge as he rode along the line. These are the precise words he made use of: 'Guards, get up and charge!' We were instantly on our legs and after so many hours of inaction and irritation at maintaining a purely defensive attitude (all the time suffering the loss of comrades and friends), the spirit which animated officers and men may easily be imagined. After firing a volley as soon as the enemy were within shot, we rushed on with fixed bayonets and that hearty *Hurrah!* peculiar to British soldiers.

It appeared that our men, deliberately and with calculation, singled out their victims, for as they came upon the Imperial Guard our line broke and the fighting became irregular. The impetuosity of our men seemed almost to paralyse their enemies: I witnessed several of the Imperial Guard who were run through the body apparently without any resistance on their parts. I observed a big Welshman by the name of Hughes, who was six feet seven inches in height, run through with his bayonet and knock down with the butt-end of his firelock, I should think a dozen, at least, of his opponents. This terrible contest did not last more than ten minutes, for the Imperial Guard were soon in full retreat, leaving all their guns and many prisoners in our hands.

The last Imperial Guard battalion to breast the ridge was the 4th Foot Chasseurs, and they were met not only by frontal fire from Maitland's brigade but by a devastating flanking fire from Colborne's 52nd Regiment, situated on Maitland's right. This incident – described by **William Leeke** (1866) of the 52nd – put paid to Napoleon's final assault, causing a shudder of anguish throughout his army, which according to William Siborne (1848), 'appeared rent asunder by some invisible power'. Wellington, looking on impassively, reputedly declared 'In for a penny, in for a pound' and ordered a general advance. The battle was won.

But Maitland still had unfinished business. Not content with victory in war, the ardent General also desired victory in love. And so, on the dark and rainy night of 16–17 October 1815, Maitland and Lady Sarah eloped. They were married at the Duke of Wellington's headquarters in Paris. Needless to say, the Duke and Duchess of Richmond were appalled: Maitland might be a hero but he was not titled and was not wealthy. But the fuss soon died down and the lovers were welcomed back into polite society.

As a postscript to Maitland's story – and indeed the Battle of Waterloo – mention should be made of the General's brother, Captain Frederick Lewis Maitland RN. He was skipper of HMS *Bellerophon* – the so-called 'Billy Ruffian' – the British ship-of-the-line that accepted Napoleon's surrender on 15 July 1815. The Emperor, unable to run the British naval blockade that prevented his escape to the USA, boarded the *Bellerophon* near Rochefort, in the hope of finding asylum in Britain. According to Captain Maitland (1904):

Buonaparte's dress was an olive-coloured great coat over a green uniform, with scarlet cape and cuffs, green lapels turned back and edged with scarlet, skirts hooked back with bugle horns embroidered in gold, plain sugar-loaf buttons and gold epaulettes; being the uniform of the Chasseurs à Cheval of the Imperial Guard. He wore the star, or grand cross of the Legion of Honour, and the small cross of that order; the Iron Crown; and the Union, appended to the button-hole of his left lapel. He had on a small cocked hat, with a tri-coloured cockade; plain gold-hilted sword, military boots, and white waistcoat and breeches. The following day he appeared in shoes, with gold buckles, and silk stockings – the dress he always wore afterwards, while with me.

On leaving the *Epervier* [a French brig], he was cheered by her ship's company as long as the boat was within hearing; and Mr Mott informed me that most of the officers and men had tears in their eyes.

General Bertrand came first up the ship's side, and said to me, 'The Emperor is in the boat.' He then ascended, and, when he came on the quarter-deck, pulled off his hat, and, addressing me in a firm tone of voice, said, 'I am come to throw myself on the protection of your Prince and laws.' When I showed him into the cabin, he looked round and said, 'Une belle chambre,' 'This is a handsome cabin.' I answered, 'Such as it is, Sir, it is at your service while you remain on board the ship I command.' He then looked at a portrait that was hanging up, and said, 'Qui est cette jeune personne?' 'Who is that young lady?' 'My wife,' I replied. 'Ah! elle est très jeune et très jolie,' 'Ah! she is both young and pretty.'

Napoleon was conducting a charm offensive. But his principal target was the British Prince Regent, to whom he had come 'like Themistocles, to throw myself on the hospitality of the British people. I place myself under the protection of their laws.' But as Vincent Cronin (1971) states in his biography of Napoleon:

> The English Government had already taken a decision totally at variance with Napoleon's hopes: the former Emperor of the French was a prisoner of State; he must never set foot on English soil; instead he must be deported to an island so remote that escape, even for him, would be virtually impossible.

Marbot
Colonel Jean-Baptiste-Antoine-Marcellin, Baron de (1782–1854)

Commander of the 7th Hussars, one of **Napoleon**'s elite light cavalry regiments, and author of the celebrated *Memoirs of Baron de Marbot*. Born of aristocratic parents – who secreted him in a girls' school to preserve him from the excesses of the French Re volution – Marbot joined the army in 1799 as a hussar trooper. Quickly gaining promotion, Marbot spent much of his early service as an aide-de-camp to Napoleon's top brass, including the likes of Augereau, Murat, Lannes and Masséna. A veteran of monster battles like Austerlitz, Jena, Eylau, Friedland Aspern–Essling and Borodino, he eventually became colonel of the 7th Hussars, via a stint with the 23rd Chasseurs à Cheval. Of all Marbot's battles, Eylau (7–8 February 1807) was perhaps the most arduous: for, by his own account, he was wounded and left for dead on the freezing battlefield, having attempted to rescue the regimental Eagle of the embattled 14th Line. According to Marbot (1900), his life was saved by Lisette, his extraordinary mare, who carried him from the thick of a savage melee to the comparative safety of the French lines – but not before ripping the face off one Russian grenadier ('making of him a living death's head, dripping with blood') and stamping another to pulp ('having torn out his entrails and mashed his body under feet, she left him dying in the snow').

This episode, however, was just one of many scrapes Marbot survived, and his memoirs remain one of the most vivid portrayals of Napoleonic warfare. A fact noted by novelist Sir Arthur Conan Doyle, who used Marbot as a model for his fictitious hussar hero Brigadier Gerard. Writing in *Through the Magic Door*, published in 1907, Conan Doyle gushed: 'the human, the gallant, the inimitable Marbot! His book is that which gives us the best picture by far of the Napoleonic soldiers.' And Marbot's reminiscences remained one of the writer's all-time favourite books (a Napoleonic enthusiast, Conan Doyle penned a short story based on the Waterloo exploits of Private **Joseph Brewer** of the Royal Waggon Train, published in 1894 and entitled, *A Straggler of '15*).

At Waterloo, Marbot led the 400 sabres of the 7th Hussars into battle, aided by Major **Victor Dupuy**. The regiment formed part of **Jacquinot**'s 1st Cavalry Division, an element of **d'Erlon**'s I Corps, and was deployed on the extreme right of the French line. According to historian A.F. Becke (1914), at 1 p.m. Marshal **Ney** was awaiting Napoleon's order to launch d'Erlon's corps against **Wellington**'s left-centre when:

> the Emperor took a last glance round, and away to the north-eastward he saw what appeared to be a dense black cloud emerging from the woods of Chapelle St Lambert. Officers on the Imperial Staff held different views concerning the composition of this apparition. But it was soon evident that it consisted of troops, although their strength and nationality remained uncertain. A reconnaissance was at once despatched, and all doubts were set at rest when a Prussian orderly officer was brought in. This officer made no attempt to conceal that the troops were the advanced guard of **Bülow**'s corps, and the corps was hastening to Wellington's

assistance. Napoleon at once realized that it was no longer a simple affair with Wellington. He would now have to reckon with Bülow's corps of 30,000 fresh troops closing round his right flank. In addition, as the prisoner also disclosed that all **Blücher**'s army had spent the previous night at Wavre, it was possible the whole Prussian Army might intervene in the battle. Nevertheless Napoleon was undismayed. Turning to **Soult** the Emperor said: 'This morning we had ninety chances in our favour. Even now we have sixty chances, and only forty against us.'

The Prussian orderly officer referred to above belonged to a regiment of hussars and was captured by Marbot's troopers. After questioning the prisoner, Marbot forwarded him to Napoleon – a scene immortalised by the artist Robert Hillingford in his painting *The Decisive Moment at Waterloo*.

In a letter dated 26 June 1815, and quoted in A.J. Butler's English translation of 1900, Marbot gives his impressions of Waterloo and its immediate aftermath:

> I cannot get over our defeat. We were manoeuvred like so many pumpkins I was with my regiment on the right flank of the army almost throughout the battle. They assured me that Marshal **Grouchy** would come up at that point; and it was guarded only by my regiment with three guns and a battalion of infantry – not nearly enough. Instead of Grouchy, what arrived was Blücher's corps. You can imagine how we were served. We were driven in, and in an instant the enemy was on our rear. The mischief might have been repaired, but no one gave any orders. The big generals were making bad speeches at Paris; the small ones lose their heads, and all goes wrong. I got a lance-wound in the side; it is pretty severe, but I thought I would stay to set a good example. If everyone had done the same we might yet get along; but the men are deserting, and no one stops them. Whatever people may say, there are 50,000 men in this neighbourhood who might be got together; but to do it we should have to make it a capital offence to quit your post, or to give leave of absence. Everybody gives leave, and the coaches are full of officers departing. You may judge if the soldiers stay. There will not be one left in a week, unless they are checked by the death penalty. The Chambers can save us if they like; but we must have severe measures and prompt action. No food is sent to us,

and so the soldiers pillage our poor France as if they were in Russia. I am at the outposts, before Laon; we have been made to promise not to fire, and all is quiet.

Butler concludes Marbot's tale with the following postscript:

In a letter written fifteen years later to General E. de Grouchy, Marbot enters more into detail. From this we learn that his regiment formed part of the force which was thrown back *en potence* on the extreme right, fronting the stream of the Dyle, as may be seen in any plan of the battle. The Emperor's instructions, conveyed to him by his old comrade, **Labédoyère**, who was then acting as aide-de-camp to Napoleon, were, while keeping the bulk of his force in view of the field of battle, to push forward his outposts towards Saint-Lambert and Ottignies; leaving a line of cavalry pickets a quarter of a league apart one from the other, so that when Grouchy arrived the news might be passed along without delay. One of these detachments reached Moustier about 1pm, and the officer in command at once sent back word that the French troops posted on the right bank of the Dyle were crossing the river – *i.e.*, falling back. This intelligence was forwarded to the Emperor, and an orderly officer soon came with orders to Marbot to push as far as possible in the direction of Wavre. Near Saint-Lambert one of his sections fell in with some Prussian cavalry, capturing an officer and a few men. These were promptly sent to the Emperor, and Marbot hastened with a squadron towards Saint-Lambert. There he saw a strong column advancing, and again sent intelligence to headquarters. But the reply was that it could be nothing but Grouchy; that the prisoners were doubtless some Prussian stragglers flying before his advance, and that Marbot might go forward boldly. Of course he had to obey orders; but soon had proof positive as to the nature of the advancing column. After hard fighting he had to retire, again reporting the circumstances to the Emperor. So possessed, however, was Napoleon with his own view of the case that he merely sent back the adjutant with orders to Marbot 'to let Grouchy know'. By this time his outposts were all falling back, and soon he was closely engaged with the English left, near Frischermont, and received the wound which he mentions in the letter already quoted.

Marshall
Sergeant Major Matthew (?–1825)

Soldier of the 6th Inniskilling Dragoons who survived 19 wounds following the charge of the Union Brigade. The Household and Union Brigades charged **d'Erlon**'s attacking I Corps about 2 p.m. on 18 June 1815. After smashing the infantry of General Marcognet, spearheading the French advance, the Inniskillings, under **Muter**, failed to rally. As a consequence, they were badly mauled by **Milhaud**'s cuirassiers and **Jacquinot**'s lancers. According to an item in *The Scots' Magazine*, quoted by Dalton (1904), Marshall,

> while sabreing a cuirassier on his right, had his bridle-arm broken by a stroke from his enemy on his left, and had not proceeded much further when he was beset by a crowd of French cavalry and hurled from his horse by a lance which penetrated his side. While he was falling, he received a heavy blow across the body, and another which broke his right thigh . . . The ground afterwards becoming somewhat clear, he espied a horse without any rider, towards which he crawled, and was about to mount, when a French trooper galloping up cut him down in the midst of his hopes, inflicting several severe wounds on his body. This part of the field being again occupied by the French, a French artilleryman made Marshall's body a resting-place for his foot while he rammed his gun. For two days and three nights, Marshall remained on the field without food or water, with nineteen lance and sabre wounds. On the regiment returning home he was discharged with two shillings per day. Resided at Belfast where he was much respected. Died there 28 September 1825.

Mercer
Captain Alexander Cavalié (1783–1868)

Commander of G Troop, Royal Horse Artillery and author of *Journal of the Waterloo Campaign* (first published in 1870). Commissioned at the age of 16, Mercer – the son of a general – was 32 at the time of Waterloo. He held the rank of Second Captain in U Troop but took over G Troop when its commander, Sir Alexander Dickson, was called away to other duties. Mercer was informed by Sir **Augustus Frazer** of **Wellington**'s order that, should the French cavalry threaten his gunners, he was to shelter them in the nearby infantry squares. But Mercer noticed that his infantry supports – the young and inexperienced troops of the Brunswick Corps – were wavering. Indeed, the officers and sergeants of these reluctant soldiers were thumping and shoving men back to their posts:

> To have sought refuge amongst men in such a state were madness
> – the very moment our men ran from their guns I was convinced,
> would be the signal for their disbanding. We had better, then, fall
> at our posts than in such a situation.

And so Mercer disobeyed Wellington's order, keeping his gunners engaged for the duration of the battle, and steadying the Brunswickers in the process. But such heroism came at a heavy cost: for G Troop sustained more casualties than any other Horse Artillery Troop (18 men and 140 horses killed or wounded). As for Mercer, he received little thanks or recognition for putting initiative before obedience. Although he eventually rose to the rank of major general, he forever maintained his decision to disobey the Duke had damaged his career.

As well as initiative, Mercer displayed cool courage at Waterloo, especially during **Ney**'s massed cavalry attacks of the late afternoon:

> At the first charge, the French column was composed of grenadiers
> à cheval and cuirassiers, the former in front. I forget whether they
> had or had not changed this disposition, but think, from the number
> of cuirasses we afterwards found, that the cuirassiers led the second
> attack. Be this as it may, their column reassembled. They prepared
> for a second attempt, sending up a cloud of skirmishers, who galled
> us terribly by a fire of carbines and pistols at scarcely forty yards from
> our front. We were obliged to stand with port-fires lighted, so that it
> was not without a little difficulty that I succeeded in restraining the
> people from firing, for they grew impatient under such fatal results.
> Seeing some exertion beyond words necessary for this purpose,
> I leaped my horse up the little bank and began a promenade (by no
> means agreeable) up and down our front, without even drawing my
> sword, though these fellows were within speaking distance of me.

This quieted my men; but the tall blue gentlemen, seeing me thus dare them, immediately made a target of me, and commenced a very deliberate practice, to show us what very bad shots they were and verify the old artillery proverb, 'The nearer the target, the safer you are.' One fellow certainly made me flinch, but it was a miss; so I shook my finger at him and called him coquin, etc. The rogue grinned as he reloaded and again took aim. I certainly felt rather foolish at that moment, but was ashamed, after such bravado, to let him see it, and therefore continued my promenade. As if to prolong my torment, he was a terrible time about it. To me it seemed an age. Whenever I turned, the muzzle of his infernal carbine still followed me. At length bang it went and whizz came the ball close to the back of my neck, and at the same instant down dropped the leading driver of one of my guns (Miller), into whose forehead the cursed missile had penetrated.

Merlen
Major General Jean-Baptiste, van
(?–1815)

Commander of the 2nd Light Brigade of **Wellington**'s Netherlands Cavalry Division at Waterloo. Van Merlen was, according to some sources, the first Allied officer to discover news of **Napoleon**'s projected invasion of Belgium. On 14 June 1815 van Merlen apparently intercepted a letter from a French officer, Baron Niel, giving details of Napoleon's

General van Merlen (?–1815)

advance into Belgium. Van Merlen dutifully passed the letter to countryman Baron **Chassé**, commander of Wellington's 3rd Netherlands Infantry Division. Chassé, in his turn, passed the letter to the Duke, who, it seems, did not credit the information it contained. Two days later, Wellington's Netherlanders were heroically staving off **Ney**'s superior French forces at Quatre-Bras.

It was here that van Merlen's brigade – consisting of the 6th Dutch Hussars and the 5th Belgian Light Dragoons – suffered heavily, sustaining some 350 casualties.

At Waterloo, on 18 June, van Merlen's brigade was initially posted in reserve with the rest of Baron de Collaert's Netherlands Cavalry Division. Most of de Collaert's brigade commanders, including van Merlen, had previously fought for the French: now they would meet their former comrades in a series of bloody cavalry combats. For, as historian Ronald Pawly writes (2002), 'the light brigades of Generals de Ghigny and van Merlen were repeatedly engaged in charge and counter-charge against the French cavalry attacks'. And it was at the head of one such charge that van Merlen was killed. According to historian Demetrius C. Boulger (1901):

> General Van Merlen had a presentiment that he would be killed in the battle. He wrote to this effect to his wife at Antwerp, and while breakfasting with General Collaert on the morning of the battle, he repeated it. Curiously enough, he figures among the 'missing' because his body was never found, despite the efforts of his family to recover it.

Milhaud
General Edouard-Jean-Baptiste, Count (1766–1833)

Commander of **Napoleon**'s IV Reserve Cavalry Corps. The youngest son of a farmer, Milhaud grew into a fierce Republican, reputedly taking part in the storming of the Bastille on 14 July 1789. By 1792 he had entered the political arena as an elected deputy to the National Convention, where he voted for the execution of Louis XVI with no right of appeal (the King was duly beheaded on 21 January 1793). A small but energetic man, Milhaud quit politics for the army in 1795. A natural leader and superb horseman, Bonaparte made him a general of brigade in 1800 – recognition for support during the 'Brumaire' coup the previous year. A veteran of Napoleonic campaigns in Central and Eastern Europe, Russia and Spain, Milhaud was obliged to retire following the Bourbon restoration of

1814 on account of his Republican past. But when Napoleon returned to power in March 1815 Milhaud rallied to the tricolour. On the eve of the Waterloo campaign Milhaud was given command of the IV Reserve Cavalry Corps, a force consisting of two cuirassier divisions under Generals Watier and **Delort**. Milhaud had never led these armoured warriors before – a point that did not go unnoticed at the time – but the diminutive firebrand had a faultless record for intelligent and responsible command. He was, in the words of General Sir Evelyn Wood (1895): 'one of the best cavalry leaders in the Grand Army'.

The cuirassiers formed the backbone of Napoleon's 'heavy' cavalry. Their name derives from the word *cuirass* – an iron shell designed to protect the wearer's front and back. French cuirassiers also wore iron helmets. These were stylish creations inspired by Ancient Greece: the iron skull cap was wrapped in a bearskin turban and topped with a copper crest, from which flowed a long horsehair 'mane'. Enormous boots and a fearsomely long sabre – designed for thrusting rather than slashing – completed the cuirassier's outfit. Massed into divisions, the cuirassiers – big men on big horses – provided Napoleon with a shock weapon of considerable power. At Waterloo Milhaud's 3,000 cuirassiers began the battle in reserve on the French right wing. After 2 p.m. Delort's division supported **Jacquinot**'s victorious counter-charge against **Uxbridge**'s intrepid British dragoons, who, having cut up **d'Erlon**'s infantry, had rashly charged the guns of Napoleon's grand battery.

But Milhaud's name is usually associated with the series of fatal French charges made against **Wellington**'s rock-solid in-fantry squares during the late afternoon. This celebrated episode is generally attributed to an error on the part of Marshal **Ney**. Apparently mistaking movements in rear of the Allied position for a general collapse (a partial retreat, an evacuation of wounded or an exodus of deserters – accounts vary), Ney decided to exploit the situation with a strong cavalry force. According to historian A.F. Becke (1914):

> Ney ordered a brigade of Milhaud's cuirassiers to attack. Farine sent two of his regiments; but his divisional commander, Delort, refused his permission, and only consented when he learned that Ney had

the Emperor's authority to make the attempt. Ney promptly repeated the order and included the whole corps of cuirassiers, whom he then led forward to carry out his premature and reckless enterprise. Unfortunately, **Lefebvre-Desnouëttes** [commander of the Imperial Guard's light cavalry division] . . . saw the cuirassiers move off, and on his own initiative he determined to support Milhaud. Ney, riding at the head of the cuirassiers, could not see the strength of the cavalry following him; and, until the attack was fairly launched, the convexity of the ground prevented Napoleon from noticing what was going on. Even if Ney had noticed Lefebvre-Desnouëttes following Milhaud, the Marshal might have concluded that the Emperor had ordered the Light Horse of the Guard to support Milhaud, and Ney would only have been confirmed in his rash resolve. The glittering mass, launched against Wellington's centre, numbered 5,000 veteran horsemen in forty-three squadrons, the finest body of horse seen on a battlefield since the time of Seydlitz.

It was about 4 p.m. when Ney led this legendary attack. Accounts vary as to the numbers involved, but they were so great that survivors spoke of being lifted from the ground with their horses in the crush. Obliged to avoid flanking fire from the bastions of Hougoumont and La Haie Sainte, the French squadrons were squashed into a compact wedge, which struggled over sticky ground towards the slopes of the Allied ridge. But Wellington's troops – while doubtless awed by the spectacle – were relieved to see the cavalry: for at last Napoleon's guns would fall silent. Meanwhile, the Allied crews stood to their own pieces and awaited the order to fire. As for Wellington's infantry, most were deployed in battalion squares (actually oblongs) on the reverse slope of the elevation, out of sight of the advancing host. Thus, as General Sir Evelyn Wood (1895), observes:

> there was not one of the cuirassiers who was not fully confident
> that he was going forward to complete a victory which had been
> practically already decided. The British infantry were not visible, and
> they were believed to be already in full retreat. Thus the immense
> mass advanced, full of confidence.

But Wellington's gunners could hardly fail to miss such an enormous target. And when the order finally came to open up, all hell broke loose. According to veteran **Edward Cotton** (1895), the Allied grape, canister and shrapnel 'rattled like hail on the steel clad warriors'. But still they came on, up to the very mouths of the guns. Cotton continues: 'Every discharge (the load was usually double) dreadfully shattered their ranks, and threw them into great disorder: but excited by the trumpets sounding the charge, they rode up to the cannons' mouths, shouting *Vive l'Empereur!'*

Much has been made of the failure to capture or at least disable the Allied batteries. Guns might have been dragged away, or 'spiked' by driving headless nails – or even bayonets – into their vents. But neither course was taken by the French. They did not even break the rammers' sponge staves. As for the crews, they fled (with the notable exception of **Mercer**'s G Troop) to the infantry squares at the last possible moment and returned to their guns when the coast was clear. Meanwhile, having rolled over the batteries, the French breasted the ridge and came upon the infantry squares – perhaps 20 in total – deployed chequerboard fashion, in order to provide mutual fire support. According to Wood (1895): 'As the Cuirassiers advanced against the squares, not a musket was fired until they came within thirty paces.' **Rees Howell Gronow** of the 1st Foot Guards recalled (Gronow 1900) that the Brits were ordered to fire low:

> so that on the first discharge of musketry, the ground was strewed with the fallen horses and their riders, which impeded the advance of those behind them and broke the shock of the charge.

Finally, Uxbridge's cavalry counter-attacked, sending the French riders back down the slope.

Across the valley at Rossomme, Napoleon was appalled by Ney's antics. Turning to Marshal **Soult**, his chief of staff, the Emperor declared: 'This is a premature movement, which may well lead to fatal results.' Soult – no friend of Ney's – replied: 'He [i.e. Ney] is compromising us as he did at Jena [a French victory over the Prussians fought on 14 October 1806].' Nevertheless, Napoleon decided that – having begun the enterprise – Ney must see it through. And so the Emperor ordered General Kellermann's III Reserve Cavalry Corps – a further 3,000 horsemen – to support Ney and Milhaud. But Kellermann – whose charge at Marengo on 14 June 1800 had saved Bonaparte's bacon – was unwilling to oblige. Like

Delort before him, Kellermann considered a cavalry charge unsupported by infantry ill-advised: especially against troops that – for the most part – appeared steady. But while Kellermann quibbled, General l'Héritier, one of his divisional commanders, set off without orders. Soon Kellermann's whole command was sucked into the vortex, to be followed by General **Guyot**'s Imperial Guard Heavy Cavalry Division.

And so the whole French cavalry – more than 10,000 sabres – was committed to a second assault on Mont St Jean. According to Captain Mercer (1927) of Wellington's horse artillery:

> The spectacle was imposing, and if ever the word sublime was appropriately applied, it might surely be to it. On they came in compact squadrons, one behind the other, so numerous that those of the rear were still below the brow when the head of the column was but at some sixty or seventy yards from our guns.

Again, the pace was slow and deliberate. Many British veterans – Gronow among them – remembered (Gronow 1900) the earth shaking beneath the beat of so many hooves:

> Not a man present who survived could have forgotten in after life the awful grandeur of that charge. You perceived at a distance what appeared to be an overwhelming, long moving line, which, ever advancing, glittered like a stormy wave when it catches the sunlight. On came the mounted host until they got near enough, whilst the very earth seemed to vibrate beneath their thundering tramp. One might suppose that nothing could have resisted the shock of this terrible moving mass.

Again the Allied gunners waited. Mercer (1927), for one, held his fire till the last moment:

> The discharge of every gun was followed by a fall of men and horses like that of grass before the mower's scythe. When the horse alone was killed, we could see the cuirassiers divesting themselves of the encumbrance and making their escape on foot. Still, for a moment, the confused mass (for all order was at an end) stood before us, vainly trying to urge their horses over the obstacles presented by their fallen comrades . . . As before, many cleared everything and

rode through us; many came plunging forward only to fall, man and horse, close to the muzzles of our guns; but the majority again turned at the very moment when, from having less ground to go over, it were safer to advance than retire, and sought a passage to the rear. Of course the same confusion . . . and slaughter prevailed as before, until gradually they disappeared over the brow of the hill. We ceased firing, glad to take breath.

Kellermann later stated: 'It's tempting to say that France's unfortunate destiny was directing the errors committed that day.'

And still the attacks continued. But so many dead and wounded encumbered the field, the latter assaults were conducted at little more than walking pace. And if William Tomkinson of the 16th Light Dragoons is to be believed (Tomkinson 1894), no serious attempt was made to penetrate the Allied infantry squares. A sentiment echoed by Gronow (1900), who recalled that:

In the midst of our terrible fire, their officers were seen as if on parade, keeping order in their ranks, and encouraging them. Unable to renew the charge but unwilling to retreat, they brandished their swords with loud cries of *Vive l'Empereur!* and allowed themselves to be mowed down by hundreds rather than yield. Our men, who shot them down, could not help admiring the gallant bearing and heroic resignation of their enemies.

A poignant example of which is given by **Thomas Morris** (1851) of the 73rd Foot:

They deliberately walked their horses up to the bayonet's point; and one of them, leaning over his horse, made a thrust at me with his sword. I could not avoid it and involuntarily closed my eyes. When I opened them again, my enemy was lying just in front of me, within reach, in the act of thrusting at me. He had been wounded by one of my rear-rank men, and whether it was the anguish of the wound or the chagrin of being defeated, I know not; but he endeavoured to terminate his existence with his own sword; but that being too long for his purpose, he took one of our bayonets, which was lying on the ground, and raising himself up with one hand, he placed the point of the bayonet under his cuirass and fell on it.

Some claim the French cavalry made 23 sorties against the Allied squares, others 14 or 12. According to historian Jac Weller (1967), however, the French could not have put in more than eight charges during the two hours the epic action lasted. For at 6 p.m., or thereabouts, the attacks ceased and the guns of Napoleon's grand battery resumed their thunder. Milhaud and Kellermann were both wounded at Waterloo. Their cavalry divisions, however, were destroyed. David Johnson (1978) highlights the tragedy of Waterloo for Milhaud and Kellermann: 'For the first time in a decade, two superb formations of the French heavy cavalry had reached a battlefield in prime condition . . . and they had been thrown away.'

After the French defeat Milhaud was one of the first to suggest peace talks with the Allies: a tactic that almost saved his career when Louis XVIII regained his throne in the wake of Napoleon's abdication. He followed this up with a florid letter to the King, expressing his desire to serve under the Bourbon banner. But branded a regicide, Milhaud could not hope to serve as a Bourbon general. Fearing banishment, imprisonment or worse, Milhaud then appealed to Louis for clemency and received it: he was suffered to remain in France – on a much reduced pension – and forced to quit the army.

Morris
Thomas (dates unknown)

Waterloo veteran and author of *Recollections of Military Service in 1813, 1814 and 1815* (first published in 1851). Often referred to as 'Sergeant Morris' in Waterloo literature, this cockney soldier fought as a private on 18 June, his promotion to sergeant coming later. Morris was a member of Captain D. Dewer's company, 2nd Battalion 73rd Foot. This battalion – almost 500 strong – formed part of Sir **Colin Halkett**'s 5th British Brigade, an element of **Alten**'s 3rd British Infantry Division. The 73rd was stationed in Wellington's front line, to the right of the crossroads atop Mont St Jean. According to historian William Siborne (1848), the battalion was one of those most exposed to 'the fierce onslaught of the French cavalry and to the continuous cannonade of their artillery'. The thunder of the guns, however, did not prevent Morris from enjoying a peaceful nap:

> As the enemy's artillery was taking off a great many of our men, we were ordered to lie down, to avoid the shots as much as possible; and I took advantage of this circumstance to obtain an hour's sleep, as comfortably as ever I did in my life.

The appearance of the steel-clad French cuirassiers, however, disturbed Morris's slumber.

Morris survived the battle unscathed, but his battalion suffered appalling casualties: some 263 men or 53 per cent of its initial strength. That night, **Wellington**'s survivors slept on the field of battle, in the midst of thousands of dead, dying and wounded men and horses. Morris recalled:

> We lay on the ground that night. I fell asleep, but awoke again about midnight, almost mad, for want of water, and I made up my mind to go in search of some. By the light of the moon, I picked my way among the bodies of my sleeping, as well as of my dead comrades; but the horrors of the scene created such a terror in my mind that I could not muster courage to go by myself, and was turning back to get my brother along with me, when on passing where a horse was lying dead, on its side, and a man sitting upright with his back against the horse's belly, I thought I heard the man call to me, and the hope that I could render him some assistance, overcame my terror. I went towards him, and placing my left hand on his shoulder, intended to lift him up with my right; my hand, however, passed through his body, and I then saw that both he and his horse had been killed by a cannon ball.
>
> I now fairly ran back again to my resting-place, and arousing my brother, begged of him to go with me for water. The thought struck us that we might find some among our comrades, who were sleeping around. We came at last to a man named Smith, who, for his foraging propensities, was called 'Cossack Smith' . . . Well, on sounding his canteen, we found it full of water, and he was sleeping with his head upon it, and the strap passed round his body. The strap we unbuckled; and gently raising his head, we

substituted an empty canteen for the full one, and retired to the spot where we had been previously lying.

We, between us, emptied the canteen, and flung it from us; and then laid down and slept till sunrise, when the first sound we heard was Smith, blustering and swearing about the loss of his water; and threatening, if he knew who had taken it, he would run him through; and I knew sufficiently of the man, to believe he would do so. In order to satisfy my own conscience about the matter, I offered him a portion of the spirits, out of my canteen; he took it, but observed, that spirits then was not like water. As he was of a very revengeful disposition, we thought it prudent to keep him in the dark, as to who the thieves were.

Müffling
General Philipp Friedrich Carl Ferdinand, Baron von (1775–1851)

Prussian liaison officer attached to **Wellington**'s headquarters during the Waterloo campaign. The son of a Saxon army officer, Müffling entered the Prussian service in 1788, eventually becoming a military surveyor and member of the Prussian General Staff. During Prussia's War of Liberation against Napoleon in 1813, Müffling – a major general by this time – served with **Blücher**. For the Waterloo campaign, however, Müffling reluctantly accepted a posting to Wellington's headquarters as a liaison officer. He was apparently selected for the job having negotiated Oliver Goldsmith's 1766 novel *The Vicar of Wakefield*, thus demonstrating his proficiency in English.

Despite his own reservations, Müffling proved to be an inspired choice, for it was largely due to his efforts that Wellington and Blücher collaborated so effectively on Waterloo Day. For a start, it was Müffling who formalised Anglo-Prussian cooperation for the battle in a plan detailing three possible scenarios. First, if **Napoleon** attacked Wellington's right, then Blücher would march on Ohain, providing the Duke with a reserve. Second, if Napoleon attacked Wellington's centre, Blücher would send one corps via St Lambert to take the French in the right flank, while another marched via Ohain to support the Duke's left wing. Third, if Napoleon marched on St Lambert (between Waterloo and Wavre), in order to drive a wedge between the Allies, Blücher would hold his ground, while Wellington advanced to attack the French rear.

By 11.30 a.m. on 18 June Napoleon's intentions became clear, and Müffling sent an aide galloping to Blücher with news that the second scenario was unfolding. As a result, Blücher sent **Bülow** and **Pirch** against the French right, **Ziethen** in support of Wellington, and left **Thielemann** at Wavre to deal with **Grouchy**. Nevertheless, Prussian progress was slow, mainly due to heavy going over a boggy landscape devoid of adequate roads. Müffling, with Wellington on the ridge of Mont St Jean, felt a sense of responsibility for the performance of his Prussian colleagues, and anxiously watched for their arrival. By late afternoon, the Duke was also becoming fretful over Prussian delays. According to veteran **Edward Cotton** (1895):

> His Grace, when he observed the diminished numbers of his brave troops, presenting still the same fearless attitude, felt there must be a limit to human endurance, and frequently turned his telescope in the direction where he expected the Prussian reinforcements to arrive, who were to cooperate more immediately with his left.

About 6 p.m. Ziethen was in sight and Wellington sent an aide-de-camp, Lieutenant Colonel **Fremantle**, to hurry him along. But far from rushing to the Duke's aid, the Prussian column turned round and began marching off in the direction of Plancenoit. Müffling, observing events from Wellington's ridge, was horrified and immediately galloped after Ziethen:

> General von Ziethen, whom fortunately I soon overtook, had received instructions from the Field Marshal [Blücher], to close up to him, and wished very properly to effect this by going by Papelotte; but he changed his intention, when one of his officers, whom he had sent forward to ascertain how the battle was going, returned with intelligence that the right wing of the English was in full retreat. This inexperienced young man had mistaken the great number of wounded (by musketry) going or being taken to the rear to be dressed, for fugitives, and accordingly made a false report. On my assuring General von Ziethen of the contrary, and undertaking to

bring the corps to the appointed place, and since in any movement
downwards from Papelotte he would not only find difficulties, but
also lose the time for cooperation, he instantly turned about and
followed me, and continued to advance until it grew dark, driving
the enemy before him. By this retrograde movement of General
von Ziethen, occasioned by this false report, the battle might
have been lost, as it would have altogether prevented the corps
from reaching the field of battle; whereas, by marching on
Papelotte, its advanced guard was in full action a quarter of
an hour later.

Having set Ziethen back on the right track, effectively saving
Wellington's bacon, Müffling then – by his own account (1853) –
took it upon himself to reinforce the Duke's hard-pressed centre.
According to Müffling:

From my station at Papelotte, I could overlook the advance of the
enemy's reserve from La Belle Alliance against the Duke's centre;
and as the advanced guard of the I Corps (General von Ziethen)
had already appeared in the position on the nearest height, I begged
Generals **Vandeleur** and **Vivian** to hasten immediately with their
six regiments of English cavalry to the assistance of the distressed
centre. On account of the arrival of the Prussian corps they were no
longer wanted on the left wing. These regiments marched off, and
reached the centre in good time to make some brilliant charges.

But the relocation of Vandeleur and Vivian from Wellington's
left to his centre receives several treatments in the literature.
According to some sources, the Duke himself ordered the movement. According to Vivian (1897), he acted on his own initiative,
writing:

About six o'clock I learnt that the cavalry in the centre had suffered
terribly, and the Prussians having by that time formed to my left,
I took upon myself to move off from our left, and moved directly
to the centre of our line, where I arrived most opportunely.

Meanwhile, historian William Siborne (1848), claimed **Uxbridge**
ordered the cavalrymen to move. But Müffling stood his ground over
this issue, adding the following note to his memoirs (1853):

This march of the brigades of Vandeleur and Vivian from the left wing to the centre of the English line of battle, is very correctly described, as far as regards time, occasion, and execution, in the report of the battle by the English Captain Siborne. But the author has been misinformed as to *who* gave directions for this movement. I should certainly make no mention of this circumstance (for it is a matter of perfect indifference to history, whether A or B issued the order), were not my report of the battle, which was written years before the appearance of Siborne's work, thereby exposed to being censured as inaccurate.

In fact, Müffling's account of Waterloo, published in Stuttgart and Tübingen in 1816, was one of the first non-English versions of the battle to appear in print. His memoirs followed long after, materialising in English in 1853 as *Passages From My Life*. In his memoirs, Müffling highlights Anglo-Prussian cooperation prior to victory at Waterloo, but hints at antagonism immediately after. Both the British and Prussians competed for ownership of the battle, which largely centred on the issue of finding a name for the great triumph. Müffling writes:

> About midnight, at Waterloo, returning from the pursuit, which I had continued with the Prussian army to Genappe, I said to the Duke, 'The Field Marshal will call the battle "Belle-Alliance".' He made no answer, and I perceived at once that had no intention of giving it this name. Now, whether he was afraid of thereby prejudicing himself or his army, I know not. Meanwhile, he had probably already called it the Battle of Waterloo in his previous report to England.

Muter
Lieutenant Colonel Joseph (?–1840)

Commanding officer of the 6th (Inniskilling) Dragoons, part of Sir **William Ponsonby**'s 2nd British (Union) Cavalry Brigade. The Inniskillings had been spared the Peninsular War, but joined

Wellington's Army of the Low Countries in time for Waterloo. Brigaded with the 1st (Royal) Dragoons and the 2nd (Royal North British) Dragoons (better known as the Scots Greys), Muter's command – consisting of some 450 sabres – was initially posted left of the Brussels road, in rear of **Picton**'s division on the reverse slope of Mont St Jean. Around 2 p.m. on 18 June 1815, however, the Inniskillings were ordered to advance, with the rest of the Union Brigade, to counter the threat posed by **d'Erlon**'s attacking infantry columns. Meanwhile, to the right of the main road, **Somerset**'s 1st British (Household) Cavalry Brigade also proceeded against the approaching French, both infantry and cavalry. According to historian William Siborne (1848), Ponsonby led the Union Brigade forward, but, unable to see the enemy on the other side of the ridge, decided to call a halt and ride on ahead to observe:

> He was accompanied by Colonel Muter, commanding the Inniskilling Dragoons, whom he desired to return, and place himself in front of the centre squadron, and to order and conduct the movement, the moment he should observe him hold up his cocked-hat as a signal.

As the riders breasted the ridge, a man in civilian clothes shouted: 'Now's your time!' This was Charles Lennox, the fourth Duke of **Richmond**, who was wandering around the battlefield as a spectator. William Siborne describes the sequel:

> The Irish 'hurrah!' loud, wild, and shrill, rent the air, as the Inniskillings, bursting through the hedge and bounding over the road, dashed boldly down the slope towards the French columns, which were about a hundred yards distant.

The 5,000 infantrymen of Donzelot's division were in a daze. Taken by surprise, they had no time to form square, but managed to fire a few shots into the ranks of their ferocious assailants. According to Sir Evelyn Wood (1895):

> The Inniskillings in the centre of the Union Brigade galloped at the rear columns of Donzelot's division, composed of the 54th and 55th Regiments, the right and centre squadrons attacking the 55th

Regiment, and the left squadron charging by itself the 54th Regiment. The feeble fire from a few men in the front did not for a moment check the Inniskillings, who, riding into the middle of the ranks, struck down a number of men, while the remainder, throwing away their muskets, asked for, and received quarter. Some three thousand men were taken by Picton's men to the rear, as prisoners.

But Ponsonby's dragoons continued to surge forward, while on their right, Somerset's swept past the farmhouse of La Haie Sainte. Sir Evelyn Wood continues:

> As the cavalry passed through the valley, they cut to pieces two field batteries, which, in trying to follow d'Erlon's corps had stuck fast in deep ground. Our men killed the gunners, drivers and teams, and destroyed the harness [sic], wrecking fifteen guns so completely that they could not be brought into action again that day.

And still the dragoons pushed on, galloping up to the muzzles of **Napoleon**'s grand battery and the waiting lances and sabres of **Milhaud**'s IV Cavalry Corps.

Now the hunters became the hunted, as with horses blown and sword-arms numb from combat, the British dragoons tried to regain their lines, pursued by deadly enemies. Losses were high among the returning riders. Muter, in a letter quoted by H.T. Siborne (1891), states that his regiment 'suffered severely . . . from peletons [i.e. platoons of 30–40 horsemen], clouds, or small bodies of French lancers'. And so triumph turned to tragedy. The two British heavy cavalry brigades had careered out of control and paid the price.

Generations of historians have searched for a scapegoat, but Muter says this of his own inexperienced men: 'flushed by extraordinary success, they went on with so much impetuosity' (Gronow 1900). As for regimental officers who should have known better, Muter exonerates them by claiming that no clear orders were received before the charge: that, in effect, no one knew how far to go. In effect, Muter – perhaps with some justification – passes the buck: but Ponsonby, the brigade commander, did not survive the charge to accept it. And neither did Lieutenant Colonel **Hamilton** of the

Scots Greys, last seen in the mad dash for the French guns. Thus, as Muter states: 'I succeeded to the command of the brigade.'

Muter rallied the survivors of the Union Brigade but was ordered forward to support Wellington's hard-pressed infantry an hour or two later. And there, according to Lieutenant Colonel Sir Arthur Clifton of the 1st Dragoons, in a letter quoted by historian Gareth Glover (2004), the brigade remained, 'amid the most galling and destructive fire, until the termination of the action'. Muter confirms this in a letter quoted by H.T. Siborne (1891):

> about four or so in the afternoon we had moved to the right of the [Brussels] road. About six I was wounded, and Sir Arthur Clifton had command of the brigade, then lieutenant-colonel of the Royals.

But despite Muter's testimony that Clifton took command of the brigade about 6 p.m., many writers have Muter charging at its head two or three hours later. The source of this anomaly is an anecdote from the pen of **Gronow**, an officer of the 1st Foot Guards, who later became a celebrated memoirist. Gronow relates how, following the repulse of Napoleon's Imperial Guard about 8.15 p.m., Major Dawson-Damer (the surname 'Damer' was added in 1829), a staff officer, was sent with orders for the Union Brigade to join Wellington's general advance. Damer apparently found the survivors of the brigade with Muter at their head, his helmet beaten in and his arm in a sling. Told to charge, Muter gave Damer a long, withering look:

> The gallant Scot . . . said nothing, but got his men together and they all broke into a sort of canter, and guided by Damer, came upon some French infantry, who were still defending themselves with a kind of desperation. As Muter gave the order to charge, the French fired a volley and hit Damer in the knee, who heard Muter grumble out in his Scotch phraseology, as he dashed amongst the French, 'I think you ha' it nu', sir'.

This oft-repeated tale would suggest Muter remained with the Union Brigade after being wounded and participated in its final charge.

Whether or not this was the case, Muter was certainly among the wounded by battle's end. His regiment suffered a total of 217 casualties. This figure represents a casualty rate of around 48 per cent, roughly echoing that of the Union Brigade as a whole. Muter survived the campaign, taking the surname Straton on succeeding to the property of his aunt, Miss Straton, in 1816. He died on 23 October 1840, leaving £70,000 to Edinburgh University.

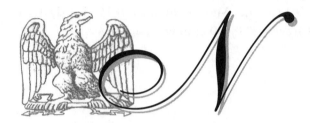

Napoleon I

(1769–1821)

Napoleon (1769–1821) – depicted in 1815

Emperor of the French and Commander-in-Chief of the French Army. Napoleon once declared himself to be a 'thing' rather than a 'person'. But he was many 'things' to many people. For some he was a thinker ('Whatever has not been profoundly meditated in all its details is totally ineffectual'); a visionary ('Imagination rules the world'); a Revolutionary ('I have fought like a lion for the Republic'); a national hero ('Everything for the French people'); a master strategist ('I see only one thing, namely, the enemy's main body: I will try to crush it, confident that secondary matters will then settle themselves'); a genius ('God has given me the power and will to overcome all obstacles'); even a superman ('Impossible – a word found only in the dictionary of fools'). For others he was an adventurer ('I aimed at the empire of the world; who in my place would not have done the same?'); a braggart ('I am not an ordinary man, and the laws of morals and of custom were never made for me'); a cynic ('Men are moved by two levers only: fear and self-interest'), a dictator ('Power is my mistress'); a butcher ('Troops are made to let themselves be killed'); a monster ('War justifies everything'); and a grand disturber ('A man like me only ceases to be formidable when he is laid in the tomb'). For the 'grumblers' of the Grand Army, however, he was 'Our Comrade' – a *confrère*, who understood soldiers and communicated in their language: 'A man does not have himself killed for a few halfpence a day . . . you must speak to the soul in order to electrify the man.'

Born at Ajaccio, Corsica, the second son of Carlo Buonaparte (a lawyer and impoverished aristocrat) and Letizia Ramolino (a local beauty who later became the formidable 'Madame Mère' of an unruly clan), Napoleone Buonaparte (the original spelling of his name before he Frenchified it) had Italian not French blood running through his veins. The Buonapartes originally hailed from Tuscany, the Ramolinos from Lombardy: but it was French-occupied Corsica that provided the backdrop to Carlo and Letizia's marriage and Napoleon's childhood. And it was to France that Napoleon was sent in 1778 to be made into a soldier. Understanding little French, Napoleon entered the Military Academy at Brienne, and later the École Militaire in Paris. A shabby foreigner who couldn't speak the lingo, Napoleon was picked on by the other boys: so he learned to talk with his fists. But that said, Napoleon was by nature a student. He excelled at mathematics and loved the classics – Alexander and Caesar were his heroes. Thus, as he stated at the time: 'With my sword by my side, and Homer in my pocket, I hope to carve my way through the world.' And he did: creating a latter-day Roman Empire from the chaos of the French Revolution, with Paris as its capital.

Exactly how Napoleon reached the top – and then blew it – is the subject of countless books: indeed, no other mortal has been written about more. In a nutshell, however, Napoleon's flight path was as follows: in 1785 he was commissioned into the French Royal Artillery: four years later the Revolution began, and having executed their Bourbon king, Louis XVI, the French found themselves at war with a coalition of European allies. In 1793 Napoleon played a significant role at the Siege of Toulon, helping to repel an Allied expeditionary force, for which he was rewarded with promotion to general. In 1796 Napoleon married Joséphine de Beauharnais before taking command of French forces in Italy and scoring a series of spectacular victories against the Austrians. In 1798 he led an expedition to Egypt. Despite initial successes the campaign foundered and Napoleon returned to France the following year to stage a successful *coup d'état*, which made him First Consul of France. In 1804 Napoleon silenced political opposition – as well as tiresome Bourbon plots against his life – by executing the hapless Duc d'Enghien, a Royalist figurehead. He then crowned himself Emperor and King of Italy.

With an outraged Europe in arms against him, Napoleon created a Grand Army, including a powerful Imperial Guard, and took on all comers. In 1805 Napoleon defeated the Austrians and Russians at Austerlitz (2 December); in 1806 he defeated the Prussians at Jena and Auerstädt (14 October); and in 1807 he defeated the Russians and Prussians at Friedland (14 June). Having dismantled the Holy Roman Empire and replaced it with a French-led Confederation of the Rhine, Napoleon proceeded to lord it over Europe, creating kingdoms for his brothers and generally kicking sand in the face of the *ancien régime*. But a trade war with Britain eventually led to disastrous campaigns in Spain and Russia, and by 1813 – having left the barren Joséphine for the fertile Austrian Marie-Louise – Napoleon was on the ropes. A monster defeat at Leipzig (16–19 October 1813), inflicted by a combined force of Russian, Prussian, Austrian and Swedish troops, effectively finished Napoleon off: but he fought to the bitter end, abdicating on 6 April 1814 after Paris fell to the Allies. With the Bourbons back on the French throne in the bulky person of Louis XVIII, Napoleon was exiled to the Mediterranean isle of Elba.

But Napoleon did not drop off the radar. Bored, listless and broke – the French royals reneged on their promise to provide a pension of 2 million francs a year – Napoleon plotted a comeback. Waiting till Sir Neil Campbell – the British Commissioner at Elba – quit the island to visit Leghorn, Napoleon slipped away on 26 February 1815. He sailed on the brig *Inconstant*, accompanied by some 1,000 followers packed into a further six vessels. Dodging the *Partridge*, a

British sloop of war, Napoleon's little flotilla made a safe landing near Cannes on 1 March.

Napoleon's return to France was like a lightning strike: it electrified many Frenchmen disillusioned with Bourbon rule, and it shocked his former enemies into a state of near nervous collapse. The following excerpts from the *Paris Moniteur* neatly summarise Napoleon's journey back to power:

> The cannibal has left his den . . . The Corsican wolf has landed in the Bay of San Juan . . . The tiger has arrived at Gay . . . The wretch spent the night at Grenoble . . . The tyrant has arrived at Lyons . . . The usurper has been seen within fifty miles of Paris . . . Bonaparte is advancing with great rapidity, but he will not set his foot inside the walls of Paris . . . Tomorrow Napoleon will be at our gates . . . The Emperor has arrived at Fontainebleau . . . His Imperial Majesty Napoleon entered Paris yesterday, surrounded by his loyal subjects.

But the 'Corsican wolf' had apparently turned into a lamb en route, for on resuming his throne, Napoleon let it be known he desired peace. Indeed, a flurry of letters was dispatched to the crowned heads of Europe assuring one and all that the Emperor had no territorial ambitions and simply wanted a quiet life. No one was listening. In fact, before Napoleon reached Paris, the Allies decreed him an outlaw, dubbing him 'the grand disturber of the peace of the world', and pledged to raise new armies for a mighty march on Paris.

But Napoleon could not wait for this avalanche of men to engulf him – he had to take the initiative. According to Philip Haythornthwaite (1999), 'his best hope of salvation was to take the offensive against the nearest Allied forces, and by securing a rapid victory, to establish a position from which he could negotiate with advantage'. The only Allied armies within striking distance were those of **Wellington** and **Blücher**, stationed in the newly created Kingdom of the Netherlands (Dutch and Belgian territories formerly annexed to France). Napoleon planned to attack, driving a wedge between Wellington and Blücher, defeating each in turn. Then, with Brussels at his mercy, his former subjects would rejoin him, the Allied coalition would crack, and Napoleon could negotiate a favourable peace. The scheme was brilliant but fraught with risk: it was Napoleon's last throw of the dice.

Looking back on the Waterloo campaign, Napoleon mused:

> I no longer felt that complete confidence in final success which accompanied me on former undertakings . . . I had no sooner gained an advantage than it was followed by a reverse.

This view of the campaign – that the French were simply defeated by bad luck – has gained ground over the years. Bad weather has been cited as a major factor, causing unavoidable confusion and delays. Unfortunate breakdowns in communication between French top brass – **Soult, Ney, d'Erlon** and **Grouchy** – have also been highlighted. And so has Napoleon's health, supposedly poor on Waterloo Day. But the inference is that Napoleon *should* have won and *would* have won had his luck not deserted him. Napoleon – unsurprisingly – was keen to promote the idea that he was defeated by a caprice of fortune, declaring: 'Everything failed me just when everything had succeeded!' and 'Look at the English! They conquered us, and yet they are far from being our equals.' And French novelist Victor Hugo later warmed to this theme, famously announcing that 'God was bored with Napoleon.' One can sympathise with this notion to an extent, but the major fiascos of the Waterloo campaign – the antics of **Bourmont**, d'Erlon, Ney and Grouchy – were more to do with bad management than bad luck: what Field Marshal Montgomery, in a later age, might have called 'lack of grip'. And despite Napoleonic spin, nothing can hide the fact that, having gleefully declared 'Now I have them, these English!' the Emperor failed to knock Wellington's polyglot army off its hill – even over the course of 12 hours.

But even if he had, Napoleon was probably doomed. Back in France, he lacked the political support necessary for a long, drawn-out war: thus, as Owen Connelly (1987) states, Waterloo was a 'glorious irrelevance'. And yet, in a sense, Napoleon *did* win at Waterloo. For as Hilaire Belloc (1931) observes, although the immediate outcome of the battle was Bonaparte's overthrow and the re-establishment of the *ancien régime* in France, the clocks could not be turned back: Napoleon, and the Revolution that unleashed him, had already become complex features in the European psyche: 'It is obvious . . . that the general political object of the

Revolutionary and Napoleonic armies was not reversed at Waterloo. It was ultimately established.' On 17 October 1815 Napoleon landed on the South Atlantic isle of St Helena. In London, the British Prime Minister, Lord Liverpool declared: 'he will soon be forgotten.'

Ney
Marshal Michel, Duke of Elchingen, Prince of Moskova (1769–1815)

Napoleon's chief lieutenant during the Waterloo campaign, and battle-field commander on 18 June 1815. The son of a barrel-maker from Saarlouis, Ney enlisted in the French Army as a hussar trooper in 1787. Commissioned as an officer in 1792, the outbreak of the Revolutionary Wars fast-tracked Ney's career and by 1796 he was a general. A fervent supporter of Napoleon,

Marshal Ney (1768–1815)

who made him a Marshal of the Empire in 1804, Ney became one of the Grand Army's best corps commanders. Nicknamed 'Le Rougeaud' on account of his red hair, Ney found fame as Napoleon's rearguard commander on the gruelling retreat from Moscow in 1812. Apparently suffering battle fatigue following grim experiences in Russia, Ney fought through further disasters during Napoleon's ruinous campaigns of 1813 and 1814. Once dubbed 'the Bravest of the Brave' by the Emperor, Ney was among those lieutenants who pressed for Napoleon's abdication in April 1814. Following Napoleon's fall Ney accepted Bourbon rule, swearing allegiance to Louis XVIII. According to historian Raymond Horricks (1995), Ney: 'served the restored Bourbons, but unhappily. He busied himself with the internal reorganisation of the army, in particular the cavalry.' But as A.G. MacDonell (1934) states:

> During the first Restoration the Bourbons contrived to make themselves distrusted, despised, and detested in an incredibly short space of time. The blunders which they committed in those few months were really remarkable.

And Napoleon, despite being incarcerated on the Mediterranean isle of Elba, was keeping tabs on events in France via a network of spies, sympathisers and informers. Concluding he had nothing to lose – especially when the Bourbons cut his cash allowance and began plotting to kidnap him (or worse) – Napoleon staged a successful escape and landed at Fréjus in the South of France on 1 March 1815. Commanding a tiny army of about 1,000 men – including a few hundred Poles under **Jerzmanowski** – Napoleon's charisma caused an avalanche as, one by one, his former generals and soldiers deserted the white flag of the Bourbons in favour of Napoleon's tricolour. In Paris, however, Ney demonstrated his loyalty to Louis by announcing that he would arrest Napoleon and bring him back in an iron cage – an unfortunate comment that Napoleon would not forget. But Ney seems to have been motivated by a desire for peace within France and beyond its borders. Hoping to avert a civil war and preserve peace in Europe, Ney marched south at the head of an army, determined to overthrow his erstwhile Emperor.

By 13 March Ney was nearing Dijon as Napoleon entered Lyons. Now Ney's force was within range of Napoleon's magnetic pull, and the Marshal could only look on as his subordinates began drifting away to the former Emperor's camp. On 17 March Ney reached Dijon, only to be told that Napoleon had slipped past him and occupied Auxerre, over 50 miles to the north-west. Ney was also informed that Napoleon wished to see him. Leaving his troops at Dijon, 'the Bravest of the Brave' set off for Auxerre, which he reached the following day. Putting up at a hotel, Ney fretted away the hours before his meeting with Napoleon, drafting a document expressing his opposition to 'tyranny' and warning Napoleon to consider the welfare of the French and 'to repair the evils his ambition had brought upon them'. Next day Ney was ushered into Napoleon's presence. He presented his missive and Napoleon promptly tore it up, murmuring to those nearby, 'This fine fellow Ney is going mad!' In the words of A.H. Atteridge (1912), Ney's biographer, Napoleon then:

turned again to Ney, and began to question him as to his troops, the state of feeling among the people in the south-eastern departments, and the experiences of his march to Dijon. Ney was embarrassed and gave brief replies. The somewhat trying interview ended by Napoleon telling him to return to Dijon, and march his troops to Paris, where the Emperor promised him that he would be at the Tuileries before him.

As good as his word, Napoleon entered Paris on 20 March to take possession of Louis XVIII's vacant throne. Having been branded an outlaw by the European Powers in congress at Vienna, Napoleon's pleas for peace on resuming the imperial mantle fell on deaf ears. And five days after his triumphant return to Paris Napoleon was faced by a new coalition ranged against him. Backed by British cash, Russia, Austria and Prussia all pledged troops to ensure Bonaparte's ruin, plotting with London to mount a grand invasion of France – a repeat performance of the campaign of 1814. Napoleon had no choice but to mobilise: his plan being to launch a strike at Brussels, defeating **Wellington** and **Blücher** in the process, before swinging his forces east to meet the threat from Russia and Austria.

On 13 June – the very eve of the Waterloo campaign – Napoleon invited Ney to dine with him, but despite feverish preparations for the coming campaign, 'the Bravest of the Brave' was not offered a command. Next day, Napoleon left for the front and Ney – still hoping for a job – followed in a hired farmer's trap. According to A.G. MacDonell (1934), Ney:

> was still in semi-disgrace, for Napoleon had not forgiven him for the iron cage. At Beaumont Ney abandoned the trap and bought two of Mortier's horses, and he was a little encouraged when the soldiers cheered him as he rode past the foot-columns, and when he heard them call out, 'Things are hotting up. There goes Le Rougeaud.'

As Ney pushed forward, the sound of gunfire met his ears, heralding the start of Napoleon's grand enterprise. Atteridge (1912) continues the story:

> Early in the afternoon he crossed the bridge of Charleroi amid moving masses of soldiery and saw the signs of the fighting in and

around the town, from which the Prussians had been driven in the forenoon. He heard that so far all had gone well, the left and centre columns driving in the Prussian detachments wherever they opposed the advance. Between two and three o'clock he at last found the Emperor, between Charleroi and Gilly, seated at a table outside a wayside inn on the slope above the Sambre, with his map and papers before him, and a group of staff officers around him, while the troops, tramping up the road in an endless column, cheered him as they passed. Here a pleasant surprise awaited Ney. He dismounted . . . and went to greet the Emperor. 'Good day, Ney,' said the Emperor, 'I am very glad to see you. You will go and take command of the 1st and 2nd Army Corps. I am giving you also the light cavalry of my Guard, but don't use it yet. Tomorrow you will be joined by Kellermann's Cuirassiers. Go and drive the enemy back along the Brussels road and take up a position at Quatre-Bras.'

Ney was back in business. But the Marshal was no longer the sharp operator he once had been. Arriving at Quatre-Bras on 16 June with over 20,000 troops, he found the crossroads held by some 8,000 Netherlanders under the Prince of **Orange**. But instead of launching an immediate assault Ney dithered. And by the time he finally got his act together troops under **Brunswick**, **Picton** and Wellington had arrived to give the French a bloody nose.

While it is generally accepted Ney blew the Battle of Quatre-Bras, some – notably A.G. MacDonell (1934) – also accuse him of compromising Napoleon's success at Ligny:

Ney's attack at Quatre-Bras was a muddled, ill-judged, ill-planned operation, but that was by far the lesser of his two blunders on that day, 16 June. His other one ruined the campaign and destroyed the Empire. For when Napoleon was hammering Blücher at Ligny, he sent for Ney's Reserve Corps to come up on the Prussian flank. **D'Erlon**, commanding the Reserve Corps, marched towards Ligny. Ney, in a wild tempestuous outburst of the temper which he had shown on the field of Borodino, cursed and swore at the Emperor and countermanded the order, and d'Erlon, obeying his immediate superior, marched back towards Quatre-Bras. The fighting at Quatre-Bras was over before he arrived, and his corps, 20,000 strong, fired not a shot all day. If d'Erlon had come to Ligny that afternoon, bringing a strong fresh corps across the right flank of the hammered Prussians, Blücher's army must have been utterly destroyed and **Grouchy**'s 33,000 men would have been under Napoleon's hand and Wellington could not have stood at Waterloo without being disastrously beaten. Ney's counter-order to d'Erlon ruined all.

A view apparently shared by Napoleon, who greeted Ney next day with the words, 'You have ruined France!'

Certainly, by 17 June, the campaign was slipping away from Napoleon: Wellington had repulsed Ney's attacks at Quatre-Bras and successfully given the Marshal the slip, retiring north to Waterloo; while Blücher – arguably a little punch-drunk after his drubbing at Ligny – was still in the ring. Having detached Grouchy to look for the Prussians, Napoleon and Ney tramped after the Anglo-Netherlanders in the pouring rain. Despite Ney's perform-ance on 16–17 June, Napoleon employed him as his battlefield commander on 18 June.

Over the years Napoleon has been criticised for taking a back seat at Waterloo and letting Ney take key tactical decisions. Writers argue that Napoleon should have led from the front, deploying the full might of his genius against Wellington. But there was noth-ing unusual in Napoleon's approach at Waterloo. For the Emperor, it was pretty much business as usual. The fact was that, whereas Wellington was a 'hands on' general, who did not trust anyone but himself to get things right, Napoleon had long been a delegator. True, Bonaparte worked out the big strategic picture, but then he relied on his corps commanders to interpret his broad brush strokes and clinch the result. And in the past, Ney had delivered the goods. At the Battle of Friedland (14 June 1807), for example, Napoleon had arrived on the battlefield to find a Russian Army trapped in a bend of the River Alle – a blunder of the first order. Having worked out a general plan of attack, Napoleon unleashed Ney: five hours later the Russians were routed, losing some 20,000 men, and the War of the Fourth Coalition was over. At Waterloo, Napoleon arrived to find Wellington with the Forest of Soignies at his back – another apparent blunder – and fully expected another Friedland.

But despite Ney's best efforts, it was not to be. According to historian R.P. Dunn-Pattison (1909):

At Waterloo the Marshal showed his old dash on the battlefield. The left wing was hurled against the Allies with a vehemence that recalled the Prince of Moskowa's conduct in the Russian campaign. But, impetuous as ever, finding he could not crush the stubborn foe with his infantry, he rushed back and prematurely ordered up 5,000 of the cavalry of the Guard. 'He has compromised us again,' growled his old enemy **Soult**, 'as he did at Jena.' 'It is too early by an hour,' exclaimed the Emperor, 'but we must support him now that he has done it.' The mistake was fatal to Napoleon's plans. In vain the French cavalry charged the English squares, still unshaken by artillery and infantry fire. Meanwhile the Prussians appeared on the Allied left. The Emperor staked his last card, and ordered the Guard to make one last effort to crush the English infantry. Sword in hand the gallant Prince of Moskowa led the magnificent veterans to the attack. But the fire of the English lines swept them down by hundreds. A shout arose, 'La Garde recule!' Ney, the indomitable, in vain seeking death, was swept away by the mass, his clothing in rags, foaming at the mouth, his broken sword in his hand, rushing from corps to corps, trying to rally the runaways with taunts of 'Cowards, have you forgotten how to die?' At one moment he passed d'Erlon as they were swept along in the rush, and screamed out to him, 'If you and I come out of this alive, d'Erlon, we shall be hanged.' Well it had been for him if he could have found the death he so eagerly sought. Five horses were shot under him, his clothes were riddled with bullets, but he was reserved for a sinister fate.

Frequently blamed for over-caution at Quatre-Bras, Ney is just as often charged with impetuosity at Waterloo. Dashing about leading charges, rallying troops and bashing British guns with a broken sword, Ney is generally depicted in the history books as a kind of gallant lunatic. More charitable writers point out that, by being constantly at the sharp end, Ney had a limited perspective on the battle; that he literally could not see the big picture and consequently misjudged the tactical situation. Fair comment perhaps. And yet the same books often praise Wellington for doing exactly the same thing – being everywhere at once and micro-managing the action. More recently, pundits argue that Ney was suffering from post-traumatic stress disorder, brought on by over 20 years of constant warfare, and that this affected his abilities on the Waterloo battlefield.

Sadly for Ney, his one success at Waterloo – the capture of La Haie Sainte – counted for little: for by 6.30 p.m. **Bülow**'s Prussians were soaking up French reserves at Plancenoit. Thus, when Ney sent his aide-de-camp, Heymès (1829), to request extra troops to exploit his success, the Emperor responded with a testy: 'Troops? Where do you expect me to find them? Do you want me to make them?' What happened next is described by Ney in a letter to the Duke of Otranto, dated 26 June 1815 and quoted by Christopher Kelly (1818):

> About seven o'clock in the evening, after the most dreadful carnage which I have ever witnessed, General **Labédoyère** came to me with a message from the Emperor, that Marshal Grouchy had arrived on our right, and attacked the left of the united English and Prussians. This general officer, in riding along the lines, spread this intelligence among the soldiers, whose courage and devotion remained unshaken, and who gave new proofs of them at that moment, notwithstanding the fatigue with which they were exhausted. What was my astonishment (I should rather say indignation), when I learned, immediately afterwards, that, so far from Marshal Grouchy having arrived to our support, as the whole army had been assured, between forty and fifty thousand Prussians were attacking our extreme right, and forcing it to retire!
>
> Whether the Emperor was deceived with regard to the time when the Marshal [i.e. Grouchy] could support him, or whether the advance of the Marshal was retarded by the efforts of the enemy longer than was calculated upon, the fact is, that at the moment when his arrival was announced to us, he was still only at Wavre upon the Dyle, which to us was the same as if he had been a hundred leagues from the field of battle.
>
> A short time afterwards, I saw four regiments of the Middle Guard advancing, led on by the Emperor. With these troops he wished to renew the attack, and to penetrate the centre of the enemy. He ordered me to lead them on. Generals, officers, and soldiers, all displayed the greatest intrepidity; but this body of troops was too weak long to resist the forces opposed to it by the enemy, and we were soon compelled to renounce the hope which this attack had for a few moments inspired. General **Friant** was struck by a ball at my side, and I myself had my horse killed, and fell under it. The brave men who have survived this terrible battle, will, I trust, do me the justice to state, that they saw me on foot, with sword in hand, during

the whole of the evening, and that I was one of the last who quitted the scene of carnage at the moment when retreat could no longer be prevented.

At the same time, the Prussians continued their offensive movements, and our right sensibly gave way. The English also advanced in their turn. There yet remained to us four squares of the Old Guard, to protect our retreat. These brave grenadiers, the flower of the army, forced successively to retire, yielded ground foot by foot, until finally overpowered by numbers, they were almost completely destroyed. From that moment the retrograde movement was decided, and the army formed nothing but a confused mass. There was not, however, a total rout, nor the cry of 'Sauve qui peut', as has been calumniously stated in the bulletin [i.e. Napoleon's account of the battle, published in the *Paris Moniteur* on 21 June 1815].

As for myself, being constantly in the rearguard, which I followed on foot, having had all my horses killed, worn out with fatigue, covered with contusions, and having no longer strength to walk, I owe my life to a corporal, who supported me in the march, and did not abandon me during the retreat. At eleven at night, I met Lieutenant General **Lefebvre-Desnouëttes**; and one of his officers, Major Schmidt, had the generosity to give me the only horse that remained to him. In this manner I arrived at Marchienne-au-Pont, at four o'clock in the morning, alone, without any officers of my staff, ignorant of the fate of the Emperor, of whom, before the end of the battle, I had entirely lost sight, and who, I had reason to believe, was either killed or taken prisoner.

Ney arrived in Paris ahead of Napoleon, on 20 June. Two days later he made an appearance in the Chamber of Peers, quashing Bonapartists like Labédoyère, who were attempting to rally support for Napoleon by glossing over events at Waterloo. Ney's speech revealed the true state of the army, widening the political sluice gates through which support for Napoleon was already seeping. Napoleon abdicated for the second and final time the same day. On 7 July the victorious Allies entered Paris and restored the Bourbon monarchy. And on 7 August Napoleon set sail for St Helena, a speck of rock in the South Atlantic.

Unlike other high ranking officers of Napoleon's final army – Lefebvre-Desnouëttes and **Vandamme**, for example, who fled to the USA – Ney remained in Paris. This was a big mistake. The Bourbons were back and they wanted blood. This was the so-called White Terror, an excuse for murder and mayhem in the name of loyalty to the crown. But it had the desired effect. In Paris, theatres began showing pre-Revolutionary plays, and any reference to the monarchy was greeted with a standing ovation. According to John R. Elting (1989), 'Anyone who failed to rise and wave a white handkerchief vigorously at such moments might be helped to fall out of the balcony.' Meanwhile it was open season on Napoleon's lieutenants and Ney was top of the list. According to historian Raymond Horricks (1995), Ney assumed he was safe from harassment on account of his German birth. He was wrong. On 3 August 1815 Ney was arrested and charged with treason. The subsequent trial was a sham, and despite pleas from Ney's supporters to the Tsar of Russia and the Duke of Wellington, begging mercy for a gallant enemy, 'le Rougeaud' was sentenced to death.

Ney resigned himself to his fate, simply asking for his flute to while away the remaining hours. On 7 December he was led to the Luxembourg Gardens to face the firing squad. According to R.P. Dunn-Pattison (1909):

> At eight o'clock in the morning the Marshal, with a firm step, was conveyed to the place of execution. To the officer who prepared to bandage his eyes he said, 'Are you ignorant that for twenty-five years I have been accustomed to face both ball and bullet?' Then, taking off his hat, he said, 'I declare before God and man that I have never betrayed my country. May my death render her happy. Vive la France!' Then, turning to the soldiers, he gave the word, 'Soldiers, fire!'

The execution was widely regarded as a crime, and some years later one of Ney's sons demanded satisfaction of Wellington in a duel – the Duke declined.

Ompteda
Colonel Christian Frederick William von, Baron (1765–1815)

Hanoverian brigade commander, ordered to make a suicidal bid to retake the farmhouse of La Haie Sainte around 6.45 p.m. on 18 June 1815. An experienced officer, Ompteda had served in the Hanoverian Guards before transferring to the King's German Legion and British service in 1807. A mental breakdown brought Ompteda back to Germany a year or so later, but by 1812 he had regained fitness, leading a battalion under **Wellington** in Spain. Ompteda saw out the remainder of the Peninsular War, and at Waterloo commanded the 2nd King's German Legion Brigade, consisting of the 1st Light, 2nd Light, 5th Line and 8th Line Battalions.

Posted to the right of the crossroads atop Mont St Jean, directly above the farmhouse of La Haie Sainte, Ompteda's brigade was almost 2,000-strong. It formed part of **Alten**'s 3rd British Infantry Division, which in turn, formed part of the Prince of **Orange**'s I Corps, and these two officers were Ompteda's immediate superiors. Ompteda's command also provided the garrison of La Haie Sainte (led by Major George **Baring**), which, starved of ammunition, was driven out by a determined French assault around 6.30 p.m. The loss of this bastion, so close to Wellington's centre, was a serious blow and Alten, the divisional commander, ordered Ompteda to launch an immediate counter-attack. But Ompteda queried the order. He had seen a body of French cuirassiers nearby, and he knew they would effortlessly carve up any infantry advance unsupported by cavalry. Alten, however, repeated his order, which was endorsed by the Prince of Orange, who apparently mistook the enemy horsemen for his own troops. Even after this mistake was pointed out, the Prince ordered Ompteda to advance, questioning his honour, and pronouncing: 'I will hear no further arguments.' After a moment's silence, Ompteda mounted his horse, and knowing he was riding to certain death, emphatically declared: 'Then I will!' Turning to Lieutenant Colonel von Linsingen, commanding the 5th Line, he added: 'Try to save my two nephews.' (The boys, Louis and Christian, were serving in the battalion as junior officers, despite being no more than 15 years old.) Then, according to Lieutenant **Edmund Wheatley** of the 5th Line (Wheatley 1964): 'Colonel Ompteda ordered us instantly into line to charge, with a strong injunction to "walk" forward, until he gave the word. When within sixty yards he cried "Charge!" we ran forward huzzaing.'

According to Captain Berger, quoted by Louis Cohen (1925), Ompteda almost made it as far as the farmhouse, riding alone into a mass of French infantry:

> I hastened to follow him as quickly as the miry state of the ground permitted. I kept my eyes on him and on the enemy. I saw that the French had their muskets pointed at the Colonel but they did not fire. The officers struck the men's barrels up with their swords. They seemed astonished at the extraordinary calm approach of the solitary horseman, whose white plume showed him to be an officer of high rank. He soon reached the enemy's line of infantry before the garden hedge. He jumped in and I clearly saw how his sword-strokes smote the shakos off. The nearest French officer looked on with admiration, without attempting to check the attack. When I looked round for my company, I found that I was alone. Turning my eyes again to the enemy, I saw Colonel Ompteda in the midmost throng of the enemy's infantry and cavalry, sink from his horse and vanish.

Meanwhile, Ompteda's prediction was realised as French cuirassiers slammed into the flank of his brigade, breaking up the attack and inflicting heavy losses. The 5th Line was particularly shaken, losing almost one-third of its men plus its sacred King's colour. The battalion's commander, Baron von Linsingen, was trapped under his wounded horse, though he managed to struggle free in time to save himself – and Ompteda's nephews – from the slaughter. Ompteda's attack having failed, La Haie Sainte remained in French hands till the end of the battle. In the grisly aftermath Ompteda's body was recovered: he had been shot in the throat at point-blank. His body was buried near the gate of the farmhouse.

Orange
William Frederick George, Prince of (1792–1849)

Commander of **Wellington**'s I Corps during the Waterloo campaign; scion of the House of Orange–Nassau, which ruled over an independent, Protestant Dutch state between 1648 and 1795. Prior to the seventeenth century, Holland and Belgium were lumped together as the Northern and Southern Netherlands respectively, an area controlled by the Spanish Bourbon monarchy. In 1568 the Dutch began their bid for independence, eventually attained in

The Prince of Orange (1792–1849)

1648 with the establishment of a republic dubbed the United Provinces of the Netherlands. Thereafter, the House of Orange dominated Dutch politics, frequently providing the nation's Governor or *Stadtholder*. Meanwhile, Belgium – or the Southern Netherlands – continued under Spanish rule until 1713, when the Habsburgs took over, creating the Austrian Netherlands. But following the outbreak of the French Revolutionary Wars, both the Dutch and the Belgians fell under French rule, and the House of Orange decamped to Britain. In 1794 Belgium was simply annexed to France, while Holland became a satellite state, known as the Batavian Republic, the following year. In 1806 **Napoleon** scrapped this republic in favour of a kingdom of Holland, placing his brother Louis on the throne. In 1810, however, this too was annexed to France. But with Napoleon's first fall from power in April 1814 the victorious Allies decided to bolt Catholic Belgium and Protestant Holland together to form a United Kingdom of the Netherlands under William Frederick of the House of Orange. And so, on 16 March 1815 – four days before Napoleon returned to Paris from exile on Elba – William Frederick was proclaimed King William I in Brussels, his new capital. His 23-year-old son, William Frederick George, thus became the hereditary Prince of Orange.

So much for the Prince's historical and political baggage, but what about the man himself? Born in Holland, William was spirited away when the French first arrived in 1794. After a sojourn in Berlin, William and his family settled in Britain. William was educated at Oxford and given a private military tutor, **Jean Victor Constant de Rebecque**, an officer in his father's service. In 1813 William joined Wellington's staff as an aide-de-camp, seeing out the final phase of the Peninsular War, which saw him an honorary lieutenant general in the British Army. With the peace that followed Napoleon's first abdication, William joined his father at Brussels, where, as the new hereditary Prince, he cut a fine figure in fashionable society: a society largely comprised of British émigrés fleeing their creditors back home. On 26 March 1815 William was given command of all Allied troops stationed in his father's kingdom, with Constant de Rebecque as his Chief of Staff. This was a post of crucial importance, considering the Allies were using the country as the launch pad for a projected invasion of Napoleonic France. But in this way, William's father – known as the 'Old Frog' to the British, with William as the 'Young Frog' – hoped to keep a guiding hand on his kingdom's fortunes.

But it was not to be. Wellington arrived at Brussels shortly after, got himself made a field marshal in the Netherlands Army, and effectively took over. Prince William was given command of the Duke's I Corps (comprising four infantry divisions under **Cooke**, **Alten**, **Perponcher** and **Chassé**), as a sop to the King's bruised ego. Meanwhile, Wellington tasked General **Rowland Hill** with preventing the 'Young Frog' (or 'Slender Billy' as he was also known) from doing anything rash with the troops under his command, for as historian David Miller (2005) states, the Prince was 'considered by all to be very brave, but little else, and certainly lacking both military command experience and maturity'. As will be seen, William displayed both bravery and lack of military tact in the fighting that followed.

At 5 p.m. on 15 June, while dressing for the Duchess of Richmond's ball, Wellington was informed that French units had crossed the Sambre and were attacking **Blücher**'s outposts along the river. Seven hours later (now at the ball), Wellington received word that Netherlands troops from his I Corps, under Lieutenant General Perponcher, were fending off Marshal **Ney** at Quatre-Bras, some 22 miles south-east of Brussels. At last, Wellington ordered the army to march. According to historian Demetrius C. Boulger (1901), the Prince of Orange arrived at Quatre-Bras ahead of Wellington, about 7 a.m. on 16 June, and immediately took charge. Boulger continues:

> Ney, having waited for Foy's division, did not begin the attack until about two o'clock, but a quarter of an hour later the action had become hot. One Dutch battalion was caught, after suffering a good deal from the French guns, by the enemy's cavalry, and only escaped destruction by rallying in the buildings of the farm of St Pierre. Things looked so desperate at three o'clock that the Prince of Orange led a battalion to the charge, had his horse shot under him, and narrowly escaped being taken prisoner. It was immediately after this incident that the approach of the cavalry brigade under **van Merlen** was signalled along the Nivelles road. At that moment the battle was practically lost. The English had not arrived, Ney was in the very act

of being reinforced . . . and nothing could gain the half-hour's respite still needed to save the position before the English troops could come up except some desperate measure. The arrival of the Dutch-Belgian cavalry brigade of van Merlen gave the Prince of Orange the means of taking it, and he did not hesitate a moment in doing so. It was his last throw. Ten minutes later, and the Perponcher division would have been ousted from Quatre-Bras.

Despite van Merlen's charge, which was met by withering French volleys plus a counter-charge by French hussars, the situation remained desperate for the Prince's 8,000 Netherlanders. About 3 p.m., however, Wellington arrived to take control, as further elements of Orange's I Corps – plus reinforcements under the Duke of **Brunswick** and Sir **Thomas Picton** – entered the battle zone. But the action remained hot, as the Allies strove to hold their ground against heavy pressure from the French (Picton was wounded during the fighting and Brunswick was killed). Late in the day, Wellington ordered Picton to deploy Sir **Colin Halkett**'s brigade – consisting of battalions from the British 30th, 33rd, 69th, and 73rd Regiments – in support of Brunswick's hard-pressed troops in and around Bossu Wood. Picton formed these troops into a chain of battalion squares, shoring up the Brunswickers' position, while offering protection against Ney's powerful cavalry: which, hidden by the uneven terrain, was awaiting a favourable moment to attack.

But Halkett's brigade was technically under the Prince of Orange's command, not Picton's, and the 23-year-old rookie outranked the 56-year-old veteran. According to historian Jac Weller (1967), the Prince resented Picton's meddling and decided to assert his authority. Seeing Halkett's battalions in squares, the Prince ordered them into line, as the Brunswickers needed as much supporting firepower as possible. Halkett, aware of the threat posed by Ney's cuirassiers, protested but was obliged to obey. Moments later French horsemen materialised, charged the vulnerable foot soldiers, and Halkett saw his troops slaughtered and scattered before his very eyes. The 69th Regiment suffered most, being wrecked as a cohesive unit and losing its King's colour – the only British colour lost by troops under Wellington's personal command. Thankfully, the arrival of more reinforcements and nightfall saved the Allies at

Quatre-Bras, allowing Wellington to retire on Waterloo in the wake of Blücher's defeat at Ligny.

But William, the Prince of Orange, had not yet finished. About 6.30 p.m. on Waterloo Day the vital outpost of La Haie Sainte fell to the French. Alten, commanding William's 3rd Division, ordered Baron **Ompteda**, one of his brigade commanders, to counter-attack and retake the farm. But in a repeat of Halkett's experience at Quatre-Bras, Ompteda spotted French cavalry waiting to carve up his men should they move. At that moment William cantered up. He insisted that the hostile horsemen were Dutch and that Ompteda – whose honour he called into question – should get on with his attack. When Ompteda continued to object, William silenced him with the words: 'I will hear no further arguments.' And so Ompteda obeyed an order that resulted in the needless destruction of his brigade and the loss of his own life. Thankfully, shortly after this event, William was wounded by a bullet in the left shoulder and obliged to quit the field.

In his official Waterloo Dispatch, Wellington describes William's Waterloo service as 'highly distinguished'. True, the Prince had displayed great bravery, and had held on at Quatre-Bras against great odds until reinforced: but at the same time, Wellington's words must have left a bitter taste in the mouths of Halkett's and Ompteda's survivors.

Percy
Major Henry (1785?–1825)

Extra aide-de-camp to **Wellington** at Waterloo. The scion of an aristocratic family (his father was Baron Lovaine and Earl of Beverley), Percy was educated at Eton College, before joining the 7th Fusiliers as a lieutenant in 1804. Two years later, Percy had reached the rank of captain, and two years after that, in 1808, he was serving on the staff of Lieutenant General Sir John Moore. Following Moore's death at Corunna in 1809, Percy returned to the Peninsula with Wellington's army. Captured by the French in 1810, he was released in 1814, when hostilities ceased. In the spring of 1815 Percy joined Wellington in Brussels as an extra aide-de-camp, attending the Duchess of Richmond's ball on 15 June. Percy was one of eight aides-de-camp employed by Wellington at Waterloo (the others being Lieutenant Colonel **Fremantle**, Lieutenant Colonel C.F. Canning, Lieutenant Colonel the Hon. Sir **Alexander Gordon**, Lieutenant Lord George Lennox, the Prince of Nassau-Usingen, Captain Lord Arthur Hill and Lieutenant Lord George Cathcart) and was the only one to emerge from the battle unscathed (Canning and Gordon died, the rest were wounded). And so, by default, it fell to Percy to return to London with Wellington's Waterloo Dispatch.

At midday on 19 June Percy took a post-chaise and four from Brussels to Ostend, clutching Wellington's dispatch and the two French Eagles captured by **Ewart**, **Clark** and/or **Styles**. There he boarded a Royal Navy sloop, HMS *Peruvian*. But halfway across the Channel the wind dropped and Percy's ship was left wallowing. Determined to reach London as soon as possible, Percy – who had not slept since 15 June – jumped in one of the *Peruvian*'s boats and, with the aid of four sailors, rowed the rest of the way, reaching Broadstairs about 3 p.m. on 21 June. Finding a fast coach, Percy reached London at 10 p.m., rattling through the streets with French flags hanging out of the windows, pursued by cheering crowds. Percy and the mob made straight for Downing Street, alarming government ministers who assumed they were being attacked by rioters. Collecting Lord Arbuthnot, who had just returned from the House of Commons, Percy then drove to Lord Harrowby's house in Grosvenor Square, where members of the Cabinet were at supper. Percy reputedly burst in on the diners crying, 'Victory! Victory! Bonaparte has been beaten!' From there he was directed to the Prince Regent, who was attending a ball at Mrs Boehm's house in St James's Square. The Prince received the dusty, dishevelled Percy, but dismissed the ladies from the room. Then Lord Liverpool, the Prime Minister, read Wellington's dispatch aloud. Percy was promoted to colonel on the spot, the Prince bursting into tears as Liverpool listed Wellington's casualties: 'It is a glorious victory,' he commented, adding: 'but the loss of life has been fearful, and I have lost many friends.'

But was Percy the first to bring news of victory to London? There is a persistent story that an agent employed by banker Nathan Rothschild reported to Lord Liverpool the day before Percy's arrival. The tale is recounted by historian Saul David (1998):

News of the great victory was carried to London by a messenger in the pay of the Rothschild banking family. But so confused was his version of events that Lord Liverpool became 'increasingly sceptical' and John Croker, the Secretary of the Admiralty, a former lawyer, was given the task of questioning him. How, asked Croker, had King Louis XVIII . . . reacted to the news? 'His Majesty embraced me, and kissed me!' replied the messenger. 'How did the King kiss you?'

'On both cheeks,' came the response. This was enough for Croker.
'My Lord, it is true,' he exclaimed.

Rothschild has been accused of withholding news of Wellington's victory long enough to take advantage of the intelligence on the stock market. Some accounts even have Rothschild receiving news of Waterloo on 19 June, courtesy of a carrier pigeon. As to making capital from his foreknowledge of events in Belgium, historian Rory Muir (1996) observes that 'the size of his profit has always been greatly exaggerated'.

As for the Waterloo Dispatch delivered by Percy, it was printed in the daily papers to a negative response. Wellington – exercising his usual restraint – managed to upset virtually everyone with his summary of the campaign, penned on 19 June after a few hours' rest, and addressed to Earl Bathurst, Secretary for War in Lord Liverpool's Cabinet (see Appendix VIII). Indeed, according to historian Andrew Roberts (2001), 'When the American envoy to London read the dispatch he found it so free of uplifting rhetoric that he assumed Wellington had actually lost the battle.' It seemed the Duke failed to satisfy patriots and veterans alike: the former by not emphasising the nation's glorious achievement; the latter by not giving sufficient praise. Baron **Chassé**, commander of the 3rd Netherlands Infantry Division at Waterloo, considered his countrymen snubbed by the Duke, and registered his dissatisfaction in a letter to his corps commander, General **Rowland Hill**. Wellington, however, refused to add or subtract anything from the Waterloo Dispatch, merely observing that

> The history of a battle is not unlike the history of a ball. Some
> individuals may recollect all the little events, of which the great result
> is the battle won or lost; but no individual can recollect the order in
> which, or the exact moment at which, they occurred, which makes all
> the difference as to their value or importance.

For Wellington, then, Waterloo was a closed subject: but the echo of his silence reverberates to this day, tantalising those who believe the Duke had something to hide. And yet, while doubtless protecting several reputations, Wellington probably felt that victory was enough, and people should be satisfied with that. As he said to

Thomas Creevey the day after the battle (Creevey 1904): 'It has been a damned nice thing – the nearest run thing you ever saw in your life.' With no mass media to answer to, and with the bulk of Britain's population not eligible to vote, Wellington's reticence should be viewed in the proper context. He was, after all, an aristocratic general, not the England football coach, so if the Waterloo Dispatch disappointed some and disillusioned others, too bad.

Nevertheless, the text of Wellington's Waterloo Dispatch is littered with errors and inaccuracies, which his detractors have since made capital out of. For example, Wellington states the battle began 'about ten o'clock': but it is generally believed that **Jérôme**'s 'diversionary' attack on Hougoumont was launched after 11 a.m., with **d'Erlon**'s opening assault on the Duke's main position occurring about 1.30 p.m. Was Wellington attempting to magnify his achievement by exaggerating the length of the combat, or was this a simple error? But then, in describing the fall of La Haie Sainte, Wellington states that:

> the enemy carried the farm house of La Haye Sainte, as the detachment of the Light Battalion of the German Legion, which occupied it, had expended all its ammunition; and the enemy occupied the only communication there was with them.

The Duke's tone implies a fault on the part of the garrison's commander, Major **Baring**, while suggesting that the farm was cut off from the main Allied position. And yet, Baring's messengers flitted between La Haie Sainte and Mont St Jean throughout the afternoon, desperately trying to obtain more bullets.

And of events following the French collapse, Wellington writes:

> I continued the pursuit till long after dark, and then discontinued it only on account of the fatigue of our troops, who had been engaged during twelve hours, and because I found myself on the same road with Marshal **Blücher**, who assured me of his intention to follow the enemy throughout the night.

But most accounts have the Anglo-Netherlands units advancing as far as the French positions around La Belle Alliance and then bivouacking as dusk fell, while Blücher's Prussians – most of whom had been on their feet since daybreak, marching and fighting – continued the pursuit.

As for the Prussian contribution, Wellington affirms:

> I should not do justice to my own feelings, or to Marshal Blücher and the Prussian Army, if I did not attribute the successful result of this arduous day to the cordial and timely assistance I received from them. The operation of General **Bülow** upon the enemy's flank was a most decisive one; and, even if I had not found myself in a situation to make the attack which produced the final result, it would have forced the enemy to retire if his attacks should have failed, and would have prevented him from taking advantage of them if they should unfortunately have succeeded.

But the phrase, 'even if I had not found myself in a situation to make the attack which produced the final result' takes the edge of the previous statements, suggesting a battle already won without Prussian aid.

Finally, Wellington's Dispatch contains several minor factual errors. For example, two French Eagles were captured at Waterloo (by Ewart, Clark and/or Styles), yet Wellington informs Earl Bathurst that he is sending 'three Eagles, taken by the troops in this action, which Major Percy will have the honour of laying at the feet of His Royal Highness'. And Sir **William De Lancey** died a week after Waterloo, though Wellington claims he was 'killed by a cannon shot in the middle of the action'. And intriguingly, no officer named 'General Van Hope' fought at Waterloo, despite Wellington being satisfied with his conduct while 'commanding a Brigade of infantry in the service of the King of the Netherlands'.

But perhaps it is unfair to subject Wellington's Waterloo Dispatch to such rigorous examination. For, as Richard Holmes (2002) observes: 'To write, largely from memory, a detailed account of the events of 15–18 June, with only a few hours' sleep and so many of his friends killed or wounded, was a prodigious accomplishment.' And we must remind ourselves that hindsight is a wonderful thing. Composed shortly after the last shots were fired, Wellington's Waterloo Dispatch is a snapshot of the Duke's level of knowledge – and fatigue – at a given moment. But his refusal to update the Dispatch or add a postscript has left Wellington open to charges of at best ingratitude, and at worst duplicity. As **Napoleon** said: 'He who fears to lose his reputation is sure to lose it.'

Perponcher-Sedlnitzky
Lieutenant General Henri-Georges, Baron (1771–1856)

Commander of the 2nd Netherlands Infantry Division during the Waterloo campaign. A Dutch nobleman who entered his country's army in 1793, Perponcher was one of those officers who, like **Constant de Rebecque**, followed the ruling House of Orange into exile following the French takeover in 1794. After a stint in British service, Perponcher

Lieutenant General Perponcher (1771–1856)

returned home in 1814, following **Napoleon**'s exile to Elba and the creation of the United Kingdom of the Netherlands. This new political entity was created by the victorious Allies, consisting of Protestant Holland and Catholic Belgium, ruled from Brussels by William I of the House of Orange–Nassau. By March 1815, however, war clouds were gathering once more with Napoleon's return to power, and the Allies' determination to crush the 'Grand Disturber' for good. Despite Allied plans for a massive assault on France, Napoleon got in first, crossing the Sambre on 15 June 1815 and driving a wedge between **Wellington**'s Anglo-Netherlands army and **Blücher**'s Prussians. Perponcher had already been given command of the 2nd Netherlands Infantry Division of the Prince of **Orange**'s I Corps. The command consisted of over 8,000 Dutch and Belgian troops, formed into **van Bijlandt**'s 1st Brigade and Major General Saxe-Weimar's 2nd Brigade.

Although informed of the French incursion late on 15 June, Wellington was initially unsure where the Emperor's main blow would fall. Fearing a Napoleonic feint, he ordered his troops to mobilise, but forbade a concentration east of Nivelles. This covered the Mons road – the likely route for an advance on Brussels – but left the crossroads of Quatre-Bras, several miles east of Nivelles, unguarded: something not to be countenanced by Constant de Rebecque, chief of staff to the Prince of Orange, who recognised its strategic importance. In essence, Quatre-Bras not only protected the southern approaches to Brussels from Charleroi, it also protected the east–west road that linked the armies of Wellington and Blücher. And so Constant de Rebecque ignored Wellington's instructions and ordered Saxe-Weimar's brigade to hold Quatre-Bras. Later that day, when it became clear that French forces were indeed advancing on Quatre-Bras from Charleroi, Perponcher also disregarded Wellington's instructions and marched to Quatre-Bras with reinforcements.

Historian Demetrius C. Boulger (1901) quotes Perponcher's official report, posted in November 1815:

> The Prince of Saxe-Weimar, who commanded my Second Brigade, having brought the remainder of his troops together at Quatre-Bras, took up an excellent strategic position in front of the village, where, after exchanging a few shots, he was left undisturbed by the enemy.
>
> In the meantime the whole of the First Brigade, with the battery of foot artillery, had been concentrated by me at Nivelles with the intention of marching on Quatre-Bras for the support of the Second Brigade, as I had been informed by some deserters and Prussians in flight that Charleroi had been evacuated, and the whole of the Prussian army had been removed to Wavre. I considered that the position at Quatre-Bras, which was now unprotected, ought to be strengthened, and that whilst awaiting there orders and reinforcements everything possible should be done to prevent the enemy from marching upon Brussels.
>
> At 2 o'clock of the morning of the 16th I marched, with the 27th Battalion of Chasseurs and the 8th Battalion of Militia, to Quatre-Bras, in order to strengthen this point and take over the command of the troops. Not knowing whether the enemy had also made an attack on Binche, in which case the entire front of my right wing would have been exposed, I left Major General van Bijlandt with the three other battalions of his brigade and the battery of foot artillery at Nivelles, with instructions to defend that point as long as possible,

and at the last extremity to retire to Mont St Jean, and to take up his position at the point where the chaussées of Nivelles and Quatre-Bras meet, and to maintain himself there until I joined him with the Second Brigade.

Immediately outside Nivelles I fell in with a detachment of fifty horse of the 2nd Silesian Regiment of Hussars, which had been cut off from the Prussian troops. Being without cavalry, I proposed to First Lieutenant Zehelin, who was in command of that detachment, to accompany me to Quatre-Bras. This young officer hesitated not an instant, and your Royal Highness himself has witnessed his courage and discernment.

On my arrival at Quatre-Bras, I found that the Prince of Saxe-Weimar had made the best possible arrangements. I somewhat extended the lines and reinforced the posts in the wood, which was the key of the position.

The Netherlanders at Quatre-Bras were faced by a far superior French force under Marshal **Ney**. But Ney and his generals simply could not believe that the puny corps facing them – no more than 8,000 Netherlanders – had been left to hold the vital crossroads. Having fought Wellington in the Peninsular War, the French top brass suspected that the Duke was hiding his true strength, as was his wont, and fearing a 'Spanish battle' advanced with great caution. This bought time for Perponcher, who was reinforced by the Prince of Orange and later Wellington.

Despite a hot action, Quatre-Bras was held until nightfall, when, having learned of Blücher's defeat at Ligny, Wellington ordered a withdrawal on Mont St Jean, south of Waterloo. According to Boulger (1901):

Wellington, in a letter to a friend, described Quatre-Bras as 'a desperate battle, in which I was successful,' but the credit of holding the position against overwhelming odds and far superior troops up to half-past three belongs to the Netherlands division of De Perponcher, serving under the personal command of the Prince of Orange.

At Waterloo, Perponcher's division was split: Saxe-Weimar defending Wellington's extreme left or eastern flank, anchored on the villages of Papelotte and La Haie; and van Bijlandt deployed left-centre, near the crossroads atop the ridge of Mont St Jean. Despite repeated charges of cowardice from British pundits, Perponcher's command suffered heavily at Waterloo while performing vital services for Wellington: van Bijlandt's 1st Brigade aiding in the repulse of **d'Erlon**'s attack of the early afternoon; and Saxe-Weimar's 2nd Brigade effectively keeping communications with the approaching Prussians open.

Petre
Lieutenant Henry William (1791–1852)

Lieutenant in the 6th Inniskilling Dragoons who, by his own account, took possession of **Napoleon**'s stallion 'Marengo' at Waterloo. Petre, son of the Hon. George Petre, was a member of Captain William F. Brown's Troop at Waterloo. His regiment, the 6th Inniskilling Dragoons, under Lieutenant Colonel **Muter**, was some 450 sabres strong. As part of Sir **William Ponsonby**'s 2nd British (Union) Cavalry Brigade, the Inniskillings took part in the successful charges of the early afternoon of 18 June 1815, against **d'Erlon**'s infantry columns, before being roughly handled by French counter-charges. By the end of the day, the regiment had sustained over 200 casualties, but still took part in the march on Paris, remaining in France till January 1816, when it finally returned to England.

It would seem, however, that thanks to Petre, the Inniskillings returned home with an important addition: Napoleon's 'favourite' stallion, Marengo. The story goes that Petre came across the wounded white Arab stallion at the close of battle, in the stables of Le Caillou, the farmstead that served as one of Napoleon's Waterloo command posts. Recognising the imperial N stamped on the horse's rump, as well as imperial motifs on the harness, Petre saved the horse from looters, apparently taking possession of it himself. Petre also nursed the stallion back to health – it had five visible wounds plus a bullet lodged in its tail – eventually shipping it back to England. And

Marengo

there, for a number of years, the trail goes cold: for it was not until 1823 – two years after Napoleon's death – that Marengo surfaced in London, hailed by Petre (on half-pay since 1819) as 'Bonaparte's Charger'. Petre's timing, however, was spot on. For despite Victor Hugo's comment that 'God was bored with Napoleon', evidently mankind was not: and ever since the Emperor's death in 1821, the world had been going crazy for all things connected with him. As the French writer Chateaubriand declared: 'In his life he failed to capture the world. When he was dead, it was his.'

And it was against the backdrop of this Napoleon-mania that Petre exhibited Marengo at the new Waterloo Rooms, 94 Pall Mall, London: admission cost 1 shilling for adults and 6 pennies for children and servants (approximately £2.50 and £1.25 in modern terms). The exhibition was a sensation, sparking extravagant stories and speculation regarding Napoleon's favourite steed: Marengo was captured during Napoleon's Egyptian crusade and carried him through all his subsequent campaigns; Marengo walked 3,000 miles in 1812, from Paris to Moscow and back; Marengo was sired in County Wexford, Ireland; Marengo was a cousin of **Wellington**'s Waterloo mount, Copenhagen. The identity of the animal – Marengo – was never questioned; neither were the claims that it was Napoelon's favourite horse, and that it carried the Emperor at Waterloo. In short, Petre's Marengo fired people's imaginations and became a star. In fact, Marengo became a superstar, destined for immortality: for when the horse died in 1832, its skeleton was sent to the London Hospital to be articulated for permanent exhibition. These bones may still be seen in London's National Army Museum.

But was the horse really Marengo? And more to the point, did Marengo ever really exist? For a full discussion of this topic, readers should consult Jill Hamilton's book, *Marengo: the Myth of Napoleon's Horse* (2000). Suffice it to say here that considerable doubt exists as to the true identity of the horse Petre brought before the eyes of the world as Marengo. Napoleon owned over 150 horses during his career and he had a clear preference for white Arab mounts. But despite the oft-repeated tale that he rode Marengo at Waterloo, no evidence from French sources backs this up. In fact, Hamilton states: 'Although it is widely believed that Marengo was Napoleon's favourite horse, no horse of this name appears in the registers of Napoleon's stables or in any primary source.' Meanwhile, French commentators highlight the extreme unlikelihood of any horse surviving all Napoleon's campaigns from Egypt to Waterloo. Finally, Hamilton speculates that Petre's Marengo was probably a horse from the imperial stable called Ali, known to have been at Waterloo (along with Cerbère, Désirée, Jaffa, Marie and Tauris), adding: 'So many of Napoleon's horses were dirty grey in colour and similar in appearance that it is easy to see how mistakes could have been made about their identification.' As to Marengo being Irish, Hamilton dismisses this as a 'wild' theory.

But presumably Petre made a tidy profit from Marengo – though little information on the Lieutenant's later life is forthcoming. In the *Waterloo Roll Call*, Dalton (1904) merely states that Petre married twice and died without issue in 1852. Marengo, however, lives on . . .

Picton
Lieutenant General Sir Thomas (1758–1815)

Commander of **Wellington**'s 5th Division at Waterloo. Born at the house later known as the Dragon Hotel in Haverfordwest, Pembrokeshire, Picton was the seventh of 12 children. He joined the army as a boy, being commissioned in 1771, and 30 years later had risen to the rank of brigadier general and Governor of Trinidad.

Fame found Picton late in life, Sir Thomas having turned 50 by the time he became a celebrity as commander of Wellington's 3rd Division during the Peninsular War. Under Picton's tenure, this element of the Duke's army became known as 'the Fighting Division', and Sir Thomas gained a reputation as a fire-eating commander and disciplinarian. He also became legendary for vulgarity, Wellington pronouncing him 'a rough, foul-mouthed devil as ever lived'. But Picton got results and when the Peninsular War was successfully concluded, in 1814, the Welshman was accorded hero status. Consequently, when **Napoleon** escaped exile in February 1815 and war clouds hovered once more, Picton was summoned to Brussels, as Wellington prepared an Anglo-Netherlands force for hostilities. But according to historian David Miller (2005), the 56-year-old fire-eater was reluctant to leave home, being troubled by premonitions of death. Before setting off for Brussels, Picton apparently amazed his companions by jumping into an open grave to try it for size, stoically observing that it was a perfect fit.

Picton arrived at Brussels on the afternoon of 15 June, several hours after Napoleon led his army across the Sambre and onto Belgian soil. But in Brussels the nobs continued to party, and on the very evening of Picton's arrival the Duchess of Richmond threw her celebrated ball: the gruff old warrior was apparently invited, but no records exist confirming his presence. Early next morning, amid reports of the French incursion, it became apparent that a small Netherlands force under General **Perponcher** was embattled at Quatre-Bras, a mere 22 miles south of the capital. As the Prince of **Orange** hurried to the scene, Picton – at the head of the 5th British Infantry Division – was instructed to follow. **Rees Howell Gronow**, an ensign of the 1st Foot Guards temporarily attached to Picton's staff, described (Gronow 1900) the moment Picton got his marching orders:

> While we were at breakfast, Colonel Canning [an aide-de-camp] came to inform the General that the Duke of Wellington wished to see him immediately. Sir Thomas lost not a moment in obeying the order of his chief, leaving the breakfast table and proceeding to the park, where Wellington was walking with **Fitzroy Somerset** and the Duke of **Richmond**. Picton's manner was always more familiar than the Duke liked in his lieutenants and on this occasion he approached him in a careless sort of way, just as he might have met an equal. The Duke bowed coldly to him and said, 'I am glad you are come, Sir Thomas, the sooner you get on horseback the better: no time is to be lost. You will take command of the troops in advance. The Prince of Orange knows by this time that you will go to his assistance.' Picton appeared not to like the Duke's manner, for when he bowed and left he muttered a few words, which convinced those who were there with him that he was not much pleased with his interview.

Picton arrived at Quatre-Bras about 3 p.m., deploying his brigades (commanded by **Kempt**, Pack and von Vincke) in support of the hard-pressed Netherlanders. The arrival of the Duke of **Brunswick**'s corps bolstered the Allied position further. And soon Wellington was commanding in person: the French, under Marshal **Ney**, having missed their chance of securing an easy victory. But at the height of the battle Picton was wounded – by a musket ball that broke two ribs according to some; by a cannonball that grazed his hip according to others. But whatever hit Picton, it inflicted a frightful wound, causing severe internal injury. And yet Sir Thomas kept quiet, bidding Tyler, his aide-de-camp, dress the wound in secret. Most British accounts explain Picton's actions as indicative of great foresight, claiming Sir Thomas predicted the coming clash with Napoleon and was eager not to miss it. But perhaps, having received a potentially mortal wound, the old warrior simply preferred to die in action rather than a hospital bed? Either way, as Wellington's army retreated on Mont St Jean next day Picton silently suffered appalling agony.

On Waterloo Day, Picton's division – almost 7,000-strong – was posted on Wellington's left-centre, on the reverse slope of the Duke's ridge, out of sight of the French. According to Charles Dalton (1904): 'one of the first questions asked by Napoleon of his staff was: "Où est la division de Picton?" A few hours later, the broken ranks and decimated companies of many French regiments answered the question.' But before the battle began, Sir Thomas went for a stroll along the line to familiarise himself with Wellington's dispositions. Wearing a shabby blue frock coat and battered beaver hat, and carrying a white umbrella, the General wandered about largely unnoticed. According to Captain **Mercer** of G Troop, Royal Horse Artillery:

> A man of no very prepossessing appearance came rambling amongst our guns, and entered into conversation with me on the occurrences of the day; he was dressed in a shabby old drab greatcoat and rusty roundhat. I took him at the time for some amateur from Brussels, of whom we had heard there were several hovering about, and thinking many of his questions rather impertinent, I was somewhat short in answering them, and he soon left us. Great was my astonishment on learning soon after that this was Sir Thomas Picton.

Although some sources blame Picton's sartorial inelegance on hasty packing or lost luggage, Sir Thomas was known for favouring non-regulation attire. For example, in 1810 Picton fought the Battle of Bussaco in his nightcap. Not that Wellington minded such eccentricities – he too was in civvies at Waterloo.

About 1 p.m. Napoleon opened the battle proper with a barrage from the grand battery sited near his forward command post at La Belle Alliance. Across the shallow valley separating the two armies, on the reverse slope of Wellington's ridge, Picton's troops were ordered to lie down to avoid the incoming cannon balls. Private Dixon Vallence, a soldier in Captain James Campbell's No. 6 Company, 79th Foot (Kempt's brigade) recalled:

> The balls from the French cannon falling very thick amongst us, we were ordered to lie down to save ourselves a little. We lay a considerable time under the dreadful fire, the cannon balls killing and wounding a great many. A cannon ball struck the ground a short distance from my head, and covered me with earth: I felt it heave up the earth under my head, another ball struck the ground a few inches

from my feet, and a soldier who was near me, observing both balls, told me to rise out of that place, as a French cannon was straight in line with me. I shifted a little of the line and another ball sunk deep in the spot where I lay only a few minutes before. Upon some of our men rising on their knees to see what was going on in front they were ordered by the officers to lie down. One man disobeyed orders and was in times taking a peep to the front. His captain ordered him to stand up and take a full view; a cannon ball struck the captain on the cheek, and tearing of the flesh, left his cheek bone bare. He lingered a short time in dreadful agony, and died.

Half an hour later Napoleon's guns – dubbed 'the Emperor's beautiful daughters' by the French – fell silent and **d'Erlon**'s four infantry divisions advanced on Picton's sector. Most British accounts of d'Erlon's attack speak of 18,000 Frenchmen marching on Picton, putting to flight a brigade of Netherlanders under **van Bijlandt** which, overwhelmed by the French tsunami, left the Brits to stiffen their upper lips and beat back the tide with cold steel. It seems, however, that **Durutte**'s division advanced no further than the village of Papelotte, while elements of **Quiot**'s division stopped off to assault **Baring**'s garrison at La Haie Sainte. This left perhaps 13,000 at most marching up the slope of Mont St Jean. And these troops did not arrive together on Picton's front, but as three staggered columns. They were halted at the crest of the ridge by artillery and musketry; then subjected to a bayonet charge; and then hacked to pieces by Sir **William Ponsonby**'s heavy cavalry. Many Frenchmen, bewildered by the storm of iron, steel and lead, simply surrendered.

Private Vallence describes Picton's glory:

Our division was led on to the charge by our gallant general, Sir Thomas Picton. We gave them three hurrahs and rushed upon them with our levelled steel and drove this powerful column into disorder and confusion. Three or four regiments of our dragoons also rushed upon the enemy and instantly cut great numbers of them down and great numbers of them surrendered themselves as prisoners, and as they came past us they cried 'Commarada! Commarada!' 'We are also all comrades now,' we replied: 'Vive l'Empereur now.' They gave us pitiful looks and shook their heads as they passed on.

As I passed a wounded Frenchman on his knees, and his knapsack open, the poor fellow looked up to me with a pitiful face, and pointed to his knapsack that I might take anything I wanted. I told him I wanted nothing, and went past him. Several of the wounded Frenchmen opened their knapsacks and showed us all they had that we might take what we wished and spare their lives. They were afraid that we would kill them as they did our wounded men. It was in this bloody strife, in defeating this powerful column of the French that we lost our gallant leader, Sir Thomas Picton.

That Picton fell at Waterloo all sources agree. But the precise time and circumstance of his death are open to question. Some accounts have Picton falling, as Charles Dalton (1904) put it, 'whilst gloriously leading a charge of infantry'. This is the version favoured by Waterloo veteran **Edward Cotton** (1895), who has Picton yelling 'Charge! Charge! Hurrah!' at the fatal moment. But Captain **Seymour**, aide-de-camp to Lord **Uxbridge**, claims (Siborne 1891):

At the moment Sir Thomas Picton received the shot in his forehead which killed him, he was calling to me to rally the Highlanders, who were for the instant overpowered by the masses of French infantry, who were moving up to the right of the high road.

Meanwhile, Captain **Leach** of the 95th Rifles, a member of Picton's division, was convinced Sir Thomas fell *after* d'Erlon's attack,

Death of Picton *by George Jones*

declaring (1831) that: 'an unlucky straggling musket-shot put a period to his existence, and thereby deprived the army of one of its most gallant, experienced, and talented generals'.

The details of Picton's death do not matter much, however, for as historian Sir Edward Creasy (1851) observes:

> Of all the brave men who were in the British Army on that eventful day, none deserves more honour for courage and indomitable resolution than Sir Thomas Picton, who . . . fell in repulsing the great attack of the French upon the British left centre. It was not until the dead body was examined after the battle that the full heroism of Picton was discerned. He had been wounded on the 16th, at Quatre-Bras . . . but he had concealed the circumstance, evidently in expectation that another and greater battle would be fought in a short time, and desirous to avoid being solicited to absent himself from the field. His body was blackened and swollen by the wound, which must have caused severe and incessant pain.

Picton's body was first interred in the family vault at St George's, Hanover Square, London. But in 1859 his remains were exhumed for reburial in St Paul's – the only Welsh bones to grace the great cathedral.

Pirch
Major General Georg Dubislaw Ludwig von (1763–1838)

Commander of **Blücher**'s II Corps during the Waterloo campaign. Not to be confused with his younger brother, Otto Karl, who commanded a division in **Ziethen**'s I Corps (the two are designated Pirch I and Pirch II in contemporary Prussian sources), Pirch joined the army at the tender age of 12. The scion of an ancient Prussian family of warriors, Pirch had a long climb up the military ladder, becoming a major general by the time of Waterloo.

Pirch's II Corps began the Waterloo campaign as Blücher's biggest asset, numbering over 30,000 officers and men. According to historian Mark Adkin (2001), the corps was badly mauled at

Ligny on 16 June 1815, losing some 6,000 men in casualties and a similar number in deserters. At noon on 18 June, Pirch set off from Wavre to St Lambert in Bülow's footsteps, arriving on **Napoleon**'s right flank after 6 p.m. Pirch's leading unit was Count von Tippelskirch's 5,000-strong 5th Infantry Brigade, which was immediately tossed into the meat grinder, as **Bülow** struggled for possession of Plancenoit. But only a fraction of Pirch's troops saw action on Waterloo Day, the bulk of them bogged down in miry country tracks behind the battlefield.

Pirch quit the army shortly after Waterloo: almost deaf, he was no longer fit for service and retired to Berlin.

Piré-Hippolyte
General Marie-Guillaume, Count (1778–1850)

Commander of the 2nd Cavalry Division in **Reille**'s II Corps. Hailing from an aristocratic background, Piré began his military career at the age of 13, fighting alongside Royalist émigrés against the Revolutionaries. In 1795 he was wounded at Quiberon, when the British Royal Navy landed 3,500 French Royalists in an abortive attempt to kindle a Bourbon uprising in Brittany. Having fought against the Revolution as an officer in the Regiment of Rohan, Piré later swapped sides: returning to France under an amnesty granted by **Napoleon** to émigrés wishing to return home. A small but energetic man, Piré was a natural leader who displayed concern for those under his command. Unsurprisingly, then, he made a smooth transition from Royalist to Bonapartist, joining Napoleon's cavalry arm and seeing service at Austerlitz, Eylau, Somo Sierra, Eckmühl, Aspern-Essling and Wagram. By 1812 Piré had become a cavalry general and commanded a brigade in Russia. The following year saw him in command of the 9th Light Cavalry Division of **Milhaud**'s 5th Cavalry Corps. During the campaign of France in 1814, Piré saw action at the Battles of Brienne, La Rothière and St-Dizier, among others. In 1815 he returned to Napoleon's colours to command the 2nd Cavalry Division of II Corps.

Consisting of a brigade of chasseurs à cheval under Baron Huber, and a brigade of lancers under Baron Wathiez, Piré's division – over 2,000 sabres in all – spearheaded II Corps' passage of the River Sambre on 15 June 1815, which heralded Napoleon's bid to crush the armies of **Wellington** and **Blücher**. Next day, Piré marched to Quatre-Bras. There he joined French forces under Marshal **Ney**, tasked with taking the crossroads from an Anglo-Netherlands force under the Prince of **Orange** and the Duke of Wellington. In the early afternoon, Piré's chasseurs supported an attack by **Bachelu**'s infantry, which beat up a battalion of Netherlands militia defending the farm of Piraumont. Next, Piré's lancers routed two regiments of Netherlands cavalry (dragoons and hussars). But despite fierce fighting, Piré's troopers could not break **Picton**'s British infantry squares. Finally, Piré hoped to join Kellermann's cuirassiers, carabiniers and dragoons in a furious charge designed to take the vital crossroads – which in the event almost succeeded – but did not receive orders in time. After such stirling service at Quatre-Bras, Piré's division was too exhausted to pursue Wellington to Waterloo on 17 June.

At Waterloo, Piré's division – which according to historian Mark Adkin (2001) was Napoleon's strongest after **Lefebvre-Desnouëttes**' Imperial Guard Light Cavalry Division – was posted on the French left, tasked with protecting the flank and supporting **Jérôme** Bonaparte's attacks on Hougoumont. Piré performed these duties admirably, his horse artillery trading fire with **Bull**'s Royal Horse Artillery Troop and, by some accounts, obliging it to retire. Later in the day, Piré's division served as supports for Jérôme's skirmishers, guarding against sudden sorties by Allied cavalry. But by 8.30 p.m. – following the Wellington's repulse of the Imperial Guard and the appearance of Prussian forces under **Bülow** and **Ziethen** – the order came for Piré to retreat. And once again, he carried out his instructions skilfully and professionally: there was no rout, but an orderly withdrawal. Then, Piré led his command across country to Genappe, in the hope that the army might rally and make a stand. But this was not to be. At Genappe, Piré's division was swept away by a flood of fugitives – all the way back to the Sambre. Back on French soil, Piré regained control of his division, conducting a controlled retreat on Paris, and besting Blücher's cavalry at Rocquencourt, south of Paris, on 1 July.

After Waterloo, Piré was obliged to quit France in fear of Bourbon reprisals – the so-called White Terror. Fleeing to Russia, he remained there till 1819, when he received permission to return home. There he worked hard on behalf of the 'Brigands of the Loire' – Napoleon's Waterloo survivors (who took refuge behind the River Loire in the aftermath of defeat), many of whom had been consigned to a life of gruelling poverty. But it was not until after the July Revolution of 1830 that Piré received an administrative post. He retired in June 1848 – on the eve of yet another revolution – and died in Paris two years later.

Ponsonby
Lieutenant Colonel Sir Frederick Cavendish (1783–1837)

Commander of the 12th Light Dragoons, part of **Vandeleur**'s 4th British Cavalry Brigade. Second son of the third earl of Bessborough, Ponsonby – an inveterate gambler who later kicked the addiction – joined the army in 1800 as a cornet in the 10th Light Dragoons. After a spell in the 60th Foot, Ponsonby obtained a majority in the 23rd Light Dragoons, before joining **Wellington**'s Peninsular Army in 1809. He became a lieutenant colonel the following year, and in 1811 was given command of the 12th Light Dragoons, remaining at their head for the remainder of the Spanish campaign through to Waterloo.

On 18 June 1815 Ponsonby's regiment – some 430 sabres – formed part of Vandeleur's 4th British Cavalry Brigade. Initially posted on Wellington's extreme left, this brigade of light cavalry was moved towards the centre in the early afternoon. Ponsonby was then ordered to cover the retirement of the 2nd British (Union) Cavalry Brigade, which, having successfully charged **d'Erlon**'s infantry, had pressed too far and was trying to extricate itself from the clutches of **Milhaud**'s lancers and cuirassiers. Ponsonby's regiment, aided by the 16th Light Dragoons, descended the slopes of Mont St Jean and entered the melee on the plain. According to historian William Siborne (1848), Ponsonby, immediately after his brilliant charge with the 12th Light Dragoons, first through a column of infantry, and then upon the right flank of the lancers, was endeavouring to withdraw his regiment from further pursuit, when he was disabled in both arms, and carried by his horse up to the crest of the French position, where, receiving a sabre cut, he was struck senseless to the ground.

Ponsonby's account of the sequel, retold by Dalton (1904) among others, is one of the great personal dramas of the battle, a testament to courage, fortitude and the sheer will to survive:

Recovering, I raised myself a little to look round, being at that time in a condition to get up and run away, when a lancer, passing by, cried out, 'Tu n'es pas mort, coquin!' [You are not dead, you rascal!] and struck his lance through my back. My head dropped, the blood gushed into my mouth, a difficulty of breathing came on and I thought all was over. Not long after, a skirmisher stopped to plunder me, threatening my life: I directed him to a small side-pocket in which he found three dollars, all I had; but he continued to threaten, tearing open my waistcoat, and leaving me in a very uncomfortable posture . . . But he was no sooner gone, than an officer bringing up some troops, and happening to halt where I lay, stooped down, and

Frederick Ponsonby Wounded *by George Jones*

addressing me, said, he feared I was badly wounded. I answered that I was, and expressed a wish to be moved to the rear. He said it was against orders to remove even their own men; but that, if they gained the day (and he understood that the Duke of Wellington was killed, and that six of our battalions had surrendered), every attention in his power should be shown me. I complained of thirst, and he held his brandy bottle to my lips, directing one of his soldiers to lay me straight on my side, and place a knapsack under my head: they then passed on into action, soon perhaps to want, though not to receive, the same assistance; and I shall never know to whose generosity I was indebted, as I believe, for my life . . .

By and by, another skirmisher came up, a fine young man, full of ardour, loading and firing: he knelt down and fired over me many times, conversing with me very gaily all the while: at last he ran off, saying, 'Vous serez bien aisé d'apprendre que nous allons nous retirer. Bonjour, mon ami.' [You will be pleased to know that we are retreating. Good day, my friend.] It was dusk, when two squadrons of Prussian cavalry crossed the valley in full trot, lifting me from the ground, and tumbling me about must cruelly . . .

The battle was now over, and the groans of the wounded all around me, became more and more audible: I thought the night would never end. About this time I found a soldier lying across my legs, and his weight, his convulsive motions, his noises, and the air issuing through a wound in his side, distressed me greatly; the last circumstance most of all, as I had a wound of the same nature myself. It was not a dark night, and the Prussians were wandering about to plunder: many of them stopped to look at me as they passed; at last one of them stopped to examine me: I told him that I was a British officer, and had been already plundered. He did not however desist, and pulled me about roughly . . . An hour before midnight, I saw a man in an English uniform, coming towards me; he was, I suspected, on the same errand. I spoke instantly, telling him who I was: he belonged to the 40th, and had missed his regiment. He released me from the dying soldier, took up a sword, and stood over me as sentinel. Day broke, and at six o'clock in the morning a messenger was sent to Hervé: a cart came for me, and I was conveyed to the village of Waterloo, and laid in the bed, as I afterwards understood from which Gordon [Lieutenant Colonel Sir **Alexander Gordon**] had just been carried out. I had received seven wounds; a surgeon slept in my room, and I was saved by excessive bleeding.

Ponsonby's belief that bleeding (known as venesection in medical circles) saved his life makes his story all the more poignant. In fact, the practice was potentially lethal. According to Dr Martin Howard (2002), Napoleonic medics bled patients in the belief they were removing impurities, thus relieving inflammation and fever. But excessive blood loss leads to shock and a dangerous drop in blood pressure and urine output, plus weakening of the pulse. As Howard states: 'Many soldiers must have died after venesection who otherwise would have lived.' That Ponsonby recovered – against all expectations – is probably thanks to the care of his sister, Caroline, who acted as his devoted nurse.

Ponsonby quit his regiment in 1820 on half-pay. Decorated with medals and prestigious orders, he went on to hold a number of administrative posts, including the governorship of Malta, and the colonelcy of several regiments. He married Lady Emily Charlotte Bathurst, daughter of the third Earl Bathurst, and together they had six children. Ponsonby died unexpectedly at the Wellesley Arms, Murrell Green, Basingstoke, on 11 January 1837.

Ponsonby
Major General Sir William (1772–1815)

Commander of **Wellington**'s 2nd British (Union) Cavalry Brigade at Waterloo (not to be confused with his second cousin, Lieutenant Colonel Sir **Frederick Cavendish Ponsonby**, who, as commander of the 12th Light Dragoons, was wounded during the great battle). Second son of William Brabazon Ponsonby, first Baron Ponsonby, Sir William purchased a captain's commission in the 83rd Foot in September 1794, upgrading three months later to become a major in the Loyal Irish Fencibles. In 1798 Ponsonby transferred to the 5th Dragoon Guards and within five years was commanding the regiment as a lieutenant colonel. In 1811 Ponsonby – now a full colonel – joined Wellington's army in Spain, serving with distinction, and rising to the command of a cavalry brigade. Two years later, in 1813, Ponsonby had attained the rank of major general. Thus, within the space of 19 years, Ponsonby had risen from captain to major general: a feat largely made possible by the purchase system, whereby wealthy British officers bought their promotions. On 2 January 1815 Ponsonby was made a Knight Commander of the Order of the Bath (KCB). Prior to the commencement of the Waterloo campaign, he received command of the 2nd British (Union) Cavalry Brigade. The command was dubbed the Union Brigade because its three regiments – the 1st (Royal) Dragoons, the 2nd Royal North British (Scots Greys) Dragoons and the 6th (Inniskilling) Dragoons – represented the Union of England, Scotland and Ireland, respectively.

At Waterloo, Ponsonby's brigade – fielding some 1,332 sabres in all – was initially placed in reserve, to the left of the Brussels high road. The dragoons were in rear of **Picton**'s 5th British Infantry Division, which became the target of a colossal French advance around 1.30 p.m.: **Napoleon**'s opening bid to breach Wellington's line and break open the Brussels road. Three French infantry divisions from **d'Erlon**'s I Corps took part in this sortie, numbering perhaps 13,000 men in all. (A fourth column, commanded by **Durutte**, broke away from the assault on Picton, hitting the village of Papelotte on Wellington's extreme left.) By 1.45 p.m. the French attack was gaining momentum, led by Donzelot's division, whose 5,000 men were reputedly packed into a tight formation 650 feet wide and 200 feet deep. D'Erlon's infantry advanced to the right of the Brussels road (i.e. Wellington's left), supported by Travers's and Dubois's heavy cavalry on the opposite side of the high road. Achieving initial success against Allied skirmishers, the French juggernaut was held on the ridge of Mont St Jean by Picton's Peninsular veterans. According to authors Uffindell and Corum (1996), this seemingly impossible feat of British pluck can be explained by the fact that d'Erlon's columns were staggered, with the effect that 'the action on the crest of Wellington's ridge was far longer and slower and fragmented than is usually realised'.

This delay played into Allied hands, allowing **Uxbridge**, Wellington's cavalry supremo, to launch a decisive counter-attack, as described by William Siborne (1848):

The Earl of Uxbridge, on perceiving the advance of the French . . .
decided upon a simultaneous charge by the heavy cavalry brigades
of Lord **Edward Somerset** and Sir William Ponsonby; the former
against the enemy's cavalry, the latter against his masses of infantry.

And so Ponsonby's brigade smashed into the leading French
columns – totalling perhaps 9,000 foot soldiers in all – wreaking
havoc and allegedly taking 2,000 prisoners. According to Major De
Lacy Evans, one of Ponsonby's aides-de-camp, the French fled 'as a
flock of sheep across the valley, quite at the mercy of the dragoons'
(Siborne 1891). Meanwhile, General Sir Evelyn Wood (1895) noted
that: 'D'Erlon's disastrous attack cost the French 5,000 men killed,
wounded or prisoners, two Eagles, and fifteen cannon wrecked.'

But success would soon turn to disaster. In the words of Waterloo
veteran **Edward Cotton** (1895):

> most of Ponsonby's brigade, with a portion of the Household
> Brigade, animated by their recent success, pursued their advantage
> too far; they crossed the valley in disorder and galloped up to the
> French position in twos and threes and groups, brandishing their
> swords in defiance, riding along the ridge, sabreing their gunners
> . . . the bugles or trumpets, sounding to rally were unheeded.

De Lacy Evans confirms Cotton's account:

> In fact our men were out of hand. The General of the brigade, his
> staff, and every officer within hearing exerted themselves to the
> utmost to re-form the men; but the helplessness of the enemy
> offered too great a temptation to the dragoons, and our efforts
> were abortive.

With Ponsonby unable to control his battle-frenzied dragoons, the
General and his staff simply got sucked into the melee.

Soon, the inevitable counter-charge materialised, as Napoleon
threw in **Jacquinot**'s hussars, chasseurs and lancers. Cotton (1895)
describes the sequel:

> The enemy's cuirassiers, lancers and chasseurs, perceiving the
> isolated and unsupported position of our broken dragoons, rushed
> forward and made serious havoc, pursuing them down the slope into

Death of Sir William Ponsonby *by George Jones*

the valley. Those of our men whose horses were blown and exhausted by their recent exertions became an easy prey.

Among their number was Ponsonby, killed by a lance thrust. The story goes that before his death, Ponsonby tried to pass his watch, and a locket containing a miniature portrait of his pregnant wife, to Captain Thomas Reignolds for safe keeping, but both men were killed. Historian William Siborne (1848) described the episode thus:

> Ponsonby might have escaped if he had been better mounted, but the groom with his chestnut charger could not be found at the moment of the charge, and he was riding a small bay hack, which soon stuck fast in the heavy ground. Seeing he must be overtaken, he was handing over his watch and a miniature to his brigade major to deliver to his family, when the French lancers came up and killed them both.

Siborne's account of Ponsonby's end has been repeated many times. For example, according to General Sir Evelyn Wood (1895):

> After Sir William Ponsonby had crossed the valley, the hack he was riding, being exhausted, could not move faster than a walk, and seeing a squadron of Jacquinot's lancers approaching, he took a

locket off his neck and gave it to his aide-de-camp, who was better mounted, with instructions that he he should, if he escaped, ensure its reaching Lady Ponsonby. Both officers were, however, speared, as were many of those overtaken in the low ground.

And Charles Dalton (1904) records that Ponsonby was killed

> from being badly mounted. Whilst leading a cavalry charge against the 'Polish Lancers' his horse stuck in a heavy ploughed field and was unable to extricate itself. He took a picture and watch out of his pocket and was just delivering them to his ADC to give to his wife when the lancers were on him.

But if Ponsonby and Reignolds were both killed, how do we know about the watch and the miniature? A clue comes from the reminscences of Corporal Dickson of the Scots Greys, a survivor of the madcap charge on Napoleon's grand battery. Making his way back across the valley with his comrades, Dickson recalled (Maughan, n.d.):

> We were returning past the edge of the ploughed field, and then I saw a spectacle I shall never forget. There lay brave old Ponsonby, the General of our Union Brigade, beside his little bay, both dead. His long, fur-lined coat had blown aside, and at his hand I noticed a miniature of a lady and his watch; beyond him, our Brigade-Major, Reignolds of the Greys. They had both been pierced by the lancers a few moments before we came up.

An eyewitness account of Ponsonby's death does exist, however, and flows from the pen of Frenchman Louis **Brô**, Colonel of the 4th Lancers. According to Brô, it was an hour after midday when Donzelot's division attacked Picton's sector. Marcognet's 4,000-strong division hurried forward into the fray, but Ponsonby's brigade appeared from behind the crest of Wellington's ridge, led by the Scots Greys. At this point, says Brô (1914), d'Erlon ordered his divisional cavalry to charge over sodden ground:

> Two minutes later the shock took place . . . The clash was dreadful . . . For a moment I was lost in a fog of gunsmoke. When it cleared I saw some English officers surrounding Lieutenant Verrand, the

Eagle-bearer. Gathering some riders I went to his aid. Sergeant Orban killed General Ponsonby with a blow of his lance. My sabre felled three of his captains. Two others fled.

Brô's account does not mention that Ponsonby was 'overtaken' as a solitary or semi-solitary rider, or that he was 'speared' while handing over his watch and a miniature portait (or locket) to Captain Reignolds. Rather, Brô's words suggest the 'clash' and 'shock' of a savage cavalry combat, with Ponsonby dying in the thick of it. Nevertheless, the idea that Ponsonby was ridden down by a posse of lancers – and Polish ones at that – persists, captured in a memorable sequence from Sergei Bondarchuk's 1970 movie *Waterloo* (Ponsonby is played by British actor Michael Wilding). But whether hunted down like a helpless animal or slain in mortal combat, Ponsonby's life appears to have been taken by a Frenchmen of Brô's 4th Lancers.

Sir William Ponsonby's body was recovered the morning after the battle and later buried at Kensington, in the Molesworth family vault: final resting place of his mother's ancestors. A national monument was erected in his honour at St Paul's Cathedral. Wellington, in his report of the battle, expressed 'grief for the fate of an officer who had already rendered very brilliant and important services, and was an ornament to his profession'. Ponsonby left one son and four daughters. The son, also named William, succeeded his uncle, John Ponsonby, as third Baron Ponsonby – a title that became extinct before the century was out.

Pozzo di Borgo
General Carlo Andrea, Count (1764–1842)

Commissioner representing Tsar Alexander I on **Wellington**'s staff at Waterloo. Born in Corsica of aristocratic parents, Pozzo di Borgo had been an early associate of the Buonaparte clan, headed by **Napoleon**'s father Carlo, a lawyer of Italian extraction and a member of the island's minor nobility. At that time, the

Mediterranean island of Corsica was controlled by France, which purchased sovereignty from the Republic of Genoa in 1768. This change of political masters was unpopular, however, and a resistance movement sprang up, centred on the powerful personality of General Pasquale Paoli (1725–1807). Pozzo di Borgo's family – like the Buonapartes – sided with Paoli, but without foreign aid the rebellion came to nothing. Paoli fled to England in 1769 (the year of Napoleon's birth) and many Corsicans saw little option but to befriend the French.

As for Pozzo di Borgo, after studying law at Pisa, he entered Corsica's political arena. Following the French Revolution of 1789, he went to Paris to sit in the National Assembly as a Corsican delegate. He remained until August 1792 when, as historian Duncan Townson (1990) states, 'militant *sans-culottes* knocked the Revolution off-course [forcing] the country's leaders to adopt policies which were contrary to the liberal reforms of the Con- stituent Assembly'. Finding the Jacobins too radical for his taste, Pozzo di Borgo returned to a Corsica governed by the newly reinstated Paoli. Appointed Chief of the Civil Government, Pozzo di Borgo echoed Paoli's dislike for the new regime in Paris and supported his anti-French revolt of 1793 – as did the British, who duly landed on Corsica and took over. Pozzo di Borgo now found himself head of the London-sponsored civil government of the island. But in 1796 French forces evicted the Brits, and Paoli and Pozzo di Borgo fled the island: the former to London, where he lived out his days; the latter to Vienna, where a new life was waiting.

Pozzo di Borgo lived in Vienna several years, before entering the Imperial Russian diplomatic service on 10 October 1805. In early 1807 (the year of Paoli's death) Pozzo di Borgo was sent on a diplomatic mission to Constantinople: but when, in July, Tsar Alexander aligned himself with Napoleon, the diplomat quit Russian service and returned to Vienna. Although Napoleon demanded his extradition, Vienna refused to comply and the Corsican fled to England, where he remained till 1812. Then, when Franco-Russian relations crashed, Pozzo di Borgo was recalled to diplomatic service by the Tsar. According to historian Alexander Mikaberidze (2005):

Pozzo negotiated with Sweden in early 1813, ensuring its alliance
against the French. He then served with the Army of the North at
Gross Beeren, Dennewitz, and Leipzig, receiving promotion to
major general on 15 September 1813.

In the wake of Napoleon's first abdication in April 1814, and
the subsequent return of the Bourbons, Pozzo di Borgo was
appointed Russian ambassador to France. He was busy helping
the monarchs of the *ancien régime* redraw the map of Europe
at the Congress of Vienna, when Napoleon escaped from Elba
in February 1815. At first, Pozzo di Borgo returned to Paris with
Louis XVIII: but with Napoleon's triumphal march on the French
capital, he ended up accompanying the bulky Bourbon to the
safety of Belgium and the city of Ghent. When Wellington arrived
at Brussels to take charge of an Anglo-Netherlands army in
April 1815, Pozzo di Borgo was appointed Russian commissioner
at the Duke's headquarters. The Corsican aristocrat attended the
celebrated Richmond Ball on 15 June, and three days later found
himself on the battlefield of Waterloo. His presence among
Wellington's suite at the start of the battle was noted by **Gronow**
(1900) of the British 1st Foot Guards:

> We had not proceeded a quarter of a mile when we heard the
> trampling of horses' feet, and on looking round perceived a large
> cavalcade of officers coming at full speed. In a moment we
> recognised the Duke himself at their head . . . The entire staff was
> close at hand: the Prince of **Orange**, Count Pozzo di Borgo, Baron
> Vincent, the Spanish General **Alava**, Prince Castel Cicala, with
> their several aides-de-camp; Felton Harvey, **Fitzroy Somerset**,
> and Delancey were the last that appeared. They all seemed as
> unconcerned as if they were riding to meet the hounds in some
> quiet English county.

And yet most of these gentleman were injured in the action, **De
Lancey** mortally. As for Pozzo di Borgo, Wellington noted that the
diplomat 'received a contusion'. But this did not prevent him from
announcing the victory at Waterloo in a letter to Louis XVIII, still at
Ghent. According to Stanhope (1888), Wellington remarked that,
following the battle, Pozzo di Borgo arrived at his quarters:

I begged him, as he was returning to Brussels, to write a letter to the King of France announcing the battle, as I wanted to go to bed. Accordingly he wrote, and he sent his letter by a Russian officer, who arrived at Ghent just when the Royal Family was sitting at breakfast. I have often thought since – there's history! Some future writer will say, it was a Russian officer that brought the despatch to Louis XVIII; it is quite clear then that the Russian generals must have had a principal share in the battle!

Quiot du Passage
General Joachim, Baron (1775–1849)

Commander of the 1st Division of **d'Erlon**'s I Corps at Waterloo. Quiot replaced General **Allix de Vaux**, who failed to turn up for the campaign (and who is often erroneously listed in published orders of battle). A veteran of campaigns in Russia, Germany and France, Quiot was a dependable commander loyal to **Napoleon**. His command, which consisted of four infantry regiments, was tasked with taking the bastion of La Haie Sainte (garrisoned by light troops from the King's German Legion under Major **Baring**) and assaulting **Wellington**'s centre. But Quiot had a tough time of it: his troops failed to take La Haie Sainte (a regiment from Marcognet's division finally stormed the place about 6.30 p.m., after the garrison ran out of bullets) and failed to pierce Wellington's centre (held by the fiery Sir **Thomas Picton**). Even worse, his regiments were roughed up by Sir **William Ponsonby**'s dragoons (the 105th Line losing its Eagle to Captain **Alexander Kennedy Clark** and/or Corporal **Styles** of the 'Royals') and at the close of the battle, fled the field.

Reille
General Honoré-Charles-Michel-Joseph, Count (1775–1860)

Commander of **Napoleon**'s II Corps. Enlisting as a private soldier in 1791 and commissioned the following year, Reille worked his way up to general of brigade within the space of 12 years. A veteran of the campaigns in Prussia, Poland and Spain, Reille joined Napoleon's staff for the Danube campaign of 1809 (having previously attained the rank of general of division), serving at the Battles of Aspern–Essling and

General Reille (1775–1860)

Wagram. The following year he went back to Spain, doing a stint as Governor of Navarre before returning to a field command. Following Napoleon's first fall in 1814, Reille accepted employment under the returning Bourbon monarchy, but rallied to the erstwhile Emperor in spring 1815. Napoleon rewarded him with command of the Army of the North's II Corps. But despite Reille's impressive track record as a gifted, fearless, and zealous commander, by 1815 he was showing signs of war-weariness and disillusionment. Poor relations with Marshal **Soult**, Napoleon's new chief of staff, did not help matters. Neither did having the Emperor's pompous and impetuous younger brother **Jérôme** as one of his subordinate generals: a circumstance which, according to historian Tony Linck (1993), was 'enough to give him the jitters'.

And in the coming Waterloo campaign Reille certainly put in something of a 'jittery' performance. First, at the Battle of Quatre-Bras on 16 June 1815, Reille warned **Ney** against a quick lunge at the vital crossroads. An old hand at fighting British redcoats – thanks to his experiences in the Peninsula – Reille advised extreme caution, emphasising the folly of being drawn into a 'Spanish battle' against Wellington. Ney was apparently convinced, for he treated the 8,000 or so troops opposite with inordinate respect, postponing an all-out attack, despite the fact that Reille's corps alone numbered 20,000 men. This dithering allowed the outnumbered **Wellington** to hurry up reinforcements and eventually fight the French to a standstill. Two days later, Reille again advised caution against Wellington – much to Napoleon's irritation. The story goes that Napoleon called a 'power breakfast' for his generals at the farmhouse of Le Caillou on the morning of the Battle of Waterloo. Reille stated his belief that the British were impregnable when defending a chosen position. He was backed up by Soult, who pronounced Wellington's infantry 'the very devil', but Napoleon rounded on his chief of staff, crying: 'Because you have been beaten by Wellington, you consider him a great general. And now I tell you he is a bad general, and the English are but poor troops!' This out-burst is frequently quoted as an example of Napoleon's contempt for Wellington – and occasionally as a symptom of failing mental faculties. But as Andrew Roberts (2001) states, 'Far from expressing over-confidence, as is constantly assumed, the Emperor was displaying his irritation at what sounded like the defeatism of a series of Peninsular generals.'

After this ear-bashing the breakfast broke up, Reille taking post with his troops, deployed on the French left wing, opposite the château of Hougoumont. His corps consisted of three infantry divisions: those of **Bachelu**, Jérôme and **Foy** (Girard's excellent 7th Infantry Division had been detached on 16 June, joining **Grouchy** for the pursuit of **Blücher**'s defeated Prussians), plus a cavalry division under **Piré**. Reille's task at Waterloo was simple: he was to launch a diversionary assault on Hougoumont, Napoleon's plan being to force the Duke to bolster this bastion by weakening his centre, the target for the main French effort. But things went awry when Jérôme Bonaparte made the seizure of Hougoumont a point of honour, throwing his 6th Infantry Division into a series of fruitless attacks against a strong garrison under **James Macdonell**. Reille should have reined in Jérôme – who turned the diversion at Hougoumont into a day-long battle-within-a-battle – but failed to do so. Overawed by Bonaparte junior, Reille looked on as both Bachelu and Foy followed Jérôme into the maelstrom, committing 15,000 French troops better employed elsewhere.

About 6 p.m. Reille was ordered to lead an assault on Wellington's right-centre, but without the support of **Milhaud**'s or Kellermann's cavalry corps – both wrecked on Wellington's infantry squares in a series of pointless charges – the sortie was repulsed with heavy losses. And yet, Reille's effort did provide a diversion for elements of **d'Erlon**'s corps to take La Haie Sainte on the opposite side of the battlefield, **Baring**'s German garrison having run out of ammunition. Finally, Reille's survivors attempted to support the Imperial Guard's last ditch assault against Wellington about 7.30 p.m. But when the Guard broke and fled, chased down the slopes of Mont St Jean by the infantry of **Chassé**, **Maitland** and Colborne, Reille's troops lost heart. Wellington's subsequent general advance – plus the advent of Prussian troops under **Ziethen** and **Bülow** – signalled a French collapse and Reille's troops were swept up by a human tsunami. That said, according to historian Harold T. Parker (1944), among others, Reille's II Corps quit the field in fairly good order. But chaos following Napoleon's defeat was profound and Reille actually got lost amid the flotsam and jetsam, rejoining Napoleon next day to find that over two-thirds of his command had disappeared – casualties or deserters.

Following Napoleon's second and final abdication on 22 June, Reille marched his remaining troops out of Paris, taking post behind the River Loire, south of the capital. Reinstated by Louis XVIII's general amnesty of 30 December 1818, Reille buried his Bonapartist sympathies and became something of a Bourbon fan. And yet, it was his association with the fallen Emperor that eventually brought Reille out of the wilderness and back into prominence. For in 1847 he was made a marshal by King Louis Philippe, eager to boost his failing popularity by fanning the flames of France's former glory. Reille survived the demise of Louis Philippe's regime to be made a senator by Bonaparte's nephew, Napoleon III.

Richmond
General Charles Lennox, fourth Duke of (1764–1819)

British aristocrat who, with his wife, hosted the famous Richmond ball on the eve of the Waterloo campaign, and who was present at the great battle as a spectator. Reputedly born in a barn (his mother apparently went into labour while out fishing), this Scottish aristocrat was the eldest son of Lieutenant General Lord George Henry Lennox. He entered the army in 1785 and four years later was appointed captain in the 2nd Foot (Coldstream) Guards by King George III. But the colonel of this elite regiment – the King's second son, Frederick Augustus, later Duke of York – apparently felt slighted that he was not consulted about Lennox's selection and protested. As a result, Lennox took umbrage and challenged the Prince to a duel, which took place on Wimbledon Common on 26 May 1789. They fought with pistols but neither party was hurt: Lennox's bullet disturbed one of Frederick's royal curls; but Frederick – who had no personal dislike of Lennox and was simply following the officer's code of honour regarding such matters – simply shot into the air. The result, however, was that Lennox transferred from the Guards to the Line – but not before fighting another duel. On 3 July 1789 Lennox demanded satisfaction from one Theophilus Swift, who had publicly criticised his character. The duel was fought near Uxbridge Road, London, and Swift was wounded. By now, Lennox had gained a measure of fame as a duellist or 'fire-eater'. But having joined his new regiment, the 35th Foot, he settled down into the life of an aristocratic British officer:

playing cricket, getting married, and taking a seat in the House of Commons.

Lennox's riches permitted him to glide through an army career, thanks to the purchase system whereby wealthy officers could buy vacant commissions: by 1795 he was a colonel, by 1805 a lieutenant general, and by 1814 a full general – even though he had no experience of command in the field (Lennox apparently requested to serve in the Peninsula under his friend the Duke of **Wellington**, but the latter declined). Meanwhile, Lennox had inherited his uncle's dukedom, making him fourth duke of Richmond, and had served for a time as Lord Lieutenant of Ireland.

By the time of the Waterloo campaign in 1815, Lennox and his wife – now the Duke and Duchess of Richmond – were living in Brussels with their children. On 15 June – the night Wellington was obliged to mobilise his army to meet **Napoleon**'s thrust into Belgium – the Richmonds hosted a celebrated ball. The event has gone down in history as both a romantic and tragic affair: the young officers of Wellington's army being called away to war still wearing their dancing pumps. Even those who attended the ball – like the husband and daughters of **Caroline Capel** – misremembered the event, claiming the venue had been full of soldiers, most of whom were later killed at Waterloo. And yet, as author David Miller states (2005), less than half of those who were present at the Richmond ball belonged to the military: perhaps 103 out of a total 238 attendees. Apart from Wellington, these included brass hats like General **Alava**, General **Pozzo di Borgo**, the Duke of **Brunswick**, and the Prince of **Orange**. And of the 103 soldiers present, only 11 were killed in the fighting between 16 and 18 June. As for the location of the ball, it seems it took place at the Richmonds' rented house on the Rue de la Blanchisserie – despite claims by nineteenth-century Belgian tour guides that the opulent Hôtel de Ville was the venue.

On Waterloo Day, Charles Lennox, the Duke of Richmond, rode out from Brussels to watch the battle as a sightseer, accompanied by his 15-year-old son, William (his son George was serving on Wellington's staff as an aide-de-camp). Attaching himself to Wellington's suite, Richmond was reprimanded by the Duke and told 'you have no business here'. Nevertheless, Richmond remained to watch the first half of the battle, wandering about the field dispensing encouragement and advice as if in command. According to historian William Siborne (1848):

> Just as the Inniskillings were on the point of advancing across the Wavre road to charge, an individual in plain clothes, on their left, called out, 'Now's your time!' This was the late Duke of Richmond, who was induced by his intimacy with the Duke of Wellington, and the interest which he naturally felt in the progress of the campaign, to repair to the field of battle; not in a military capacity, for he held no rank in the army, but merely *en amateur*. He was accompanied by his son, the present Lord William Lennox, then a Cornet in the Blues, and extra aide-de-camp to Major General **Maitland**. Lord William had, a few days before the battle, met with a violent accident, by a fall from his horse in the park of Enghien: his right arm was severely fractured, the sight of his right eye destroyed, and his life despaired of; but hearing, when on the sick list at Brussels, that his brother aide-de-camp, Captain Lord James Hay, had been killed at Quatre-Bras, he decided on accompanying his father to the field on the 18th. Here he presented himself to General Maitland, who, however, would not permit his lordship to remain with him, deeming a boy of fifteen, with a maimed arm, bandaged eye, and weak frame of body, but ill calculated to prove an efficient aide-de-camp. Lord William then joined his father, who rode about the field, unmindful of the frequently heavy fire to which he became exposed, conversing with his friends, and passing his remarks as if on actual service. After witnessing the brilliant cavalry charge on the left, his Grace proceeded towards the right, but finding the fire had become very heavy, and the ground strewed with the slain, he and his son returned leisurely to Brussels.

But the Duke of Richmond was not the only non-combatant at Waterloo. For although the locals had abandoned their homes and farms before the battle to hide in the Forest of Soignes, a few remained stuck on the battlefield. One was the farmer's wife at Mont St Jean, who, concerned for the safety of her animals, refused to quit. She spent the day hiding in her attic. Another was the gardener at Hougoumont, still tending the grounds, though the château was unoccupied. He had intended to leave before the battle, but being a conscientious worker, left it too late. He remained with the garrison throughout the day, exposed to shot, shell and fire for almost

10 hours. Meanwhile, Napoleon is known to have pressed local men, **Jean Decoster** and Joseph Bourgeois, into service as guides. And an apocryphal story has Wellington using hapless civilians as battlefield messengers: according to Elizabeth Longford (1969), the Duke enlisted a Swiss haberdasher and a cockney commercial traveller as unofficial aides-de-camp. The latter is supposed to have approached Wellington with: 'Please Sir, any orders for Todd and Morrison?' Eliciting the laconic reply: 'No; but will you do me a service? Go to that officer and tell him to refuse a flank.' These non-combatants, like the Duke of Richmond, all survived the great battle.

But despite coolness under fire, Richmond lost his composure when, a few months later, his daughter – Lady Sarah Lennox – ran off to marry Maitland, the impecunious and untitled major general referred to above.

Saint-Denis
Louis Étienne (1788–1856)

Napoleon's manservant at Waterloo. Born at Versailles of humble parents – his father worked in the palace stables, his mother in the kitchens – Saint-Denis entered Napoleon's service as a valet in 1806, at the age of 18. Initially put under the care of the Emperor's celebrated Mameluke servant, Roustam, Saint-Denis was promoted 'Second Mameluke' in 1811. Saint-Denis – or 'Ali' as he was now known – accompanied Napoleon to Russia and throughout the campaigns of 1813 and 1814. Having replaced Roustam as Napoleon's principal manservant in the wake of the first abdication (Roustam quit to become a minor Parisian celebrity and memoirist of dubious veracity), Saint-Denis followed his master into exile on Elba. At Waterloo, he remained the faithful valet, carrying the Emperor's writing materials, sealing wax, dividers and telescope. Determined not to be jettisoned in the aftermath of battle, Saint-Denis accompanied Napoleon on the mad dash for Philippeville and the French frontier:

> Night was covering the battlefield with its shades when Marshal **Blücher** entered our lines, carrying disorder into some French

regiments; and as this disorder gradually spread, it became general in a short time. It was necessary for the Guard to change its front and then it was formed into squares, in one of which the Emperor and his suite sought refuge from the Prussian cavalry, which was flooding the field. **Bülow**'s corps, which had taken the offensive once more, was threatening to cut us off completely . . .

In the long column of soldiers of all arms, of all corps, of all regiments, who were retreating, each one going his own way, the small group of which the Emperor was the centre marched with all the rest, going to Philippeville. It was a summer night without a moon; one could see, but not clearly. Bivouac fires could be seen here and there on the road, and around them men were resting, worn out and dying of hunger. We went on calmly and quietly, the horses at a walk.

During the 19th, in the middle of the day, we arrived at Philippeville. The Emperor, extremely fatigued, not only by the long journey but by the events of the 18th and the small amount of sleep the night before, went to a shabby inn and got a room. I half undressed him and he went to bed to try to get some rest. He was very sad, and above all, much absorbed in thought.

According to Saint-Denis (1926), Napoleon remained at Philippeville until early evening. It was here the Emperor wrote his final Bulletin and issued orders for the troops to rally at Laon, halfway point between Paris and the Belgian border.

Leaving **Soult** to salvage the wreck of the army, Napoleon continued his journey to the capital. Speed was essential, for the Emperor knew he had to reach Paris ahead of Waterloo news, to stave off the very real threat of deposition at the hands of political enemies (notably Fouché, the Minister of Police). Saint-Denis says that Napoleon clambered into a two-seater barouche at Philippeville, accompanied by General Bertrand, Grand Marshal of the Palace. Once again, the loyal, steadfast Saint-Denis was hell-bent on following, spending much of the journey clinging for dear life to the back of the Emperor's coach:

When the hour for departure came the post horses were hitched to the carriage, which could not hold more than two people and which had no box seat. As I was determined to accompany the Emperor at any cost, I was very much embarrassed. How was I to go? As there

345

were iron spikes on the ledge behind the carriage I could not sit there. Yet I saw no option but to perch behind, after the manner of footmen, holding myself up by the aid of two straps, which were on the top, and there was only just room for my two feet on the ledge . . . I hoped, as soon as daylight came, to find a more agreeable mode of travelling. The Emperor and the Grand Marshal got into the carriage, I settled myself as well as I could, and we started. The other carriage remained a good way behind, so we might appear to be travelling separately and not attract the eyes of curious people whom we might meet. I suffered a great deal during the whole journey. I constantly feared that the straps might break or come loose, and that I should fall over backward, with my feet caught on the iron spikes. The road was very rough and exhausted me terribly. It was a long time to spend in a most trying position. But I kept up my courage, always hoping to relieve my pain at the first opportunity.

Saint-Denis remained loyal to the end, being among the small band of 'companions in misfortune' who accompanied Napoleon into final exile on St Helena. There he performed the functions of copyist, librarian, manservant and nurse to the fallen Emperor. He also found time to marry a certain Mary Hall in 1819, with whom he had three daughters. Following Napoleon's death in 1821, Saint-Denis and his newfound family returned to France. Named as a beneficiary in the Emperor's will, he settled down to a comfortable life at Sens, penning a remarkable portrait of the years spent as 'Ali', Napoleon's 'Second Mameluke'.

Saltoun
Alexander George Fraser, Lord (1785–1853)

Commander of the light companies of the 1st Foot Guards and one of the defenders of Hougoumont. Eldest son of the fifteenth Lord Saltoun of Abernethy, he succeeded his father while still a minor. Educated at Eton College, Saltoun entered the army as an ensign in 1802. Within two years he had become a captain –

thanks to the British practice of purchasing commissions – transferring to the 1st Foot Guards from the 35th Foot. A veteran of the campaigns of Sicily, Corunna, Walcheren and the Iberian peninsula, Saltoun returned to England in 1814, following **Napoleon**'s first fall from grace. During the Waterloo campaign he commanded the light companies of Byng's 2nd British (Guards) Brigade, part of Major General **George Cooke**'s 1st British Infantry (Guards) Division.

Saltoun's troops, drawn from the 2/2nd and 2/3rd Foot Guards, held the garden and orchard of Hougoumont against repeated attacks by **Jérôme** Bonaparte's 6th Infantry Division (**James Macdonell** of the 2nd Foot Guards held the château complex itself). At the close of the action Saltoun apparently returned to his place in **Wellington**'s line with only one-third of his original command, the remainder having gone down as casualties. Saltoun himself had four horses shot under him during the battle. In a letter quoted by William Siborne (1848), Saltoun describes the see-saw battle for the outer perimeter of Hougoumont, including his abortive attempt to silence a French howitzer, deployed in woods south of the château:

> The whole was a succession of attacks against the front of that
> post attended with more or less partial success for the moment,
> but in the end always repulsed; and it was in one of these attacks
> when I had been driven from the front hedge of the orchard to the
> hollow way in the rear of it, that they occupying the outward
> side of the front hedge with infantry, brought a gun . . . This gun
> I endeavoured to take, but failed. I, however, regained the front
> hedge of the orchard, and from which I never was again driven.

After Waterloo Saltoun was showered with honours and promotions. An accomplished musician as well as soldier (he later became President of the Madrigal Society of London and Chairman of the Musical Union), Wellington considered him 'a pattern to the army both as a man and a soldier'.

Sandham
Captain Charles F. (?–1869)

Commander of the battery of five 9-pounders and one 5½-inch howitzer that reputedly fired the first Allied salvo at Waterloo. According to writers Julian Paget and Derek Saunders (1992): 'it is strange that it is still not certain when the first shot was fired in anger on 18 June 1815. Various individuals who were there gave times ranging from 10 a.m. to midday.' But historian A.F. Becke (1914) seems untroubled by such doubts: 'At 11.30 **Napoleon** began the battle with the assault on Hougoumont. The French advanced, some of their guns opened fire.' Napoleon, then, fired the first shot: a barrage in support of brother **Jérôme**'s attack on Hougoumont. The first Allied shot came almost immediately after, in direct response: 'Sandham's Field Brigade answered,' continues Becke, 'the first round from our position at the attacking infantry, a spherical case, was effective.' But how effective? Becke states that three Frenchmen were hit by this opening shot from one of Sandham's five 9-pounders, but as usual sources vary. According to eyewitness Daniel Mackinnon (1833), the round from Sandham's gun 'made a gap for a moment in the head of the column commanded by Prince Jérôme Bonaparte, as it moved to the attack on Hougoumont'.

Scott
Sir Walter (1771–1832)

Famous bard and novelist who, following a tour of the Waterloo battlefield in 1815, penned the poem *The Field of Waterloo*. Born in Edinburgh of middle-class parents, Scott contracted polio in his youth, which left him permanently lame in his right leg. He studied law at Edinburgh University and qualified as an advocate in 1792, pursuing a legal career until retirement in 1830. But Scott was a man of romantic imagination, and inspired by the traditional Border ballads of his boyhood, began producing his own epic poems. The first of these, *The Lay of the Last Minstrel*, was published in 1805 to immediate critical acclaim. In 1807 Scott's publisher paid him 1,000 guineas (approximately £52,000 in modern reckoning) as an advance on the poem *Marmion*, which appeared a year later. And in 1810 Scott eclipsed *Marmion* with the hugely popular *The Lady of the Lake*. Now Scott was a celebrated poet, competing with the likes of Byron and Southey.

Perhaps the most prolific poet of the period, Scott was also one of the wealthiest, his literary endeavours enabling him to build his very own Gothic castle at Abbotsford, near Galashiels. Within the space of a few years, however, sales of Scott's poetry was on the wane: indication, perhaps, of a subtle change in literary tastes and public mood. Now obliged to support a baronial lifestyle, Scott – the 'Laird of Abbotsford' – dabbled in fiction, in an attempt to earn big bucks, and confirm his ascendancy over Byron. It proved an inspired move, as his first novel, *Waverley* – published anonymously in 1814 – was a runaway success (interestingly, the character of Fergus MacIvor is reputedly based on **James Macdonell**, who later found immortal fame in his own right at Waterloo). As a writer, Scott's mind was full of romantic images from Scotland's bloody past. He had always taken a keen interest in warfare and even considered himself something of a military man. And to prove it, Scott formed the Royal Edinburgh Volunteer Light Dragoons – a kind of Home Guard outfit composed of part-timers – in 1797. Despite his lameness, Scott filled the post of quartermaster, but according to biographer A.N. Wilson (1980), the poet was merely playing at soldeirs: 'He never saw action, except to do riot duty. He helped to take a few shots at some rebellious miners at Cross Causeway, and threatened some mill workers with the sabre at Moredun Mill.'

Following news of **Wellington**'s victory at Waterloo, which appeared in the *London Gazette Extraordinary* of 3 July 1815, Scott was inspired by thoughts of seeing a real battlefield and meeting Wellington, the great hero and saviour of Europe. As the Continent had been closed to the British for 10 years, and as Scott had never ventured abroad before, his excitement may be imagined. And so, accompanied by three countrymen, the bard sailed on 28 July. But Scott's Waterloo adventure was not motivated by idle curiosity: on a spiritual level, visiting the scene of his country's ultimate triumph over tyranny would be a sublime experience for the poet; on a lowlier plane, publishers John Murray and Archibald Constable had commissioned an account of the journey. For Scott, then, the road to Belgium was a pilgrimage, an artistic endeavour and a business opportunity.

Scott's party arrived at Waterloo during the first week of August, by which time most of the corpses had been burned or buried. But this did not stop Scott describing heaps of mangled bodies – 'ghastly evidences' – for the benefit of Murray, Constable and their readers. In fact, although Scott was among the first British civilians to visit the battlefield, there was not a great deal to see, the whole area having been stripped by local peasants: only rubbish was left, stuff not worth looting. Nevertheless, Scott selected a soldier's pocket-book for a battlefield souvenir, and bought bullets, buttons and a French cuirass at the tourist market in Waterloo village. Scott's guides were Captain Campbell, General **Adam**'s aide-de-camp, and Major Pryse Gordon. But it was the encounter with local innkeeper **Jean Decoster** – the man Napoleon had pressed into service as his reluctant guide – that excited Scott most. Despite Decoster's dubious narrative of events, Scott soaked up his stories and worked them into his own lively travelogue, destined to be published as *Paul's Letters to His Kinfolk* in 1816.

After his tour of the battlefield and Waterloo village – including the grave of Lord **Uxbridge**'s right leg, buried in the garden of 214 Chaussée de Bruxelles – Scott journeyed to Paris. Here Wellington held court and Scott duly paid homage, entering the social whirl with gusto, having packed his blue and red militia uniform for the occasion. Scott would later claim that of all the men he had met, only Wellington left him awed and abashed. For his part, Wellington thought Scott 'a very agreeable man, full of anecdote'. But according to Stanhope (1888), the Duke qualified this observation by adding that the bard 'was a little too fond of his own preconceived notions'. But then the Duke had little time for writers, once famously remarking that: 'If writers would adhere to the golden Rule for an Historian, *viz*. To write nothing which they did not know to be true, the Duke apprehends they would have nothing but little to tell.' Needless to say, when an excited Scott announced his intention of writing a history of the Battle of Waterloo and asked for Wellington's cooperation, he got short shrift: 'You have my published report,' replied the Duke, 'is not that enough?' But for Scott – and many others – Wellington's Waterloo Dispatch was *not* enough. As Philip Shaw (2002) writes: 'Reactions to the dispatch ranged from bafflement to outright hostility. Wellington had not only neglected to honour the heroes of Waterloo, he had also failed to address the transcendent significance of the event.'

Thrown back on his own resources, Scott resolved to celebrate the victory, fathom its divine message and honour its heroes himself. To achieve this, he would return to his literary roots and the bardic form of epic poetry. As a final flourish, Scott would not only commemorate the fallen, he would also succour their families: for the proceeds of his Waterloo rhapsody would be donated to a subscription fund for soldiers' widows and orphans. Amounting to almost 3,500 words, *The Field of Waterloo* (Turner would exhibit a painting of the same title three years later) was published on 23 October 1815, with an initial print run of 6,000 copies. Beginning with the lines:

> Fair Brussels, thou art far behind,
> Though, lingering on the morning wind,
> We yet may hear the hour
> Pealed over orchard and canal,
> With voice prolonged and measured fall,
> From proud St Michael's tower . . .

Scott proceeded to unravel a tale of cannon-roaring, trumpet-braying, steel-gleaming slaughter on a field 'fetlock-deep in blood'. In other words, as Philip Shaw observes, Scott consigned the great battle 'to the pleasurable charms of verse romance'.

The following extract, describing the onset of the French massed cavalry charges, is typical of the Scott treatment:

> On came the whirlwind – like the last
> But fiercest sweep of tempest-blast
> On came the whirlwind – steel-gleams broke
> Like lightning through the rolling smoke;
> The war was waked anew,
> Three hundred cannon-mouths roared loud,

And from their throats, with flash and cloud,
Their showers of iron threw.
Beneath their fire, in full career,
Rushed on the ponderous cuirassier,
The lancer couched his ruthless spear,
And hurrying as to havoc near,
The cohorts' eagles flew.
In one dark torrent, broad and strong,
The advancing onset rolled along,
Forth harbingered by fierce acclaim,
That, from the shroud of smoke and flame,
Pealed wildly the imperial name.

In his biography of Scott, A.N. Wilson (1980) dismisses *The Field of Waterloo* as the author's 'worst poem' and leaves it at that. Back in 1815 critical response was exceedingly cool, most of the London literati playing dumb – disarmed by the poem's undoubted good cause. For the Great British Public, however, such niceties were of little consequence and Scott received a mauling. Typical was the following sally, from the *Morning Chronicle* of 4 December 1815:

Then comes Waterloo
With a haloa ballou!
Of legions disabled and slain;
But you are not content
With the blood they have spent,
Will mangle them over again.
Ah! Teaze our good folks
No more with this hoax,
which JOHN BULL in a doze could not see
But now wide awake
This tax will not take,
He's determined to live, Sir; SCOTT free.

Or this anonymous jibe:

On Waterloo's ensanguined plain
Full many a gallant man was slain,
But none, by sabre or by shot,
Fell half so flat as Walter Scott.

Unimpressed by Scott's poetic treatment of Waterloo, an increasingly literate population wanted straightforward prose. Indeed, Waterloo's true literary capital was realised not by poets but by publishers like John Booth, who presented readers with reports from participants or 'near observers'. Thus, Waterloo marked not only Napoleon's fall from grace, but also Scott's – as a poet that is. For Scott's public drubbing over *The Field of Waterloo* did not finish his literary career, it marked its true beginning, as Philip Shaw (2002) explains: 'Henceforth, what the public demanded, and what the public would get, would be the serial production of historical novels.' In other words, Scott accepted the fact that Waterloo represented a change in direction: effectively killing his old career as poet and kick-starting a new one as novelist. And a good thing too, for Scott went on to create some of the most enduring classics of English literature: *Rob Roy* (1817), *Ivanhoe* (1819), *Kenilworth* (1821) and *Redgauntlet* (1824). And in their day, Scott's novels sold: turning the erstwhile poet into an international celebrity and, as Philip Shaw states, launching 'a literary career that would revolutionise the publishing industry'.

Meanwhile, Scott remained fascinated by Waterloo and its heroes: he was a major supporter and champion of the Waterloo Subscription; he was instrumental in bringing home the remains of Corporal **John Shaw** – the celebrated boxer who died from wounds following the charge of the Household Brigade – for a hero's burial; and he lionised Sergeant **Charles Ewart** – the man who took the Eagle of **Napoleon**'s 45th Regiment during the charge of the Union Brigade, organising a lecture tour for the bashful paladin. And despite Wellington's refusal to cooperate on a definitive history of the Battle of Waterloo, Scott always considered him 'a most wonderful man'.

Seymour
Captain Horace Beauchamp (?–1851)

Officer of the 18th Hussars who served as aide-de-camp to Lord **Uxbridge** at Waterloo. According to historian Charles Dalton (1904),

Seymour was 'the strongest man in the British Army, who is said to have slain more men at Waterloo than any other single individual'. Dalton goes on to state that Seymour 'was taken prisoner on 18 June, but rescued by some of our cavalry, sent by **Wellington** himself for the purpose'. In fact, Seymour performed several notable acts at Waterloo: rallying the Highlanders of **Picton**'s division during **d'Erlon**'s assault of the early afternoon; sending Corporal **Brewer** of the Waggon Train to Hougoumont with ammunition for the garrison in the mid-afternoon; and escorting the wounded Uxbridge to the rear in the evening.

But Seymour's most celebrated act occurred around 5 p.m., when Uxbridge noted one of his cavalry regiments quitting the field without orders. The regiment in question was the Duke of Cumberland's Hussars, a Hanoverian unit composed of some 500 gentleman-volunteers. Despite being 'owned' by Ernst Augustus, Duke of Cumberland and King of Hanover, the regiment was commanded by a certain Lieutenant Colonel Hake (or 'Hacke'), who may have been English – accounts vary. Kept in reserve for most of the battle, as soon as French shot and shell fell among them, these gentlemen became unsettled, and after sustaining some 60 casualties from the enemy's cannonade, they quit – presumably feeling they had done enough to satisfy honour. But Uxbridge was appalled and sent Seymour after Hake. Seymour describes the sequel in a letter dated 21 November 1842, quoted by Siborne (1891):

> Lord Anglesey [i.e. Uxbridge], seeing that regiment moving to
> the rear (about five o'clock), desired me immediately to halt it.
> On delivering the order to the Colonel, he told me that he had no
> confidence in his men, that they were volunteers, and the horses
> their own property. All this time the regiment continued moving to
> the rear, in spite of my repeating the order to halt, and asking the
> second in command to save the character of the regiment by taking
> command and fronting them. I was unsuccessful, and in the exigence
> of the moment I laid hold of the bridle of the Colonel's horse, and
> remarked what I thought of his conduct; but all to no purpose.
>
> I then returned to Lord Anglesey, and reported what had passed.
> I was again ordered to deliver the message to the commanding
> officer of the regiment, that if they would not resume their position
> in the Line, that he was to form them across the high road out of fire.

They did not even obey this order, but went, as was reported, altogether to the rear.

In fact, some of the hussars joined other units and fought on, but the remaining fugitives rode back to Brussels, spreading panic and alarm with tales of an Allied defeat. Hake was court-martialled in August 1815 and dismissed.

Shaw
Corporal John (1789–1815)

Soldier of the 2nd Life Guards, killed at Waterloo. John or 'Jack' Shaw was the son of a Nottinghamshire farmer. Born near the village of Cossall and educated at Trowell Moor School, Shaw grew into a tall, large-limbed, muscular youth. First apprenticed to a wheel-wright, Shaw went to work as a carpenter at Wollaton Hall, home of Lord Middleton. He volunteered for the 2nd Life Guards 16 October 1807, aged 18 (some sources have him enlisting at the Nottingham Goose Fair, others in London).

Shaw took to army life. Already something of a giant at 6 foot – the average height for a man being 5 feet 7 inches in those days – Shaw was put through a punishing programme of weight training and sword exercises, turning him into a killing machine. The army also encouraged Shaw in his passion for boxing, which was something of a mania in Regency England. According to historian Beresford E. Chancellor (1926):

> During the first half of the nineteenth century pugilism was rampant in this country. It was the favourite amusement among all classes in practically every county, each of which possessed its particular prize-fighters patronised by the gentry and regarded with a sort of wondering admiration by the lower classes . . . The fact is that the sport had taken so great a hold on the people that in spite of laws and regulations, little interference was made with prize-fights, and although these often took place in localities and at times, ostensibly selected in order to evade notice, the crowd duly assembled with impunity to witness the combats.

Shaw had demonstrated his prowess in the ring before enlisting. Once in the army – where he quickly gained an extra half inch in height – Shaw was identified as a potential champion. Major Knollys (1880), Shaw's biographer, takes up the story:

> Shaw, on joining the Life Guards, found himself quite in his element, for pugilism was much cultivated by the Household Cavalry, and very few months had elapsed before he was recognised by his comrades as a bruiser of the first water. His prowess soon stood him in good stead. At the beginning of the century, as now, the soldier was exposed to the vulgar insolence of the lower classes, and was often saluted with cries of 'lobster', 'a shilling a day to be shot at', and similar silly chaff. Occasionally, the would-be wits got a severe lesson for their impertinence, and seldom was it more severe than the one administered by Shaw, under the following circumstances. He was quartered in Portman Street barracks when three strongly-built roughs assailed him with various uncomplimentary epithets. His blood was up in an instant, and before they could guess his purpose, the three jokers were sprawling in the gutter. Seeing themselves, however, three to one, they, on recovering their legs, set upon the young Life Guardsman. But they had caught a Tartar, and in less than five minutes Shaw had given them such a drubbing, that they were obliged to take refuge in flight.

Shaw's exploit became widely known and Colonel Barton – a celebrated boxing impresario – took the young man under his wing, introducing him to the Fives' Court, London's most famous 'temple' to the art of pugilism. Standing over 6 feet tall, weighing some 15 stone, and with arms strong as steel, Shaw was put through his paces by Barton, who pitted him against the best boxers of the day.

Steadily, his speed and technique improved, and Shaw the novice became Shaw the prizefighter. Major Knollys continues:

> The public began now to take him up, and he justified their favour by defeating the celebrated Molineaux in a contest with the gloves . . . He came off conqueror in a fight with the gloves with Captain Barclay, the well-known amateur pedestrian and boxer; but Barclay was avenged a few days after by Tom Belcher, brother of Jem

Belcher, whose advice had stood Shaw in such good stead on the occasion of his first fight. The encounter was with gloves, and Shaw, notwithstanding his strength, reach, pluck and skill, was soon disposed of by the veteran pugilist.

Undaunted by this defeat, Shaw later climbed back into the ring, disposing of a West Countryman by the name of Burrows in a mere 17 minutes. It was a bare-knuckle fight and Shaw gave Burrows such a drubbing that the latter could not find his way out of the ring, and had to be led off by his seconds.

With this fight, Shaw established himself as a contender for the crown of the mighty Tom Cribb, bare-knuckle champion of England. But on 18 April 1815 Shaw entered the ring for the last time, in a match against Ned Painter, a recently released convict. The event took place on Hounslow Heath, a vast crowd gathering to witness the contest and place bets on the outcome. Knollys continues:

Shaw and Ned Painter . . . peeled and stepped into the ring. In appearance Painter was very inferior to his antagonist, for though he weighed thirteen stone, he was only 5 feet 9¾ inches in height. Moreover, he had but that morning come out of the Fleet Prison, and could not, therefore, have been in good training . . . According to contemporary accounts, Painter set to work with great gaiety, at first seemed to hold his own very fairly, and gave and received terrific hits. Shaw's reach and weight, however, soon began to tell; and we are told that it was piteous to witness the punishment which Painter received, and the gameness with which he bore it astonished all beholders. Shaw soon seemed to do what he liked with his opponent, and gave him ten knock-down blows in succession. Painter was urged to give in, as he had not the faintest chance of victory; but he still struggled pluckily on till, at the end of a sharp twenty-eight minutes, he was quite unable to come to time.

Shaw's title match with Cribb seemed closer than ever, but events in a larger ring interposed. **Napoleon** had escaped from Elba and **Wellington** had gone to Brussels to prepare an invasion of France. Twelve days after defeating Painter on Hounslow Heath, Shaw and the Life Guards quit London for Belgium. Two squadrons from the

1st and 2nd Life Guards joined Wellington's army in Belgium in May 1815, forming part of the Household Brigade under Major General Lord **Edward Somerset**. Corporal Shaw, the celebrated pugilist and 'fancy man', was probably the most famous character in the British Army after Wellington himself.

In the early afternoon of Waterloo Day, Shaw's regiment took part in Somerset's charge against **d'Erlon**'s corps, clashing with steel-clad cuirassiers west of the La Haie Sainte farm complex. Shaw killed nine Frenchmen in single combat, during a spree that some claimed was fuelled by alcohol. According to Sergeant **Thomas Morris** of the 73rd Foot, Shaw was drunk at the time of the charge, and 'running a-muck at the enemy, was cut down by them as a madman'. Drunk or not, Shaw galloped to the aid of Captain **Edward Kelly**, cutting at the cuirassiers till the sword broke in his hand. Beset by numerous attackers, Shaw was reduced to fending them off with his helmet. Eventually the prizefighter was unhorsed and fatally wounded (run through by a colonel of cuirassiers according to **Rees Howell Gronow**, hit by a bullet from a carbine according to **Edward Cotton**). Shaw managed to crawl to the farmhouse, where, propped up against the wall, he died from loss of blood.

Corporal John Shaw of the Life Guards *by George Jones*

Next day, Shaw was buried near La Haie Sainte, Edward Cotton, later proprietor of the Waterloo Museum, being among the burial party. But Shaw's body was later exhumed and returned to Britain at the instigation of Sir **Walter Scott**, who had met the boxer at the studio of artist Benjamin Haydon, where Shaw posed as a model. A memorial to Shaw and other Waterloo heroes was erected in the parish churchyard at Cossall in 1877.

Simmons
Lieutenant George (1785–1858)

Veteran of **Wellington**'s army, who compiled a celebrated memoir from private letters and journals. A comrade of **John Kincaid**, **Jonathan Leach** and 'Harry' **Smith**, Simmons served in the 1st Battalion 95th Regiment at Waterloo, a lieutenant in Captain Charles Beckwith's company. Simmons started the day felling trees to form an abbattis across the Brussels high road south of La Haie Sainte. In the late afternoon he was wounded skirmishing near the farmhouse. Hit by a voltigeur's bullet, which lodged in his body after smashing two ribs, Simmons describes how: 'Most of the men with me were killed, so it was some time before any officer noticed me, and not until I had been trampled over many times.' Eventually, Simmons was carried to a house in the rear, where the bullet was extracted – without the aid of anaesthetic, which was then unknown – and his wound dressed.

Several days later, Simmons wrote to his parents:

> I now began to feel my miseries. Sergeant Fairfoot was also here wounded in the arm. He got me everything he could, and said he would go and knock some French prisoner off his horse for me in order to get me off. The balls were riddling the house we were in. He got me a horse. They tried to lift me upon it, but I fainted; some other officer took it. In consequence of a movement the French made with all their forces, our people were obliged to retire. If I stayed I must be a prisoner, and being a prisoner was the same as being lost. Poor Fairfoot was in great agitation. He came with

another horse. I remember some Lifeguardsman helped me on. Of what I suffered! I had to ride twelve miles. I forgot to tell you the ball went through my ribs, and also through my body. The motion of the horse made the blood pump out, and the bones cut the flesh to a jelly. I made my way to the house I had been billeted on – very respectable people. I arrived about 10 o'clock on that doleful night. The whole family came out to receive me. The good man and his wife were extremely grieved. I had everything possible got for me, a surgeon sent for, a quart of blood taken from me, wrapped up in poultices, and a most excellent nurse. In four days I had six quarts of blood taken from me, the inflammation ran so high in my lungs. At present everything is going on well. I am so weak, if I lift my head from the pillow I faint. I have sent you a five-pound note. This business has bothered me, but I shall get a year's pay, and most likely a pension, which will enable me to make you comfortable. My love to you all.

When Simmons retired from the army (with the rank of major) he used his journals and letters as the basis of a war memoir. Sadly, however, Simmons died before finishing his task. The manuscript was eventually completed by Lieutenant Colonel Willoughby Verner and published in 1899 as *A British Rifleman: The Journals of Major George Simmons*.

Smith
Captain Sir Henry George Wakelyn (1787–1860)

Staff officer and author of the celebrated *Autobiography of Sir Harry Smith* (first published in 1901). Born at Whittlesea, Cambridgeshire, 'Harry' Smith was the son of a local surgeon. He was commissioned in the 95th (Rifle) Regiment in 1805, later serving in the Peninsular War alongside fellow memoirists **John Kincaid** and **George Simmons**. It was there that he famously met and fell in love with Juana Maria de los Dolores de Léon, who, in the disgraceful orgy of pillage following **Wellington**'s successful storming of Badajoz, approached Smith seeking protection. Smith married his Spanish beauty in short order, and the two were rarely separated, even on campaign.

At Waterloo, Smith was in constant danger. He served as a brigade major (the principal staff officer attached to a brigade) in Sir John Lambert's 6th British Infantry Division: a post that involved galloping around the battlefield with messages, orders and reports. Amid the carnage, Smith protected himself with a personal mantra:

> I repeated to myself a verse from the Psalms of that day – 91st Psalm, 7th verse: 'A thousand shall fall beside thee, and ten thousand at thy right hand, but it shall not come nigh thee.'

It worked: Smith emerging from the fight unscathed – which is more than can be said for many of his comrades on the staff, or indeed their horses:

> Every staff officer had two or three (and one four) horses shot under him. I had one wounded in six, another in seven places, but not seriously injured. The fire was terrific, especially of cannon.

The arrival of night and the Prussians put an end to the Battle of Waterloo and Smith, like many others, was deeply moved by the final tableau:

> The whole field from right to left was a mass of dead bodies. In one spot, to the right of La Haye Sainte, the French cuirassiers were literally piled on each other; many soldiers not wounded lying under their horses; others, fearfully wounded, occasionally with their horses struggling upon their wounded bodies. The sight was sickening, and I had no means or power to assist them.

Smith was promoted to lieutenant colonel after the battle, and later found fame as Governor of Cape Colony, South Africa (1847–52). The town of Ladysmith was named in his wife's honour.

Smith
Admiral Sir William Sidney (1764–1840)

One of the Royal Navy's bravest and, at the same time, vainest commanders. According to author David Miller (2005), Smith was 'a man of great zeal and undoubted courage, but with a fatal penchant for pomposity, self-aggrandizement and endless story-telling'. Having retired from active service in 1814, Smith followed **Wellington**'s troops to Belgium, attaching himself to the English colony there, and making unauthorised visits to army camps. On 18 June 1815 he rode from Brussels to Waterloo, finding Wellington on the ridge of Mont St Jean late in the day: 'though I was not allowed to have any of the fun, I had the heartfelt gratification of being the first Englishman that was not in the battle who shook hands with him'. But Wellington was unimpressed, later declaring: 'of all the men I ever knew who have any reputation, the man who least deserves it is Sir Sidney Smith . . . I cannot believe that a man so silly in all other affairs can be a good naval officer.'

Somerset
Major General Lord (Robert) Edward Henry (1776–1842)

Commander of **Wellington**'s 1st British (Household) Cavalry Brigade at Waterloo. Fourth son of the fifth Duke of Beaufort (and elder brother of **Fitzroy Somerset**, Wellington's military secretary), Somerset joined the army in 1793 as a cornet in the 10th Light Dragoons. A wealthy background inevitably led to speedy promotion, thanks to the purchase system prevalent in the British Army at the time. Thus, by 1799, Somerset was a major and aide-de-camp to the Duke of York. Two years later he was a lieutenant colonel, having switched to the 4th Dragoons via the 12th Light Dragoons. And by 1810 Somerset was a full colonel and aide-de-camp to the King. But Somerset was not simply a blue-blooded brass hat: he was a natural leader, distinguishing himself during the Peninsular War – notably at the Battles of Salamanca

(1812), Vitoria (1813), Orthez and Toulouse (both 1814). Thus, by 1815, Somerset had received the Peninsular Gold Cross, the thanks of Parliament for his part in the Spanish victory, and a knighthood.

A distinguished soldier favoured by Wellington, he was the obvious choice to lead the Duke's 1st British (Household) Cavalry Brigade during the Waterloo campaign. The Household Brigade was composed of the 1st and 2nd Life Guards, the Royal Horse Guards (Blues), and the 1st or King's Dragoon Guards. At Waterloo the brigade numbered perhaps 1,300 sabres, and was initially held in reserve, on the right of the Brussels high road, a few hundred yards in front of the farm of Mont St Jean. To Somerset's left, on the other side of the paved high road, was Sir **William Ponsonby**'s 2nd British (Union) Cavalry Brigade.

At about 1.30 p.m. **d'Erlon** launched his attack on Wellington's right-centre. Lord **Uxbridge** – Wellington's cavalry supremo – ordered Ponsonby and Somerset to advance, finally unleashing them against the French about 30 minutes later: the former against several infantry columns, the latter against **Dubois**'s cuirassiers (part of **Milhaud**'s IV Cavalry Corps). According to Somerset's account, quoted by H.T. Siborne (1891):

> the 1st Cavalry Brigade . . . advanced in line (the Blues supporting) to the attack of the enemy's cavalry, which was met on the ridge of the hill, and was completely defeated and driven back with considerable loss. In the first instance, the 1st Life Guards had a severe conflict with the enemy near La Haye Sainte, where they did great execution, and succeeded in forcing them back to the opposite height, pursuing them to the foot of the French position.

General Sir Evelyn Wood's version (1895) of this action is a touch more enthusiastic:

> The 1st Life Guards and the French cuirassiers collided, as an eye-witness declares, 'like two walls' but the result was never for a moment doubtful. The cuirassiers had already been engaged, and although they had achieved a brilliant success in cutting up the Lüneburg Battalion, were naturally not as steady as before that combat. The British troopers were far better trained, were mounted

on much bigger horses, and with all the advantage of the descending slope, had passed over just enough distance to obtain momentum without their horses being exhausted. After the collision the cuirassiers turned, and many tried to escape by galloping down the Genappe–Brussels road. The 2nd Life Guards and the left squadron King's Dragoon Guards now struck into Dubois' right Regiment. As it advanced, it crossed the Genappe–Brussels road at the cutting, from which the squadrons were emerging in some confusion as our men galloped at them. Organised resistance was hopeless under these circumstances, and the cuirassiers fled, while the 2nd Life Guards, bringing up their right shoulders, crossed the road, and eventually became mingled with the Union brigade.

But once Somerset's victorious dragoons became mingled with Ponsonby's battle-mad troopers all cohesion was lost, and a headlong dash for **Napoleon**'s grand battery ensued. Attacked in turn by d'Erlon's 1st Cavalry Division under **Jacquinot**, the British horsemen were hunted down by lancers and obliged to make their way back to the Allied lines as best they could. Somerset's brigade sustained severe casualties – perhaps some 50 per cent – among them Lieutenant Colonel **Samuel Ferrior**, commander of the 1st Life Guards, and celebrity boxer **John Shaw** of the 2nd Life Guards.

Somerset survived the charge unscathed – but only just. According to **Gronow** (1900) of the 1st Foot Guards, Somerset 'had a very narrow escape. His horse was killed, and he had only just time to creep through a thick hedge and leap on another horse before the enemy were upon him.' Historian Charles Dalton (1904) puts a little flesh on the bones of Gronow's story:

> In the first cavalry charge at Waterloo, Lord Edward Somerset lost his cocked hat, and went to the charge bare-headed. On his return, whilst looking for his hat, a cannon-ball took off the flap of his coat and killed his horse. He donned a Life Guard's helmet and wore it during the battle.

As for the casualties among the Household Brigade's horses, those which survived the battle were returned to England and sold by auction. The sale was apparently attended by Sir Astley Paston

Cooper, the great surgeon, who purchased 12 badly injured beasts. In his *Life of Sir Astley Cooper* (1843), Bransby B. Cooper relates how:

> Having had them conveyed, under care of six grooms, to his park in the country, the great surgeon followed, and, with the assistance of his servants, commenced extracting bullets and grape-shot from the bodies and limbs of the suffering animals. In a very short time after the operations had been performed, Sir Astley let them loose in the park; and one morning, to his great delight, he saw the noble animals form in line, charge and then retreat and afterwards gallop about, appearing greatly contented with the lot which had befallen them. These manoeuvres were repeated generally every morning to his great satisfaction and amusement.

Soult
Marshal ('Nicolas') Jean-de-Dieu
(1769–1851)

Marshal Soult (1769–1851)

Chief of Staff to **Napoleon**'s Army of the North. The son of a notary, Jean-de-Dieu Soult (although he became known as 'Nicolas' it was not his official name) joined the French Army in 1785. Thanks to the Revolution of 1789 Soult rapidly advanced through the ranks, becoming a general of division by 1799. Serving in the Revolutionary Wars in Germany, Switzerland and Italy, Napoleon made him a Marshal of the Empire in 1804. A veteran of classic Napoleonic battles like Austerlitz, Jena and Friedland, Soult – like **Ney** – became a star of the Grand Army and a noted corps commander. But then he was sent to Spain – the graveyard of French reputations. First, Soult was beaten by British tragic hero Moore at Corunna (1809); then he was beaten by Beresford (another Brit) at Albuera (1811); and finally he was beaten (repeatedly) by **Wellington**. And yet it is generally accepted that Soult performed well in the latter phase of the Peninsular War, which saw Wellington's redcoats battling across the Pyrenees into southern France. That said, Wellington made the following unflattering assessment of Soult's abilities, quoted by Stanhope (1888).

> Soult was not the ablest general ever opposed to me; the ablest after Napoleon was, I think Masséna. Soult did not quite understand a field of battle; he was an excellent tactician – knew very well how to bring his troops to the field, but not so well how to use them, when he had brought them up.

Finally, Soult's reputation has been tarnished by his liking for plunder: war being something of a pretext for enhancing his collection of fine art.

Following Napoleon's first overthrow in 1814, Soult became Minister of War under the incoming Bourbon regime. But when the Emperor returned the following spring, Soult rallied to the tricolour. Napoleon apparently thought Soult 'the ablest tactician in the Empire' – but instead of giving him an army to command, the Emperor gave him a desk. For in May 1815 – just weeks away from the planned foray into Belgium – Napoleon made Soult chief of staff to the Army of the North. According to historian Tony Linck (1993), many myths have since appeared regarding his suitability for, and his performance in, this post. Frequently compared unfavourably with Marshal Berthier, the Emperor's chief of staff of the glory years, Soult generally gets a bad press in histories of the campaign. For example, he is often criticised for not ensuring Napoleon's orders were dispatched in triplicate – or at least in duplicate – but as Linck points out, this was standard practice and Soult's subordinates – in particular his deputy, General **Bailly de Monthion** – might just as easily take the blame. Soult has also been censured for **d'Erlon**'s wanderings on 16 June, when I Corps spent the day marching and counter-marching between the Battles of Quatre-Bras and Ligny, fighting at neither. The truth behind this fiasco is obscured by a blizzard of contradictory accounts, frequently partisan in nature (for a persuasively lucid account see Linck 1993, p. 300). But suffice to say that

Napoleon, Ney, d'Erlon and **Labédoyère** have all been accused of orchestrating the blunder.

Was Soult made a convenient scapegoat for the failings of others? Perhaps. For having seconded Berthier in 1813 it is unfair to say he had no experience of staffwork. And Napoleon, for his part, thought Soult 'excellent' as a chief of staff. But it is true to say that Soult was no Berthier. While the latter made an ideal military secretary – all Napoleon really wanted from a chief of staff – Soult was a battlefield commander of skill and experience. He was also familiar with the Belgian countryside, which Napoleon was not. But the Emperor chose not to exploit Soult's gifts: thus, in a sense, his performance at Waterloo was as good as Napoleon allowed it to be.

Soult stuck close to Napoleon at Waterloo. And when defeat could no longer be ignored, Soult, Kipling-like, kept his head when all around were losing theirs. And so, while French brass hats like Ney and Labédoyère dashed about trying to get killed, Soult took the bridle of Napoleon's horse and led the Emperor from the field. Later, when the Emperor quit the army for Paris, Soult took charge, imposed order, and conducted something resembling a methodical retreat. If nothing else, Soult deserves some credit for steadying the wreck of the French Army and steering it back to its home port.

On 24 June, however, Soult received news of Napoleon's second and final abdication, prompting him to resign on the spot and hand over to Marshal **Grouchy**: an action that historian Linck describes as 'shameful'. And he has a point. For no sooner had Soult quit when he popped up in Paris, loudly declaring his support for Bourbon rule. Fearing Royalist retribution, however, Soult decamped to Düsseldorf and attempted to write his memoirs – a task he quickly abandoned. Soult returned to France in 1819 but kept a low profile for the next ten years. But with the advent of a new regime, following the July Revolution of 1830, Soult experienced a renaissance: rising, phoenix-like, to become Minister of War, ambassador to London and eventually Marshal General of France.

Styles
Corporal Francis (?–1928)

Referred to as 'Stiles' in many accounts, this soldier of the 1st (Royal) Dragoons was involved in the capture of a French Eagle at Waterloo. Two of these regimental standards were taken by British troops during the battle: the first, that of the 45th Regiment, was won by Sergeant **Ewart** of the Scots Greys; the second, that of the 105th Regiment, was reputedly taken by Captain **Alexander Kennedy Clark** of the 1st Dragoons, with the help of Corporal Styles.

French Eagles (designed by the sculptor Chaudet in 1804 and based on the imperial eagle of Ancient Rome) weighed about 4 pounds and were fixed to flagpoles some 6 feet in length. Dubbed 'cuckoos' by French troops, they were supposed to embody a regiment's spirit – much like traditional battalion colours. As such they were highly prized and their loss was considered a catastrophe. Ewart bagged his Eagle after a bloody contest with the 45th's standard bearer. Once the Eagle was in his possession, Ewart was ordered back to Brussels with his trophy. But Clark's capture of the 105th's Eagle seems less straightforward. This is due to the fact that written accounts by the two men concerned – Clark and Styles – do not add up. That said, it is Clark's version (recorded in a letter to William Siborne and paraphrased in his history (1848) of the campaign) that has been accepted as fact. And according to Clark, Styles was a mere bit player in the drama.

Clark's story goes like this. When, at around 2 p.m., the 2nd British (Union) Cavalry Brigade was deployed against **d'Erlon**'s infantry columns, the 1st (Royal) Dragoons came in contact with the 105th Regiment. Captain Clark, commanding the centre squadron of the 'Royals', spotted the regiment's Eagle and made a dash for it, crying, 'Right shoulders forward – attack the Colour!' By his own account (Clark 1975), Clark ran the standard bearer through and the Eagle fell awkwardly across his horse's neck. William Siborne continues:

> He [Clark] endeavoured to catch it with his left hand, but could only touch the fringe of the colour, and it would probably have

fallen to the ground and have been lost in the confusion of the moment, had it not been saved by Corporal Stiles, who, having been standard-coverer, and therefore posted immediately in rear of the squadron-leader, came up at the instant, on Captain Clark's left, and caught the colour as it struck, in falling, against his own horse's neck.

According to Siborne, Styles handed the trophy to Clark, who tried to separate the Eagle from its pole: 'Pray, sir, do not break it', Styles is supposed to have said, Clark replying, 'Very well, carry it to the rear as fast as you can – it belongs to me.' And so it was Styles who bore the Eagle out of the melee. And it was Styles who, having handed the trophy to an officer in the rear, was initially credited with its capture. Clark remained in action until 6.15 p.m. when he quit the field, having been twice wounded and had two horses killed under him. Lying in his sickbed, Clark recalled the Eagle and claimed its capture, maintaining that he had given it to Styles for safe keeping.

At some point Sir Arthur Clifton, commanding officer of the 1st Dragoons, must have demanded clarification on the matter, for Dalton (1904) quotes the following letter by Styles to a certain Lieutenant George Gunning, dated 31 January 1816:

> This day Colonel Clifton sent for me about the taking of the Eagle and colours. He asked me if I had any person that see [*sic*] me take the Eagle; I told him that you see me, I believe, as the officer of the French was making away with it. I belonged to your troop at that time, and you gave me orders to charge him, which I did, and took it from him. When I stated it to him [Colonel Clifton] this day he wants to know the particulars about it, and me to rite [*sic*] to you for you to state to him how it was. I would thank you to rite to the Colonel, as you was the nearest officer to me that day. Sir, by doing so you will much oblige.

Styles's letter is interesting because it strongly implies that it was he, not Clark, who took the Eagle of the 105th, on Gunning's orders. In fact, Clark is not mentioned at all in Styles's missive, which describes Gunning as 'the nearest officer to me that day'. Sadly, Dalton does not say if Gunning ever replied to Styles. Dalton does, however, emphatically state that Clark took the Eagle and handed it over to Styles. And so the facts remain unclear.

Interestingly, Styles – who had been promoted to sergeant after the battle – was promoted again following his interview with Clifton, receiving an ensigncy (the lowest commission for an infantry officer) in the 6th West India Regiment. He was placed on half-pay on 28 December 1817 and died in London on 9 January 1828. Clark was knighted in the wake of Waterloo and eventually became a general and aide-de-camp to Queen Victoria. The Eagle of the 105th, meanwhile, rests in the National Army Museum, London.

Thielemann
General Johann Adolf, Baron von (1765–1824)

Commander of the Prussian III Corps during the Waterloo campaign. Saxon by birth, Thielemann (sometimes the name is spelt Thielmann in the literature) was one of those men – like **Alava** and **Chassé** – who fought against **Napoleon** in 1815, having fought for him in previous years. Indeed, Thielemann had served with the Emperor's Grand Army as recently as 1812, distinguishing himself at the Battle of Borodino. Commanding the 1st Brigade of the 7th Cuirassier Division, part of IV Cavalry Corps, Thielemann led his Poles and Saxons in a celebrated charge against the Raevsky Redoubt. The capture of this formidable Russian battery was a brilliant feat, but Thielemann was robbed of the credit, as Napoleon always maintained the bastion had been taken by French troops. The kingdom of Saxony was allied to Napoleon from 1807 to 1814, but Thielemann defected to the Allies on 12 May 1813. At first he commanded a force of Cossacks, defeating Napoleon's cavalry supremo, **Lefebvre-Desnouëttes** at Altenburg on 28 September 1813. At the beginning of 1815, however, Thielemann entered the Prussian service with the rank of *Generalleutnant*.

In the Waterloo campaign Thielemann commanded the III Corps of **Blücher**'s Army of the Lower Rhine. After the Prussian defeat at Ligny on 16 June (during which Thielemann's corps was badly mauled), Blücher and **Gneisenau** regrouped at Wavre, several miles east of Waterloo, and from there marched to **Wellington**'s aid on 18 June. But with **Grouchy**'s 30,000 Frenchmen on Blücher's tail, Thielemann's corps was left at Wavre as a rearguard. Guarding the banks of the River Dyle, Thielemann's troops spent a tranquil day, until about 2 p.m., when the approach of **Vandamme**'s advance guard heralded the Battle of Wavre, destined to rage for the next two days. Thielemann had already sent six of his battalions to join Blücher's march on Waterloo when the action began, leaving him with about 15,000 men to hold off Grouchy. According to historian E.F. Henderson (1911):

> Twice that day . . . General Thielemann was to send word to Blücher that he could not hold his own against such frightful odds; but Blücher's answers were worthy of a Spartan commander. Thielemann must manage as best he could; he must hold fast Grouchy as long as possible and then, if need be, retire; but no troops could be spared from the battle with Napoleon.

And so, outnumbered two to one, Thielemann clung on for the rest of the day, embarrassing French attempts to force a passage of the Dyle over two stone bridges at Bierge and Limale. But the dawn of 19 June saw further French attacks by troops of Vandamme's and **Gérard**'s corps. Finally, Thielemann gave way, pulling his troops back to allow Grouchy 30 minutes of glory: for by mid-morning news of Napoleon's defeat at Waterloo transformed the strategic situation, Grouchy having little option but to retreat.

Thielemann's achievement at Wavre was considerable: for 20 hours he held an army twice the size of his own at bay, covering Blücher's march to Wellington's aid at Waterloo.

Thornton

James (1787–1854)

Wellington's personal cook at Waterloo. The sixth of seven children, Thornton was apprenticed to a London chef at the age of 13, no doubt with high hopes of making a good living: the highest-paid male cooks at that time commanding salaries up to £500, or approximately £25,000 in modern terms. Having qualified, Thornton was offered a position on the staff of the Duke of Wellington, and in 1811 quit London for Lisbon. Arriving at the Duke's headquarters, Thornton – who had been trained by French émigrés in London – found little to challenge him. Wellington dined simply, even frugally, frequently making do with boiled eggs stuffed in his pockets. Nevertheless, Thornton organised dinners for the Duke and his headquarters staff, procuring local supplies out of his own purse. In 1814, following victory in the Peninsula, Thornton returned home. But 12 months later, when Napoleon escaped from Elba and Wellington was sent to Brussels to organise an Anglo-Netherlands army, Thornton was again engaged. The cook remained in the Duke's employ until 1820, when he apparently walked out of Wellington's residence at Apsley House, following a dispute with the Duchess over the kitchen budget.

But what of Thornton's Waterloo experiences? At daybreak on 18 June 1815 Thornton rode to Waterloo market to purchase ingredients for the Duke's 'hot dinner', returning later to his master's headquarters at the inn of Jean de Nivelles. According to Louis Cohen (1925):

> Most interesting was the house where the Duke of Wellington took up his quarters before the battle commenced, and that interest was created not so much by the great commander as the commander's cook. During the battle, as from hour to hour thousands on thousands of fugitives poured along towards Brussels, or at least towards the Forest of Soigne [*sic*], crying that all was lost – the English beaten – the French victorious, and coming – the incredulous cook continued unmoved his preparations for his master's dinner. 'Fly!' cried one after another, 'the French are coming, and you will be killed!' But the imperturbable cook, strong

in his faith of invariable victory, only replied, 'No, I have served my master while he has fought a hundred battles, and he never yet failed to come to his dinner.' So he cooked on, in spite of flying thousands of 'brave Dutch' and Hanoverians; and the Duke came, though rather late!

This story seems to have originated after the Duke's death in 1852, when a French chef began claiming he had cooked for Wellington at Waterloo, remaining at his post while all around fled. Thornton was mortified and responded with a letter to *The Times*:

> Having seen in your widely circulated paper that the late and ever-to-be-honoured Duke of Wellington had a French cook at Waterloo who is reported to have said, 'He knew that the Duke would return to his dinner'. I beg most respectfully to inform you that I cooked his dinner on the day.

Not that Wellington was particularly hungry or convivial after 12 hours of carnage. Nevertheless, according to Thornton: 'his Grace rode up after the battle, and on getting off his horse Copenhagen he saw me and said, "Is that you? Get dinner."' Christopher Hibbert (1997) describes how: 'The dinner table was laid in the Duke's bedroom upstairs. Various members of the staff who had not been wounded were there; so were **Alava** and **Müffling**; and so were Lord Apsley and Sir Sidney Smith.' But even so, many places were empty at Wellington's table, and Hibbert goes on to say that: 'the Duke looked up quickly every time the door opened, hoping to see a familiar face; but no other officer appeared'.

'T.S.'
(1790–?)

Anonymous author of a celebrated journal describing experiences as a foot soldier during the Peninsular War and at Waterloo. According to Sir Charles Oman (1913), this volume – entitled *Journal of T.S. of the 71st Highland Light Infantry, in Memorials of the Late Wars* (1828) –

stands out from all the rest for its literary merit – it is the work of a man of superior education, who had enlisted in a moment of pique and humiliation to avoid facing at home the consequences of his own conceit and folly.

But the identity of the author has always remained a mystery. The only clues in the *Journal* are the initials T.S. (the T apparently standing for Thomas) and the writer's rank: private. Interestingly, despite the initials T.S., some have speculated the author was a certain Thomas Howells, but on checking the Waterloo muster roll for the 71st, no man of that name could be found. That said, a Private Thomas Howie is listed in Captain D. Campbell's company. Meanwhile, the battalion muster roll throws up several private soldiers named Thomas with a surname that begins with S: Thomas Syme, Thomas Smith, Thomas Seagrove, Thomas Stevenson, Thomas Scott and Thomas Springate.

Born in Edinburgh in 1790, 'T.S.' came from an impoverished background, his parents apparently subsisting on 11 shillings a week (about £27.50 in modern reckoning). Nevertheless, they invested in their son's education, hoping he would become 'a man of letters'. But Thomas broke his mother's heart by running away to join a troupe of actors. Failing his audition on account of stage fright, Thomas could not bring himself to return home in humiliation:

> I wandered the whole night. In the morning early, meeting a party of recruits about to embark, I rashly offered to go with them. My offer was accepted and I embarked at Leith with seventeen others, for the Isle of Wight in July 1806.

Thomas received a bounty of 11 guineas – almost half his parents' yearly income. Keeping £4 for himself, he sent the remainder to his grieving kinfolk. But Thomas soon 'began to drink the cup of bitterness', as he had not bargained for the brutal life of a soldier. His comrades, bemused by his refusal to drink alcohol, gamble or swear, nicknamed him 'Saucy Tom' and 'The Distressed Methodist'. Having entered the ranks of the 71st Regiment, campaigns in South America, Spain and Holland followed. In January 1815 the 71st was earmarked for service in America, but bad weather kept the troops at home. Consequently, when **Napoleon** escaped from Elba on

26 February, the regiment's 1st Battalion – with 'T.S.' among its number – was ordered to Belgium.

At Waterloo, the battalion was commanded by Colonel Thomas Reynell. Forming part of **Adam**'s 3rd British Brigade, it numbered over 900 men. According to Reynell, writing in 1834 and quoted by William Siborne (1848), the 71st bivouacked in a field on the far right of **Wellington**'s line the night before battle. On the morning of 18 June, the battalion:

> lay upon their arms in the rear of a rising ground, upon which, soon after, a Brigade of British Foot Artillery was posted, which, attracting the Enemy's attention, brought down a heavy fire of shot and shell, very destructive in its consequences.

The battalion later advanced to a position in rear of Hougoumont, where it formed square.

A little after 8 p.m. the 71st took part in Wellington's general advance, reputedly capturing a French battery and firing the final shot of the battle. Colonel Reynell recalled that:

> When all apprehension of further annoyance from the Enemy's Cavalry had ceased, we . . . directed our march upon two Columns of French Infantry, which from the first had appeared at the bottom of the hill. These Columns did not wait our approach, but made off, and from the circumstance of our finding an immense quantity of arms lying against the walls of the houses in the village of Caillou, I should incline to the belief that they had broken without order and dispersed . . . After scouring Caillou, where we came in contact with the Prussian advance, we gave up the pursuit to them, and having retired a little to the right to a cornfield that had been cut, bivouacked there for the night.

In his *Journal*, 'T.S.' gives the following resumé of the battle:

> About twelve o'clock we received orders to fall in . . . We then marched up to our position, where we lay on the face of a brae, covering a brigade of guns. We were so overcome by the fatigue of two days' march that, scarce had we lain down, until many of us fell asleep. I slept sound for some time while the cannon balls, plunging in amongst us, killed a great many. We lay thus, about an hour and a

half, under a dreadful fire, which cost us about sixty men, while we had never fired a shot. The balls were falling thick amongst us . . .

About two o'clock a squadron of lancers came down, hurraying, to charge the brigade of guns. They knew not what was in the rear. General Barnes [Major General Sir Edward Barnes, Wellington's fire-eating adjutant-general] gave the word, 'Form Square'. In a moment the whole brigade were on their feet, ready to receive the enemy . . . Down they came upon our square. We soon put them to the right-about.

Shortly afterwards, we received orders to move to the heights. Onwards we marched and stood for a short time in square, receiving cavalry every now and then. The noise and smoke were dreadful. At this time I could see but a very little way from me, but all around the wounded and slain lay very thick. We moved on in column for a considerable way and formed line, gave three cheers, fired a few volleys, charged the enemy and drove them back.

At this moment a squadron of cavalry rode furiously down upon our line. Scarce had we time to form. The square was only complete in front when they were upon the points of our bayonets. Many of our men were out of place. There was a good deal of jostling, for a minute or two, and a good deal of laughing. Our quartermaster lost his bonnet in riding into the square, got it up, put it on, back foremost, and wore it thus all day. Not a moment had we to regard our dress. A French general lay dead in the square; he had a number of ornaments upon his breast. Our men fell to plucking them off, pushing each other as they passed, and snatching at them . . .

We stood in square for some time, whilst the 13th Dragoons and a squadron of French dragoons were engaged. The 13th Dragoons retiring to the rear of our column, we gave the French a volley, which put them to the right-about; then the 13th at them again. They did this for some time; we cheering the 13th, and feeling every blow they received. When a Frenchman fell we shouted; and when one of the 13th, we groaned. We wished to join them but were forced to stand in square.

The whole army retired to the heights in the rear, the French closely pursuing to our formation, where we stood, four deep, for a considerable time. As we fell back, a shot cut the straps of the knapsack of one near me; it fell and was rolling away. He snatched it up, saying, 'I am not to lose you that way; you are all I have in the world,' tied it on the best manner he could and marched on . . . Shortly the whole army received orders to advance. We moved forwards in two columns, four deep, the French retiring at the same time. We were charged several times in our advance. This was our last effort; nothing could impede us. The whole enemy retired, leaving their guns and ammunition and every other thing behind. We moved on towards a village and charged right through, killing great numbers, the village was so crowded. We then formed on the other side of it and lay down under the canopy of heaven and wearied to death. We had been oppressed all day by the weight of our blankets and greatcoats, which were drenched with rain and lay upon our shoulders like logs of wood.

Scarce was my body stretched upon the ground when sleep closed my eyes . . . Next morning, when I awoke I was quite stupid. The whole night my mind had been harassed by dreams. I was fighting and charging, re-enacting the scenes of the day, which were strangely jumbled with the scenes I had been in before. I rose up and looked around, and began to recollect. The events of the 18th came before me, one by one; still they were confused, the whole appearing as an unpleasant dream. My comrades began to awake and talk of it; then the events were embodied as realities. Many an action had I been in wherein the individual exertions of our regiment had been much greater and our fighting more severe; but never had I been where the firing was so dreadful and the noise so great. When I looked over the field of battle it was covered and heaped in many places, figures moving up and down upon it. The wounded crawling along the rows of the dead was a horrible spectacle; yet I looked on with less concern, I must say, at the moment, than I have felt at an accident, when in quarters. I have been sad at the burial of a comrade who died of sickness in the hospital and followed him almost in tears; yet have I seen, after a battle, fifty men put into the same trench, and comrades amongst them, almost with indifference. I looked over the field of Waterloo as a matter of course, a matter of small concern.

The 71st sustained 202 casualties at Waterloo, including Colonel Reynell, who was wounded.

Thomas returned to Edinburgh in the winter of 1815. Having plucked up the courage to confront his long-lost parents, he made his way home, only to discover they had 'flitted long ago'. He went to a nearby tavern to make enquiries:

The landlord knew me. 'Tom,' said he, 'Are you come back safe? Poor fellow! Give me your hand.' 'Does my mother live?' 'Yes, yes,

come in and I will send for her, not to let the surprise be too great.'
Away he went. I could not remain but followed him and, the next
minute, I was in the arms of my mother.

Unable to find work in the depression that hit Britain in the wake
of the Napoleonic Wars, Thomas lived for a time with his married sister. But by 1818 his luck had not changed and, in despair, Thomas recorded his wartime experiences, in the hope of
raising a modest sum. Last seen among a party of road menders,
'T.S.' disappeared before Constable & Co. finally published the
book in 1828.

Turner
Joseph Mallord William (1775–1851)

Celebrated artist commissioned to paint an 'official' Waterloo
picture, marking Britain's victory over Napoleonic France. A
Londoner who never lost his cockney accent, Turner rose from
a humble background (his father was a barber) to become a
world-class artist. A child prodigy who excelled at drawing, Turner
earned a place at the Royal Academy School of Art at the age of 15.
His bold experiments in depicting pure forms of light and colour
anticipated the work of the Impressionists, changing the nature of
art by freeing painters from dogma and tradition. By the time of
Waterloo, the 40-year-old Turner was a celebrity, hailed as a genius.

Victory at Waterloo gave birth to a new concept for many Britons:
peace. The country had been at war with France for 23 years, and
for many people war was normal. Indeed, before the cataclysm of
the First World War, Britons referred to the struggle against
Revolutionary and Napoleonic France as 'the Great War'. And the
cost was immense, both in lives and capital. Over the whole period of
the conflict, Britain lost some 225,000 soldiers (although only about
10 per cent were killed in battle, the rest dying from wounds and
sickness). Thus, as David Gates (1997) has observed: 'Britain lost as
many men as a proportion of her population in the struggle against

Napoleon as she was to in that against the *Kaiser* 100 years later.' France, meanwhile, lost over 900,000 soldiers, prompting Gates to conclude:

> For the generation born between 1790 and 1795, this constitutes a mortality rate of 38 per cent, which is 14 per cent higher than the casualties inflicted on the generation of 1891–5 in the First World War, widely regarded as the most devastating conflict in French history.

Across Europe, says Gates, the Napoleonic Wars claimed some 5 million deaths: 'the same proportion of Europe's population as was to be claimed by the conflict of 1914–18'. And in financial terms, the cost of war was crippling. According to Charles J. Esdaile (1995), Britain coughed up a hefty £1.5 billion to defeat France: a sum that must be multiplied by a factor of at least 50 for a modern equivalent. No wonder news of Waterloo crashed over the country in a wave of euphoria.

But how should the great victory be celebrated? For the villagers of Denby Dale in Yorkshire, the answer was simple: bake a big pie 18 feet long, 6 feet wide and 18 inches deep, containing 3 tons of beef and 1½ tons of potatoes. For the government, too, there was an obvious solution: build more churches. Not content with peace, pie and piety, however, Britons soon began looking for a way of immortalising victory, of translating it into a symbol capable of nourishing the national psyche. And then, as now, people looked to pop stars for inspiration. And the pop stars of the Waterloo generation were poets. But neither Southey, the Poet Laureate, nor **Scott**, the popular bard, succeeded in pleasing the public palate. Byron, meanwhile, did not even try: a confirmed Bonapartist, he took to driving around in a replica of **Napoleon**'s coach after Waterloo (the original had been exhibited at London's Egyptian Hall in 1816) and threatening suicide. Meanwhile, a row had broken out between the Royal Academy and the British Institution over the commissioning of an official Waterloo painting, resulting in the latter body offering a 'premium' to any artist capable of conveying the patriotic significance of the battle. Enter the country's coolest artist, Joseph Mallord William Turner. Short and pugnacious, Turner could not be described as a romantic figure. But he had the Regency equivalent of 'street cred', his language, as Peter Ackroyd (2005) states, being 'the language of the street'. Yet Turner was an acknowledged master of his profession, and high hopes were entertained for his Waterloo project.

Turner set sail from Margate for Ostend in the summer of 1817, managing to lose a bag containing his razor, waistcoat, cravats and guide book to Belgium en route. At Ostend he stayed at the Hôtel de la Cour Impériale, where he was 'badly served' a breakfast costing 2 francs – an outrageous sum in Turner's eyes (Captain **Gronow** recalled paying the same for a three-course dinner in Paris after Waterloo). He then took a carriage to Brussels via Ghent. Turner spent a day inspecting the battlefield of Waterloo, jotting down a series of grisly notes: '1,500 killed here' and '4,000 killed here'. The result of the artist's diligent research was a painting entitled *The Field of Waterloo* – an appellation borrowed from Scott's 1815 poem. But the picture was not the flag-waving, drum-beating slab of patriotism the British Institution had anticipated. Instead, Turner depicted a field full of corpses at sunset. It was first shown in May 1818, and in the exhibition catalogue, printed alongside the picture's number, was stanza 28 from canto III of Byron's *Childe Harold's Pilgrimage*:

> The thunderclouds close o'er it, which when rent
> The earth is covered with other clay
> Which her own clay shall cover, heaped and pent
> Rider and horse – friend, foe, in one red burial blent!

According to Peter Ackroyd, Turner's canvas was 'not necessarily a paean against warfare as such – in some respects Turner was a profound patriot and would not have regretted the result of the battle – but rather a description of the lamentable effects of human strife'. In other words, the picture was rooted in reality, in the corporeal, not in the abstract or the sublime: and that was not what people wanted. By focusing on the immediate effects of Waterloo – death, pain and suffering – rather than its national significance, Turner had failed in his brief. At best, the painting met with a lukewarm response. Some critics admitted it was 'solemn and striking', but in general the work was considered too 'realistic'. Thus, by confronting his audience with the reality of war, Turner had transgressed the taste barrier. And even worse, by featuring a verse from Byron – whose idol was Napoleon – Turner appeared to be presenting, as Philip Shaw (2002) observes, 'a critique of the ravages of Waterloo'.

And so, like Scott and Southey before him, Turner had aimed his creative powers at the Battle of Waterloo and missed the mark – at least in the eyes of the Art Establishment. Indeed, having won the military victory at Waterloo, the British could only stand aside and watch a succession of French writers and artists like Hugo, Stendhal and Bellangé claim the artistic laurels. Thus, in the aftermath of their great victory, perhaps the most substantial celebratory offering enjoyed by Britons was a slice of Denby Dale pie . . .

Uchelen
Lieutenant van (dates unknown)

Netherlands prisoner of war who allegedly raised the town of Chareloi against the French after **Napoleon**'s defeat at Waterloo. According to historian Demetrius C. Boulger (1901), when **Gneisenau**'s Prussians entered Charleroi on 19 June 1815, in pursuit of Napoleon's vanquished Waterloo army, they found the place under the control of a certain Netherlands officer named Lieutenant van Uchelen. This man had apparently been captured by the French on 17 June, arriving at Charleroi next day:

> There he was forgotten by the French, and during the night of the 18th–19th he raised the townspeople, organised them into a police, and was in possession when the victors arrived on the 19th.

Presumably van Uchelen's task was easy, given the eagerness of the French to quit, and the locals' need to convince the Prussian 'liberators' of their loyalty. For Napoleon's appearance at Charleroi on 15 June 1815 – after victorious clashes with **Ziethen**'s Prussians at the nearby villages of Gilly and Gosselies – not only presented the Emperor with the military initiative, it also presented him with a demonstration of Belgian loyalty. Indeed, Napoleon's arrival at Charleroi – a tiny town of some 2,500 souls, 5 miles north of the River Sambre – was something of a triumph. The locals, who like other Belgians had been 'French' for the past 20 years (France annexed the former Austrian province in October 1795), welcomed Napoleon with acclamations and flowers, while the Emperor – no doubt warmed by this display of affection – warned his erstwhile subjects to flee before a 'big battle' began. A battle he was confident of winning: for while at Charleroi, Napoleon printed a proclamation to the Belgian people announcing a great victory. Prematurely dated from the Palace of Laecken at Brussels, Napoleon called on the Belgians to join his cause (the following translation is taken from E.F. Henderson (1911):

> The momentary success of my enemies had detached you for a brief space from my empire. In my exile on a rock in the sea I heard your laments. The God of weapons has determined the fate of your fine provinces. Napoleon is in your midst! Rise in a body! Join my invincible phalanxes to annihilate the remnants of the barbarians who are your enemies as well as mine! They have taken to flight with rage and despair in their hearts.

Needless to say, it was the French who took flight 'with rage and despair in their hearts' following defeat at Waterloo, 20 miles up the road from Charleroi. The disaster was so complete that by nightfall on 18 June Napoleon's army had degenerated into a mass of demoralised fugitives, flying back to Charleroi and the French border.

Gneisenau, leading the Prussian pursuit, records (Gneisenau 1815) the sequel:

> About 40,000 men in the most complete disorder, the remains of the whole army, saved themselves by retreating through Charleroi, partly without arms, and carrying with them only twenty-seven pieces of their numerous artillery.

And Napoleon was among their number. According to most French accounts – including those of **Coignet** and **Jardin** – the Emperor entered Charleroi at dawn on 19 June, having swapped his carriage for a swift steed (ditched in a traffic jam a few miles up the road at Genappe, much to the delight of Major **von Keller**'s pursuing

Prussians). Napoleon paused at Charleroi for an hour: long enough to convince some doubting generals of his need to fly; and to dictate an update for **Grouchy**, still embattled with **Thielemann**'s Prussians at Wavre. Then, in the words of Jean-Roch Coignet (1928), a soldier of the Imperial Guard: 'He asked for a glass of wine; it was handed to him on a large tray; he drank it, then saluted us, and started off. We were never to see him again.'

Meanwhile, Charleroi had degenerated into hellish anarchy, as the wreck of Napoleon's army hit town in full flight. Although the Prussians were some way behind, such was the psychological collapse of the French that every false alarm ignited a fresh stampede. A single steep and narrow street – the Rue de la Montagne – led down to Charleroi's only bridge, resulting in a crush of men, horses and carriages, all desperate to push through. Some vehicles were involved in an accident on the bridge, aggravating the traffic jam behind and tightening the bottleneck. Napoleon's paymaster despaired of getting his treasure-waggons through. Terrified of losing the Emperor's gold to Prussian pursuers, he decided to open the chests and distribute the bags (20,000 francs-worth of gold coins in each) among his men and the troops of the imperial escort. But someone shouted 'The Prussians are coming!' and the crowd surged forward, engulfing the poor paymaster, his waggons and his treasure chests. The entire fortune was plundered in the panic by a mass of seething soldiery. It was amid this bedlam that, as historian John Naylor (1960) states: 'the officer in charge of the carriage carrying the state papers ordered his men to tear up and scatter the most important documents'.

The Prussians finally entered Charleroi at midday on 19 June. It was then that, according to Boulger (1901), they found the place under the control of the forgotten prisoner of war, Lieutenant van Uchelen. Despite van Uchelen's apparent orgnisational skills, Charleroi still presented a sorry sight: littered as it was with the debris of a broken army, as well as innumerable copies of Napoleon's 'victory' proclamation: trampled underfoot like the flowers thrown at the Emperor's feet less than 100 hours before.

Uxbridge
Henry William Paget, second Earl
of (1768–1854)

Lord Uxbridge (1768–1854)

Wellington's second-in-command at Waterloo. Described by Baron Stockmar as 'a tall, well-made man', with 'a great deal of ease in his manners', Uxbridge was known as Lord Paget until 1812, when he inherited his father's title. Perhaps the best British cavalry commander of the period, he made his name in Sir John Moore's Corunna campaign of 1808–9, inflicting spectacular defeats on the French at Sahagun and Benevente. Having established himself as a commander of the first rank, Uxbridge pressed the 'self-destruct' button by deserting his wife and children to elope with Lady Charlotte Wellesley, wife of Wellington's brother Henry. The couple eventually obtained divorces and married, but the damage was done: precluded from service with Wellington, Uxbridge was obliged to spend the next five years in the doldrums. But when **Napoleon** escaped from Elba in February 1815 to rattle the collective cage of Europe's ruling elite, Uxbridge was rehabilitated. Highly regarded as a commander by the Prince Regent and his brother, the Duke of York, Uxbridge was thrust upon Wellington as his cavalry supremo and nominal second-in-command. And so, on 15 April 1815 – much to Wellington's chagrin – Uxbridge took command of some 13,000 Allied cavalrymen.

According to historian Sir Charles Oman (1913), 'Wellington never, till the Waterloo campaign, had an officer of proved ability in chief command of his cavalry.' But a major part of Uxbridge's brief was to direct operations against Napoleon should Wellington become a casualty. Not unreasonably, Uxbridge wanted to know something of the Duke's plan of campaign. He got a frosty response: 'Buonaparte has not given me any idea of his projects, and as my plans depend on his, how can you expect me to tell you what mine are?' As for the cavalry, Wellington simply gave Uxbridge carte blanche, the Earl later noting: 'These are all the orders I ever received from the Duke during this short campaign.'

And so, on 18 June 1815, Uxbridge had complete control of Wellington's cavalry at Waterloo, leading several charges in person. The first of these occurred in the early afternoon, in response to **d'Erlon**'s attack on Wellington's left-centre. As the French infantry advanced up the shallow incline of Mont St Jean, driving **van Bijlandt**'s and **Picton**'s skirmishers before them, Uxbridge ordered his heavy cavalry – positioned behind the ridge and consisting of the Household Brigade under Lord **Edward Somerset** and the Union Brigade under Sir **William Ponsonby** – to form line. Then, taking his place in the first line, he put the whole in motion: Ponsonby advancing on the left of the Brussels high road against d'Erlon's infantry; Somerset advancing on the right of the high road against the supporting cavalry. Uxbridge recorded later that the French were so astonished by the sudden appearance of the British dragoons, crashing over the crest of the ridge, 'that no very great resistance was made, and surely such havoc was rarely made in so few minutes'. And according to Uxbridge's descendant, the Marquess of Anglesey (1961),

> The effect of this immortal charge was such that in a very short space of time the French columns had dissolved into a mere pack of fugitives. Perhaps never in all military annals has there ever occurred a more spectacular, speedy and complete destruction of formed infantry by cavalry.

Indeed, for Uxbridge's troopers inflicted several thousand casualties, bagged a similar number of prisoners, and captured two French Eagles (that of the 45th Regiment was taken by Sergeant **Ewart** of the Scots Greys, that of the 105th by Captain **Alexander Kennedy Clark** and/or Corporal **Styles** of the Royals). But flushed with their success, and by all accounts possessed by battle-frenzy, the British dragoons failed to rally, and charged through the intervals of the oncoming French columns towards the guns of Napoleon's grand battery. After sabreing a few gunners and terrorising some waggon drivers, Uxbridge's 'heavies' were cut up in the inevitable French counter-charge. Many were killed – including Ponsonby and

Lieutenant Colonel **James Inglis Hamilton** – and the survivors played little part in the rest of the day's proceedings.

In the aftermath of the charge Wellington reputedly greeted Uxbridge with a sour, 'Well, Paget, I hope you are satisfied with your cavalry now.' But Uxbridge blamed himself for the fiasco, later admitting (Anglesey 1961):

> I committed a great mistake in having myself led the attack. The
> *carrière* once begun, the leader is no better than any other man;
> whereas, if I had placed myself at the head of the 2nd line, there
> is no saying what great advantages might not have accrued
> from it.

In the dying moments of the battle Uxbridge was hit by one of the last artillery rounds fired by the French. The accepted version of this episode, repeated countless times, has Uxbridge trotting alongside Wellington when the cannonball strikes: 'My God, sir! I have lost my leg!' exclaims the doughty Earl, to which Wellington, momentarily lowering his telescope, replies: 'My God, sir, you have!' Having suggested that Uxbridge's leg was torn off by the missile, some sources – in a bizarre twist of logic – then describe how the limb was amputated without anaesthetic, Uxbridge's steady pulse being unaffected by the trauma. In truth, it seems more likely that Uxbridge was struck on the right knee by grape-shot, as described by his aide-de-camp, Captain Thomas Wildman of the 7th Hussars. Nevertheless, it was a serious wound: though Uxbridge remained in the saddle until carried to the rear by six Hanoverian infantrymen aided by Captain **Horace Seymour**.

Uxbridge was taken to the village of Waterloo, where, at 214 Chaussée de Bruxelles (the home of a certain Monsieur Paris) his injured leg was scrutinised by medics. Captain Wildman describes (Capel and Uxbridge 1955) the sequel:

> When the surgeons examined it, they all agreed that it would be at
> the imminent danger of his life to attempt to save the limb. He only
> said 'Well gentlemen I thought so myself and if amputation is to take
> place the sooner it is done the better.' He wrote a short note to Lady
> Uxbridge, saying that if he had been a young single man he would

probably have run the risk, but that he would preserve his life for her & his children if possible. During the operation, he never moved or complained, no one even held his hands. He said once quite calmly that he thought the instrument was not very sharp. When it was over his nerves did not appear the least shaken, and the surgeon observed his pulse was not altered. He said smiling, 'I have had a pretty long run, I have been a beau these forty-seven years and it would not be fair to cut the young men out any longer,' and then asked us if we did not admire his vanity. I have seen many operations, but this neither Lord Greenock nor myself could bear. We were obliged to go to the other end of the room. I thank God he is doing as well as possible. There has been no fever and the surgeons say nothing can be going on more favourably.

Despite Wildman's testimony, Dr Martin Howard – while recognising Uxbridge's undoubted bravery – doubts the pulse could remain unaffected by surgery. Dr Howard (2002) writes:

We have no reason to doubt Lord Uxbridge's bravery . . . but the whole episode is more reminiscent of a Victorian melodrama than an emergency operation . . . It seems inconceivable that even one of the most admired officers in the British Army could have a limb amputated without any change in pulse.

Whatever the state of Uxbridge's metabolism, the operation was a success, and the Earl survived. The amputated limb was appropriated by Uxbridge's host, Monsieur Paris, who placed it in a wooden casket and buried it in his garden. In due course, an elaborately inscribed 'tombstone' was erected over the 'grave' and a willow planted. The site subsequently became a tourist attraction, visited by the likes of Sir **Walter Scott**, and Monsieur Paris became a minor celebrity. Meanwhile, on hearing of Uxbridge's ordeal, the Prince Regent sent Lady Charlotte over to Belgium on the royal yacht. The couple returned to London on 9 July 1815. The one-legged Uxbridge was greeted as a hero, the Prince Regent dubbing him Marquess of Anglesey. Uxbridge was also awarded an annual pension of £1,200 (approximately £60,000 in modern reckoning), which he politely refused, settling for an articulated artificial leg, the first ever devised, which subsequently became known as the 'Anglesey leg'. As for Uxbridge's 'Waterloo leg', it was exhumed in 1854 on the occasion of the Earl's death, and returned to its former owner for interment – presumably something of a blow for the Waterloo tourist industry.

Vandamme
General Dominique-Joseph-René, Count (1770–1830)

Commander of **Napoleon**'s III Corps during the Waterloo campaign. Born near at Cassel near Dunkirk, Vandamme entered the French Army in 1786. An able and courageous soldier, Vandamme's career was fast-tracked by the Revolution of 1789, and within 10 years he was a general of division. A loyal Bonapartist, Vandamme was selected by Napoleon to mentor his

General Vandamme (1770–1830)

youngest brother **Jérôme** during the Polish campaign of 1806–7. Talented, brave, audacious, Vandamme's career was blighted by two failings: a love of loot and a loathing of authority. The first character flaw led to instances of brigandage and embezzlement, punished by periods of suspension. The second fault led to numerous quarrels with superiors and a reputation for insubordination. Thus, although he worked hard for a marshal's baton, Vandamme was dogged by 'financial irregularities' and the unpleasant consequences of an uncontrollable temper.

After Napoleon's first abdication in 1814, Vandamme was exiled to Cassel by the hated Bourbons. But when the Emperor returned to power a year later, Vandamme returned to the colours. Napoleon reward Vandamme with the command of III Corps, consisting of three infantry divisions, **Domon**'s cavalry division, four batteries of foot artillery and one troop of horse artillery. But Vandamme wanted a marshal's baton and was livid not to have received one: this resentment would seriously affect his relationship with the newly promoted **Grouchy** in the coming campaign. At the Battle of Ligny on 16 June 1815, Vandamme led attacks on **Blücher**'s right wing, capturing the key village of St Armand. But thereafter, Vandamme was put under Grouchy's command (with **Gérard** and **Exelmans**) and sent in pursuit of Blücher's retreating Prussians, while Napoleon marched after **Wellington** with the bulk of the army. This was an unfortunate decision on the part of the Emperor: for Vandamme would undoubtedly have been better employed at Waterloo on 18 June, instead of slogging up the road to Wavre, bickering with a commander he loathed.

In his dealings with Grouchy between 16–18 June, historians have accused Vandamme of sluggishness at best, insubordination at worst. Tasked with dogging the defeated Prussians and preventing them joining Wellington, Grouchy stubbornly stuck to tailing after the Prussian rearguard, even when the sound of Napoleon's Waterloo guns reached his ears. Vandamme and Gérard urged Grouchy to march directly to the Emperor, but in such a tactless manner as to guarantee resistance on the part of their superior. According to historian Charles Chesney (1868):

> In spite of warm remonstrances, the march on Wavre was continued and a little before 2 p.m. Vandamme's infantry, preceded by Exelmans' horse, reached Baraque, 2 miles south from the town, and became engaged soon after with a considerable force of Prussians.

At this point, Vandamme shifted gear, launching an immediate attack on **Thielemann**'s Prussian rearguard – holding the line of the

River Dyle – without a thorough reconnaissance. In his attempt to rush the bridges over the Dyle, Vandamme succeeded in getting his men caught in a hail of Prussian fire from the opposite bank, wasting lives as a result. Grouchy, quoted by Christopher Kelly (1818), describes the action thus:

> I fell in with the enemy as I was marching on Wavre. He was immediately driven into Wavre; and General Vandamme's corps attacked that town, and was warmly engaged. The portion of Wavre on the right of the Dyle was carried; but much difficulty was experienced in debouching on the other side . . . In this state of things, being impatient to co-operate with your majesty's army on that important day, I detached several corps to force the passage of the Dyle, and march against **Bülow**. The corps of Vandamme, in the mean time, maintained the attack on Wavre, and on the mill, whence the enemy showed an intention to debouch, but which I did not conceive he was capable of effecting . . . Night did not permit us to advance further, and I no longer heard the cannon on the side where your majesty was engaged. I halted in this situation until daylight.

Thus, despite being outnumbered by his French attackers, Thielemann hung on throughout 18 June, delaying Grouchy and covering Blücher's march on Waterloo. But the following day Vandamme pushed across the Dyle and occupied Wavre. Grouchy describes the sequel:

> The Prussians were repulsed, and the village of Bielge taken . . . General Vandamme then passed one of his divisions by Bielge, and carried with ease the heights of Wavre, and, along the whole of my line, the success was complete. I was in front of Rozierne, preparing to march on Brussels when I received the sad intelligence of the loss of the battle of Waterloo. The officer who brought it informed me, that your majesty was retreating on the Sambre, without being able to indicate any particular point on which I should direct my march. I ceased to pursue, and began my retrograde movement.

In effect, no sooner had Vandamme secured Wavre when news of Napoleon's defeat at Waterloo threw him into reverse. By mid-day on 19 June Vandamme was following the rest of Grouchy's force back to the French border. There, at Namur, Vandamme commanded Grouchy's rearguard, successfully holding off the pursuing Prussians till Grouchy made good his escape into France. Grouchy again:

> We entered Namur without loss. The long defile which extends from this place to Dinant, in which only a single column can march, and the embarrassment arising from the numerous transports of wounded, rendered it necessary to hold for a considerable time the town, in which I had not the means of blowing up the bridge. I entrusted the defence of Namur to General Vandamme, who, with his usual intrepidity, maintained himself there till eight in the evening; so that nothing was left behind, and I occupied Dinant. The enemy has lost some thousands of men in the attack on Namur, where the contest was very obstinate; the troops have performed their duty in a manner worthy of praise.

This was Vandamme's last assignment for the Emperor. Fearful of Bourbon reprisals, Vandamme quit France for America (like **Lefebvre-Desnouëttes**), and although he returned a few years later, was never employed in his country's service again.

Vandeleur
Major General Sir John Ormsby (1763–1849)

Commander of **Wellington**'s 4th British Cavalry Brigade. According to General Sir Evelyn Wood (1895), Vandeleur joined the 5th Foot in 1781 and after advancing to the rank of captain some 11 years later,

> transferred to the 8th Light Dragoons, to the command of which he succeeded in 1798. As a colonel he commanded a brigade of cavalry in India in 1803–5, where he distinguished himself greatly on one occasion, taking 2,000 prisoners by a flank charge. In the Peninsula he commanded a brigade in the Light (Infantry) Division. Towards the end of that war he was transferred to the command of a cavalry brigade, and held a similar position at Waterloo.

Vandeleur's Waterloo command consisted of the 11th Light Dragoons (under Lieutenant Colonel James Wallace Sleigh), the 12th Light Dragoons (under Lieutenant Colonel the Honourable **Frederick Ponsonby**) and the 16th Light Dragoons (under Lieutenant Colonel James Hay): over 1,000 sabres in all. The brigade began the battle on Wellington's left wing, which, along with **Vivian**'s hussars, it was tasked with protecting. About 2 p.m., however, **Uxbridge** – commanding Wellington's cavalry – sent the Household and Union cavalry brigades crashing into **d'Erlon**'s advancing columns: the former, under Lord **Edward Somerset**, charging on the right of the great Brussels road; and the latter, under Sir **William Ponsonby**, charging on the left. Vandeleur and Vivian, watching these events unfold from their station, were joined by Wellington's Prussian liaison officer, Baron **von Müffling**. The Prussian urged them to advance in support of the Union Brigade but they refused to move without Wellington's orders (even though the Duke had given Uxbridge carte blanche with regard to the cavalry).

Convinced that neither commander would move, Müffling galloped off in despair. But, as General Sir Evelyn Wood describes:

After Müffling had ridden away, Vandeleur changed his mind. His brigade was drawn up to the east of the Papelotte–Verd–Cocu road, which cuts through the ridge on which Wellington's army stood. To move directly south, and cross where the cutting was no longer an obstacle would have brought the brigade under close fire of **Durutte**'s skirmishing line, and so Vandeleur turned northwards for about a quarter of a mile, and came back to the front through Best's Hanoverians; but by this time the Scots Greys had suffered great loss, and the commander of the Union Brigade had been killed . . . When Vandeleur's brigade at last came over the ridge, the 12th Light Dragoons, leading, saw in their front that the only remaining intact column (46th Regiment) of Marcognet's division was moving back steadily and in order. The scattered men of the Union Brigade were being followed so closely by some lancers, that the order was given to the 12th Light Dragoons, 'Squadrons right half wheel, charge.' The 46th Regiment attempted to stand when the dragoons were seen approaching, but being caught on its right flank it broke up, and the 12th, galloping right through the crowd, without pausing to reform, struck into the flank of some squadrons of **Jacquinot**'s lancers.

Keeping the 11th Light Dragoons in reserve, Vandeleur led the 16th in a charge against the lancers' leading squadrons. Moments later, Vandeleur's men were chasing the fleeing French into the shallow valley that separated the two armies. According to Sir Evelyn Wood:

> The survivors of the heavy cavalry now drew back, the retreat of the Union Brigade being covered to some extent by Vandeleur's brigade, and a regiment of Dutch-Belgian cavalry, which advanced about half way down the slope to the valley. The British squadrons reformed on the position they had previously occupied, but d'Erlon's disorganised corps was withdrawn out of sight to the southward of 'La Belle Alliance.' The crowd of shouting and fighting men disappeared, and no troops remained on the slopes on which Wellington's Staff had witnessed one of the most brilliant successes ever achieved by horsemen over infantry.

As a matter of interest, Müffling remained ignorant of Vandeleur's charge for years afterwards. He once discussed the matter with Wellington, describing how Vandeleur and Vivian had refused to budge without orders. Wellington, having forgotten Vandeleur's triumphant charge (as well as Uxbridge's role as cavalry supremo) declared he 'would have tried either of them by court martial had they moved, even if they were successful'.

During Wellington's general advance – the final act of the Waterloo drama, following the repulse of **Napoleon**'s Imperial Guard about 8 p.m. – Uxbridge was wounded by one of the last rounds fired by the French artillery and forced to quit the field. Vandeleur immediately took control of the Allied cavalry arm, command of his brigade passing to Lieutenant Colonel James Wallace Sleigh of the 11th Light Dragoons. It was Sleigh, then, who in the dying moments of the battle led the final charges, during which the bulk of the brigade's casualties were sustained. By his own account – published in Siborne's *Waterloo Letters* (1891) – Sleigh describes how the brigade advanced with Vivian's hussars to its left:

> We took the last battery, and received their last fire, which was given when the brigade, then under my command, was so close that I saw the artillerymen fire their guns; fortunately the ground was undulating, and we only lost by the fire Lieutenant Phillips

[Phelips?] of the 11th Dragoons, and Hay of the 16th Dragoons. It was after this, when continuing our advance, that the 1st Hussars [of the King's German Legion, one of Vivian's regiments] came up in the rear of the brigade, and from its being nearly dark were all but in collision with the 11th and 16th, which regiments, knowing there was a brigade of French cavalry on our right, went threes about, and were in the act of charging, when they recognised the 1st Hussars by knowing their cheer; it was very dark, and the men knew of the French brigade being behind them.

And according to Captain William Tomkinson of the 16th Light Dragoons:

Here the pursuit ended, it being ten o'clock, and the brigade was ordered to retire. The ground was covered with muskets, thrown-away guns, ammunition waggons, tumbrils, brandy, etc. We came across some of the latter, and got as much as the men required. We retired to the edge of the wood near the Observatory, and not half a mile from the point where we charged the infantry, and there bivouacked for the night.

Vivian
Major General Sir Richard Hussey (1775–1842)

Commander of **Wellington**'s 6th British Cavalry Brigade at Waterloo. Born in Truro, the eldest son of John Vivian, 'Hussey' (as he was known) entered the army in 1793 as an infantry ensign. Quickly promoted to lieutenant, Vivian transferred to the 7th Light Dragoons in 1799. He saw much service during the Peninsular War, including Moore's arduous Corunna campaign of 1808–9. When hostilities with France were rekindled by **Napoleon**'s return to power in March 1815, Vivian was recalled to the colours, despite a Peninsular War wound that kept his right arm in a sling. Vivian embarked on 16 April 1815, arriving in the Netherlands on 3 May to take command of Wellington's 6th British Cavalry Brigade, consisting of the 7th, 10th, and 18th Hussars. At the end of May,

Vivian lost the 7th Hussars to Major General Sir Colquhoun Grant's 5th British Cavalry Brigade, but gained the 1st Hussars of the King's German Legion. Vivian's brigade was completed by the addition of Captain Sir Robert Gardiner's E Troop, Royal Horse Artillery.

On 15 June Vivian attended the Duchess of Richmond's ball in Brussels, before taking a circuitous route over bad roads to Quatre-Bras next day. Vivian's 40-mile trek to the front prevented him from assisting at the Battle of Quatre-Bras, though his brigade covered Wellington's retreat to Waterloo on 17 June, conducted during a violent thunderstorm. At Waterloo, Vivian's brigade fielded some 1,500 sabres, and was tasked with holding Wellington's extreme left, or east, flank. Having bivouacked near the Forest of Soignies the previous night, the brigade took post on the Wavre road, the Duke's line of communication with **Blücher**'s Prussians. Vivian's hussars saw little action throughout the day, but early evening saw them committed to the desperate battle boiling around Wellington's centre. The question of who ordered Vivian's brigade to move from the left to the centre is debatable. Some historians say Wellington issued the order; Baron von **Müffling**, the Duke's Prussian liaison officer, claimed he told Vivian and **Vandeleur** to move; but Vivian always maintained that he acted on his own initiative. Entering the maelstrom after 6 p.m., Vivian wheeled his brigade into 'the most dreadful fire of shot and shell, and musketry that it is possible to imagine'. And there his hussars remained, putting heart into hard-pressed infantrymen, who had been subjected to alternating artillery barrages and mass cavalry attacks for several hours. Some two hours after Vivian's redeployment, Napoleon's Imperial Guard attacked and was repulsed.

Having successfully survived this final trauma, Wellington ordered his line to advance and Vivian sent his hussars down the slopes of Mont St Jean and into the shallow valley beyond. There Vivian unleashed a series of charges, which he recalled in his memoirs (1897):

> I charged with the 10th and as soon as we were well into the enemy and mixed up, the French making off, I gave the word 'Halt,' and galloped off to the 18th. En route, I was attacked by one of the cuirassiers whom we had passed. I was fortunate enough to give him

a thrust in the neck with my left hand (for my right was in a sling and I was just capable of holding the reins with it only), and at that moment I was joined by my little German orderly, who cut the fellow off his horse . . . With the 18th I charged a second body of cuirassiers and chasseurs that were supporting a square of Imperial Guards; and the 18th not only defeated them, but took fourteen pieces of cannon that had been firing grape at us during our movement . . . I ordered the 10th to charge a square of infantry still steady and close to us. They did this most gallantly, and as gallantly was the attack received . . . Here we took prisoner Count **Lobau**, who commanded one of the corps d'armée; and here was fired the last shot for the night.

Vivian's statement regarding the capture of Count Lobau, the commander of Napoleon's VI Corps, is of note: for according to historian Tony Linck (1993), among others, Lobau was picked up by Prussian horsemen the day after the battle, in the vicinity of Genappe (although he was later handed over to the British).

Meanwhile, flushed with success, Vivian began blabbing about how he had turned the fate of the battle. According to William Tomkinson (1894) of the 16th Light Dragoons, who met Vivian at the close of the battle: 'Sir Hussey told me he had *turned* the fate of the day by charging with his brigade.' Tomkinson then inserts the following acid drop: 'The place he charged at was two miles out of the position and half an hour after the enemy retired.' Vivian, however, seems convinced of his central role in the outcome of the battle, writing on 23 June 1815:

Whether the Duke will do my brigade justice or not, I know not, but . . . the Colonel of the 3rd Chasseurs, who lodged the night before last in the house I occupied last night, told the proprietor that two regiments of British Hussars decided the affair. The third regiment I kept in reserve.

After the battle, Vivian received a mention in Wellington's Dispatch, the thanks of the British Parliament, plus honours from Austria and Russia. In 1897 his grandson, the Hon. Claud Vivian, published *Richard Hussey Vivian, First Baron Vivian, A Memoir.*

Waterloo
Frederica M'Mullen (1815–?)

Allegedly present at Waterloo on 18 June, carried in her mother's womb, and born in an Antwerp hospital several days later. In a tale recounted by Kelly (1818):

> A private of the 27th Regiment, who was severely wounded, was carried off the field by his wife, then far advanced in pregnancy; she also was severely wounded by a shell, and both of them remained a considerable time in one of the hospitals at Antwerp in a hopeless state. The poor man had lost both his arms, the woman was extremely lame, and here gave birth to a daughter, to whom it is said the Duke of York has stood sponsor, and who has been baptized by the name of Frederica M'Mullen Waterloo.

According to the *Waterloo Medal Roll* there were two private soldiers named McMullen in the 27th (Inniskilling) Foot: Peter and William. The 1st Battalion of the regiment suffered appalling losses: 463 men of its complement of 750 becoming casualties. As Ian Fletcher observes in *Wellington's Regiments*, 'Such is the price of glory'.

Weir
Sergeant John (?–1815)

Pay-sergeant of the 2nd Royal North British Dragoons (Scots Greys) who, though his duties might have excused him, requested to ride into combat with his comrades on Waterloo Day. A native of Ayrshire, Scotland, Weir was mortally wounded in the melee with **Milhaud**'s cuirassiers and **Jacquinot**'s lancers, following the Greys' initial success against Marcognet's infantry. Knowing death to be imminent, Weir determined to make his identity known, to prove he had not absconded with his comrades' pay. His body was found with 'Weir' daubed on the forehead, apparently written by his own hand, in his own blood.

Wellington
Field Marshal Sir Arthur Wellesley, first Duke of (1769–1852)

Wellington (1769–1852) by Francisco Goya

Commander of the Army of the Low Countries. Son of the first Earl of Mornington, Wellington (as he was known from 1809) was reputedly born in Dublin, but no one knows exactly where (some sources cite Merrion Street, but it did not matter much to Wellington, who never considered himself Irish anyway). Despite an aristocratic background, money was tight; so after studies at Eton College and a French military college, Wellington was pushed into the army and expected to make the best of it. He was not expected to shine, his mother apparently observing, 'Anyone can see he has not the cut of a soldier.' But thanks to the British system of purchasing commissions, Wellington did make progress: entering the army as an ensign in 1787, he was a lieutenant colonel by 1793.

Wellington first saw action in the Netherlands (1794–5) where, by his own account, he learned how *not* to conduct a campaign. Two years later Wellington was commanding British troops in India, where he scored a string of victories against the Mahrattas. Returning to Britain in 1805, he dabbled in politics until 1808, when British involvement in the Peninsular War ensured him a command under Generals Burrard, Dalrymple and Moore. Within months, however, Burrard and Dalrymple had been recalled to London and Moore had died a hero's death at Corunna. Effectively in charge, Wellington set about winning the war: liberating Portugal and Spain before invading the South of France via the Pyrenees.

Wellington received his title in 1809 (the name 'Wellington' coming from Wellesley family estates in Somerset), following his victory at Talavera (27–28 July 1809). First he was made a viscount, then an earl, then a marquess and finally, in May 1814, a duke – by which time he was also a field marshal. Thus, within the space of 27 years, Wellington had progressed from the army's lowest commissioned rank to its highest. He was, in effect, Britain's top soldier.

The abdication of **Napoleon** on 6 April 1814 technically ended hostilities with France – although news did not reach Wellington till after his victory at Toulouse on 10 April. The following month saw Louis XVIII restored to Paris and Napoleon incarcerated on Elba. After 22 years of war and over 5 million deaths Europe heaved a sigh of relief. On 1 November 1815 Allied diplomats gathered at Vienna to sort out the mess and rebuild Europe on secure foundations. Peace was shattered, however, by Napoleon's escape from exile on 26 February 1815 and subsequent return to French soil. Louis XVIII fled to the Netherlands and on 20 March Napoleon strolled back into the Tuileries. According to Arthur Bryant (1950):

> The Sovereigns of Europe assembled at Vienna refused to accept the outrageous *fait accompli* . . . they proclaimed the escaped prisoner an outlaw and 'disturber of the peace of the world.' Thereafter they ordered an immediate mobilisation of the Continent's armies and appointed the Duke of Wellington to command the advance guard in the Low Countries.

The Duke arrived in Brussels on 4 April to take command of scratch British units, newly raised Netherlands militia, and a sprinkling of Hanoverians and assorted Germans. Most of the Duke's Peninsular veterans had been sent to fight the Americans, leaving the Duke to lament: 'I have got an infamous army, very weak and ill equipped, and a very inexperienced Staff.' The so-called Army of the Low Countries consisted of four major elements: the I Corps was commanded by the Prince of **Orange** (a political appointment designed to please King William I of the Netherlands); the II Corps was commanded by Wellington's Peninsular sidekick Lord **Hill**; and a strong Reserve Corps remained under Wellington's own hand. Finally, a Cavalry Corps over 10,000 strong was placed under Lord **Uxbridge**'s orders. Suspicious of his Dutch and Belgian troops – some of whom had served in Napoleon's Grand Army when their nations were annexed to France – Wellington mixed them up with the Brits and Germans and hoped for the best. Very roughly speaking, one-third of Wellington's troops were British, one-third Germans (including the Hanoverians of the King's German Legion) and one-third Netherlanders.

Meanwhile, the Duke was joined in Belgium by a Prussian army under Field Marshal **Blücher**. With Wellington's troops spread out in cantonments west of Brussels, Blücher's boys took post east of the capital. The two armies were supposed to act together in a projected invasion of France, boosted by contingents from Austria and Russia. But Napoleon got in first, crossing the Sambre at Charleroi on 15 June with the intention of prising Wellington and Blücher apart, defeating each in turn, then marching on Brussels. It was a long shot, perhaps, but as a pariah Napoleon had little to lose and everything to gain: besides, he had gambler's blood in his veins. According to Hilaire Belloc (1931): 'Wellington . . . was both misinformed and confused as to the nature and rapidity of the French advance into Belgium.' Belloc is just one of a battalion of historians who accuse Wellington of dilatoriness in the opening phase of the campaign; and of failing to appreciate the importance of Quatre-Bras, the crossroads south of Brussels that linked the Duke's army in the west with that of Blücher's in the east (fortunately **Constant de Rebecque**, Chief of Staff to the Prince of Orange, sent Netherlands troops to occupy the place on his own initiative). Meanwhile, Peter Hofschroer (1999) suggests Wellington deliberately dragged his heels, thereby ensuring Blücher clashed with Napoleon first.

But it seems the Duke was initially fearful of Napoleonic feints and stratagems, and simply refused to move until he was sure where the main blow would fall. By midnight on 15 June Wellington was satisfied and – after attending the Duchess of Richmond's ball – finally swung into action, ordering a concentration on Nivelles and Quatre-Bras. As the Duke later admitted in conversation: 'I have always avoided a false move. I preferred being too late in my movements to having to alter it.' In the event both Blücher and Wellington were attacked on 16 June: the former by Napoleon at Ligny, the latter by Marshal **Ney** at Quatre-Bras. Both Allied commanders had their hands full and could not cooperate. Next day Blücher retreated north to Wavre, having received a bloody nose courtesy of the Emperor, while Wellington – who had successfully seen off Ney – followed suit and retired on Waterloo. In the words of historian Edward S. Creasy (1851), Wellington:

> slept a few hours at his headquarters in the village of Waterloo;
> and rising on the 18th, while it was yet deep night, he wrote several
> letters, to the Governor of Antwerp, to the English Minister at
> Brussels, and other official personages, in which he expressed his
> confidence that all would go well; but, 'as it was necessary to provide
> against serious losses should any accident occur,' he gave a series of
> judicious orders for what should be done in the rear of the army in
> the event of the battle going against the Allies. He also, before he left
> the village of Waterloo, saw to the distribution of the reserves of
> ammunition which had been parked there, so that supplies should be
> readily forwarded to every part of the line of battle where they might
> be required. The Duke, also, personally inspected the arrangements
> that had been made for receiving the wounded and providing
> temporary hospitals in the houses in the rear of the army. Then,
> mounting a favourite charger, a small thoroughbred chestnut horse,
> named 'Copenhagen', Wellington rode forward to the range of hills
> where his men were posted. Accompanied by his Staff and by the
> Prussian General **Müffling**, he rode along his lines, carefully
> inspecting all the details of his position. Hougoumont was the object
> of his special attention. He rode down to the south-eastern extremity
> of its enclosures, and, after having examined the nearest French
> troops, he made some changes in the disposition of his own men
> who were to defend that important post. Having given his final
> orders about Hougoumont, the Duke galloped back to the high
> ground in the right centre of his position, and, halting there, sat
> watching the enemy on the opposite heights and conversing with

his staff with that cheerful serenity which was ever his characteristic in the hour of battle.

Twelve hours later it was all over. Having withstood attacks by **d'Erlon**'s columns, **Milhaud**'s cuirassiers and **Drouot**'s Imperial Guard, Wellington launched a general advance as Prussian units under **Bülow**, **Pirch** and **Ziethen** pitched into the French right flank: Napoleon fled, as did most of his soldiers, and victory was complete. Three days later Napoleon abdicated for good. Three weeks later the Allies were in Paris. As Wellington's biographer, William Hamilton Maxwell (1904) states: 'The decisive results of Wellington's success may be estimated from the inability of every attempt made by the wreck of the French Army to arrest the Allied march upon the capital.'

In the years following Waterloo Wellington morphed into the Great Duke – a kind of British institution. Widely viewed as the superhero saviour of Europe, he took on the role of diplomat, statesman and guru to the young Queen Victoria. He also found time to serve as British Prime Minister (1828–30) and Commander-in-Chief of the British Army (1827–8 and 1842–52). Of Waterloo the Duke once said: 'I never took so much trouble about any battle, and was never so near being beat.' And yet, considering his achievement at Waterloo, Wellington has been taken to task by historians ever since. Accused of everything from accepting battle in a bad position

Wellington and his Staff *by George Jones*

to duplicity in his dealings with Blücher, Wellington's reputation has taken its share of knocks. Napoleon was one of the first to chip away at the Duke's renown, claiming that 'The position of Mont St Jean was ill-chosen.' Under the false impression Wellington had been instrumental in sending him to St Helena, Napoleon exacted revenge by writing a poisonous critique on the Duke's Waterloo strategy. In a neat twist of logic, the erstwhile Emperor concluded that Wellington won because the Forest of Soignies in his rear made retreat impossible. In truth, the forest did not constitute a barrier to Wellington's army, but Napoleon was adamant: 'such is the bizarre course of human events – that the poor choice of his battlefield . . . was the cause of his victory'. Meanwhile, Wellington had already soured relations with the Prussians (**Gneisenau** loathed him anyway) by refusing to accept 'The Battle of La Belle Alliance' as a sobriquet for the Great Battle, insisting the victory be named after his headquarters at Waterloo. He also ruffled a flock of feathers with his Waterloo Dispatch, which was so downbeat that, as Andrew Roberts (2001) observes, the American envoy to London 'assumed that Wellington had actually lost the battle'. Wellington blotted his copybook further by refusing to intervene on behalf of the hapless Marshal Ney, sentenced to death by the Bourbons after Waterloo for his part in Napoleon's swansong. And if any would-be historian – including literary superstar Sir **Walter Scott** – sought Wellington's cooperation in a definitive history of Waterloo, the Duke remained ferociously tight-lipped – giving rise to suspicions he had something to hide.

Even today the Duke has his supporters and detractors. Readers keen to keep up with the debate might consult the following: Jac Weller, *Wellington at Waterloo* (1967), Peter Hofschroer, *1815 The Waterloo Campaign: The German Victory* (1999), Andrew Roberts, *Napoleon and Wellington* (2001), Richard Holmes, *Wellington, the Iron Duke* (2002) and Peter Hofschroer, *Wellington's Smallest Victory* (2004). But to give Wellington the last word, here is his tearful postscript to Waterloo, as witnessed by Lady Shelley (1912):

> I hope to God I have fought my last battle. It is a bad thing to be always fighting. While in the thick of it, I am much too occupied to feel anything; but it is wretched just after. It is quite impossible to

think of glory. Both mind and feelings are exhausted. I am wretched even at the moment of victory, and I always say that next to a battle lost, the greatest misery is a battle gained.

Wheatley
Lieutenant Edmund (1793–1841)

British officer in the 5th Line Battalion, King's German Legion, captured near La Haie Sainte. Wheatley was a love-struck Londoner, besotted with a certain Eliza Brookes. But as an impecunious junior officer in the King's German Legion (KGL), Wheatley was considered an unsuitable match by Eliza's parents, who forbade the couple to meet or correspond. And so Wheatley went to war lovelorn, confiding his thoughts, feelings and experiences to a diary, which he dedicated to Eliza.

Soldiers of the King's German Legion, 1815

Wheatley's corps, the KGL, mainly consisted of Hanoverians loyal to Britain's George III, still technically the Elector of Hanover. These Germans made their way to Britain following the French invasion of their homeland in 1803, determined to fight for freedom under the Union Flag. According to historian Sir Charles Oman (1913):

> Men soon began to follow in considerable numbers, and after two provisional infantry regiments had been formed in August, a larger organisation, to be called the King's German Legion, was authorised in December. It included light and line infantry, heavy and light cavalry, artillery and engineers. All through 1804 new units were being rapidly created, mainly from Hanoverians, but not entirely, for other recruits of German nationality were accepted. But all the officers, nearly all the sergeants, and the large majority of the rank and file came from the old Electoral army.

Wheatley joined the King's German Legion in November 1812, and as Christopher Hibbert states in his introduction to *The Wheatley Diary* (1964), 'despite the distinguished service of various of its regiments . . . it was at that time considered an unsuitable corps for an English gentleman to join'. In fact, most of the Legion's officers were German, described by Wheatley as 'sometimes haughty and reserved'. Indeed, it seems that Wheatley's only friend in the battalion was a drunken Welshman named Llewellyn.

On Waterloo Day, Wheatley awoke cold, hungry, miserable and wet from the previous night's downpour. Comforting himself with thoughts of Eliza and home, Wheatley's mood mellowed. Turning his attention to the French soldiers massing across the valley, he concluded that they were 'commendable characters' and undeserving of his animosity. But before the day was out, Wheatley would have good cause to revise this opinion. For, like fellow Waterloo veterans **George Drummond Graeme** and **Jean-Baptiste Jolyet**, Wheatley would suffer abuse as a prisoner of war. Wheatley's battalion was situated atop the ridge of Mont St Jean, in rear of the farm of La Haie Sainte, which guarded the approach to **Wellington**'s centre. When this bastion fell to a concerted French attack in the early evening (the KGL garrison under **Baring** having run out of ammunition), Wheatley was wounded in the abortive counter-attack led by Baron **Ompteda**. Wheatley was then captured and taken to the farmhouse, which he found 'completely destroyed, nothing but the rafters and props remaining . . . The carnage had been very great in this place.' He was then escorted to the French rear by a soldier who robbed him on the way. Eventually arriving at the village of Genappe, several miles behind the battlefield, Wheatley discovered the place crammed with French wounded. By now it was late in the day, and the tide of the battle had turned against the French. Consequently, Wheatley was appallingly maltreated by his captors: stripped, beaten, cruelly denied water, and forced to march barefoot to Charleroi at bayonet point. And adding insult to injury, a grenadier of the Imperial Guard forced Wheatley to write a recommendation for him, should he fall into British hands:

> I scrawled the following words: 'I Edmund Wheatley, Lieutenant in the German Legion, write this on a bundle of bricks, June 19th 1815, at the entrance of Charleroi in the middle of the retreating French Army.' Cold, wounded, barefooted, bareheaded, like a dog in a fair, everyone buffets me *ad libitum*. If the bearer, named Rivière, is in your power, prove to him how differently an Englishman can treat a poor unhappy victim of human instability.

Happily, Wheatley managed to give his tormentors the slip amid the chaos of the French retreat, setting off across country to find his regiment, which he rejoined 10 days later, on 29 June. And so Wheatley survived Wellington's campaign, returning home to pursue his own crusade for the hand of Eliza Brookes. His cause was not helped when, in April 1816, the KGL was disbanded and he was placed on half-pay. Nevertheless, despite all odds, the couple married in February 1820. Unable to survive on 4 shillings a day (about £10 a day in modern terms), Wheatley and Eliza went abroad, first to Belgium and then to France, where they raised a family of four daughters.

Whinyates
Captain Edward Charles (1782–1865)

Commander of O Troop, Royal Horse Artillery, also known as the 'Rocket Troop'. Apparently related to Oliver Cromwell (1599–1658) on his mother's side, Whinyates was the son of an army officer from Devon. Educated at the Royal Military Academy, Woolwich, Whinyates entered the Royal Artillery in 1798 as a second lieutenant. A veteran of campaigns in Holland and Denmark, Whinyates served in **Wellington**'s Peninsular Army as a captain in the Royal Horse Artillery, distinguishing himself at the Battles of Bussaco and Albuera. In 1814 he joined O Troop, which he commanded at Waterloo. There were eight Troops of Royal Horse Artillery at the great battle, under the overall command of Lieutenant Colonel Sir **Augustus Frazer**. Each Troop was known by a letter of the alphabet or the name of its commander: A Troop (commanded by Lieutenant Colonel Sir Hew Dalrymple Ross); D Troop (commanded by Major George Beane); E Troop (commanded by Lieutenant Colonel Robert Gardiner); F Troop (commanded by Lieutenant Colonel James Webber Smith); G Troop (commanded by Captain **Alexander Cavalié Mercer**); H Troop (commanded by Major William Norman Ramsay); I Troop (commanded by Major **Robert Bull**); and of course, Whinyates's O Troop.

In addition to the usual five 6-pounders and one $5\frac{1}{2}$-inch howitzer, Whinyates's troop was also equipped with Congreve rockets: fairly primitive missiles consisting of gunpowder charges mounted on long sticks – like large fireworks – and named after their inventor, Colonel William Congreve (who adapted Indian rockets captured during clashes with Tipoo Sultan in the 1790s). Rockets varied in size, from 6-pounders up to immense 300-pounders, but the principle was the same: missiles were fired at an angle from an adjustable 'bombarding frame' or simply sent fizzing along the ground. Either way, rockets behaved erratically, but as Philip Haythornthwaite (1979) notes, their main purpose was not to destroy precise targets, but 'to shatter enemy morale'. Wellington, however, remained sceptical – even scornful – of Congreve's missiles, caustically observing: 'I do not wish to set fire to any town, and I do not know of any other use for rockets.' And so the Duke ordered Whinyates to

*Trooper of the British
Mounted Rocket Corps*

leave his rockets behind for the Waterloo campaign. When informed
that this would break Whinyates's heart, Wellington replied: 'Damn
his heart; let my orders be obeyed.' But in the event Whinyates took
his rockets to Waterloo – with Wellington's (reluctant) approval
according to some, without it according to others.

Attached to Sir **William Ponsonby**'s 2nd British (Union)
Cavalry Brigade, Whinyates advanced in support about 2 p.m., when
the British dragoons smashed into **d'Erlon**'s attacking columns.
According to some pundits, Whinyates deployed rockets on his own
initiative, but in a letter to Sir Hew Dalrymple Ross, dated 10 March
1841 and quoted by Siborne (1891), Whinyates states:

> I suddenly received a communication that the cavalry was going
> to advance, and that I was to move forward . . . At this moment,
> however, Colonel MacDonald of the Horse Artillery came up, and
> ordered me to leave my guns and advance with the Rocket Sections,
> which I did, down the slope in front of the position until the ground
> on the French side gave a more favourable chance of effectual rocket
> practice . . . On dismounting to fire the ground rockets some very
> high grain crops interposed and screened the enemy's line, and after

firing some discharges of rockets I received an order to rejoin the position. The Troop accordingly moved back, steadily and in perfect order and unpursued, and rejoined their guns.

It should be noted that Whinyates refers to 'ground rockets' – a fact ignored by some contemporary artists, who depicted rockets streaking across the smoke-filled Waterloo sky.

But even if the spectacle of Whinyates's rockets – snaking through the tall standing crops – may not have been as impressive as some Waterloo prints would have us believe, their effect on the French was dramatic enough. According to G.R. Gleig (1812), a Peninsular War veteran who later produced books on Wellington and Waterloo, 'the confusion created in the ranks of the enemy beggars all description', a fact highlighted by Lieutenant F. Warde of Ross's Troop who, in a letter dated 27 May 1840 and quoted by Siborne (1891), describes how:

> The Rocket Troop was . . . told off into thirteen sections, each section carrying eight 6-pound rockets. Soon after coming into position, Major Whinyates [the Captain was promoted after Waterloo] received orders to advance with the thirteen sections, with the view of checking the advance of a brigade of the enemy's cavalry. Major Whinyates moved at a trot within a range of 300 yards, and fired volleys of rockets, and in ten minutes the French brigade were in total disorder and dispersed.

Warde goes on to contradict his own estimate of 104 rockets deployed by O Troop (i.e. 'thirteen sections, each section carrying eight 6-pound rockets') by declaring that as many as 300 missiles were fired 'during the commencement of the action'. But according to historian Mark Adkin (2001), only some 52 rockets were fired by O Troop at Waterloo, though Whinyates's men were kept busy throughout the day serving their guns: apparently loosing off over 300 cannon balls and 236 rounds of spherical case or shrapnel.

As for Whinyates, according to historian Charles Dalton (1904), the Captain had: 'three horses shot under him, was struck by a round shot on the leg and severely wounded in the left arm towards the close of the day'. Whinyates was rewarded with promotion to major and a Waterloo medal. He was later knighted, promoted to colonel, and rose to command of the Horse Artillery at Woolwich.

Woodford
Lieutenant Colonel Alexander George (1782–1870)

Commander of the 2nd Battalion, 2nd Foot (Coldstream) Guards, who aided **Macdonell** in the defence of Hougoumont on 18 June 1815. Born in London, Woodford was the elder son of Lieutenant Colonel John Woodford (d.1800). He attended Winchester College and then the Royal Military Academy at Woolwich, obtaining an ensign's commission in the 9th Foot in 1794. Transferring to the elite 2nd Foot (Coldstream) Guards a few years later, by 1810 Woodford held a guards rank of captain and an army rank of lieutenant colonel. A veteran of campaigns in the Mediterranean and the Iberian Peninsula, Woodford commanded the 2nd Battalion of the 2nd Foot Guards at Quatre-Bras on 16 June and at Waterloo two days later (his younger brother, Lieutenant Colonel John Woodford, was on **Wellington**'s staff). And it was at Waterloo that Woodford found fame as one of the defenders of the fourteenth-century château of Hougoumont, lying some 12 miles south of Brussels, at the foot of the ridge of Mont St Jean.

On 18 June 1815 Hougoumont was a vital bastion protecting Wellington's right flank. Essentially a farmstead, the place consisted of a clutch of buildings enclosing two courtyards and surrounded by walls. On the south side of the complex stood a small brick-built chapel containing a fifteenth-century figure of the crucified Christ. Flanking the château on its eastern side was a walled garden, and beyond that, a large orchard. Meanwhile, to the south, lay a dense wood. Owned by absentee landlord the Chevalier de Louville (a resident of nearby Nivelles), the place was let to local farmer, Antoine Dumonceau, though on Waterloo Day it was unoccupied and unfurnished. The battle for Hougoumont began around 11.30 a.m. with a French assault meant to be a mere diversion: it ended nine hours later with the collapse of **Napoleon**'s army and its flight up the Charleroi road. And so Hougoumont was a battle-within-a battle, during which **Jérôme** Bonaparte's 6th Infantry Division, part of **Reille**'s II Corps, launched several separate assaults to no avail.

Napoleon had conceived the assault on Hougoumont as a means of obliging Wellington to weaken his centre by sending troops to its defence. But the Duke – while committing some reinforcements and supporting units to the château – refused to fall for the Emperor's ploy, preferring to rely on the strength of the bastion and the fighting qualities of the troops within it. The result was a reversal of Napoleon's intended outcome: the French threw away precious manpower at Hougoumont, while the Allies stood firm on all fronts. As historian Tony Linck (1993) observes: 'Jérôme had totally misread Napoleon's plan and throughout the day continued to batter away at Hougoumont.' In all, the French used over 15,000 men in their assaults against the château, which was held by perhaps 3,000 troops with a further 4,000 in supporting units. Total casualties numbered some 6,500, leading Victor Hugo – writing in his 1862 novel *Les Misérables* – to describe Jérôme's 'diversion' as a 'conflagration, massacre, carnage, a rivulet formed of English blood, French blood, German blood mingled in fury'. According to veteran **Edward Cotton** (1895), the château 'never before sustained such a succession of desperate attacks: the battle began with the struggle for its possession, which struggle only terminated in the utter defeat and rout of the enemy'.

By his own account, Woodford arrived at Hougoumont shortly after midday at the head of his battalion, which counter-attacked French forces attempting to storm the stronghold. In a letter dated 14 January 1838, and quoted in by Siborne (1891), Woodford describes the scene:

> At the time I was sent down to Hougoumont (about twelve o'clock or a little after), the enemy had nearly got into the farmyard. We found them very near the wall, and charged them, upon which they went off, and I took the opportunity of entering the farm by a side door in the lane.

Although Woodford was the senior officer at Hougoumont, he declined to exercise his prerogative to command, permitting regimental comrade **James Macdonell** to remain in charge. His letter continues:

> there was much *tiraillerie*, some cannon and howitzer shots . . .
> The *tirailleurs* on the rising ground along the eastern hedge never distinctly showed themselves, though they annoyed us very much by firing at the door which communicated between the courtyard and garden, and of which they could see the top. Several cannon shots went into the centre of the building, where some wounded officers were lying.

About 3 p.m. the howitzer Woodford refers to – deployed in the wood immediately south of the château around 1.30 p.m. – was still in action, despite attempts by **Saltoun**'s light troops to silence it. Around this time, Woodford notes that 'a shell or carcass was thrown into the great barn, and smoke and flames burst out in a most terrific manner, and communicated with rapidity to the other outbuildings'. According to Private **Clay** (1853) of the 3rd Guards:

> The fire unobstructed continued its ravages, and having been unnoticed by us in the eagerness of the conflict, destroyed many of the buildings, where (in the early part of the action) many of the helpless wounded of both armies had been placed for security.

This fact was not lost on Woodford, who recalled:

> The heat and smoke of the conflagration were very difficult to bear. Several men were burnt, as neither Colonel MacDonell nor myself could penetrate to the stables where the wounded had been carried.

Observing the smoke and flames, Wellington ordered the garrison to hold on as long as possible, but not to endanger life needlessly. According to Woodford:

> Some officers attempting to penetrate into the stables to rescue some wounded men, were obliged to desist, from the suffocation of the smoke, and several men perished. The flames, as is well known, stopped at the little chapel.

But not just at the chapel: at the very feet of the life-sized figure of Christ suspended above the door. A fact confirmed by G.D. Standen,

415

an ensign in the 3rd Foot Guards, again quoted by Siborne (1891): 'The anecdote of the fire burning only to the foot of the Cross is perfectly true, which in so superstitious a country made a great sensation.' Indeed it did, for, as Elizabeth Longford (1969) states: 'Hougoumont had received such a terrible visitation at 3 p.m. that the peasants universally believed that it was saved by a miracle.' Or perhaps by sheer bravery and tenacity, for as veteran Coldstreamer Daniel Mackinnon (1833) states, Woodford and his 'Gentlemen's Sons' of the British foot guards (aided by Nassauers, Lünebergers and Hanoverians), 'maintained the post amidst the terrible conflagration within, and the murderous fire of the enemy from without'.

Next morning, Hougoumont was a smouldering ruin. It was visited by Captain **Mercer** of the Royal Horse Artillery, who recorded (1927) the following, memorable description:

> The immediate neighbourhood of Hougoumont was more thickly strewn with corpses than most other parts of the field – the very ditches were full of them. The trees all about were most woefully cut and splintered, both by cannon-shot and musketry. The courts of the chateau presented a spectacle more terrible even than any I had yet seen. A large barn had been set on fire, and the conflagration had spread to the offices, and even to the main building. Here numbers, both of French and English, had perished in the flames, and their blackened swollen remains lay scattered about in all directions. Amongst this heap of ruins and misery many poor devils yet remained alive, and were sitting up endeavouring to bandage their wounds. Such a scene of horror, and one so sickening, was surely never witnessed.

According to Julian Paget and Derek Saunders (1992), the wreck of the château was sold shortly after the battle to a Count François de Robiano for 40,000 francs. Today, the chapel (still a consecrated church), the gardener's house and the south gate are all that survive of the original building. Sadly, as historian Mark Adkin (2001) informs us, the lower right leg of the miracle-working figure has disappeared: broken off and stolen by trophy-hunters.

Ziethen
Lieutenant General Hans Ernst Karl, Count von (1770–1848)

Commander of **Blücher**'s I Corps in the Waterloo campaign. A veteran of the monster 'Battle of the Nations' at Leipzig in 1813, Ziethen took the field in 1815 as one of Prussia's top generals. His I Corps took the brunt of **Napoleon**'s advance into Belgium on 15 June, General **Bourmont** of Napoleon's 14th Infantry Division having already presented the Prussian general with the Emperor's plan of campaign. Next day, Ziethen's corps was in the thick of the fighting at Ligny, and afterwards retired north on Wavre with the rest of Blücher's defeated army.

In the early morning of 18 June – having already lost some 40 per cent of its strength in the first three days of the campaign – Ziethen's corps set off west from Wavre to link with **Wellington**'s left wing at Waterloo (**Bülow** and **Pirch** taking the south-westerly route to Plancenoit on Napoleon's extreme right, while **Thielemann** remained at Wavre to check the advance of **Grouchy**). About 6 p.m. Ziethen's advance guard reached the village of Ohain, some 9 miles from Wavre and 3 miles from Wellington. Despite appeals by **Fremantle**, Wellington's aide-de-camp, Ziethen refused to budge further until his whole corps had formed up. Ziethen has been criticised by British commentators ever since, but his apologists point out that he was merely following the military textbook of the day. But worse was to come. One of Ziethen's staff officers – apparently mistaking the movements of wounded, deserters and prisoners – reported that Wellington was in full retreat. Consequently, Ziethen turned the head of his column about and began marching away from the hard-pressed Wellington to join Bülow in the battle for Plancenoit. Only the timely arrival of Baron **von Müffling**, Wellington's Prussian liaison officer, retrieved the debacle, setting Ziethen back on course for Mont St Jean.

And so, at about 7.30 p.m., advanced elements of Ziethen's corps – perhaps 4,500 men – emerged near Wellington's left flank, in the vicinity of Smohain, La Haie and Papelotte. According to historian E.F. Henderson (1911):

> There was an unfortunate moment when Ziethen, taking some of the Duke's own Nassau soldiers for the enemy, fired into their midst and drove them from the village of Smohain in such a panic that they had gone a quarter of a mile before the error could be explained. Ziethen's advance from this unexpected quarter . . . was the last straw that broke Napoleon's resistance.

In fact, Ziethen's approach had already been spotted by Napoleon, who is reputed to have sent his aide-de-camp, **Labédoyère**, to spread the false rumour that Grouchy's reinforcements were arriving – the Emperor's idea being to stiffen morale long enough for the Imperial Guard to smash Wellington's centre. But Ziethen's deployment, with that of Bülow and Pirch, brought the total number of Prussians engaged in the battle to about 50,000, leaving the French hopelessly outnumbered. The historian Hilaire Belloc (1931) describes the impact of Ziethen's arrival from Napoleon's viewpoint:

> At the far end of the long ridge of Mont St Jean, more than a mile away, this last great body and newest reinforcement of the Emperor's foes had emerged from the walls and thickets of Smohain and, new to the fighting, was already pushing in the weary French line that had stood the carnage of six hours.

Although some British pundits have played down Ziethen's contribution, his arrival on Wellington's left wing allowed troops from that sector (including the cavalry brigades of **Vandeleur** and **Vivian**) to reinforce the Allied centre – a crucial factor in resisting Napoleon's last-ditch attempts to force a breakthrough. Furthermore, Ziethen's appearance had a huge psychological impact on the French, who threw in the towel less than an hour later, following the abortive assault on Mont St Jean by elements of the Imperial Guard. Finally, in the words of historian Peter Hofschroer (1999): 'Once the French line began to disintegrate . . . Ziethen's Reserve Cavalry started to move up . . . with the battle won, Ziethen alone took over the pursuit.'

Appendix I

Chronology of major political events

1814   **6 April** Napoleon abdicates for the first time.

3 May Louis XVIII enters Paris to reclaim the Bourbon throne.

4 May Napoleon is exiled to the Mediterranean isle of Elba.

30 May The Treaty of Paris concludes 22 years of war between Europe and France.

21 June The Allies declare their intention to cement Catholic Belgium to Protestant Holland in the United Kingdom of the Netherlands.

1 November The Congress of Vienna opens to redraw the map of Napoleonic Europe.

1815   **26 February** Napoleon escapes from Elba.

1 March Napoleon lands in the South of France in a bid to regain power.

16 March Prince William Frederick of the House of Orange-Nassau is proclaimed King William I of the Netherlands. His eldest son, William, is proclaimed hereditary Prince of Orange.

20 March Napoleon enters Paris in triumph as Louis XVIII and his court flee to Belgium.

25 March Europe rallies against Napoleon, declaring him an outlaw and forming the Seventh Coalition.

4 April Wellington arrives at Brussels to take command of Allied forces preparing for war with Napoleon.

12 June Napoleon leaves Paris for France's north-eastern frontier as his 'Army of the North' prepares to march on Brussels.

15 June Napoleon crosses the Sambre and enters Charleroi.

16 June Napoleon defeats Blücher at Ligny, while Marshal Ney fails to crush Wellington at Quatre-Bras. As a result, Blücher retreats north to Wavre, while Wellington retires on Mont St Jean, several miles south of Brussels and Waterloo.

18 June Napoleon is defeated at Waterloo by Wellington and Blücher, while Marshal Grouchy battles Thielemann's Prussians at Wavre.

19 June Wavre finally falls to Grouchy, but news of Waterloo obliges the French Marshal to retreat.

22 June Napoleon abdicates for the second time.

7 July The Allies re-enter Paris.

15 July Napoleon surrenders to Captain Maitland of HMS *Bellerophon*.

7 August Napoleon is transported to the South Atlantic isle of St Helena.

20 November The Second Treaty of Paris finally concludes a lasting European peace.

7 December Marshal Ney is executed by the Bourbons for treason.

1821   **21 May** Napoleon dies at St Helena.

1840   **15 December** Napoleon's body is interred in Les Invalides in Paris.

Appendix II

Chronology of the Waterloo campaign

According to Ensign William Leeke (1866) of the 52nd Foot:

> It is very difficult to calculate time during the progress of a battle; one officer told me that the whole action only appeared to him to last two hours, whereas it commenced exactly at twelve o'clock at noon, and lasted till a quarter after nine at night.

In fact, eyewitness accounts of the Battle of Waterloo differ widely when it comes to the timing of events. For a start, there was no such thing as standard time in 1815. Instead, people went by solar time, setting clocks and watches when the sun reached its highest point in the sky and pronouncing this 'noon'. Needless to say, the precise occurrence of 'noon' varied according to location: if officers on campaign failed to allow for this, their watches would become increasingly inaccurate as the miles passed on the march. At Waterloo it is clear British officers had not synchronised their watches, survivors quoting anywhere between 10 a.m. and 1.30 p.m. as the hour at which the battle began. And with no official journal of the day's events to act as a chronological guide, we are left with the personal recollections of individuals apparently equipped with faulty timepieces. In the table that follows, then, times given are necessarily approximate.

15 June **3 a.m.** Napoleon's 'Army of the North' crosses the Sambre at Charleroi.

3 p.m. Having evicted Ziethen's Prussians from Charleroi, Napoleon gives Marshal Ney command of his left wing, with orders to secure Quatre-Bras, the vital crossroads linking the armies of Wellington and Blücher.

5 p.m. At Brussels, Wellington is informed that French troops have attacked Prussian outposts along the Sambre.

10 p.m. Wellington, still at Brussels, is unsure where Napoleon's main blow will land. He attends the Duchess of Richmond's ball but puts his Anglo-Netherlands army on high alert, forbidding any concentration east of Nivelles.

12 p.m. At the ball Wellington receives word that General Perponcher – having disobeyed instructions – has gathered Netherlands troops east of Nivelles at Quatre-Bras, which he is holding against superior French forces. Wellington orders the army to march on Quatre-Bras.

16 June **7 a.m.** The Prince of Orange arrives at Quatre-Bras to reinforce Perponcher.

9.30 a.m. Wellington arrives at Quatre-Bras but finds Ney's French troops quietly cooking. The Duke takes this opportunity to visit Blücher.

Noon Wellington and Blücher meet at Brye. The Duke promises to aid the Prussians unless attacked, then returns to Quatre-Bras.

2 p.m. Ney attacks in earnest at Quatre-Bras.

2.30 p.m. Napoleon attacks Blücher at Ligny.

4 p.m. Ney's advance at Quatre-Bras is checked by the arrival of Picton's division.

6 p.m. D'Erlon's corps – supposedly marching to support Ney at Quatre-Bras – unexpectedly appears at Ligny, causing panic among Napoleon's troops and temporarily halting French operations.

7 p.m. D'Erlon fails to deploy at Ligny, then – apparently responding to a recall order from Ney – turns round and marches back to Quatre-Bras. Napoleon, outnumbered by Blücher, deploys the Imperial Guard.

8.30 p.m. Napoleon pierces the Prussian centre at Ligny. Blücher falls from his horse, and command of the Prussian Army temporarily passes to Gneisenau.

9 p.m. Napoleon is victorious at Ligny but the Prussians, untroubled by effective pursuit, retreat unmolested. The Emperor assumes Blücher will head east along his line of communication with Germany, but Gneisenau orders a northerly withdrawal on Wavre, which Blücher later confirms.

Fighting ceases at Quatre-Bras with both sides occupying their original positions.

17 June **7 a.m.** At Quatre-Bras, Wellington receives news of Blücher's retreat on Wavre. The Duke announces his decision to retire on Mont St Jean, south of Brussels and Waterloo: there he will make a stand, providing Blücher can offer support.

9.30 a.m. Napoleon inspects the Ligny battlefield.

10.30 a.m. Wellington begins his withdrawal from Quatre-Bras.

11 a.m. Napoleon, still at Ligny, sends Marshal Grouchy with over 30,000 troops to pursue Blücher.

1 p.m. Grouchy begins his pursuit of Blücher, unsure of which route to follow.

2.30 p.m. Napoleon arrives at Quatre-Bras, amid a thunderstorm, to find the place held by Wellington's cavalry, while Ney's troops settle down to lunch.

3 p.m. Wellington receives confirmation of Blücher's support for a stand at Mont St Jean.

Grouchy receives word of Blücher's line of retreat and marches on Gembloux.

5 p.m. Wellington's army takes post on the ridge of Mont St Jean. The Duke garrisons the château of Hougoumont and the farm of La Haie Sainte.

6.30 p.m. Napoleon's advance guard reaches the farm and inn of La Belle Alliance on the southern heights of the Waterloo battlefield.

Across the valley, Wellington's troops have taken post.

10 p.m. Having arrived at Gembloux, Grouchy sends word to Napoleon announcing his intention of marching north on Wavre next day.

11 p.m. Blücher's army concentrates at Wavre and prepares to march to Wellington's aid at dawn.

18 June 1 a.m. Napoleon sets up his headquarters at the farm of Le Caillou, on the southern edge of the Waterloo battlefield.

3 a.m. Wellington sets up his headquarters at the village of Waterloo. There he receives confirmation of Blücher's support.

4 a.m. Napoleon plans to attack Wellington at 6 a.m. as the torrential rain of the previous night's storm finally ceases.

Blücher's Prussians break camp at Wavre and begin an arduous cross-country march to the Waterloo battlefield.

5 a.m. Nassau and Hanoverian troops relieve the British foot guards in Hougoumont's orchard.

6 a.m. With his army still arriving on the battlefield, Napoleon postpones his attack on Wellington until 9 a.m.

Wellington quits his HQ for the front line at Mont St Jean.

7 a.m. Wellington inspects Hougoumont.

8 a.m. At Gembloux, Grouchy's march on Wavre hits setbacks and delays caused by sodden ground and a lack of good roads.

Nassauers and Hanoverians advance from Hougoumont's orchard to occupy the wood facing the French.

At Le Caillou, Napoleon breakfasts with his generals, dismissing Wellington as a 'bad general' and the British as 'bad troops'.

Soldiers of the 1/2nd Nassau Regiment reinforce the garrison at Hougoumont.

9 a.m. Napoleon arrives at La Belle Alliance, his forward command post. The Emperor's troops are still assembling, so battle is postponed until 11 a.m. Across the valley, on the opposite ridge, Wellington completes his deployment.

10 a.m. Napoleon dictates his plan of attack: d'Erlon is to secure the ridge of Mont St Jean prior to a march on Brussels. The Emperor then drafts an order to Grouchy, informing the Marshal that his proposed march on Wavre is 'conformable to His Majesty's wishes'.

At Sart-les-Walhain, Grouchy stops for breakfast en route for Wavre. He sends word to Napoleon, confirming the march on Wavre.

11 a.m. At La Belle Alliance, Napoleon postpones d'Erlon's attack until 1 p.m. To boost morale and kill time, the Emperor holds a grand review of his army.

11.30 a.m. As Napoleon's Imperial Guard forms up, the Emperor orders a bombardment of Wellington's line. This is quickly followed by the first French attack on Hougoumont.

With Napoleon's intentions now apparent, Baron Müffling, Wellington's Prussian liaison officer, sends word to Blücher requesting urgent support. According to a prearranged plan, Bülow and Pirch will march on Napoleon's right-rear, while Ziethen will reinforce Wellington, arriving on the Duke's left flank. Thielemann will remain at Wavre to oppose Grouchy.

At Sart-les-Walhain, Grouchy hears the guns of Waterloo, but despite strong objections from his subordinates, decides to continue the advance on Wavre.

Noon At Hougoumont, the French launch a second assault. MacDonnell closes the great north gate.

At Mont St Jean, General Perponcher orders van Bijlandt's Netherlands brigade – isolated and exposed to gunfire on the forward slope of Wellington's ridge – to retire on Picton's division.

At St Lambert, French hussars capture a Prussian horseman from Bülow's advance guard, who tells of the Prussian approach.

1 p.m. At Hougoumont, a third French attack is launched. A howitzer is brought up to shell the château.

At Rossomme, Napoleon spots Bülow's Prussian on his distant right. The Emperor sends cavalry under Domon and Subervie to reconnoitre his right flank, and drafts another order to Grouchy, informing the Marshal of this development and bidding him 'not to lose a moment in drawing near to us, and effecting a junction with us, in order to crush Bülow'.

1.30 p.m. D'Erlon's attack on Wellington's left-centre is launched, supported by cavalry under Travers and Dubois.

1.45 p.m. At Hougoumont, Lord Saltoun launches an abortive bid to silence the French howitzer.

D'Erlon's columns close on Picton's sector of Wellington's line. The French assault is held and then repulsed. Picton is killed.

2 p.m. At Hougoumont, a fourth French attack, led by Foy, is launched. Wellington reinforces the garrison and the orchard is secured once more.

Cuirassiers under Travers and Dubois push beyond La Haie Sainte in support of d'Erlon's infantry. Uxbridge launches the Household and Union Brigades in a devastating cavalry attack on d'Erlon's infantry. The Eagles of the French 45th and 105th Regiments are captured.

Leading elements of Grouchy's force reach Baraque, 2 miles from Wavre, where Thielemann's Prussians guard the line of the River Dyle.

2.15 p.m. Uxbridge's Household and Union Brigades career out of control and charge the French lines, including Napoleon's grand battery. They are counter-charged and badly mauled by 20 squadrons of French cavalry. Sir William Ponsonby is killed.

2.30 p.m. At Hougoumont, a fifth French assault, led by Bachelu and Foy, approaches from the south-east. The attack is broken up by Allied artillery fire.

3 p.m. Bülow's Prussian corps begins its passage of the Bois de Paris.

At Hougoumont, the château is set on fire by French incendiary shells.

At La Haie Sainte, Baring's garrison beats off a French attack, which fails to penetrate the farm complex.

Napoleon returns to his rear headquarters at Le Caillou – to dictate dispatches announcing victory according to some, to have his piles treated according to others. Marshal Ney is in effective control of the battle against Wellington.

At Mont St Jean, Chassé's Netherlanders arrive at new positions on the Nivelles road. Mercer's G Troop, RHA, advances in support of the Brunswick infantry.

4 p.m. Bülow's Prussians emerge from the Bois de Paris at Frischermont on Napoleon's right flank. Skirmishing begins with the outposts of Lobau's VI Corps.

Ney apparently mistakes the movement of wounded, prisoners and deserters to Wellington's rear for a general retreat and orders a cavalry assault.

Grouchy arrives at Wavre. He receives Napoleon's orders of 10 a.m., informing him to 'direct his movements on Wavre' and concludes he has acted correctly.

4.30 p.m. Blücher arrives at the rear of Bülow's corps, ordering an immediate attack in support of Wellington.

5 p.m. Baring's garrison is running out of ammunition at La Haie Sainte, despite pleas for a replenishment.

Bülow, with only half his corps assembled, obeys Blücher's order to attack, pushing Lobau back on the village of Plancenoit.

5.30 p.m. Ney commits his whole cavalry force against Wellington but without success. Reille's infantry provides belated support but is repulsed.

Bülow launches some 6,000 troops against Plancenoit and evicts the French defenders. Napoleon sends Duhesme's Young Guard to retrieve the situation.

6 p.m. Ney's cavalry attacks cease, to be replaced by a heavy cannonade from Napoleon's grand battery.

At Plancenoit, Duhesme's Young Guard retakes the village. To the north, Lobau's VI Corps holds its ground.

6.30 p.m. La Haie Sainte is successfully stormed by the French as Baring is obliged to evacuate for want of bullets. Ney, eager to exploit this success, requests reinforcements from Napoleon, but the Emperor's reserves are occupied with Bülow's Prussians at Plancenoit.

6.45 p.m. Ompteda's brigade is launched into a doomed counter-attack to retake La Haie Sainte. Casualties are high, leaving a gaping hole in Wellington's centre.

7 p.m. Wellington reinforces his line with Brunswick and Chassé's Netherlanders.

Ziethen's I Corps arrives at Papelotte on Wellington's left flank, bringing the total number of Prussians committed to over 30,000.

Observing Ziethen's approach, Napoleon spreads the false news that Grouchy has arrived.

At Wavre, Grouchy is still embattled with Thielemann. He receives Napoleon's orders of 1 p.m., informing him of the Battle of Waterloo, of Bülow's appearance on his right flank, and directing him to march on the Emperor's right flank. But it is now too late for Grouchy to obey.

7.30 p.m. Bülow launches yet another ferocious assault on Plancenoit, having received reinforcements. Perhaps as many as 50,000 Prussians are now fighting in the Waterloo area.

Napoleon decides to throw 3,500 infantrymen from his Imperial Guard at Wellington, in an effort to pierce the Duke's centre.

8 p.m. Napoleon's Guard is repulsed by Wellington. Ziethen and Bülow bite into the French right flank. French morale collapses, and the Duke orders a general advance.

8.30 p.m. Wellington's advance gains momentum as Napoleon's army evacuates the battlefield, some units conducting an orderly retreat, others fleeing up the Charleroi road in a rabble.

9 p.m. Bülow finally secures Plancenoit, scene of the day's bitterest fighting.

9.30 p.m. As the sun sets, Prussian troops threaten to cut Napoleon's line of retreat. The Old Guard makes a last stand as the Emperor quits the field, making for Philippeville via Genappe and Charleroi.

10 p.m. Wellington and Blücher meet at or near La Belle Alliance and agree the Prussians should pursue Napoleon's fugitive army.

10.45 p.m. Wellington arrives at his headquarters in the village of Waterloo.

11 p.m. Grouchy finally overwhelms Thielemann's Prussians at Wavre, ignorant of Napoleon's defeat at Waterloo.

Midnight At Waterloo village Wellington is joined by Prussian liaison officer, Baron Müffling, who tells of a ruthless pursuit conducted by Gneisenau.

19 June **4 a.m.** Napoleon crosses the Sambre at Charleroi.

Noon Prussians enter Charleroi.

21 June **7 a.m.** Napoleon arrives in Paris. The following day the Emperor abdicates for the second and final time.

Appendix III

Order of battle: Napoleon's Army of the North

The following is an attempt to list the units that comprised Napoleon's forces at Waterloo. It is not – and perhaps cannot be – definitive, as much confusion is apparent in secondary sources. For example: some sources list the 7th Infantry Division of II Corps as present at the battle, others do not (likewise with the 40th and 47th Line Regiments); some sources refer to the 51st Line, others the 31st Line; the units that made up the four reserve cavalry corps – and their whereabouts – is also a matter of debate; while a question mark apparently hangs over the leadership of the 13th Cavalry Division: Watier or St-Alphonse? And so on . . .

Napoleon began the campaign with some 116,000 troops. About 8,000 were lost at Ligny on 16 June 1815, a further 30,000 being detached to chase the vanquished Prussians (Vandamme's III Corps, Gérard's IV Corps and Exelmans's II Reserve Cavalry Corps). This leaves an approximate figure of 78,000 soldiers at Waterloo, apparently supported by some 250 guns.

Records do not exist for Napoleon's Waterloo casualties, but it has been speculated that the Emperor lost over 40 per cent of his army in 'missing' (i.e. deserters), prisoners, wounded and killed.

Army of the North

Commander-in-Chief: The Emperor Napoleon I

I Corps: General Drouet, Count d'Erlon

- 1st Infantry Division: General Allix
  - 1st Brigade: 54th Line and 55th Line
  - 2nd Brigade: 28th Line and 105th Line

- 2nd Infantry Division: Baron Donzelot
  - 1st Brigade: 13th Light and 17th Line
  - 2nd Brigade: 19th Line and 51st (31st?) Line
- 3rd Infantry Division: Baron Marcognet
  - 1st Brigade: 21st Line and 46th Line
  - 2nd Brigade: 25th Line and 45th Line
- 4th Infantry Division: General Durutte
  - 1st Brigade: 8th Line and 29th Line
  - 2nd Brigade: 85th Line and 95th Line
- 1st Cavalry Division: General Baron Jacquinot
  - 1st Brigade: 7th Hussars and 3rd Chasseurs à Cheval
  - 2nd Brigade: 3rd Lancers and 4th Lancers
- Corps Artillery: five foot batteries, one horse battery, Engineers

II Corps: General Count Reille

- 5th Infantry Division: General Baron Bachelu
  - 1st Brigade: 3rd Line (2nd Light?) and 61st Line
  - 2nd Brigade: 72nd Line and 108th Line
- 6th Infantry Division: Jérôme Bonaparte
  - 1st Brigade: 1st Light and 2nd Light (3rd Line?)
  - 2nd Brigade: 1st Line and 2nd Line
- 7th Infantry Division: General Baron Girard
  - 1st Brigade: 11th Light and 82nd Line
  - 2nd Brigade: 12th Light and 4th Line
- 9th Infantry Division: General Foy
  - 1st Brigade: 92nd Line and 93rd Line
  - 2nd Brigade: 4th Light and 100th Line
- 2nd Cavalry Division: General Count Piré
  - 1st Brigade: 1st Chasseurs à Cheval and 6th Chasseurs à Cheval
  - 2nd Brigade: 5th Lancers and 6th Lancers
- Corps Artillery: five foot batteries, one horse battery, Engineers

III Corps: General Count Vandamme (not present at Waterloo)

IV Corps: General Baron Gérard (not present at Waterloo)

VI Corps: General Count Lobau

- 19th Infantry Division: General Baron Simmer
  - 1st Brigade: 5th Line and 11th Line
  - 2nd Brigade: 27th Line and 84th Line
- 20th Infantry Division: General Baron Jeanin
  - 1st Brigade: 5th Light and 10th Line
  - 2nd Brigade: 107th Line (47th Line not present at Waterloo)

- 21st Infantry Division: General Baron Teste
  - 1st Brigade: 8th Light (40th Line not present at Waterloo)
  - 2nd Brigade: 65th Line and 75th Line
- 3rd Cavalry Division: General Baron Domon (attached from III Corps?)
  - 1st Brigade: 4th Chasseurs à Cheval and 9th Chasseurs à Cheval
  - 2nd Brigade: 12th Chasseurs à Cheval
- Corps Artillery: four foot batteries, one horse battery, Engineers

I Reserve Cavalry Corps: General Count Pajol

- 4th Cavalry Division: General Baron Soult
  - 1st Brigade: 1st Hussars and 4th Hussars
  - 2nd Brigade: 5th Hussars
- 5th Cavalry Division: General Baron Subervie
  - 1st Brigade: 1st Lancers and 2nd Lancers
  - 2nd Brigade: 11th Chasseurs à Cheval
- Corps Artillery: two horse batteries

II Reserve Cavalry Corps: General Count Exelmans (not present at Waterloo)

III Reserve Cavalry Corps: General Count Kellermann

- 11th Cavalry Division: General Baron L'Héritier
  - 1st Brigade: 2nd Dragoons and 7th Dragoons
  - 2nd Brigade: 8th Cuirassiers and 11th Cuirassiers
- 12th Cavalry Division: General Baron d'Hurbal
  - 1st Brigade: 1st Carabiniers and 2nd Carabiniers
  - 2nd Brigade: 2nd Cuirassiers and 3rd Cuirassiers
- Corps Artillery: two horse batteries

IV Reserve Cavalry Corps: General Count Milhaud

- 13th Cavalry Division: General Watier? General St-Alphonse?
  - 1st Brigade: 1st Cuirassiers and 4th Cuirassiers
  - 2nd Brigade: 7th Cuirassiers and 12th Cuirassiers
- 14th Cavalry Division: General Baron Delort
  - 1st Brigade: 5th Cuirassiers and 10th Cuirassiers
  - 2nd Brigade: 6th Cuirassiers and 9th Cuirassiers
- Corps Artillery: two horse batteries

Imperial Guard: General Count Drouot

- Grenadier Division: General Count Friant
  - Old Guard: 1st Grenadiers and 2nd Grenadiers
  - Middle Guard: 3rd Grenadiers and 4th Grenadiers

- Chasseur Division: General Morand
  - Old Guard: 1st Chasseurs à Pied and 2nd Chasseurs à Pied
  - Middle Guard: 3rd Chasseurs à Pied and 4th Chasseurs à Pied
- Young Guard Division: General Count Duhesme
  - 1st Division: 1st Tirailleurs and 1st Voltigeurs
  - 2nd Division: 3rd Tirailleurs and 3rd Voltigeurs
- Imperial Light Cavalry Division: General Count Lefebvre-Desnouettes
  - Chasseurs à Cheval
  - 2nd Chevaux-Légers Lanciers (Red Lancers)
- Imperial Heavy Cavalry Division: General Count Guyot
  - Grenadiers à Cheval
  - The Empress's Dragoons
  - Gendarmerie d'Élite
- Artillery Reserve: four foot batteries

As stated above, Vandamme's III Corps, Gérard's IV Corps, and Exelmans's II Reserve Cavalry Corps were not present at Waterloo, being engaged against the rearguard of Blücher's army at Wavre on 18 June 1815.

Sources

Adkin, Mark, *Waterloo Companion*, London 2001

Haythornthwaite, Philip, Cassin-Scott, Jack and Chappell, Michael, *Uniforms of Waterloo*, London 1974

Holmes, Richard, *Army Battlefield Guide: Belgium and Northern France*, London 1995

Siborne, Captain W., *History of the War in France and Belgium in 1815*, London 1848

Wootten, Geoffrey, *Waterloo 1815*, Oxford 1992

Appendix IV

Order of battle: Blücher's Army of the Lower Rhine

The following is a rough outline of Prussian forces at Waterloo: however, numbers quoted in secondary sources vary so wildly, a precise breakdown is almost impossible.

Blücher began the campaign with perhaps 130,000 men. Over half were regulars, the remainder militia or *Landwehr*. Some 20,000 were lost on 16 June 1815 at the Battle of Ligny, with a further 10,000 deserting on the retreat to Wavre. Thus, on 18 June, Blücher had around 100,000 men. Although most of this force set off for Waterloo, only 50,000 made it in time to join the battle: the rest were either struggling to catch up or embattled at Wavre, where Thielemann's III Corps held Marshal Grouchy at bay.

In fact, Bülow's command was the only Prussian corps to fight in its entirety at Waterloo, debouching from the Bois de Paris on Napoleon's right flank shortly after 4 p.m. Bülow was reinforced by leading elements of Pirch I's II Corps two or three hours later. The advance guard of Ziethen's I Corps arrived on Wellington's left flank around 7 p.m., the final Prussian troops to pitch into the French. Thus, Blücher's army arrived in packets: by 4.30 p.m. he had about 16,000 troops and 60 guns in action; by 6.30 p.m. this force had doubled; and by 7.30 p.m. 50,000 were committed, aided by over 100 guns. In all, Blücher sustained some 7,000 casualties at Waterloo: half as many as Wellington. But the Prussian intervention was decisive, as explained by H.T. Parker (1944): 'From the time the Prussians appeared within the field of observation, Napoleon was fighting two battles, an offensive one against Wellington, a defensive one against Blücher.'

Army of the Lower Rhine

Commander-in-Chief: Field Marshal Gebhard Leberecht von Blücher

I Corps: Lieutenant General Count von Ziethen
- 1st Infantry Brigade: Major General von Steinmetz
- 1st Cavalry Brigade: Major General von Treskow

II Corps: Major General von Pirch I
- 5th Infantry Brigade: Major General Count von Tippelskirch
- 6th Infantry Brigade: Major General von Krafft
- 7th Infantry Brigade: Major General von Brause
- 2nd Cavalry Brigade: Lieutenant Colonel von Sohr

IV Corps: General Baron von Bülow
- 13th Infantry Brigade: Lieutenant General von Hake
- 14th Infantry Brigade: Major General von Ryssel
- 15th Infantry Brigade: Major General von Losthin
- 16th Infantry Brigade: Colonel Hiller von Gartringen
- 1st Cavalry Brigade: Colonel Count von Schwerin
- 2nd Cavalry Brigade: Lieutenant Colonel von Watzdorff
- 3rd Cavalry Brigade: Major General von Sydow
- Artillery Reserve: Major General von Braun

As stated above, the remaining Prussian units, including Thielemann's III Corps, were either fighting at Wavre on 18 June or en route for the Waterloo battlefield.

Sources

Adkin, Mark, *Waterloo Companion*, London 2001

Haythornthwaite, Philip, Cassin-Scott, Jack and Chappell, Michael, *Uniforms of Waterloo*, London 1974

Holmes, Richard, *Army Battlefield Guide: Belgium and Northern France*, London 1995

Siborne, Captain W., *History of the War in France and Belgium in 1815*, London 1848

Wootten, Geoffrey, *Waterloo 1815*, Oxford 1992

Appendix V

Order of battle: Wellington's Army of the Low Countries

Wellington's Anglo-Allied force numbered over 100,000 in total, but only 67,000–73,000 served at Waterloo (estimates vary – see Adkin 2001, pp. 36–7). The remainder – largely consisting of Colville's 4th British Infantry Division and Prince Frederick's Netherlands Corps – were strategically placed to guard the Duke's right flank, his rear depots, and his communications with the coast. Of the Waterloo army, about 70 per cent were foot soldiers, 25 per cent cavalrymen, and 5 per cent artillerymen or support services. Roughly speaking, about one-third of Wellington's troops were British, one-third ethnic Germans (including the 8,000 men of the King's German Legion), and one-third Dutch-Belgian. Although frequently described as 'raw recruits', Wellington's 'infamous army' of legend contained plenty of veterans: perhaps as many as 50 per cent. Wellington's force was augmented by 157 guns. Total Waterloo losses were perhaps 15,000.

Army of the Low Countries

Commander-in-Chief: The Duke of Wellington

I Corps: HRH The Prince of Orange
- 1st British Infantry (Guards) Division: Major General George Cooke
  - 1st Brigade (2/1st Foot Guards, 3/1st Foot Guards): Major General Peregrine Maitland
  - 2nd Brigade (2/2nd Foot Guards, 2/3rd Foot Guards): Major General Sir John Byng
  - Artillery (Sandham's Battery, Kuhlmann's Troop): Lieutenant Colonel S.G. Adye
- 3rd British Infantry Division: Lieutenant General Sir Charles Alten
  - 5th British Brigade (2/30th Foot, 33rd Foot, 2/69th Foot, 2/73rd Foot): Major General Sir Colin Halkett

- 2nd KGL Brigade (1st Light Btn, 2nd Light Btn, 5th Line Btn, 8th Line Btn): Colonel Baron C. Ompteda
- 1st Hanoverian Brigade (Osnabrück, Grubenhagen, Bremen, Verden, Lüneberg Field Btns): Major General Count Kielmansegge
- Artillery (Lloyd's and Cleeves's Batteries): Lieutenant Colonel J.S. Williamson

• 2nd Netherlands Infantry Division: Lieutenant General Baron Perponcher-Sedlnitzky
- 1st Brigade (27th Dutch Jäger, 7th Belgian Line, 5th Dutch Militia, 7th Dutch Militia, 8th Dutch Militia): Major General Count W.F. van Bijlandt
- 2nd Brigade (2nd Nassau Regiment, Regiment of Orange–Nassau): HSH Prince Bernard of Saxe-Weimar
- Artillery (van Bijleveld's and Stievenart's Batteries): Major van Opstall

• 3rd Netherlands Infantry Division: Lieutenant General Baron Chassé
- 1st Brigade (35th Belgian Jäger, 2nd Dutch Line, 4th Dutch Militia, 6th Dutch Militia, 17th Dutch Militia, 19th Dutch Militia): Colonel H. Detmers
- 2nd Brigade (36th Belgian Jäger, 3rd Belgian Line, 12th Dutch Line, 13th Dutch Line, 3rd Dutch Militia, 10th Dutch Militia): Major General A.K.J.G. d'Aubremé
- Artillery (Krahmer's and Lux's Batteries): Major J.L.D. van der Smissen

II Corps: Lieutenant General Lord Hill

• 2nd British Infantry Division: Lieutenant General Sir Henry Clinton
- 3rd British Brigade (1/52nd Foot, 71st Foot, 2/95th Foot (Rifles), two companies 3/95th Foot (Rifles)): Major General F. Adam
- 1st KGL Brigade (1st Line Btn, 2nd Line Btn, 3rd Line Btn, 4th Line Btn): Colonel G.C.A. du Plat
- 3rd Hanoverian Brigade (Bremenvörde, Osnabrück, Quackenbrück, Salzgitter Landwehr Btns): Colonel Hew Halkett
- Artillery (Bolton's and Sympher's Troops): Lieutenant Colonel C. Gold

• 4th British Infantry Division: Lieutenant General Sir Charles Colville (not present at Waterloo)
- 4th British Brigade (3/14th Foot, 23rd Foot, 1/51st Foot): Lieutenant Colonel H.H. Mitchell
- 6th British Brigade* (2/35th Foot, 1/54th Foot, 2/59th Foot, 1/91st Foot): Major General Johnstone
- 5th Hanoverian Brigade* (Lauenberg Field Btn, Calenberg Field Btn, Nienberg Landwehr, Bentheim Landwehr, Hoya Landwehr): Major General Sir James Lyon
- Artillery (von Rettberg's and Brome's* Batteries): Lieutenant Colonel J. Hawker

• Netherlands Corps*: Prince Frederick of the Netherlands
- Indian Brigade: Lieutenant General C.H.W. Anthing
- 1st Netherlands Division: Lieutenant General J.A. Stedman
- Artillery (Riesz's and Wijnands's Batteries)

(* These units not present at Waterloo)

Reserve Corps: The Duke of Wellington

- 5th British Infantry Division: Lieutenant General Sir Thomas Picton
  - 8th British Brigade (28th Foot, 32nd Foot, 79th Foot, six companies 1/95th Foot (Rifles)): Major General Sir James Kempt
  - 9th British Brigade (3/1st Foot, 42nd Foot, 2/44th Foot, 92nd Foot): Major General Sir Denis Pack
  - 5th Hanoverian Briagde (Gifhorn Landwehr, Hameln Landwehr, Hildesheim Landwehr, Peine Landwehr): Colonel von Vincke
  - Artillery (Rogers' Troop and Braun's Battery)

- 6th British Infantry Division: Lieutenant General Sir Galbraith Lowry Cole (not present at Waterloo, replaced by Major General Sir John Lambert)
  - 10th British Brigade (1/4th Foot, 1/27th Foot, 1/40th Foot, 2/81 Foot*): Major General Sir John Lambert
  - 4th Hanoverian Brigade (Verden Landwehr, Lüneberg Landwehr, Munden Landwehr, Osterode Landwehr): Colonel C. Best

  (* These units not present at Waterloo)

- Brunswick Contingent: HSH The Duke of Brunswick (killed at Quatre-Bras, replaced by Colonel Olfermann)
  - Advance Guard Btn: Major von Rauschenplat
  - Light Infantry (Life Guard Btn, 1st Light Btn, 2nd Light Btn, 3rd Light Btn): Lieutenant Colonel von Buttlar
  - Line Infantry (1st Line Btn, 2nd Line Btn, 3rd Line Btn): Lieutenant Colonel von Specht
  - Cavalry (2nd Hussars, Lancers): attached to Uxbridge's Cavalry Corps (see below)
  - Artillery (von Heinemann's Troop and Moll's Battery): Major Mahn

- Nassau Contingent:
  - 1st Nassau Regiment (1st Btn and 2nd Btn plus Landwehr Btn): Major General A.H.E. von Kruse

- Reserve Artillery
  - A Troop, RHA: Lieutenant Colonel Sir H. Ross
  - D Troop, RHA: Major G. Beane
  - Morrison's Foot Battery*
  - Hutchesson's Foot Battery*
  - Ilbert's Foot Battery*

  (* These units not present at Waterloo)

Cavalry Corps: The Earl of Uxbridge

- 1st British (Household) Cavalry Brigade: Major General Lord Edward Somerset
  - 1st Life Guards
  - 2nd Life Guards
  - Royal Horse Guards
  - 1st Dragoon Guards

- 2nd British (Union) Cavalry Brigade: Major General Hon. Sir William Ponsonby
  - 1st (Royal) Dragoons
  - 2nd (Royal North British) Dragoons (Scots Greys)
  - 6th (Inniskilling) Dragoons

- 3rd British Cavalry Brigade: Major General Sir Wilhelm Dörnberg
  - 23rd Light Dragoons
  - 1st (KGL) Light Dragoons
  - 2nd (KGL) Light Dragoons

- 4th British Cavalry Brigade: Major General Sir John Vandeleur
  - 11th Light Dragoons
  - 12th Light Dragoons
  - 16th Light Dragoons

- 5th British Cavalry Brigade: Major General Sir Colquhoun Grant
  - 7th Hussars
  - 15th Hussars
  - 13th Light Dragoons
  - 2nd (KGL) Hussars

- 6th British Cavalry Brigade: Major General Sir Hussey Vivian
  - 10th Hussars
  - 18th Hussars
  - 1st (KGL) Hussars

- 7th British Cavalry Brigade: Lieutenant Colonel Sir F. Arentschildt
  - 13th Light Dragoons: attached to 5th British Cavalry Brigade (see above)
  - 3rd (KGL) Hussars

- Hanoverian Cavalry Brigade: Colonel Baron Estorff (not present at Waterloo)
  - Prince Regent's Hussars
  - Bremen and Verden Hussars
  - Duke of Cumberland's Hussars

- Royal Horse Artillery: Lieutenant Colonel A. MacDonald
  - E Troop: Lieutenant Colonel Sir R. Gardiner
  - F Troop: Lieutenant Colonel J. Webber-Smith
  - G Troop: Captain A.C. Mercer
  - H Troop: Major W.N. Ramsey
  - I Troop: Major R. Bull
  - O Troop (2nd Rocket Troop): Captain E.C. Whinyates

- Netherlands Cavalry Division: Lieutenant General Baron J.A. de Collaert
  - Heavy Brigade (1st Dutch Carabiniers, 2nd Belgian Carabiniers, 3rd Dutch Carabiniers): Major General A.D. Trip
  - 1st Light Brigade (4th Dutch Light Dragoons, 8th Belgian Hussars): Major General Baron C. de Ghingy
  - 2nd Light Brigade (6th Dutch Hussars, 5th Belgian Light Dragoons): Major General J.B. van Merlen
  - Artillery (Petter's and van Pittius's Troops)

- Brunswick Cavalry
  - Hussar Regiment
  - Lancer Regiment

Sources

Adkin, Mark, *Waterloo Companion*, London 2001

Haythornthwaite, Philip, Cassin-Scott, Jack and Chappell, Michael, *Uniforms of Waterloo*, London 1974

Holmes, Richard, *Army Battlefield Guide: Belgium and Northern France*, London 1995

Siborne, Captain W., *History of the War in France and Belgium in 1815*, London 1848

Wootten, Geoffrey, *Waterloo 1815*, Oxford 1992

Appendix VI

British Waterloo regiments: strengths and losses

According to Haythornthwaite (1974):

> It is difficult to determine exactly how many members of the British Army fought at Waterloo. The statistics published by William Siborne [1848] . . . are deceptive in that although taken from the 'morning state' of the army for 18 June . . . they do not show the grand total of each unit's personnel. Siborne lists only the rank and file, excluding sergeants, drummers, trumpeters and officers; yet he includes in the total men on detached duty ('on command') in the rear areas . . . and those wounded men unfit to take their place in the ranks but still carried on the regimental muster rolls.

This point is also noted by Mark Adkin (2001), who suggests the total of Wellington's Waterloo army may have been 'about 6,000 higher than many writers have suggested'.

The following table represents estimated strengths and losses for Wellington's British contingent at Waterloo, including the 8,000 Hanoverians of the King's German Legion. It is based on adjustments to Siborne's statistics suggested by Haythornthwaite (1999). That said, I would stress that these figures, like others quoted in this book, can only be considered approximate.

British Waterloo regiments: strengths and losses

Unit	Strength	Losses	Commander
Royal Artillery	5 259	303	Colonel Sir George Adam Wood
Royal Engineers	47	1	Lieutenant Colonel James Carmichael-Smyth

Royal Sappers & Miners	755	0	(As above)
Royal Waggon Train	301	0	Lieutenant Colonel Thomas Aird (?)
Royal Staff Corps	274	2	Lieutenant Colonel William Nicolay (?)
1st Life Guards	255	65	Lieutenant Colonel Samuel Ferrior (killed)
2nd Life Guards	235	155	Lieutenant Colonel Hon. Edward Lygon
Royal Horse Guards	277	98	Lieutenant Colonel Sir Robert Hill (wounded)
1st Dragoon Guards	583	275	Colonel William Fuller (killed)
1st Dragoons	435	194	Lieutenant Colonel Arthur Clifton
2nd Dragoons	444	199	Lieutenant Colonel James Hamilton (killed)
6th Dragoons	453	217	Lieutenant Colonel Joseph Muter (wounded)
7th Hussars	362	155	Colonel Sir Edward Kerrison
10th Hussars	478	94	Colonel George Quentin (wounded)
11th Light Dragoons	442	63	Lieutenant Colonel James Sleigh
12th Light Dragoons	430	111	Lieutenant Colonel Hon. Frederick Ponsonby (wounded)
13th Light Dragoons	455	117	Colonel Patrick Doherty
15th Hussars	450	82	Lieutenant Colonel Leighton Dalrymple (wounded)
16th Light Dragoons	440	36	Lieutenant Colonel James Hay (wounded)
18th Hussars	447	104	Lieutenant Colonel Hon. Henry Murray
23rd Light Dragoons	341	80	Colonel, the Earl of Portarlington
1st KGL Light Dragoons	540	153	Lieutenant Colonel John von Bülow (wounded)
2nd KGL Light Dragoons	520	78	Lieutenant Colonel Charles de Jonquières (wounded)
1st KGL Hussars	605	10	Lieutenant Colonel Augustus von Wissell
3rd KGL Hussars	712	130	Lieutenant Colonel Frederick Meyer (killed)

Regiment	Strength	Losses	Commander
2/1st Guards	781	157	Colonel Henry Askew (wounded)
3/1st Guards	847	335	Colonel Hon. William Stuart (wounded)
2/2nd Guards	1 098	315	Colonel Alexander Woodford
2/3rd Guards	1 100	248	Colonel Francis Hepburn
3/1st Regiment	457	138	Lieutenant Colonel Colin Campbell (wounded)
1/4th Regiment	677	134	Lieutenant Colonel Francis Brooke
3/14th Regiment	640	29	Lieutenant Colonel Francis Tidy
23rd Regiment	741	99	Colonel Sir Henry Walton Ellis (killed)
1/27th Regiment	750	463	Major John Hare (wounded)
28th Regiment	557	177	Colonel Sir Charles Belson
2/30th Regiment	635	229	Lieutenant Colonel Alexander Hamilton (wounded)
32nd Regiment	503	174	Lieutenant Colonel John Hicks
33rd Regiment	566	187	Lieutenant Colonel William Elphinstone
1/40th Regiment	862	227	Major Arthur Heyland
42nd Regiment	338	44	Lieutenant Colonel Sir Robert Macara (killed)
2/44th Regiment	494	61	Lieutenant Colonel John Hamerton (wounded)
51st Regiment	626	29	Lieutenant Colonel Samuel Rice
1/52nd Regiment	1 167	190	Colonel Sir John Colborne
2/69th Regiment	565	79	Colonel Charles Morice (killed)
71st Regiment	936	202	Colonel Thomas Reynell (wounded)
2/73rd Regiment	498	263	Colonel William Harris (wounded)
79th Regiment	445	162	Lieutenant Colonel Neil Douglas (wounded)
92nd Regiment	422	110	Colonel John Cameron (killed)
1/95th Regiment	418	144	Colonel Sir Andrew Barnard (wounded)
2/95th Regiment	666	233	Lieutenant Colonel Amos Norcott (wounded)

3/95th Regiment	205	50	Lieutenant Colonel John Ross (wounded)
1st KGL Line Battalion	478	121	Major William Robertson (wounded)
2nd KGL Line Battalion	521	109	Major George Müller
3rd KGL Line Battalion	589	147	Lieutenant Colonel Frederick von Wissell
4th KGL Line Battalion	478	112	Major Frederick Reh
5th KGL Line Battalion	503	161	Lieutenant Colonel William von Linsingen
8th KGL Line Battalion	525	151	Lieutenant Colonel J. von Schroeder
1st KGL Light Battalion	478	145	Lieutenant Colonel Lewis von dem Bussche
2nd KGL Light Battalion	432	202	Major George Baring
Total	36 538	8 349	

Sources

Adkin, Mark, *Waterloo Companion*, London 2001

Haythornthwaite, Philip J., *Waterloo Men*, London 1999

Siborne, Captain W., *History of the War in France and Belgium in 1815*, London 1848

Appendix VII

The British purchase system

Promotion for officers in the British Army during the Napoleonic period could happen in one of two ways. In the first instance, where deaths in action created vacancies, regimental officers were advanced according to seniority without money changing hands. But in the second instance, where retirement from the service created vacancies, officers could simply buy any commissions available. In this case, money was paid not to the government but rather to the retiring officer.

The system favoured the wealthy, because although – in theory – prices of commissions were fixed (see the table below), a premium was often added, making the sale of commissions a lucrative business. Sir Charles Oman, the celebrated author of *Wellington's Army 1809–1814* (1913), explains the system in detail:

> When a lieutenant-colonelcy, majority, or captaincy was vacant, the senior in the next lower rank had a moral right to be offered the vacancy at the regulation price. But there were many cases in which more than the regulation could be got. The officer retiring handed over the affair to a 'commission broker' and bidding was invited. A poor officer at the head of those of his own rank could not afford to pay the often very heavy price, and might see three or four of his juniors buy their way over his head, while he vainly waited for a vacancy by death, by which he would obtain his step without having to pay cash . . . It is said that one young officer, who had the advantages of being wealthy, a peer, and possessed of great family influence in Parliament, was worked up from a lieutenancy to a lieutenant-colonelcy in a single year. This, of course, was a very exceptional case, and happened long ere the Peninsular War began; but it may be remembered that Wellington himself, was, through

similar advantages on a smaller scale, enabled to move up from ensign on March 7, 1787, to lieutenant colonel in September, 1793 – five steps in seven years, during which he had been moved through as many regiments – two of horse and five of foot. He was only nineteen months a captain and six months a major, and he had seen no war service whatever when he sailed for Flanders in command of the 33rd at the age of twenty-three!

But what was the 'regulation price' for commissions? The following table, based on figures set by the Royal Warrant of 1821, gives some indication. All prices are in pounds sterling, and must be multiplied by a factor of at least 50 for a modern equivalent.

Regiment	Ensign/Cornet	Lieutenant	Captain	Major	Colonel
Foot	450	700	1800	3200	4500
Cavalry	840	1190	3225	4575	6175
Life Guards	1260	1785	3500	5350	7250
Horse Guards	1200	1600	3500	5350	7250
Foot Guards	1200	2050	4800	8300	9000

Appendix VIII

Wellington's Waterloo Dispatch to Earl Bathurst, as printed in the *London Gazette Extraordinary* of 3 July 1815

MY LORD,

Buonaparte, having collected the 1st, 2nd, 3rd, 4th, and 6th Corps of the French Army, and the Imperial Guards, and nearly all the cavalry, on the Sambre, and between that river and the Meuse, between the 10th and 14th of the month, advanced on the 15th and attacked the Prussian posts at Thuin and Lobbes, on the Sambre, at daylight in the morning.

I did not hear of these events till in the evening of the 15th; and I immediately ordered the troops to prepare to march, and, afterwards to march to their left, as soon as I had intelligence from other quarters to prove that the enemy's movement upon Charleroi was the real attack.

The enemy drove the Prussian posts from the Sambre on that day; and General Ziethen, who commanded the corps which had been at Charleroi, retired upon Fleurus; and Marshal Prince Blücher concentrated the Prussian Army upon Sombref, holding the villages in front of his position of St Amand and Ligny.

The enemy continued his march along the road from Charleroi towards Bruxelles; and, on the same evening, the 15th, attacked a brigade of the army of the Netherlands, under the Prince de Weimar, posted at Frasne, and forced it back to the farm house, on the same road, called Les Quatre Bras.

The Prince of Orange immediately reinforced this brigade with another of the same division, under General Perponcher, and, in the morning early, regained part of the ground which had been lost, so as to have the command of the communication leading from Nivelles and Bruxelles with Marshal Blücher's position.

In the mean time, I had directed the whole army to march upon Les Quatre Bras; and the 5th Division, under Lieut. General Sir Thomas Picton, arrived at about half past two in the day, followed by the corps of troops under the Duke of Brunswick, and afterwards by the contingent of Nassau.

At this time the enemy commenced an attack upon Prince Blücher with his whole force, excepting the 1st and 2nd Corps, and a corps of cavalry under General Kellermann, with which he attacked our post at Les Quatre Bras.

The Prussian Army maintained their position with their usual gallantry and perseverance against a great disparity of numbers, as the 4th Corps of their army, under General Bülow, had not joined; and I was not able to assist them as I wished, as I was attacked myself, and the troops, the cavalry in particular, which had a long distance to march, had not arrived.

We maintained our position also, and completely defeated and repulsed all the enemy's attempts to get possession of it. The enemy repeatedly attacked us with a large body of infantry and cavalry, supported by a numerous and powerful artillery. He made several charges with the cavalry upon our infantry, but all were repulsed in the steadiest manner.

In this affair, His Royal Highness the Prince of Orange, the Duke of Brunswick, and Lieut. General Sir Thomas Picton, and Major Generals Sir James Kempt and Sir Denis Pack, who were engaged from the commencement of the enemy's attack, highly distinguished themselves, as well as Lieut. General Charles Baron Alten, Major General Sir C. Halkett, Lieut. General Cooke, and Major Generals Maitland and Byng, as they successively arrived. The troops of the 5th Division, and those of the Brunswick Corps, were long and severely engaged, and conducted themselves with the utmost gallantry. I must particularly mention the 28th, 42nd, 79th, and 92nd Regiments, and the battalion of Hanoverians.

Our loss was great, as your Lordship will perceive by the enclosed return; and I have particularly to regret His Serene Highness the Duke of Brunswick, who fell fighting gallantly at the head of his troops.

Although Marshal Blücher had maintained his position at Sombref, he still found himself much weakened by the severity of the contest in which he had been engaged, and, as the 4th Corps had not arrived, he determined to fall back and to concentrate his army upon Wavre; and he marched in the night, after the action was over.

This movement of the Marshal rendered necessary a corresponding one upon my part; and I retired from the farm of Quatre Bras upon Genappe, and thence upon Waterloo, the next morning, the 17th, at ten o'clock.

The enemy made no effort to pursue Marshal Blücher. On the contrary, a patrol which I sent to Sombref in the morning found all quiet; and the enemy's vedettes fell back as the patrol advanced. Neither did he attempt to molest our march to the rear, although made in the middle of the day, excepting by following, with a large body of cavalry brought from his right, the cavalry under the Earl of Uxbridge . . . This gave Lord Uxbridge an opportunity of charging them with the 1st Life Guards, upon their *débouché* from the village of Genappe, upon which occasion his Lordship has declared himself to be well satisfied with that regiment.

The position which I took up in front of Waterloo crossed the high roads from Charleroi and Nivelles, and had its right thrown back to a ravine near Merke Braine, which was occupied, and its left extended to a height above the hamlet Ter la Haye, which was likewise occupied. In front of the right centre, and near the Nivelles road, we occupied the house and gardens of Hougoumont, which covered the return of that flank; and in front of the left centre we occupied the farm of La Haye Sainte. By our left we communicated with Marshal Prince Blücher at Wavre, through Ohain; and the Marshal had promised me that, in case we should be attacked, he would support me with one or more corps, as might be necessary.

The enemy collected his army, with the exception of the 3rd Corps, which had been sent to observe Marshal Blücher, on a range of heights in our front, in the course of the night of the 17th and yesterday morning, at about ten o'clock, he commenced a furious attack upon our post at Hougoumont. I had occupied that post with a detachment from General Byng's Brigade of Guards, which was in position in its rear; and it was for some time under the command of Lieut. Colonel Macdonell, and afterwards of Colonel Home; and I am happy to add that it was maintained throughout the day with the utmost gallantry by these brave troops, notwithstanding the repeated efforts of large bodies of the enemy to obtain possession of it.

This attack upon the right of our centre was accompanied by a very heavy cannonade upon our whole line, which was destined to support the repeated attacks of cavalry and infantry, occasionally mixed, but sometimes separate, which were made upon it. In one of these the enemy carried the farm house of La Haye Sainte, as the detachment of the Light Battalion of the German Legion, which occupied it, had expended all its ammunition; and the enemy occupied the only communication there was with them.

The enemy repeatedly charged our infantry with his cavalry, but these attacks were uniformly unsuccessful; and they afforded opportunities to our cavalry to charge, in one of which Lord E. Somerset's brigade, consisting of the Life Guards, the Royal Horse Guards, and 1st Dragoon Guards, highly distinguished themselves, as did that of Major General Sir William Ponsonby, having taken many prisoners and an eagle.

These attacks were repeated till about seven in the evening, when the enemy made a desperate effort with cavalry and infantry, supported by the fire of artillery, to force our left centre, near the farm of La Haye Sainte, which, after a severe contest, was defeated; and, having observed that the troops retired from this attack in great confusion, and that the march of General Bülow's corps, by Frischermont, upon Planchenois and La Belle Alliance, had begun to take effect, and as I could perceive the fire of his cannon, and as Marshal Prince Blücher had joined in person with a corps of his army to the left of our line by Ohain, I determined to attack the enemy, and immediately advanced the whole line of infantry, supported by the cavalry and artillery. The attack succeeded in every point: the enemy was forced from his positions on the heights, and fled in the utmost confusion, leaving behind him, as far as I could judge, 150 pieces of cannon, with their ammunition, which fell into our hands.

I continued the pursuit till long after dark, and then discontinued it only on account of the fatigue of our troops, who had been engaged during twelve hours, and because I found myself on the same road with Marshal Blücher, who assured me of his intention to follow the enemy throughout the night. He has sent me word this morning that he had taken 60 pieces of cannon belonging to the Imperial Guard, and several carriages, baggage, &c., belonging to Buonaparte, in Genappe.

I propose to move this morning upon Nivelles, and not to discontinue my operations.

Your Lordship will observe that such a desperate action could not be fought, and such advantages could not be gained, without great loss; and I am sorry to add that ours has been immense. In Lieut. General Sir Thomas Picton His Majesty has sustained the loss of an officer who has frequently distinguished himself in his service, and he fell gloriously leading his division to a charge with bayonets, by which one of the most serious attacks made by the enemy on our position was repulsed. The Earl of Uxbridge, after having successfully got through this arduous day, received a wound by almost the last shot fired, which will, I am afraid, deprive His Majesty for some time of his services.

His Royal Highness the Prince of Orange distinguished himself by his gallantry and conduct, till he received a wound from a musket ball through the shoulder, which obliged him to quit the field.

It gives me the greatest satisfaction to assure your Lordship that the army never, upon any occasion, conducted itself better. The division of Guards, under Lieut. General Cooke, who is severely wounded, Major General Maitland, and Major General Byng, set an example which was followed by all; and there is no officer nor description of troops that did not behave well.

I must, however, particularly mention, for His Royal Highness's approbation, Lieut. General Sir H. Clinton, Major General Adam, Lieut. General Charles Baron Alten (severely wounded), Major General Sir Colin Halkett (severely wounded), Colonel Ompteda, Colonel Mitchell (commanding a brigade of the 4th division), Major Generals Sir James Kempt and Sir D. Pack, Major General Lambert, Major General Lord E. Somerset, Major General Sir W. Ponsonby,

Major General Sir C. Grant, and Major General Sir H. Vivian, Major General Sir O. Vandeleur, and Major General Count Dörnberg.

I am also particularly indebted to General Lord Hill for his assistance and conduct upon this, as upon all former occasions.

The artillery and engineer departments were conducted much to my satisfaction by Colonel Sir George Wood and Colonel Smyth; and I had every reason to be satisfied with the conduct of the Adjutant General, Major General Barnes, who was wounded, and of the Quarter Master General, Colonel De Lancey, who was killed by a cannon shot in the middle of the action. This officer is a serious loss to His Majesty's service, and to me at this moment.

I was likewise much indebted to the assistance of Lieut. Colonel Lord Fitzroy Somerset, who was severely wounded, and of the officers composing my personal Staff, who have suffered severely in this action. Lieut. Colonel the Hon. Sir Alexander Gordon, who has died of his wounds, was a most promising officer, and is a serious loss to His Majesty's service.

General Kruse, of the Nassau service, likewise conducted himself much to my satisfaction; as did General Tripp, commanding the heavy brigade of cavalry, and General Van Hope, commanding a Brigade of infantry in the service of the King of the Netherlands.

General Pozzo di Borgo, General Baron Vincent, General Muffling, and General Alava, were in the field during the action, and rendered me every assistance in their power. Baron Vincent is wounded, but I hope not severely; and General Pozzo di Borgo received a contusion.

I should not do justice to my own feelings, or to Marshal Blücher and the Prussian Army, if I did not attribute the successful result of this arduous day to the cordial and timely assistance I received from them. The operation of General Bülow upon the enemy's flank was a most decisive one; and, even if I had not found myself in a situation to make the attack which produced the final result, it would have forced the enemy to retire if his attacks should have failed, and would have prevented him from taking advantage of them if they should unfortunately have succeeded.

Since writing the above, I have received a report that Major General Sir William Ponsonby is killed; and, in announcing this intelligence to your Lordship, I have to add the expression of my grief for the fate of an officer who had already rendered very brilliant and important services, and was an ornament to his profession.

I send with this dispatch three eagles, taken by the troops in this action, which Major Percy will have the honour of laying at the feet of His Royal Highness. I beg leave to recommend him to your Lordship's protection.

I have the honour to be, &c. WELLINGTON

Appendix IX

The Battles of Waterloo and Quatre-Bras, as reported by *The Times*

DOWNING STREET, JUNE 22 1815

The Duke of WELLINGTON'S Dispatch, dated Waterloo, the 19th of June, states, that on the preceding day BUONAPARTE attacked, with his whole force, the British line, supported by a corps of Prussians: which attack, after a long and sanguinary conflict, terminated in the complete Overthow of the Enemy's Army, with the loss of ONE HUNDRED and FIFTY PIECES of CANNON and TWO EAGLES. During the night, the Prussians under Marshal BLÜCHER, who joined in the pursuit of the enemy, captured SIXTY GUNS, and a large part of BUONAPARTE'S BAGGAGE. The Allied Armies continued to pursue the enemy. Two French Generals were taken.

Such is the great and glorious result of those masterly movements by which the Hero of Britain met and frustrated the audacious attempt of the Rebel Chief. Glory to WELLINGTON, to our gallant Soldiers, and to our brave Allies! BUONAPARTE'S reputation has been wrecked, and his last grand take has been lost in this tremendous conflict. TWO HUNDRED AND TEN PIECES OF CANNON captured in a single battle, put to the blush the boasting column of the Place de Vendome. Long and sanguinary, indeed, we fear, the conflict must have been; but the boldness of the Rebel Frenchmen was the boldness of despair, and conscience sate [*sic*] heavy on those arms which were raised against their Sovereign, against their oaths, and against the peace and happiness of their country. We confidently anticipate a great and immediate defection from the Rebel cause. We are aware that a great part of the French nation looked to the opening of this campaign with a superstitious expectation of success to a man, whom, though many of them hated, and many feared, all had been taught to look on as the first captain of the age. He himself went forth boasting in his strength, and still more in his talents. He had for many years ridiculed CARNOT'S plan of a Northern Campaign, and had openly avowed at Paris his intention to break through the centre of the Allied Armies, instead of moving round both their flanks. With as little reserve had he declared that he would open the campaign on the Meuse and Sambre. In short, by a refinement in finesse, he had exposed his true plan, imagining that nobody would believe that such was his real intention. We do not deny that his plan might have been one of considerable ability; but he did not take into the account that he was to be opposed by abilities superior to his own. That unpalatable truth his vanity would not allow him to believe, nor would it easily find credit with his admirers; but the 18th of June, we trust, will satisfy the most incredulous. Two hundred and ten pieces of cannon! When, where, or how is this loss to be repaired? Besides, what has become of his invincible guard, of his admired and dreaded cuirassiers? Again, we do not deny that these were good troops; but they were encountered by better. We shall be curious to learn with what degree of coolness, or personal courage, and self-possession BUONAPARTE played this stake, on which he must have been well aware that his pretensions to Empire hung. It is clear that he retreated; nor are we prepared to hear that he fled with haste or cowardice; but we greatly suspect that he did not court an honourable death. We think his valour is of the calculating kind, and we do not attribute his surviving the abdication at Fountainebleau entirely to magnamity.

To the official Bulletin we have as yet little to add. The dispatches, we understand, were brought by Major PERCY, Aide-de-camp to the Duke of WELLINGTON; and we have heard, but we hope the statement is premature, that among the British slain was that gallant and estimable officer Sir THOMAS PICTON. But whoever fell on this glorious day cannot have fallen in vain. The fabric of rebellion is shaken to its base. Already, we hear, numerous desertions have taken place from the Rebel Standard; and soon, it is to be hoped, the perjured wretches NEY and DESNOUETTES, and EXCELMANS, and LALLEMAND, LABEDOYERE, and their accomplices in baseness and treason, will be left alone, as marks for the indignation of Europe, and just sacrifices to insulted French honour.

Those who attended minutely to the operations of the Stock Exchange yesterday, were persuaded that the news of the day before would be followed up by something still more brilliant and decisive. Omnium rose in the course of the day to 6 per cent, premium, and some houses generally supposed to possess the best information were among the purchasers. For our own parts, though looking forward with that confidence which we yesterday expressed, we frankly own this full tide of success was more than we had anticipated. We were very well satisfied that Mr. SUTTON'S account, so far as it went, was correct – that BUONAPARTE'S grand plan had been frustrated, and that he had not only been prevented from penetrating between the English and Prussian armies, but forced to fall back again behind the Sambre. How far the Duke of WELLINGTON and Prince BLÜCHER might have thought it prudent to pursue him, was a point on which we did not conceive ourselves warranted to form any decisive opinion from the evidence before us. We had no doubt that he would be harassed in his retreat, and perhaps ultimately be driven into his entrenched camp, or under the guns of his fortresses; but without some distinct official information, we repeat, that we could not have ventured to anticipate such a triumphant result as that on which we have now to congratulate our country and the world.

Among the rumours which obtained some credit in the city yesterday, was one of an insurrection in Paris. We are not much inclined to give credit to this, conceiving that the Parisians will not move until the tyrant's force in the field is broken. We know, however, that a spirit of hostility to his usurpation is very generally and very boldly expressed in the French capital. We have received from thence a paper which has obtained extensive circulation there, and which will be found in another of our columns. It contains an address to the inhabitants of the Fauxbourgs St. Antoine and St. Marceau, and a Declaration in the name of the Duke of ORLEANS. Both these documents are plainly and ably drawn up. The one successfully opposes the ferocious doctrines of the Jacobins, the other the more insidious views of those who seek to cover their criminality with the respect justly due to a brave and honourable Member of the House of Bourbon. Whether his Serene Highness has authorised this avowal of his sentiments, we know not; but it is one, which appears perfectly congenial with that fair and manly conduct which he has always observed. The Duke of ORLEANS has never at any time given the least countenance to those criminal projects, which under the specious pretence of attachment to himself, would as completely break down the principle of legal succession, as if a BUONAPARTE or a ROBESPIERRE were the object of election. That principle once violated, the faction assuming today the right of choosing any given Sovereign, might tomorrow, with equal authority, assume the right of cashiering him. Nothing would be permanent or secure. Neither King, nor Dynasty, nor form of Government, would be certain of lasting a twelve month; the intolerable perpetuity of change would necessitate the ultimate submission to despotism; and none would be more miserably the sufferers then those unfortunate personages who might be mocked with the capricious grant of a delusive sovereignty by the paramount authority of faction.

Yesterday his Royal Highness the PRINCE REGENT held a Council at Carlton House, which was unexpectedly summoned. It was attended by the Lord President, the Lord Privy Seal, the First Lord of the Treasury, the Chancellor of the Exchequer, the First Lord of the Admiralty, the Master General of the Ordnance, the three Secretaries of State, the President of the Board of Control the Chancellor of the Duchy of Lancaster, the Master of the Mint, the Commander in Chief, &c.

Among other important proceedings, and Order in Council for reprisals and letters of marque against the French was agreed upon, and signed by all the members of the Council present, in consequence of hostilities having commenced.

His Royal Highness gave audience to the Earls of LIVERPOOL, HARROWBY, Viscount SIDMOUTH, and Mr. BATHURST. The Rev. Dr. LUXMORE, the late Bishop of Hereford, did homage before the PRINCE, upon his being translated from the Bishopric of Hereford to the Bishopric of St. Asaph.

We have seen a gentleman who left Brussels on Sunday evening, at which time the people were manifesting the greatest joy for a decisive victory gained by the Duke of WELLINGTON on that day. The wounded were beginning to be brought in, in waggons, as this gentleman quitted Brussels.

Many of the British Officers present in the affair of the 16th, declared that they never witnessed more severe fighting in the Peninsula than that which took place on the plains of Fleurus and its vicinity. What made the fate of the 79th and 42nd Regiments so severe was their having been taken by surprise by a strong force of cuirassiers, who lay in ambush for them in a road, the sight of which was completely intercepted by fields of corn immensely high. With such fury was the 79th Regiment attacked, that most of them were cut to pieces, and the whole were in danger of being destroyed, but for the coming up of the brave 42nd. This latter regiment formed itself into a square, and five times were they broken. On the sixth attack they formed the plan of opening a passage to the enemy; and the moment he effected it, they changed their position, and so hemmed in the cuirassiers, that not a single man was suffered to escape: thus was the destruction of one of BUONAPARTE'S finest regiments completed. Col. CAMERON; says our informant, was killed at the head of the gallant 42nd. Next day, Saturday, when the 79th was mustered, the men amounted to no more than 54, and two officers. A few more were, however, expected to be brought in. General PICTON'S division did wonders; and the gallant General himself fought at the head of it in a manner to astonish the greatest veterans. The Duke of WELLINGTON exposed himself as usual to imminent danger; the bullets, says our informant, were whizzing about him in every direction.

Bibliography

Ackroyd, Peter, *Turner*, London 2005

Adkin, Mark, *Waterloo Companion*, London 2001

Anglesey, Marquis of, *One Leg: The Life and Letters of Henry William Paget, First Marquess of Anglesey, K.G., 1768–1854*, London 1961

Anon., *Vicissitudes in the Life of a Scottish Soldier Written by Himself*, London 1828

Anton, James, *Retrospect of a Military Life*, Edinburgh 1841

Atteridge, A.H., *Bravest of the Brave: Michel Ney, Marshal of France*, London 1912

Aubry, Capitaine, *Souvenirs du 12e Chasseurs (1799–1815)*, Paris 1899

Beamish, N.L., *History of the King's German Legion*, London 1832–7

Becke, A.F., *Napoleon and Waterloo*, London 1914

Bell, Charles, *Letters of Sir Charles Bell*, London 1870

Belloc, Hilaire, *Six British Battles*, London 1931

Blathwayt, George, *Recollections of My Life, including Military Service at Waterloo* (ed. Gareth Glover), Cambridge 2004

Blond, Georges, *La Grande Armée*, Paris 1979

Booth, John, *Additional Particulars to the Battle of Waterloo, Also of Ligny, and Quatre Bras, With Circumstantial Details by a Near Observer, Containing a Register of the Names of the Officers who Served in the Campaign of the Netherlands, 1815*, London 1817

Boulger, Demetrius C., *Belgians at Waterloo*, London 1901

Bourrienne, F. de, *Memoirs of Napoleon Bonaparte*, London 1905

Boutflower, Charles, *Journal of an Army Surgeon During the Peninsular War*, London 1912

Brack, General F. de, *Light Cavalry Outposts: Recollections of General F. de Brack*, London 1876

Brett-James, A., *The Hundred Days From Eyewitness Accounts*, London 1970

Brô, L., *Mémoires du Général Brô (1796–1844)*, Paris 1914

Brock, Russell Claude, *The Life and Work of Astley Cooper*, Edinburgh and London, 1952

Bryant, Arthur, *The Age of Elegance*, London 1950

Buckland, C. (ed.), *Waterloo Medal Roll*, London 2001 (reissue)

Burney, Frances, *Journals and Letters* (ed. P. Sabor and L.E. Troide), London 2001

Capel, Caroline Paget, Lady, and Uxbridge, Jane Champagne Paget, Countess of, *The Capel Letters: Being the Correspondence of Lady Caroline Capel and her Daughters with the Dowager Countess of Uxbridge from Brussels and Switzerland 1814–1817*, London 1955

Carman, W.Y., *Dictionary of Military Uniform*, London 1977

Chancellor, Beresford E., *Life in Regency and Early Victorian Times*, London 1926

Chandler, David G., *Campaigns of Napoleon*, London 1966

Chandler, David G., *Dictionary of the Napoleonic Wars*, London 1979

Chandler, David G., *Waterloo: The Hundred Days*, London 1980

Chandler, David G. (ed.), *Napoleon's Marshals*, London 1987

Chesney, Colonel Charles, *Waterloo Lectures*, London 1868

Clark, Captain A.K., *Attack the Colour: The Royal Dragoons in the Peninsula and at Waterloo*, London 1975

Clay, Matthew, *Narrative of the Battles of Quatre-Bras and Waterloo; with the Defence of Hougoumont*, Bedford 1853

Cohen, Louis, *Napoleonic Anecdotes*, London 1925

Coignet, J., *Notebooks of Captain Coignet, Soldier of the Empire*, London 1928

Connelly, Owen, *Blundering to Glory*, Wilmington DE 1987

Cooper, Bransby Blake, *The Life of Sir Astley Cooper, Bart., interspersed with sketches from his note-books of distinguished contemporary characters*, London 1843

Costello, E., *Adventures of a Soldier*, London 1841

Cotton, E., *A Voice From Waterloo*, Brussels 1895

Craan, W.B. de, *References to and Memoir of the Field of Waterloo*, without imprint, *c*.1817

Creasy, Edward S., *Fifteen Decisive Battles of the World*, London 1851

Creevey, Thomas, *The Creevey Papers*, London 1904

Cronin, Vincent, *Napoleon*, London 1971

Crumplin, M.K.H., and Starling, P., *A Surgical Artist at War: The Paintings and Sketches of Sir Charles Bell 1809–15*, London 2005

Dallas, Gregor, *1815: The Roads to Waterloo*, London 1996

Dalton, Charles, *Waterloo Roll Call*, London 1904

David, Saul, *Prince of Pleasure*, London 1998

De Lancey, Lady, *Week at Waterloo in 1815*, London 1906

Dobbs, John, *Recollections of an Old 52nd Man*, London 1863

Dunn-Pattison, R.P., *Napoleon's Marshals*, London 1909

Dupuy, Victor, *Souvenirs Militaires de Victor Dupuy 1794–1816*, Paris 1892

Duthilt, Pierre, *Mémoires du Capitaine Duthilt*, Lille 1909

Eaton, Charlotte Anne, *Narrative of a Residence in Belgium During the Campaign of 1815; and of a Visit to the Field of Waterloo by an Englishwoman*, London 1817

Eaton, Charlotte Anne Waldie, *Waterloo Days: the Narrative of an Englishwoman Resident at Brussels in June 1815*, London 1888

Elting, John R., *Swords Around a Throne*, London 1989

Esdaile, Charles J., *The Wars of Napoleon*, London 1995

Esposito, Vincent J., and Elting, John R., *Military History and Atlas of the Napoleonic Wars*, London 1999

Fleury de Chamboulon, *Mémoires pour servir à l'histoire de la vie privée, du retour et du règne de Napoléon en 1815*, Paris 1908

Fletcher, I., *Wellington's Regiments*, London 1994

Fletcher, I., and Poulter, R., *Gentlemen's Sons*, London 1992

Foy, Maximilien, *Vie Militaire du Général Foy*, Paris 1900

Fraser, E., *War Drama of the Eagles*, London 1912

Frazer, Sir Augustus Simon, *Letters of Colonel Sir Augustus Simon Frazer, K.C.B., Commanding the Royal Horse Artillery in the Army under the Duke of Wellington, Written during the Peninsular and Waterloo Campaigns*, London 1859

Fuller, J.F.C., *Decisive Battles of the Western World 1792–1944*, vol. 2, London 1954

Funck, Ferdiand von, *In the Wake of Napoleon 1807–09*, London 1931

Gardiner, Samuel Rawson (ed.), *A School Atlas of English History*, London 1892

Gates, David, *The Napoleonic Wars 1803–1815*, London 1997

Gleig, G.R., *The Subaltern*, London 1812

Glover, Gareth (ed.), *Letters from the Battle of Waterloo*, London 2004

Glover, Gareth (ed.), *Narrative of the Battles of Quatre-Bras and Waterloo; with the Defence of Hougoumont by Matthew Clay*, Cambridge 2006 (reissue)

Glover, Gareth (ed.), *Reminiscences of Waterloo: The Correspondence Between Henry Leathes and Alexander Mercer of G Troop RHA*, Cambridge 2004

Glover, M., *Wellington's Army in the Peninsula 1808–1814*, London 1977

Gneisenau, General Count, *Life and Campaigns of Field-Marshal Prince Blücher*, London 1815

Gomm, W., *Letters and Journals of Field Marshal Sir William Maynard Gomm from 1799 to Waterloo 1815*, London 1881

Grant, Charles, and Youens, Michael, *Royal Scots Greys*, Oxford 1972

Gronow, Rees Howell, *Reminiscences and Recollections of Captain Gronow*, London 1900

Hamilton, Archibald James, *At Waterloo with the Scots Greys* (ed. Stephen Maughan), Napoleonic Archive, no date

Hamilton, Jill, *Marengo: The Myth of Napoleon's Horse*, London 2000

Haythornthwaite, Philip J., *Armies of Wellington*, London 1994

Haythornthwaite, Philip J., *Napoleonic Sourcebook*, London 1990

Haythornthwaite, Philip J., *Waterloo Men*, London 1999

Haythornthwaite, Philip J., *Weapons and Equipment of the Napoleonic Wars*, London 1979

Haythornthwaite, Philip J., *Who Was Who In the Napoleonic Wars*, London 1998

Haythornthwaite, Philip, Cassin-Scott, Jack, and Chappell, Michael, *Uniforms of Waterloo*, London 1974

Henderson, E.F., *Blücher And the Uprising of Prussia Against Napoleon 1806–1815*, New York and London 1911

Herold, J. Christopher, *The Mind of Napoleon*, New York 1955

Heymès, *Relation de la Campagne de 1815*, Paris 1829

Hibbert, Christopher, *Waterloo: Napoleon's Last Campaign*, London 1967

Hibbert, Christopher, *Wellington, A Personal History*, London 1997

Hofschroer, Peter, *Wellington's Smallest Victory*, London 2004

Hofschroer, Peter, *1815 The Waterloo Campaign: The German Victory*, London 1999

Holmes, Richard, *Army Battlefield Guide: Belgium and Northern France*, London 1995

Holmes, Richard, *Wellington: The Iron Duke*, London 2002

Horricks, Raymond, *Napoleon's Elite*, New Brunswick and London 1995

Houssaye, Henri, *Waterloo*, London 1900

Howard, Martin, *Wellington's Doctors*, London 2002

Howarth, David, *Waterloo: A Near Run Thing*, London 1968

Hughes, Kristine, *Everyday Life in Regency and Victorian England*, Cincinnati 1998

Hugo, Victor, *Les Misérables*, London 1976 (Paris 1862)

Johnson, David, *French Cavalry 1792–1815*, London 1989

Johnson, David, *Napoleon's Cavalry and Its Leaders*, New York 1978

Jolyet, Jean-Baptiste, 'Souvenirs de 1815', *Revue de Paris*, October 1903

Jomini, Baron de, *Art of War*, London 1992

Keegan, John, *The Face of Battle*, London 1976

Kelly, Christopher, *A Full And Circumstantial Account of the Memorable Battle of Waterloo*, London 1818

Kennedy, General Sir James Shaw, *Notes on the Battle of Waterloo*, London 1865

Kincaid, J., *Adventures in the Rifle Brigade in the Peninsula, France and the Netherlands, from 1809 to 1815*, London 1847

Knesebeck, E. von dem, *The Life of Baron Hugh von Halkett*, Stuttgart 1865

Knollys, H., *Shaw the Lifeguardsman: An Exciting Narrative*, London c.1880

Korngold, Ralph, *The Last Years of Napoleon*, London 1960

Kukiel, Maryan, *Dzieje Oreza Polskiego w Epoce Napoleonskiej* (trans. Ewa Haren), Poznan 1912

Lachouque, Henry, and Brown, Anne S.K., *Anatomy of Glory: Napoleon and his Guard*, London 1978

Laffin, John, *Brassey's Battles*, London 1986

Lagneau, Louis-Vivant, *Journal d'un chirurgien de la Grande Armée 1803–1815*, Paris 1913

Lawrence, William, *The Autobiography of Sergeant William Lawrence, a Hero of the Peninsular and Waterloo Campaigns*, London 1886

Leach, J., *Rough Sketches of the Life of an Old Soldier*, London 1831

Leeke, William, *The History of Lord Seaton's Regiment (the 52nd Light Infantry) at the Battle of Waterloo*, London 1866

Leroy-Dupré, L.A.H., *Memoirs of Baron Larrey, Surgeon in Chief of the Grand Army*, London 1862

Linck, Tony, *Napoleon's Generals: The Waterloo Campaign*, Chicago 1993

Longford, Elizabeth, *Wellington: Years of the Sword*, London 1969

Macbride, Mackenzie (ed.), *With Napoleon at Waterloo, and Other Unpublished Documents from the Peninsular War and Waterloo Campaign*, London 1911

MacDonell, A.G., *Napoleon and his Marshals*, London 1934

McGrigor, Sir J., *Autobiography and Services, etc.*, London 1861

Mackinnon, D., *Origin and Services of the Coldstream Guards*, London 1833

McLynn, F., *Napoleon: A Biography*, London 1997

Maitland, Rear-Admiral Sir Frederick, *The Surrender of Napoleon*, London 1904

Marbot, Baron de, *Memoirs of Baron de Marbot* (trans. A.J. Butler), London 1900

Maughan, Stephen (ed.), *Scots Greys at Waterloo: Letters and Records of the 2nd Royal North British Dragoons*, Napoleonic Archive, no date

Maughan, Stephen (ed.), *With the 69th in the Waterloo Campaign*, Napoleonic Archive, no date

Maxwell, W.H., *Life of Wellington*, London 1904

Mercer, Cavalié, *Journal of the Waterloo Campaign*, London 1927

Mikaberidze, A., *The Russian Officer Corps in the Revolutionary and Napoleonic Wars, 1792–1815*, Staplehurst 2005

Miller, David, *The Duchess of Richmond's Ball, 15 June 1815*, Staplehurst 2005

Mokhtefi, Elaine, *Paris: An Illustrated History*, New York 2002

Monick, S., *A Voice from Waterloo*, Uckfield 2001

Morgan, Matthew, *Wellington's Victories*, London 2004

Morris, Thomas, *Recollections of Military Service in 1813, 1814 and 1815*, London 1851

Mudford, William, *An Historical Account of the Campaign in the Netherlands, in 1815, under His Grace the Duke of Wellington, and Marshal Blücher, Comprising the Battles of Ligny, Quatre Bras, and Waterloo*, London 1817

Müffling, Friedrich Karl von, *Passages From My Life, Together With Memoirs of the Campaigns of 1813 and 1814*, London 1853

Muir, Rory, *Britain and the Defeat of Napoleon*, New Haven and London 1996

Myerly, Scott Hughes, *British Military Spectacle*, London 1996

Naylor, John, *Waterloo*, London 1960

Nofi, Albert, *Waterloo Campaign*, London 1993

Oman, Sir Charles, *Wellington's Army, 1809–1814*, London 1913

O'Meara, B., *Napoleon in Exile*, London 1822

Oxford Dictionary of National Biography, 2004–7, at www.oxforddnb.com

Paget, Julian, and Saunders, Derek, *Hougoumont*, London 1992

Palmer, Alan, *Encyclopaedia of Napoleon's Europe*, London 1984

Panton, Kenneth, *London: A Historical Companion*, London 2001

Parker, Harold T., *Three Napoleonic Battles*, Durham NC 1944

Pattison, Frederick Hope, *Personal Recollections of the Waterloo Campaign*, Glasgow 1873

Pawly, Ronald, *Red Lancers*, London 1998

Pawly, Ronald, *Wellington's Belgian Allies 1815*, Oxford 2001

Pawly, Ronald, *Wellington's Dutch Allies 1815*, Oxford 2002

Pivka, Otto von, *Black Brunswickers*, Oxford 1973

Pivka, Otto von, *Brunswick Troops 1809–15*, Oxford 1985

Pivka, Otto von, *Napoleon's German Allies: Nassau and Oldenburg*, Oxford 1976

Pivka, Otto von, *Napoleon's Polish Troops*, Oxford 1974

Roberts, Andrew, *Napoleon and Wellington*, London 2001

Roberts, Andrew, *Waterloo: Napoleon's Last Gamble*, London 2005

Robinaux, Pierre, *Journal de Route du Capitaine Robinaux, 1803–1832*, Paris 1908

Saint-Denis, Louis Étienne ('Ali'), *Souvenirs du Mameluck Ali sur l'Empereur Napoléon*, Paris 1926

Schaumann, A.L.F., *On the Road with Wellington*, London 1924

Scott, Walter, *Paul's Letters to his Kinsfolk*, Edinburgh and London 1816

Scott, Walter, *The Journal of Sir Walter Scott* (ed. W.E.K. Anderson), Oxford 1972

Shaw, Philip, *Waterloo and the Romantic Imagination*, London 2002

Shelley, F., *Diary of Lady Frances Shelley, 1787–1815*, London, 1912

Siborne, H.T., *Waterloo Letters: A Selection from Original and Hitherto Unpublished Letters Bearing on the Operations of the 16th, 17th, and 18th June, By Officers Who Served in the Campaign*, London 1891

Siborne, Captain W., *History of the War in France and Belgium in 1815*, London 1848

Simmons, G., A British Rifleman: The Journals of Major George Simmons (ed. Lt Colonel Willonghby Verner), London 1899

Smith, Digby, *Greenhill Napoleonic Wars Data Book*, London 1998

Smith, H., *Autobiography of Lieutenant General Sir Harry Smith*, London 1901

Stanhope, Philip Henry, *Notes of Conversations with the Duke of Wellington*, London 1888

Stouff, L., *Essai sur le Lieutenant Général Baron Delort*, Dijon 1905

Sultana, Donald, *From Abbotsford to Paris and Back: Sir Walter Scott's Journey of 1815*, Far Thrupp 1993

Sutcliffe, Victor, *The Sandler Collection*, Cambridge 1996

Taylor, Thomas William, *Letters of Captain Thomas William Taylor of the 10th Hussars, During the Waterloo Campaign*, Tetbury 1895

Teissedre, F. (ed.), *Souvenirs et correspondance sur la Bataille de Waterloo*, Paris 2000

Thackeray, William Makepeace, *Vanity Fair*, London 1848

Thorburn, W.A., 'The Royal Scots Greys at Waterloo', 1998, at www.napoleonic-alliance.com/articles/scotsgreys.htm

Thornton, J., *Your Most Obedient Servant: James Thornton, Cook to the Duke of Wellington*, Exeter 1985

Thoumas, General Charles, 'Les Trois Colberts', *La Revue de Cavalerie*, Paris 1888

Tomkinson, William, *Diary of a Cavalry Officer in the Peninsular and Waterloo Campaigns*, London 1894

Townson, Duncan, *France in Revolution*, London 1990

T.S., *Journal of T.S. of the 71st Highland Light Infantry, in Memorials of the Late Wars*, Edinburgh 1828

Uffindell, A., and Corum, M., *On the Fields of Glory*, London 1996

Uffindell, A., and Corum, M., *Waterloo*, London 2003

Urban, Mark, *The Man Who Broke Napoleon's Codes*, London 2001

Urban, Mark, *Rifles: Six Years with Wellington's Legendary Sharpshooters*, London 2003

Usher, George, *Dictionary of British Military History*, London 2003

Vallence, Dixon, *At Waterloo with the Cameron Highlanders* (ed. Stephen Maughan), Napoleonic Archive, no date

Vivian, Claude, *Richard Hussey Vivian, First Baron, A Memoir*, London 1897

Weigley, Russell F., *The Age of Battles*, London 1993

Weller, Jac, *Wellington at Waterloo*, London 1967

Wheatley, E., *Wheatley Diary*, London 1964

Wheeler, Harold F.B., *The Mind of Napoleon: As Revealed in his Thoughts, Speech and Actions*, London 1910

Wheeler, W., *Letters of Private Wheeler*, London 1951

Wilson, A.N., *The Laird of Abbotsford: A View of Sir Walter Scott*, Oxford 1980

Windrow, M., and Mason, F.K., *Concise Dictionary of Military Biography*, London 1990

Wood, General Sir Evelyn, *Cavalry in the Waterloo Campaign*, London 1895

Wootten, Geoffrey, *Waterloo 1815*, Oxford 1992